MAINE

EASTPORT
FT. SULLIVAN

FT. BRADY
MACKINAC

PLATTSBURG

VERMONT

NEW HAMPSHIRE

PORTLAND

FT. PREBLE

FT. CONSTITUTION (PORTSMOUTH)

FT. INDEPENDENCE (BOSTON)

TERRITORY

GREEN BAY

SACKETT'S HARBOR

FT. NIAGARA

NEW YORK

Hudson River

MASSACHUSETTS

CONN.   R.I.

FT. WOLCOTT

BRENTON'S POINT (NEWPORT)

FT. TRUMBULL (NEW LONDON)

TRONG   CHICAGO

DETROIT

PENNSYLVANIA

NEW JERSEY

FT. COLUMBUS
FT. LEWIS
FT. WOOD

NEW UTRECHT POINT (NEW YORK)

ILLINOIS

INDIANA

OHIO

DEL.

M.D.

FT. DELAWARE (PEA POINT ISLAND)

Ohio River

KENTUCKY

VIRGINIA

FT. MC HENRY (BALTIMORE)

FT. SEVERN (ANNAPOLIS)

FT. WASHINGTON (WASHINGTON)

FORTRESS MONROE (OLD POINT COMFORT)

FT. CALHOUN (HAMPTON ROADS)

TENNESSEE

NORTH CAROLINA

CHICKASAW BLUFFS

SMITHVILLE

FT. JOHNSTON

SOUTH CAROLINA

MISSISSIPPI

CHOCTAW FACTORY

ALABAMA

GEORGIA

FT. MITCHELL

CHARLESTON   FT. MOULTRIE

FT. JOHNSON

SAVANNAH

FT. JACKSON

FLORIDA TERRITORY

ST. AUGUSTINE

PENSACOLA

MOBILE POINT

DAUPHIN ISLAND

RIGOLETS

CHEF MENTEUR

FT. ST. PHILIP

FT. JACKSON

ST. MARKS

CANTONMENT BROOK

MILITARY MAP of the UNITED STATES in 1818-1825

Principal posts and fortifications existing or under construction on JANUARY 1, 1818 shown in black; those established during CALHOUN'S Administration of the WAR DEPARTMENT shown in red. Works abandoned before 1825 not shown, except Indian Trading Posts, all abolished in 1822. Boundary Lines as of MARCH 4 1825.

Coastal Fortifications

Frontier Army Posts

Government-operated Indian Trading Posts or Factories

Posts or Forts for which Congressional approval was withdrawn

JOHN C. CALHOUN

Nationalist, 1782-1828

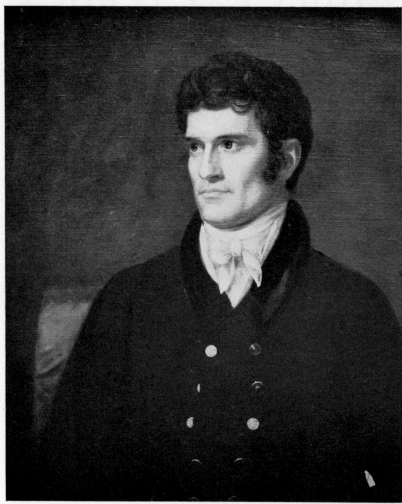

JOHN C. CALHOUN
by Charles B. King

JOHN C. CALHOUN

NATIONALIST, 1782-1828

by

Charles M. Wiltse

THE BOBBS-MERRILL COMPANY, INC.

Publishers

INDIANAPOLIS NEW YORK

TABLE OF CONTENTS

CHAPTER   PAGE

   I   Long Canes 11

  II Yale and Litchfield 25

 III Upcountry Lawyer 40

 IV The War Hawks 53

  V New England Objects 67

 VI The Strategy of Obstruction 80

 VII Peace Without Victory 92

VIII Nationalism Triumphant 103

 IX Subsidized Industry 114

  X Binding the Republic Together 127

 XI The War Department 142

 XII Jackson Disregards Orders 155

XIII Military Policy 164

XIV Depression and Reaction 175

 XV A Fire Bell in the Night 188

XVI The Gage Is Thrown Down 198

XVII The Campaign Begins 211

XVIII The Glittering Crown 225

XIX Candidate 240

 XX Calhoun Fights Back 249

XXI Mostly Personal 264

XXII Candidate No Longer 272

TABLE OF CONTENTS—*Continued*

CHAPTER   PAGE

XXIII   NATIONALISM CRUMBLES 285

XXIV   CLAY MAKES A PRESIDENT 299

XXV   A VICE PRESIDENT IN OPPOSITION 315

XXVI   ONSLOW AND PATRICK HENRY 328

XXVII   PLANTERS AND PLAIN REPUBLICANS 340

XXVIII   DEMOCRACY ADVANCES 352

XXIX   THE TARIFF OF ABOMINATIONS 365

XXX   SOUTH CAROLINA OBJECTS 375

XXXI   CALHOUN TAKES HIS STAND 387

APPENDIX A 401

APPENDIX B 403

APPENDIX C 404

NOTES 405

BIBLIOGRAPHY 443

PERSONAL ACKNOWLEDGMENTS 454

INDEX 457

LIST OF ILLUSTRATIONS

John C. Calhoun, by Charles B. King *(Permission The Corcoran Gallery of Art, Washington, D. C.)* . . . *Frontispiece*

FACING
PAGE

Map of South Carolina 30

View of the City of Washington about 1812, looking down the Potomac from Georgetown *(From a contemporary woodcut in the Library of Congress)* 31

Langdon Cheves *(From a portrait by Hal Morrison)* . . . 96

Henry Clay *(From a portrait by Charles Wilson Peale in possession of the Historical Society of Pennsylvania)* . . . 96

James Madison *(From a portrait by Gilbert Stuart)* . . . 96

James Monroe *(From a portrait by Gilbert Stuart)* 96

John C. Calhoun, about 1818, by John Wesley Jarvis *(Original in possession of Yale University)* 97

Andrew Jackson, by Thomas Sully *(The Corcoran Gallery of Art)* 128

William Harris Crawford, by John Wesley Jarvis *(Courtesy of the Pennsylvania Academy of the Fine Arts)* 129

The Old House of Representatives, by Samuel F. B. Morse *(The Corcoran Gallery of Art)* 224

"Oakly," the Calhoun home in Georgetown *(Print from the Pictorial Archives of Early American Architecture, Library of Congress)* 225

John Quincy Adams, by Thomas Sully *(National Gallery of Art)* 256

Calhoun as Secretary of War, by Rembrandt Peale *(National Gallery of Art)* 257

Mrs. John C. Calhoun *(From a miniature believed to be by Charles Fraser)* 320

LIST OF ILLUSTRATIONS—*Continued*

FACING
PAGE

Calhoun as Vice President, from a miniature by John Trumbull
(Courtesy of Yale University Art Gallery) 321

George McDuffie *(Source of portrait unknown. Reproduction
by L. C. Handy Studios)* 352

Daniel Webster, by Joseph Wood *(Courtesy of the New
Hampshire Historical Society)* 352

Martin Van Buren, by Henry Inman *(New York City Hall)* . 352

John Randolph of Roanoke, by Chester Harding *(The Corcoran Gallery of Art)* 352

Sketch of Calhoun, by Rembrandt Peale *(Reproduced by permission of the owner, Mr. Charles Coleman Sellers)* . . 353

JOHN C. CALHOUN

Nationalist, 1782-1828

CHAPTER I

LONG CANES

1

To THE end of a long and tempestuous life, Andrew Jackson regretted that he had not hanged John C. Calhoun. To the direct, blunt mind of the old soldier the doctrine that a state might nullify an act of Congress was treason, and those who ruled the growing industrial empire of New England and the middle states agreed with him. Relieved by successive tariffs of the restraining influence of competition, their enterprises had grown strong and profitable, and there were those among them to whom higher and ever higher tariffs seemed to mean unlimited wealth and boundless power. By 1828 these industrial interests dominated Congress, and in the Tariff of Abominations Calhoun read the doom of the cotton-growing South.

The tall, magnetic Scotch-Irish planter from South Carolina who sacrificed his own dearest ambition to champion the cause of the cotton states was one of the brilliant leaders of American democracy. Again and again his gifts of mind and character carried him to the very threshold of the White House, and as often he turned away while the Presidential mantle settled upon the shoulders of lesser men. He spoke for an economic interest whose exploitation by the new union of government and industry was threatening its existence, and in so doing he spoke for all minorities in all democratic states. The issue was as old as government itself, though it was phrased, as it always is, in language familiar to the given day and age.

2

Peace had returned to the South Carolina highlands by 1782, though the British held Charleston still. The fort at Ninety Six bore the scars of siege, and farther to the north armies remained in

11

the field; but so far as the pine barrens and rolling hills of the middle and upper country were concerned, the Revolution was over. A newly elected legislature met at Jacksonborough in January to restore civil government to the state, while farmers and artisans resumed their accustomed tasks. It was in this new independent America that John Caldwell Calhoun was born on March 18, 1782, near Abbeville in Ninety Six District, which his father, Patrick Calhoun, represented in the legislature.

The Calhouns were a family to whom political protest was second nature. Descended from the Scottish clan of Colquhoun, land hunger first drove them to northern Ireland, and after a generation of religious and economic friction sent them on again across the sea. In 1733 they settled near the Potomac River in western Pennsylvania, most of which was then included in Lancaster County. Pat Calhoun was six years old and the youngest of a clan that included his father, also named Patrick; his mother, Catherine Montgomery; three older brothers, William, James and Ezekiel; and a married sister, Mary Noble, with John Noble, her husband.[1] They were not a people to be long content in any community guided by other hands than their own, but they were industrious and frugal. When old Patrick died in 1741, he left an estate worth more than £150, including land, stock and tools.

Three or four years later the Calhouns moved down the long valley of the Shenandoah to the southern part of Augusta County, Virginia, at that time a princely domain which extended from the Appalachian foothills to the Mississippi. No doubt it was a group migration, including Montgomerys, Nobles, Pickenses, and many others besides Calhouns, some of them tempted by the prospect of mild climate and rich soil, some merely restless and others going because their friends and neighbors went. Carrying tools and equipment, food and seed for the planting, and driving cattle and sheep ahead of them, they continued southward to the valley of the New River, in what is now Wythe County. At Reed Creek, a few miles from the present town of Wytheville, they halted and began to take up land.

The first official mention of the family in their new home is an entry in the Augusta County court records for September 19, 1746, which committed James, Ezekiel, William and Patrick Colhoon for the November court on the charge that they were "divulgers of

false news to the great detriment of the inhabitants of the colony."
Later in the same year the Calhoun brothers appear among those
ordered to work on a road from "Reed Creek to Eagle Bottom and
thence to the top of the ridge that parts the waters of New River
and those of the south fork of Roanoke."[2] Thereafter the names of
the four brothers, and of others associated with them or related to
them, are mentioned over and over again in order books, will books,
deed books, and court records of the county. James Calhoun
became a constable in 1747, and qualified as captain of a troop of
horse in 1750. All of the brothers were now and again involved in
litigation, and they served frequently as witnesses or sureties for
others. Land was granted to them and bought and sold by them.
James, Ezekiel and William married; and John Noble died, leaving four sons and a daughter.[3] Quite obviously the family prospered; and before they had been in Virginia a full ten years, their
holdings amounted in all to three thousand acres of fertile bottom
land, stretching for several miles up and down Reed Creek, and as
much or more running up into the hills.[4]

The Calhouns might have remained permanently in the peaceful
valley of the New River, along with their Scotch-Irish neighbors,
had circumstances permitted. But the struggle between European
powers for empire and world domination was in one of its more
active phases in the mid-eighteenth century, and France and England chose to make the New World a battleground. The French
and Indian War broke out in 1754, and its first result was a wave of
Indian depredations, incited by the French, along the whole Appalachian frontier. Intrenched at Fort Duquesne, the French sent
bands of marauding savages against the English settlements in
ever-increasing numbers, and it became obvious even to the colonial
officials safe at the seaboard that something must be done. They
chose to wrest Fort Duquesne from the French; and when Braddock failed in his attempt to take that stronghold in 1755, he turned
loose upon the back country of Pennsylvania and Virginia the full
horror of Indian war.

3

In the same year an earlier agreement between the colonial government of South Carolina and the Cherokee Nation was reaf-

firmed, by which a fort was to be built beyond the mountains to protect the Indians against the French, and in return the colony acquired title to all lands to the south and east of Long Cane Creek. The nearest important settlement to this newly opened country was at Waxhaw, then in South but now in North Carolina, and it was probably on a visit there that Pat Calhoun heard about it. He lost no time in carrying the news back to Reed Creek, and the Calhouns prepared once more to move.[5]

Pressure from the Indians along the Virginia frontier must indeed have been severe, for the party set out in midwinter with their heavy wagons, their livestock, and their household goods. Besides Patrick, who led the caravan, there was seventy-year-old Catherine, the three older brothers and their families, Mary Noble and her children, and perhaps others related by blood or marriage. They were soon followed by many friends and neighbors, forming part of a mass migration from Pennsylvania and Virginia.

As far south as Waxhaw the road was passable for teams of oxen, following most of the way the well-traveled Catawba Path, main trading route to the West. Below Waxhaw the trail was less definite and progress must have been slow, but the Calhouns were not the first to come this way. They merely extended the fringe of population a few miles farther west. There were settlements along Waxhaw Creek and the Catawba River, growing less frequent as they followed the high ground south to Rocky Creek. Turning west again they crossed the Broad River near the mouth of the Enoree and went up into the highlands, where they forded Little River and the Saluda to reach the trading post of Ninety Six. There they left the last white man behind as they pushed on to Long Cane Creek.[6]

After the long, rough journey, this country of gently rolling hills, covered with a thick growth of canes from five to thirty feet in height, must indeed have seemed the promised land. The climate, even in February, was mild. The soil was rich and game was plentiful. Deer and buffalo roamed the canebrakes, and wild turkeys flew up in noisy alarm from the thickets.[7]

The main body of emigrants stopped at Long Cane Creek and built there the Long Canes settlement. The Calhouns, however, pushed on a few miles farther west to the stream now called Little

River, but then regarded as a branch of Long Cane Creek. About
three miles from the mouth of a small tributary stream, which soon
came to be known as Calhoun's Creek, the Calhoun settlement was
located. Just above the settlement the creek divided into North and
South Forks, and it was on the north side of the South Fork that
Patrick Calhoun selected his land and built his log cabin.

At some point in the travels of the family, probably in Virginia,
Pat had learned surveying, and was presently commissioned by the
Surveyor General as his deputy for the new settlement. The surveying was under way by summer, though formal applications for
land warrants were not made until 1758. Ezekiel Calhoun received
five hundred acres, William four hundred, James three hundred
and fifty, Mary Noble three hundred, and Patrick two hundred in
the first distribution; and all of them got additional grants at later
dates, placing their individual holdings substantially above the
average for the upper country.[8]

By the end of 1758 more than fifty plats had been surveyed. A
mill was in operation on Calhoun's Creek, and there was a wagon
road clear to the forks of the Edisto, two-thirds of the way to
Charleston. The community was already one of the largest in all
the upper country.

4

The Long Canes settlement lay west of the creek whose "dividing waters" marked the Indian boundary, and the Cherokees looked
upon its growth with increasing alarm. Within two years game had
become so scarce that the Indians could no longer keep their villages
supplied. Such was the situation when a belated British victory at
Fort Duquesne drove a new wave of savages to the South. Clashes
soon occurred in the Long Canes region, and by the winter of
1759-1760 affairs had become menacing.

Although they might easily have fortified their homes against
attack, the settlers chose flight instead. Early on the morning of
February 1, 1760, a party of two hundred and fifty, some fifty or
sixty of them armed men, set out for Augusta, fifty miles away.
James Calhoun was the leader of the expedition.

The journey was uneventful for the first few hours, and when the heavily loaded wagons turned to cross Long Cane Creek, no member of the party thought to warn of danger. Beyond the creek the wagons mired and the men of the party laid aside their weapons while they strove to get the ponderous wheels once more on solid ground. Then without warning a band of Cherokees swept down upon them, killing and scalping while the men struggled desperately to reach their guns.

Fifty persons were killed or captured in the massacre. Among the dead were James Calhoun and his aged mother. Two daughters of William Calhoun were killed and another taken into captivity, from which she escaped after fourteen years.[9] Thirteen loaded wagons were also lost.

The survivors pushed on to Augusta, but Patrick Calhoun went back to bury the dead. Three weeks later he was in Charleston, urging aid for the stricken settlement in the tangible guise of fighting men. It was Patrick, too, who erected stones to mark the scene of the massacre, one of them a memorial to his mother.

The appeal of the settlers for help was not unheeded. A regiment of twelve hundred Highlanders and a third as many provincials under Colonel Montgomerie left Charleston April 1 and reached Fort Prince George early in June. On his way to Fort Loudoun, however, Montgomerie was ambushed and defeated by the Cherokees. Fort Loudoun surrendered in August and its garrison was massacred, after accepting a guarantee of safe-conduct from the Indians. Thus in South Carolina as in Virginia and Pennsylvania, the Americans learned that if they were to be protected at all, they must protect themselves. The British soldier of that day was regarded as the finest fighting man in Europe, but along the Appalachian foothills he was looked upon with something bordering on contempt.

A new expedition under Colonel Grant the following year made generous use of the upcountry militia and won a decisive victory. The resulting treaty redrew the Indian boundary to validate the encroachments of the Long Canes settlers, but the gesture was needless. The final British victory in the French and Indian War came in 1763 and removed the last barrier to English settlement beyond the mountains. No further effort was made to observe any treaty line with the Cherokees, who kept up a desultory border warfare until after the Revolution.

In October of 1764 we find the assembly voting six months' pay
for a company of rangers, or mounted riflemen, to protect the Long
Canes settlement. The company was to consist of twenty men, a
sergeant, and a captain, the last to serve without pay. The captain
was Patrick Calhoun.[10]

5

The Indian uprisings of 1760 and 1761 fell with particular fury
upon the Long Canes settlement, and many of those who lived there
moved north to the greater security of the more populous region
around Waxhaw. One of these was Ezekiel Calhoun, and it was
there that his daughter Rebecca met her future husband, Andrew
Pickens, one day to become a general in the Revolutionary Army.
It was presumably also at Waxhaw that Patrick Calhoun discovered a cultured and by no means unattractive woman in the person
of Jean Craighead, whom he had probably known when she was a
child in Augusta County. Jean was the daughter of the Reverend
Alexander Craighead, who had gone from Ulster to western Pennsylvania about the same time as the Calhouns, and may indeed have
been of the same party. He followed to Augusta County in 1749
and joined the flight from the Virginia border after Braddock's
defeat. He was now settled at Sugar Creek, just over the line in
North Carolina, but his daughter Nancy was married to Glasgow-
bred William Richardson, pastor of the Waxhaw Church, and her
sisters were much in her company.

Dr. Richardson was the only minister in those troubled times
who regularly served an upcountry congregation. He visited Long
Canes in 1764 to preach and to help organize a church, and he found
many a devout Presbyterian family eagerly awaiting his coming.
So long had they been without the offices of the church that sixty
children were awaiting baptism. He performed the marriage service for not a few upcountry couples too, probably Pat Calhoun and
Jean Craighead among them.[11]

In the early 1760's Patrick Calhoun was one of the most active
and industrious citizens of the whole upper country. His duties as
Indian fighter and as surveyor kept him almost constantly on the
move, and he could have found little time in these crowded years to
attend to his farms or to enjoy the companionship of his young

bride. The Long Canes community was growing, both in numbers and in the variety of its cultural and political life. New settlers of Scotch-Irish ancestry arrived in long wagon trains from Pennsylvania and Virginia, or direct from Ireland by way of Charleston. From France, for conscience' sake, came a band of Huguenots, and from Germany came the Palatines. For all of these Pat Calhoun surveyed homesteads, and often enough helped to build houses, too. Sometimes he served as commissary, and always as instructor in the ways of the frontier.[12]

Undoubtedly these newcomers from southern and central Europe left their impress upon the culture of the upper country, just as the peculiar geographic and economic conditions of the region molded in some measure the characters of those who came to dwell in it. The times were troublous and hard, and the upcountry was soon to need the services of all her adopted sons, French, German, and Ulster-Scot alike. So too was Pat Calhoun to need the emotional outlet of hard labor at exacting tasks. Later in life than all his brothers he had waited to start a family of his own, but Jean Craighead did not survive her first confinement. Virtually all we know of her is contained in the brief, cryptic notice of her death in the *South-Carolina Gazette* of Monday, October 13, 1766:

"Long Canes, Sept. 24, 1766

"Of a Miscarriage of Twins, on the 10th Instant, died here, in the 24th Year of her age, one of the most pious and accomplished young Women in these Parts, in the Person of Mrs. Calhoun, the Wife of *Patrick Calhoun,* Esq.; and Daughter of the Rev. *Alexander Craighead.*"[13]

The twins did not survive their mother, and Patrick Calhoun threw himself with all the restless energy of grief into the political struggle then coming to an issue between wealthy and powerful coastal planters and the more numerous but unrepresented small farmers of the upcountry districts.

6

Among the proprietors of the original South Carolina colony was the philosophically minded Earl of Shaftesbury, who asked his friend and counselor, John Locke, to draw up a Fundamental Constitution for the new settlement. The document Locke produced sought to avoid a "numerous democracy"; and although its terms were never completely carried out—it had the fatal defect of providing for more officeholders than there were people in the colony— a landed aristocracy came shortly into being. The rich coastal plain was cut up into huge plantations, thousands and often tens of thousands of acres in extent; and the labor needed to make them productive was presently supplied by the importation of African slaves. Profits from rice, from indigo, and later from cotton, were large and wealth accumulated rapidly.

By the middle of the eighteenth century, when the rolling hills of the piedmont and the fertile plateaus of the Blue Ridge itself were thrown open to settlement, the low country already had a well-developed social organization, an established church, a culture and a cohesion all its own. It had, too, a fair degree of representative government functioning through the colonial assembly and an entirely adequate system of courts. Local government was organized on the basis of parishes, but many of its functions were actually exercised by the plantations, each of which was a community in itself.

Between the wealthy slaveholding planters of the low country, many of them descendants of Cavaliers and members of the Church of England, and the hardy but less privileged Scotch-Irish of the upper settlements, stanchly republican and almost fanatically Presbyterian, there was no common bond. Social, commercial and political interests were alike concentrated in Charleston; and it was hardly to be expected that the lowland aristocracy would surrender any part of its power to small farmers who held no slaves and had scarcely been in America long enough to shake the dust of Ulster from their feet. The upcountry resented its exclusion from public affairs, and resentment grew to cold fury when the Commons in 1757 refused to pay any part of the cost of building Fort Loudoun. The planters and merchants who made up the lower house feared that such an expenditure would set "a bad precedent by opening a door to great impositions from people who live so very remote." Yet the upcountry settlers were taxed the same forty shillings per acre for their small, diversified farms as were the lowland planters whose profit was infinitely more. Neither would the coastal parishes send militia to aid the western districts in the Cherokee war, although they expected the upcountry farmers to be ready to rush to the defense of the coast when a slave uprising was feared in 1765.

Even after the piedmont could claim a preponderance of the population, it remained without representation and with no legally constituted local government. There were neither schools nor churches except such as the inhabitants provided for themselves, and there were no courts of any description outside the capital city of Charleston. To sue or to answer a summons, however small the cause, the upcountry settler must travel two or three hundred miles to Charleston. If he wished to clear and claim new land, he must first secure his warrant at the seat of government. He must pay as much for a grant of one hundred acres as the low-country planter paid for ten thousand; and if he fell heir to a small estate, the fee for administration bore no relation to the amount of property involved. If he stood on his common-law right to a jury trial, he must still plead his case in Charleston before jurymen who knew nothing of his district and cared nothing for his people. If he would marry in accordance with the laws of the colony, he must get a license in Charleston. He could not even know the law by which he was bound without journeying to the capital, for there was no printed code; and since the upcountry boasted no courts, it had no lawyers.

A petition asking redress of these intolerable grievances reached the capital in 1767. It differed from others that had preceded it only in the determination of its four thousand upcountry backers, who would have delivered it personally but for the assurance of Lieutenant Governor Bull, in whom alone they had confidence, that they would get a fair hearing. While the petition was pondered in Charleston, conditions grew steadily worse in the upcountry. Outlaws and fugitives from the justice of other colonies swarmed into this safe haven where they could count on no interference from the law because there was no law.

Early in 1768 the men of the upcountry took things into their own hands. Calling themselves "Regulators," they rounded up and publicly whipped suspected thieves and destroyed the houses in which they had sheltered. The victims promptly sued, and the Regulators were ordered to pay heavy damages. At this point the Governor stepped in, dismissing all but eight of the cases; but the released Regulators were rearrested without the formality of warrants.

Any lingering faith that might have remained as to the prospect of reform vanished forthwith, and by fall the upcountry was in open rebellion. The service of processes from Charleston was forcibly prevented by the Regulators. The militia refused to obey its low-country commanders, and word came through to the rebels that three thousand armed men from the North Carolina highlands would come to their aid should troops be sent against them.[14]

In the thick of this fight was Patrick Calhoun, Justice of the Peace, erstwhile Captain of Rangers, and Deputy Surveyor.

7

In the circumstances the legislators in Charleston concluded they had gone too far. A circuit-court act was hastily drafted to bring the law to the upcountry, but it provided that judges should serve during good behavior instead of for life; and this obvious insult to officers of the Crown was met by royal disallowance. In the upcountry, men reached again for their muskets and sent angry petitions to the King's representative in the colony. Sponsors for the petitions from Long Canes were Patrick and William Calhoun. The law was redrawn to meet His Majesty's objections and was approved, but not until November 1769. Thereafter the court met three times a year in Charleston and twice a year in each of six other judicial districts into which the colony was divided.

Meanwhile, an election for members of the lower house of the colonial legislature was held in October 1768, but elaborate precautions were taken to keep upcountry men from voting. The polling places were fixed near the coast, and in many cases the wrong place was indicated, or the wrong date was given to the unrepresented farmers. In at least one instance the would-be voter was allowed to go only a few miles before hired thugs attacked his home, a circumstance which served as an effective check to any of his neighbors who might have considered casting a ballot. Nevertheless, when the votes were counted the upcountry was found to have elected one of the fifty members of the Commons.

The following spring in another bitterly contested election, Patrick Calhoun was sent to the Assembly as its second upcountry member, representing Prince William's Parish. The voting place was within twenty-five miles of Charleston, and according to legend he and a band of his neighbors made the long journey to the polls carrying their guns to make sure that their right to vote was not challenged.

Still in his early forties, Patrick Calhoun was perhaps the most prominent man in all the upper country, and he was ready to settle down again. In June of 1770 he married Martha Caldwell, born in Charlotte County, Virginia, whither her forebears had migrated like the Calhouns from Scotland by way of Ulster.[15] Over the next fifteen years a daughter and four sons were born of this marriage. The fourth child and third son was John Caldwell Calhoun.

8

After the Stamp Act, "liberty" and the "rights of Englishmen" were phrases on all men's lips, and a new spirit of independence began to animate the provincial legislatures. The first Assembly of which Patrick Calhoun was a member took a decisive stand in favor of free speech and a free press, voting £1500 for the defense of John Wilkes, the quondam editor of the *North Briton,* whose prosecution for libel was a *cause célèbre* throughout the empire. When the appropriation was rejected by the Council, the Commons refused to vote money for carrying on the business of the colony. The argument proved unanswerable, and the Commons made good their sole power of appropriation against all the legal batteries of the Crown.

Patrick Calhoun remained in the colonial legislature only until 1772, but he was back as a member of the first Provincial Congress, which met on January 11, 1775. His brother-in-law, Major John Caldwell, represented the region between the Broad and Saluda Rivers, and although his name does not appear in the list of members, William Calhoun was also present in time to sign the resolutions of the Congress a few days later.[16] Patrick was re-elected to the second Provincial Congress, which came together in November, and was presumably present when a constitution was adopted and the members resolved themselves into the first General Assembly of the State of South Carolina. He remained in the legislature until his death in 1796.

Aside from his services in the assembly, little is known of Patrick Calhoun's activities during the Revolution. He was nearing fifty when the war broke out, and seems to have been content to leave the fighting to younger men. His sympathy with the cause of independence was beyond question; but the old differences were not forgotten by the survivors of the "Regulation." The Crown had been more generous to the upcountry than had the lowland planters, and they wanted to be quite sure that revolution would bring reform.

Long Canes escaped the worst ravages of war, and even as the troops moved up and down the state, Patrick Calhoun continued to acquire land. The return of peace found him the owner of more than a thousand acres, five times the average upcountry holding, and possessed of slaves in corresponding numbers.[17] Honored and respected throughout the state, he was the first citizen of his section, but he was not satisfied. Independence had brought no change in the relations between the coastal parishes and the more populous highlands, and so it had not brought freedom to the upper country.

Conscious of an impending crisis, the legislature voted in 1786 to move the capital to Columbia, hoping to pacify, at least for a time, the embattled upcountry farmers. Before the change could go into effect, however, the Philadelphia Convention completed its work, and the South Carolina delegates were back with a new Federal Constitution on which they asked the state to pass judgment. The legislature voted unanimously for a convention to consider the document, but Charleston rather than Columbia was chosen as the place of meeting. The upcountry delegates, among them Joseph Calhoun, a nephew of Patrick, honored the convention with their presence, but almost to a man they voted nay. Ratification was secured by 149 to 73, but the vote was along strict sectional lines.[18] The upcountry had so far gained little from a state government only two hundred miles away and saw no reason to expect more from a federal government whose seat was remote Philadelphia. Objections to the new Constitution were various, but if one could be taken as fundamental, it was that expressed by Patrick Calhoun, that it permitted the taxation of South Carolinians by someone

other than themselves and so violated the principle of the Revolution.[19]

Disagreement over a form of government for the Union could
not fail to fan into flame once more the smoldering sectional quarrel within the state, nor could it fail to leave its impress on the
eager mind of John Caldwell Calhoun. Patrick talked freely of
political matters before his family, and John Caldwell when past
sixty still remembered his father's conviction that good government
meant the maximum of individual liberty compatible with life in
society.[20] John was in his eighth year when the long-awaited state
constitutional convention met in Columbia, May 12, 1790. The
low country sought to maintain a century-old vested economic interest against sheer weight of numbers, while the upcountry demanded political equality which would carry with it the power to
rectify the economic inequality between the sections. It was to this
sectional struggle in South Carolina that Calhoun recurred forty
years later when the prosperity of the entire South was challenged
by a numerically stronger interest. It was an important influence in
determining his future career and in molding his political creed.

When the convention met, Charles Pinckney, Governor at thirty-
two, was in the chair. He handled his office so well that, though the
low-country aristocracy to which he himself belonged branded him
a traitor and dubbed him "blackguard Charlie," a compromise acceptable to both sections was worked out and passed. Upcountry
representation was increased somewhat in the state senate, and increased by sixty-seven percent in the lower house. The arrangement
still left the low country with a safe majority in each chamber, but
the upcountry was for the time being content to accept the gain and
not to demand representation proportionate to its population. As a
further concession to the democratic and Presbyterian highlands,
the new constitution abolished primogeniture and granted complete
religious equality. Thus early in his life, John Calhoun learned the
value of compromise and the worth of purposeful resistance in
bringing it about.

CHAPTER II

YALE AND LITCHFIELD

1

FOR ALL its growing respectability and its new-found political power, the upcountry was only meagerly supplied with schools. There was no "academy" in all the Carolina piedmont in the 1790's, and no school of any sort save those conducted for a few weeks or months at a time by itinerant teachers. John Calhoun attended one of these "field schools" long enough to learn the three R's,[1] but until he was nearly grown the best of his education was acquired at home. Working in the fields with his playmate Sawney, son of Pat Calhoun's first slave, he learned the value and dignity of labor; and his father, who had fought for freedom against royal and republican governments alike, taught him to prize liberty above all other possessions.

While John was imbibing the elements of political dissent along with Calvinistic theology and applied agriculture, a new preacher put in an appearance at Abbeville, which had become the center for the district. His name was Moses Waddel and he came from Appling, Georgia, fifty miles away, where he had recently become headmaster of a school for boys. The combined responsibilities of teacher and minister seemed to weigh down the young preacher not at all. The fatiguing ride every week end in no way lessened the brilliance of his conversation, nor yet the animation of his glance, if all accounts be true. As was the custom in frontier communities, the minister was always the house guest of the more well-to-do members of the community, and Waddel stayed often at Patrick Calhoun's. It was soon obvious to all that he had his reasons, and no one was surprised when he married Catherine Calhoun, Patrick's only daughter.[2]

Waddel had early been impressed with the bright look and eager questions of his future brother-in-law, and a few months after the marriage, arrangements were made to send the boy to Carmel Academy, as the school near Appling was called. John was thirteen years old when his formal education began late in 1795, but his studies were of brief duration. On January 15, 1796, Patrick Calhoun died, in his sixty-ninth year, and was followed within two months by Moses Waddel's young bride of a year.[3]

The bereaved minister promptly closed the school, but John remained in his household, eagerly pursuing a newly discovered taste for books. Waddel was often away, carrying his own sustaining faith to a dozen upcountry communities in Georgia and South Carolina, but he left behind a circulating library of which he had charge. In this library the young scholar spent all his waking hours, bending his tousled head over current works of history and philosophical classics as long as daylight lasted, and on into the evening by candlelight. He spent altogether fourteen weeks in Dr. Waddel's library, and curious indeed is the list of books he read. There was Rollin's *Ancient History,* newly translated from the French, and treating in eight substantial volumes of Egypt, Carthage, Assyria, Babylon, Medea and Persia, Macedonia and Greece. There was the learned William Robertson's monumental history of the reign of the Emperor Charles V, a three-volume edition of which had been published in Philadelphia as early as 1770, and the same author's work on the discovery of America and the conquest of Mexico and Peru. No doubt he found the more sprightly style of Voltaire's history of Charles XII, King of Sweden, a pleasant relief ; and he was probably fascinated, as many a boy has been since, by the voyages of Captain James Cook.

Then he turned to John Locke's ponderous *Essay Concerning Human Understanding;* but by the time he reached the chapter on Infinity about midway in Book II, his eyes were inflamed and he had grown thin and sallow from too much close application and too little air and exercise. Returning home to find his young charge in such a state, Waddel wrote in alarm to Martha Calhoun, and John was hastily recalled to the healthier atmosphere and more robust duties of the farm.[4]

2

The next four years were lived out of doors, hunting and fishing, working in the fields, and taking part in the familiar country sports with his younger brother, Patrick. When the older brothers were away, John looked after the business of the plantation and presently became its manager when William and James left home to enter business.[5]

During all this time he had little contact with books, but there were newspapers from Charleston and Augusta, filled with the doings of the legislature and of the Congress at Washington, the activities of President Adams and of his arch-opponent, a loose-jointed farmer from the Virginia back country named Thomas Jefferson. The papers kept alive the taste for politics aroused by Pat Calhoun's example and fostered by his own reading of history. The innate ability of this tall, gangling youth with his shining brown eyes and his thick, unruly hair was evident to all who knew him, and gradually the conviction grew in the family and among the neighbors that John Calhoun ought to have an education.

When James came home for a visit in the summer of 1800 he proposed that John should enter a profession. The younger brother seized the idea eagerly but asked for seven years of preparation. He favored the bar, but he would rather remain a planter than become a half-educated lawyer. The other members of the family were probably thinking in terms of Dr. Waddel's newly reopened academy,[6] but they quickly adjusted themselves to John's more ambitious plans. His mother's consent was freely given, and James agreed to manage the property and provide the funds.

So it fell out that in June of 1800, on the very eve of the "wonderful century," young Calhoun set off for Appling to begin his education. The road led past fields of cotton where the wild cane had stood twenty feet in height within his own memory. Singing Negroes worked in the same broad meadows where his father had fought the Cherokees, and the very road he followed had been a buffalo trail when the Calhouns first came to South Carolina forty-odd years ago. But of these things he was probably quite oblivious. His thoughts were for the future rather than the past.

If there was wonder in the gray eyes of Moses Waddel as he welcomed his onetime brother-in-law, it was more for the change he saw in him than for the fact that he had come. The awkward, shaggy-haired lad, who had left the school only a little more than four years before, now towered nearly half a foot above his teacher.

His hair was shaggy still, and shaggy it remained to the end of his life, though it lost its chestnut color with the passing years. While seemingly combed back, it stood straight up and added an appearance of even greater height to his six feet and two inches. His features were regular and strong, and his deep-set brown eyes seemed to kindle as he talked until all color vanished and only light remained. In his nineteenth year, Calhoun was already a commanding figure of a man.

Moses Waddel was also a leader of men in his own special way. Those who came under his tutelage were not all men when they came to him, but all were men when they left. If there was any spark there, he found it and fanned it into flame. If there was the stuff of character there, he went unerringly to it and wrought his magic upon it. Pre-eminently he was a teacher, whose school at Willington on the South Carolina side of the Savannah, to which he moved in 1804, became one of the most famous in the South. It had no buildings to speak of—only rude log cabins, often enough built by the boys themselves, scattered over a few acres of field and woodland—but it left its impress again and again in the more enduring architecture of the living spirit. Among the more famous of Waddel's pupils, in addition to Calhoun, were William H. Crawford, Hugh Legaré, James L. Petigru, George McDuffie, Thomas W. Cobb and A. B. Longstreet.

No boy in the school was ever held back because some slower or less industrious lad could not keep up. Each moved ahead as fast as his own qualities would take him, constantly spurred on by the strict but kindly teacher to do better than his best. In that day corporal punishment was the very basis of most educational endeavor. Not only was rigid discipline maintained by abundant use of the rod, but lessons were learned from day to day for fear of the certain thrashing that would follow if they were not. This method Waddel never used. Discipline was strict and was enforced in the approved manner; but lessons were learned not for fear of any whipping but because it was a prime disgrace to fail in an assignment, and the opprobrium of one's fellows has always been the most condign of punishments.

The scholastic pace was rapid for all, and especially so for those like Calhoun who were both older than the average and endowed with superior intelligence. The training of the day was almost exclusively classical, and Moses Waddel, with his ministerial background, was even more strictly a classicist than most. So great was the emphasis on the works of the ancient world that to construe a mere 150 lines of Virgil or Horace as a day's assignment was considered next thing to failing altogether. The school's record was set a few years after the removal to Willington when George McDuffie prepared for one recitation 1,212 lines of Virgil.[7]

Into this atmosphere of antiquity came John C. Calhoun, unversed in Latin or in Greek and with a scholastic background mainly drawn from fourteen weeks of reading history and metaphysics by himself; yet in two years' time he was ready to leave the academy to enter Yale College as a junior.

Before he left for New Haven, Calhoun's mother died;[8] but James carried out to the letter the obligations he had assumed, while William, now a planter, backed him up and Patrick, youngest of the brothers, took over responsibility for the plantation. Leaving behind him such faith in his ability, John had no choice but to succeed.

3

Calhoun arrived in New Haven sometime in October 1802, shortly before the opening of the fall term, and found himself plunged without warning into an atmosphere of intellectual ferment such as he had never known before. The two severe, oblong dormitories—ivy-covered Connecticut Hall or "Old College," and Union Hall or "New College"—had long since been outgrown; and the students, overflowing into rooming houses in the town, had communicated to the little port of New Haven something of their own ebullient spirits. Here was no medieval scholasticism, but a university already aware of the nineteenth century and alive to the new spirit of the times.

Symbolic of a Puritan heritage, the chapel with its tall spire and clear-toned bell stood midway between the two dormitories, and with the smaller, low-built dining hall behind Old College completed the full quota of buildings. No, not quite the full quota, for already the walls of another building were rising above unusually deep foundations: the Lyceum, soon to house the library, the four thousand volumes of which were now miserably cramped on the upper floor of the chapel; new classrooms; and in the basement, to the confusion of traditionalism and the glory of the age, a chemical laboratory! Adjoining the Lyceum was soon to be a new dormitory too, to take care of the rapidly increasing number of students. At the commencement of 1804 it was named Berkeley Hall in honor of the great philosopher who had given his library to the college nearly three-quarters of a century before.

Hovering over it all, and breathing the spirit of learning and of life into the piles of brick and timber, was the guiding genius of Timothy Dwight, embarking upon his eighth year as president of Yale College. Tough, intolerant, bigoted, but aware as were few men of his generation of the potency for good or for evil of the new forces of science and democracy, Dwight brought to his task all of the sincerity, the eloquence and not a little of the genius of his grandfather, Jonathan Edwards. He brought also a rugged will that was more than a match for illness and failing sight, and an instinct for leadership. Under Dwight the college achieved a national reputation, no easy matter in those days of slow communication and sharp cultural differences; and it was this reputation that attracted students from as far away as the Carolinas and Georgia.[9]

Calhoun could not have been long a stranger to the college or to his fellow students. He made friends readily, adapting himself easily and eagerly to new and stimulating surroundings. And stimulating indeed they must have been to this tall, angular young planter of twenty who was experiencing his first contact with the alien culture of the North. He was not much if any above the average age of his classmates, nor was his feat of entering as an upperclassman at all unusual. Few young men in those days had the advantage he had enjoyed of formal preparation for college in a school or academy. Most were tutored by the local minister, and when he deemed them ready they entered the college of their choice as lower or upperclassmen according to their own degree of advancement.

New students were assigned by lot to one of the two campus societies, and so Calhoun became a member of Linonia, though most of the other Southerners belonged to the Brothers in Unity.

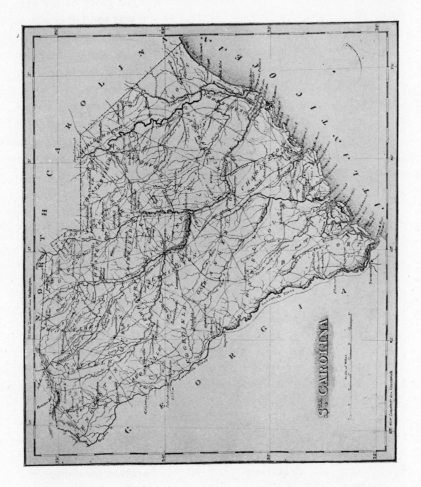

View of the City of Washington about 1812, looking down the Potomac from Georgetown

The rules did not permit transfer of allegiance but it probably made little difference. It was not for the social life Calhoun had come to Yale, and he took small part in Linonian affairs. More to his taste was Phi Beta Kappa, of which he also became a member in his first year on the campus, serving on various of its committees.[10] His temperament was suited to a college where life in the main was serious and even austere.

Students were expected to attend prayers morning and evening and two full services on Sundays and fast days; but though a third or more of her graduates still entered the ministry, Yale was approaching a truly secular status and, politics excepted, was almost liberal. The commencement of 1802 saw Benjamin Silliman take office as professor of chemistry and natural history, and a few months earlier Elizur Goodrich had assumed the duties of a newly established professorship of law. The curriculum also included political science and modern languages. Law and politics claimed almost as many members of the class of 1804 as did the church.

Calhoun's interests as a student accurately forecast those of his maturity. He took pleasure in philosophy and mathematics and was among those who attended Silliman's first lectures in natural science,[11] but it was history and politics to which he devoted himself most assiduously. He was among the subscribers to John Marshall's *Life of Washington*,[12] and followed as closely as news sources permitted the course of contemporary events both at home and abroad. He was planning a political career and was preparing himself for it with the systematic thoroughness that was one of his distinguishing characteristics.

In the circumstances he could hardly have chosen otherwise. The intellectually minded youth of his generation, unless he had strong scientific leanings, was almost forced to choose between the ministry and the law. In the South this was especially true, and there even more than in New England the law was the gateway to a political career. The memory of his father's battle against the low-country aristocracy was still vivid when Calhoun found himself on the defensive in the very center of New England Federalism, and he saw in the quarrel between Jefferson and his opponents the same quarrel he had lived through in South Carolina.

In New Haven at this time lived Pierpont Edwards, youngest son of the great New England theologian and an uncle of Timothy Dwight, but representing the opposite pole in politics. Edwards was the leader of the Jeffersonians in Connecticut and controlled the party patronage for the state. Henry W. Edwards, one of his sons, though already through school and practicing law, was about Calhoun's age and was most probably one of his friends. The town was not so large nor Republicans so plentiful that young men of like minds could not know each other. The Jeffersonians among the students made up in ability what they lacked in numbers, and political discussion was not allowed to languish for want of partisans.

Most popular of all the collegiate activities of the day were the weekly "disputations" of the Junior and Senior years. In these debates groups of eight students participated by turns, with Silliman and Dwight acting as judges for the Juniors and Seniors respectively. The topics debated were often political, and the decisions as often motivated by the forthright Federalist prejudices of the president and his faculty. Elizur Goodrich had even served in Congress as a Federalist and had been named by President Adams during the dying hours of his administration to be Collector of Customs for New Haven, only to be summarily removed from that office by Jefferson. Though democracy had triumphed in the nation, Yale remained obstinately unregenerate, and those who came professing Republicanism were quickly forced to defend their faith or to renounce it.

True to the political creed he had absorbed as a boy from his father, Calhoun was one of those who defended the Jeffersonian cause, so ably as to attract the special notice of Timothy Dwight himself. As the story is told, Dwight asked him in the course of a recitation what he believed to be the legitimate source of political power. Calhoun replied that it could come only from the people themselves, and the resulting argument consumed the rest of the allotted time. Dwight is said to have remarked afterward that the young Carolinian had talent enough to be President of the United States, and predicted that he would one day reach that office. The incident became the theme of a song which swept New Haven in the 1840's:

"John C. Calhoun my Jo, John!
   When we were first acquaint
You were my chum at Yale, John,
   And something of a Saint—
And Doctor Dwight, God bless him John!
   Predicted as you know
You'd be the Nation's President,
   John C. Calhoun, My Jo!"[13]

Politics was, indeed, the standard fare for all Americans in those turbulent days of Jefferson's first administration. Politics was the breath of life to the small farmer and petty tradesman whose votes for Jefferson had raised them to new dignity and power. Politics filled the newspapers and found further outlet in broadsides and pamphlets by the thousands. Politics contested with justice for the attention of the courts, and politics now and again made its presence known even in the pulpit. So universal a theme could hardly fail to occupy much of the time of students and faculty alike. Even Timothy Dwight, who preached so eloquently in the college chapel that one forgot the cold of the unheated building, stood menacingly in heavy brown greatcoat and pounded mittened fists upon the pulpit as he denounced the "blockheads and knaves" who had brought chaos to the land, not sparing his own cousin, Vice President Aaron Burr. "Pope" Dwight, as he was known to the unregenerate, made no effort to conceal his Federalist convictions, and found ways to bring them into sermon and lecture alike.

Democracy in New England was very much on trial, and many believed that anarchy and civil conflict were near. The Jeffersonians were "Jacobins" when they were not called by less complimentary names, and they were distinctly unacceptable in Federalist households. In this atmosphere of vigorous opposition Calhoun made warm friends, even among those with whom he disagreed; yet he remained true to his father's creed, and as eager as Pat had been to fight for a principle. As the commencement exercises drew near, he prepared to speak on "the qualifications necessary to constitute an ideal statesman."[14]

The oration was never delivered, and in spite of his hopes Calhoun was not present on September 12, 1804, when President Dwight presented diplomas to sixty-five other members of the class. A month before the graduation he became ill, and although he fancied himself recovering nicely before the end of August, he was still too ill when the long-awaited time arrived "to participate either in the pleasures or exercises of the day."[15] The illness was probably yellow fever.

4

It was at the time of his graduation from Yale that Calhoun first became intimate with the family of his cousin, Floride Bonneau Calhoun, who soon came to occupy in his affections the place of the mother he had lost. Mrs. Calhoun was the widow of John Ewing Colhoun, son of Patrick's brother Ezekiel. He was thus first cousin to John Caldwell, although he was a full generation older and retained a different spelling of the name. His widow, however, was always known as Mrs. Calhoun—or "old Mrs. Calhoun" to distinguish her from her daughter, after the latter became John Caldwell's wife—and her name will be so spelled in this work. John Ewing Colhoun was graduated from Princeton in 1774 and set about the study of law, but the Revolution intervened, and it was nine years before he was admitted to the bar. He practiced in Charleston long enough to marry Floride Bonneau, a low-country heiress of Huguenot extraction, in 1786, but soon thereafter he gave up law for the life of an upcountry planter. He was a member of the South Carolina Assembly from 1778 until 1800, and was in the state senate when he was chosen in 1801 to speak for South Carolina in the Senate of the United States. He died in 1802 in Pendleton, having attended only one session of Congress.[16]

After her husband's death, Mrs. Calhoun took up her residence at Bonneau's Ferry on the Cooper River, about twenty miles above Charleston, where she lived with her three surviving children. She lived there, that is, when she was not in Charleston, or Pendleton, or in some northern watering place, or traveling—and she could well afford to travel. The summer of 1804 she spent at Newport, less than one hundred miles from New Haven. News of her impending visit to Rhode Island was duly passed along to Calhoun; and sometime after her arrival there, she wrote her young cousin extending him an invitation to visit her. Her letter found him wracked with fever, but he hastened to reply. He hoped to be well by commencement, and he hoped "above all . . . to recover in order that I may visit New Port, which, with the indulgence of health, I shall do immediately after Commencement."[17]

It was near the end of September before he put in an appearance at the already fashionable resort where his cousin and her family were staying, and the impression seems to have been immediately favorable on both sides. Calhoun soon became a favorite, not alone with his cousin but also with her two boys, John Ewing and James Edward. What impression he made upon twelve-year-old Floride, his cousin's only daughter, we do not know; but within five years she had consented to become his wife.

Calhoun found Newport as pleasant a spot as he had ever visited, though the age of its buildings gave it a melancholy aspect in his eyes. Nevertheless, he remained until well into October; and then, still in the company of Mrs. Calhoun, he visited Boston, all the time regaining his strength and observing the life of the people around him. Shortly before the middle of November he sailed with his cousin and her family for Charleston.

The day before Christmas 1804 he entered the law office of De Saussure and Ford as a student. The fee of one hundred guineas was presumably paid by his brother James, who was in business in the city.[18] Henry William De Saussure was attorney for Mrs. Floride Calhoun and was the guardian of her children. He was also one of the outstanding lawyers of the South, a future chancellor of the state, and a Federalist. No young man preparing for the South Carolina bar could do better than study law in De Saussure's office, but only those from well-to-do families could afford the fee.

It was not Calhoun's intention, however, to content himself with the conventional reading for the bar in a lawyer's office, even that of the most distinguished lawyer in the state. The winter of 1804-1805 was only a sort of prelude to his legal education, which was to begin in earnest in the summer at the famous law school of Judge Tapping Reeve in Litchfield, Connecticut.

This time the trip to New England was made in the private coach of Mrs. Calhoun, who was again on her way to Newport for the summer. They probably used the well-traveled coastal route, which ran from New York, where it joined the Boston Post Road, all the way to Savannah. It was one of the best of the early American highways, where a good private coach might make twenty or thirty miles a day, if the weather was fine, if the streams were not unduly swollen, and if the coachman had the skill and strength to avoid the innumerable ruts, boulders, fallen branches or trunks of trees, and other hazards, any one of which might upset the coach or break a horse's leg.

Doubtless the trip was made at a leisurely pace, for the sake of comfort and for greater safety on the road, since Mrs. Calhoun's three children were in the party. One of these children, James Edward Calhoun, said many years later that a detour had been made on the journey through Virginia so that John Caldwell might call at Monticello and pay his respects to President Jefferson, who detained him overnight and spoke highly of him the next day. The incident would be an important one in Calhoun's life, if only it were true; but the weight of evidence is all against it. It rests solely on an octogenarian's memory of an event supposed to have occurred when he was seven years old, and when, as a matter of fact, the President was in Washington. Calhoun himself never mentions any such visit to Jefferson, as he undoubtedly would have, for political purposes if for no other, had it actually taken place.[19]

After a rest in Philadelphia, the Calhouns directed their course to Princeton, where a son of De Saussure was a student. Calhoun wrote an account of the visit to the father, who hastened to express his pleasure.[20] From Princeton they pushed rapidly on to Newport, spending only a few hours in New York.

5

As he hurried from Newport to Litchfield in mid-July of 1805, Calhoun must have noted with keen interest a fellow passenger who boarded the stage at Hartford—a well-preserved gentleman of sixty, whose broad face was framed by thick, curling gray hair which hung to his shoulders, and who peered through his spectacles at those about him with a mixture of abstraction and interest. Calhoun soon recognized the stranger as Judge Reeve himself, and

lost no time in presenting his letter of introduction. On the journey to Litchfield the judge proved "open and agreeable," and the
young student looked forward with pleasure to "the cultivation of
Blackstone's acquaintance."[21]

The Litchfield Law School was the most famous—almost the
only—institution of its kind then in existence in the United States,
and it drew pupils from the far corners of the Union. Altogether,
Reeve and his partner, James Gould, trained more than a thousand young men for admission to the bar; and a surprisingly large
proportion of them held distinguished public offices. The school
dated its origin from 1774, when Aaron Burr, Reeve's brother-in-
law, became the first student. Others followed, their number increasing until Reeve was forced in 1782 to give up individual
training and substitute a course of lectures. Two years later he
built a small, unheated frame building to accommodate the fifteen
or twenty students he then had, and the building was still his lecture room when Calhoun matriculated in 1805.[22]

Here again he was under the tutelage of ardent, if not violent,
Federalists. Both Reeve and Gould belonged to a group of Litchfield Tories who adhered closely to the more famous "Essex Junto."
Gould was the son-in-law of Federalist Senator Uriah Tracy; and
Reeve had gone so far as to predict that, should Jefferson be elected,
it would not be two years before the streets would run with blood.
As late as January 1801, he was conspiring with Federalist members of Congress to elect Burr rather than Jefferson to the first
office; and only a year and a half before Calhoun's enrollment at
the school, he had expressed his readiness to co-operate in breaking up the Union, should the Federalists decide to take the road to
secession.[23] So high did feeling run that when Selleck Osborne of
the *Witness* was jailed in Litchfield in 1805, some fifteen hundred
Jeffersonians saluted at the window of his cell, among them young
John Calhoun, who was still following in the tradition of his
father.[24] A few months later Reeve himself was indicted by a
Federal grand jury for libeling the President in the *Monitor,* but
the action was dropped at Jefferson's request.

In spite of his political prejudices, Judge Reeve appears to have
been a very good teacher, excelled only by his colleague and former
pupil, suave and lucid James Gould. Somehow the two teachers

managed to keep politics out of their lectures: at least Calhoun gives no hint of any political discussions or disagreements in his frequent letters to his future mother-in-law. But neither the learning of Reeve nor the logic of Gould could arouse in him any real enthusiasm for the subject they taught. Before he had been at Litchfield three weeks, he was writing to Mrs. Calhoun of his "dry and solitary journey through the exterior fields of law"; and to his cousin Andrew Pickens he was even more specific a few months later. "Many things I study for the love of study, but not so with law. I can never consider it, but as a task which my situation forces on me. I therefore, often lay it aside for the more delicious theme of the muses, or interesting pages of history." Yet from this aversion to the law he drew a motive for industry. "It must be done, and the sooner the better is often my logick."[25] In the same letter he speaks with keen interest of the rising fortunes of Napoleon Bonaparte.

Whatever his inclinations may have been, Calhoun did not stray often from his legal studies. He could find no time to visit, even briefly, with Mrs. Calhoun and her family, although they remained in Newport throughout the winter. There were lectures every weekday, lasting about an hour and a half, and examinations every Saturday afternoon. But it was in connection with the Moot Court held on Monday evenings that he particularly distinguished himself, and it was there that he first developed facility as an extemporaneous speaker. The remainder of the student's time was at his own disposal, but most of it had to be devoted to study, in spite of the attractions of Litchfield's unusually gay social life and the Female Academy kept by Miss Sally Pierce.

With the background he had acquired in De Saussure's office, Calhoun was able to complete the required course in exactly a year, although the usual time was fourteen to eighteen months. He remained at Litchfield, however, until the regular vacation in August, and returned to the school the next month after visiting Newport. He found classes again in session and the judge lecturing on an important subject, so he stayed on for still another month or two[26] before taking the stage for Philadelphia. There he bought a horse, which he rode for the remainder of the journey. He chose the upper or more westerly road, which closely approximated the route by which his father had migrated to South Carolina.

He spent a few weeks in Abbeville with his brothers and friends and then proceeded to Charleston, where he resumed his place in the law office of De Saussure and Ford. So busy was he in his new situation that it was almost Christmas before he found time to write an account of his southward journey to his cousin in Newport.[27]

CHAPTER III

UPCOUNTRY LAWYER

1

CHARLESTON in 1806, with her 21,000 inhabitants, was on the way to becoming third city in the United States. Culture and distinction she had always had, as well as hurricanes and fevers, but now her wharves were piled high with bales of cotton and her warehouses were bursting with more cotton still. Her trade in rice and indigo remained as well, and since the Revolution her market had been not England alone but all the world. The trade winds and the Gulf Stream favored her ships, and there seemed no limit to the wealth and influence that might be hers. She could not know that steam-powered boats like that even then being built in New York by Robert Fulton and Chancellor Livingston would ultimately overcome her advantages of wind and current and turn commerce to the shorter sea lanes from New York and Boston; nor could she anticipate Mr. Jefferson's embargo.

At this time goods for all parts of the state passed through the Charleston customhouse, and Charleston merchants levied their toll upon it before it moved by boat and wagon train to its inland destination. The wagons and boats returned from the upper country loaded with cotton and with rice, with lumber and flour and iron pigs, which were funneled in their turn through the hands of the Charleston merchants, and in their turn paid toll. The merchants grew prosperous and positive; and although they were regarded as socially inferior by the planters, who usually owed them money, their power increased with their means. Still another source of wealth had come their way in 1804, when the slave trade was reopened, and they made the most of it during the four years that it lasted. Between 1804 and the end of 1807, two hundred slave ships entered the port, and thirty thousand Africans were sold, to pile still higher the bales of cotton crowding Charleston's wharves, and add still more to the affluence and importance of that bustling city.[1] So great was the value of merchandise passing through Charleston that the Phoenix Insurance Company of London maintained its own fire engine in the city to protect its risks.[2]

Calhoun boarded in the family of a French Protestant minister, Mr. Detarguey, in Church Street, and lived much to himself. His brother James had closed out his Charleston business to establish himself in Augusta,[3] and his cousin remained at Newport. He had, to be sure, many friends and acquaintances in the city, but he was first of all a student, and to his studies he gave the best of his time and energy. The life of Charleston was more like that of European cities than it was akin to any American counterpart, but to Calhoun it was intemperate and debauched.[4] Calvinist he had been reared, and Calvinist he remained in spirit long after he had ceased to be concerned with dogma.

Already mature in body and in mind, he moved through the vivid city with its gay society and crowded commerce, its cultural pretensions and its sordid trade in human beings, its contrasts and its color, thinking more of morals than of gaiety and more concerned with politics than with the law. The moderate Federalism of De Saussure influenced him no more than had the extreme partisanship of Dwight and Reeve. Republican by birth, breeding and tradition, his years of training under teachers of opposite leaning made him Republican by conviction also.

2

When the damp, stifling heat of the Charleston summer set in, Calhoun fled to Abbeville to complete his legal training in the office of George Bowie, a cousin by marriage and the pioneer lawyer in the district.

His thoughts and energies, however, were soon turned in directions other than the law. On June 22, 1807, the British frigate *Leopard* fired upon the American *Chesapeake,* a war vessel which had refused the British commander permission to board and search for deserters. Public reaction to the outrage was instantaneous and overwhelming, for the *Chesapeake* incident was but the final link in a long chain of abuses. The united anger of all Americans everywhere was compounded not alone of indignation at a violation of national sovereignty. It recalled commercial abuses going back to the Revolution itself: impressment of American seamen, the humiliation of the Jay Treaty, the arrogant denial by Britain of freedom of the seas. It included old scores chargeable to France as well as to England: the X Y Z negotiations and the persistent interference of Bonaparte with American commerce. This deliberate and unprovoked act of war on the part of a British commander, acting under explicit orders from his admiral, committed within sight of Hampton Roads, became the symbol of all the losses, all the indignities, and all the wanton acts of thievery and malice of which England and France alike had been guilty since their own titanic struggle on the continent began.

When news of the *Chesapeake's* fate was received, all sectional and party differences were forgotten and a true nationalism was born in America. In coastal cities and frontier villages from Maine to Georgia and west to the Mississippi, Americans of all ranks and all persuasions met to demand suitable reprisal. The citizens of Abbeville were as prompt as any to denounce the British and to pledge support to the administration. Resolutions were called for, and a committee appointed which included John C. Calhoun. It was the young law student who prepared the draft, and who spoke for the committee when the resolutions were presented. The meeting was large and the occasion was Calhoun's first public address. His brothers were there to hear him, as were friends and neighbors from miles around. No lawyer about to begin his practice could ask for a better chance to show his wares. No youth ambitious for a political career could ask a better opportunity to make his talents known. What he said in his maiden political speech we do not know, but the sequel showed that he did not fail.[5]

3

Calhoun was admitted to the bar early in 1808[6] and celebrated the event by a visit to the Bonneau's Ferry plantation of his cousin. Floride was in her seventeenth year and, with the early maturity of her French ancestry, had grown to womanhood in the year and a half since he had seen her. No doubt it was then that he first beheld in her something more than a mere relative. Before long he was head over heels in love, and his future mother-in-law was acting as adviser in his undeclared suit.[7]

In the practice of the law, meanwhile, he was almost immediately successful, and soon shared with Bowie and Benjamin Yancey the legal business of the district. As early as 1809 he was conceded to be the most promising young attorney in all the upper country, but no degree of success could make him like the law, which he found increasingly confining.[8] In the spring of 1809 Mrs. Calhoun visited the highlands, but she saw little of her young cousin, who sent his apologies by letter. He felt himself "almost as a slave chained down to a particular place and course of life." Though his practice was as large as he could handle, he had lost none of his aversion to the law and was determined to give it up as soon as he had won a competence from it. He could not argue a cause in which he did not believe, nor convince himself of the necessary righteousness of the side prepared to pay the larger fee. On one occasion, as junior counsel in a murder case, he admitted that his client was guilty of manslaughter, but his colleague won an acquittal for the prisoner on a plea of self-defense. The story is told to illustrate the eloquence of the older man, but it reveals as well the intellectual integrity of the younger.[9]

Almost from the very beginning of his legal career, Calhoun had students reading law in his office. One of these was his cousin Patrick Noble, with whom he formed a partnership in 1809. The others of whom we have record were Nathaniel Alcock Ware and Robert Cunningham, son of one of the Revolutionary Tories of that name. These students and colleagues of his three years at the bar testify to Calhoun's extraordinary personal magnetism, and to his natural qualities of leadership. George Bowie's younger brother, the future chancellor of Alabama, tells how he and the other law students used to gather in the summer evenings on Calhoun's piazza, together with the young lawyers in whose offices they studied. Calhoun and Yancey led the conversation, which the younger men found a rare source of improvement. Bowie is also authority for a foot race in which Calhoun defeated the more athletic Yancey. Throughout their lives these students and colleagues remained personally devoted to Calhoun, even though some of them, like Robert Cunningham, broke with him politically during the nullification controversy.[10]

Lawyers in those pioneer days rode circuit with the judges before whom they pleaded, and the pressure of business at each court session made judge and jury alike impatient of delay. Brevity and conciseness of argument rather than fancy rhetoric and rolling oratory were the qualities demanded of a lawyer where simplicity of speech and dress were universal and where court dockets were so crowded that two juries were kept in continuous service, one listening to the arguments of counsel while the other considered a verdict.[11] Calhoun's strength lay in reasoning rather than in declamation, and he was never verbose, qualities which endeared him to upcountry farmers and businessmen and attracted favorable notice from harassed and overworked judges.

4

It was through the eyes of the farmers, the merchants, and the manufacturers who were his clients that Calhoun saw the effects of the embargo, adopted a few days before Christmas 1807.

He saw the rising prosperity of Charleston and its agricultural and manufacturing hinterland come to an abrupt halt. Hardly had the news been received when cotton and rice dropped to a half or a third of their normal value. Idle ships clogged the bay, once busy warehouses were padlocked, and grass actually grew on the wharves. Planter, farmer, and small manufacturer alike felt the effects of Charleston's inactivity. No class was spared, and all sections were equally distressed.[12]

Calhoun did not fail to note and ponder these results of a policy intended as a substitute for war. His brother James was in business, William and Patrick were planters of cotton, and the Bonneau's Ferry plantation was devoted to rice. To the young upcountry lawyer the embargo seemed of doubtful efficacy, and fraught with dangerous political possibilities. He accepted it only as a stopgap to buy time for preparation before hostilities should begin.[13]

With the pros and cons of the embargo we are not here concerned, save only as the measure served to accentuate those sectional and economic differences which were in time to be decisive, both for Calhoun and for the Union. When commerce with Europe was cut off, the prices of manufactured articles rose precipitously, and Northern capital began to be withdrawn from less productive enterprises to be risked in manufacturing ventures, with their promise of fabulous profits. In the South there was no money available for any such purpose, for investment there was in land and slaves. The four years preceding the embargo were the years of the reopened slave trade, into which the speculative capital of the South had gone, even to the extent of mortgaging homes and plantations.[14] Much of the profit from the trade went to New England, where it was available for investment when new opportunity offered.

So manufacturing did not develop in the South, except in the form of some slight expansion of the "household" system of the upper country. The Southern planter had bought new slaves in anticipation of an expanding market for cotton, and he could not now turn to a system into which his slaves would not fit.[15] Economic differences between North and South became more pronounced, and the stage was made ready for the coming controversies over the tariff. By the time nonintercourse succeeded the embargo, the war spirit aroused over the *Chesapeake* had cooled and the spirit of faction had taken its place.[16]

5

The embargo came at a time of internal crisis in South Carolina, confronted once more by rising sectional antagonism. The constitutional compromise of 1790, although it temporarily pacified the upper country and thereby avoided civil turmoil, did not remove the differences between the two sections of the state. There remained two distinct and often hostile societies: one wealthy, aristocratic, cultured and in control of the machinery of government; the other four times as populous, rugged, independent, self-contained, but economically and politically in vassalage to the other. For two generations the low country had feared the potential dominance of the nonslaveholding upcountry farmers, while the latter had resented with growing bitterness their enforced subjection.

The compromise of 1790 had scarcely found its way into the State Constitution before agitation for further revisions began, accompanied by increasing violence and disorder.

It was the fateful impact of technology that was at last to eliminate the differences between upper and lower Carolina, and in the end to fuse the entire South into a single cultural and economic whole. Cartwright's power loom and Whitney's cotton gin brought about an almost fabulous increase in the demand for textile fibers, and the early 1800's saw cotton culture move back from tidewater, above the fall line, on beyond the mountains and out across the Mississippi valley. In those same years were sown the seeds of disunion and civil war, of economic exploitation and moral obloquy, of sectional and racial and class hatreds. The seeds were the green seeds of the upland cotton, and they were placed in the earth by slaves. When the slave trade was reopened and maintained by the votes of upcountry representatives, the major difference between the sections was gone.

In December of 1807, about the time Jefferson's embargo message reached the National Legislature, the General Assembly and the Senate of South Carolina, each with only two dissenting votes, approved a resolution calling for a special session to deal with the question of representation. In record time the compromise of 1808 was brought in and passed by the necessary two-thirds of each house. It provided that half of the 124 members of the assembly were to be chosen on the basis of population, and half on the basis of property, as indicated by taxation. To become a part of the State Constitution, the compromise had still to be submitted to the public three months before the next election, and ratified by a two-thirds vote of the legislature then chosen.

The embargo, with all its attendant distress and political unrest, tended to focus public attention upon national and international rather than local issues; but it served also to unify the state, to show that low country and upcountry were dependent upon each other, and to insure in consequence the final approval of the reapportionment. In Abbeville District the compromise was an election issue, along with the policies of Jefferson's administration. Both were approved, and so the choice of a representative to go to the General Assembly was almost predetermined. In October of 1808 John C.

Calhoun, twenty-six years old and less than a year a member of the
bar, was elected to the legislature from his native district, and on
the fourth Monday in November he began his public career.

6

The election resulted in an overwhelming victory for the Jeffersonians throughout the state, following a bitter campaign in which
the Federalists made the most of the embargo issue. The lower
house was topheavy with Republicans, many of them serving their
first terms, and most of them young.[17] Among the more prominent
members at this time were Langdon Cheves, already marked for
political advancement, and Joseph Alston, son-in-law of Aaron
Burr. William Lowndes, who was to become Calhoun's most intimate friend, was also a member, but was not present at this
session, though the compromise which was its principal business
had originated with him.[18]

Calhoun had not been in Columbia more than a few days before
he was summoned to a party caucus, to select nominees for President and Vice President of the United States. James Madison had
long been understood to be Jefferson's choice, and was accepted as
such by the Republicans of South Carolina; but to the renomination
of George Clinton there was some opposition, in which Calhoun
joined. It offered him an opportunity to state his views on national
questions, and he had come prepared to do just that. His thesis
was that the embargo would not work, and that war with Great
Britain was inevitable. Party unity was therefore of the first
importance, yet discontented Republicans were already rallying
around Clinton. He believed that, should the Vice President be
re-elected, the leadership of this discontented element would ultimately pass to his capable and ambitious nephew, DeWitt Clinton.[19]
The speech made Calhoun from the outset one of the leaders of the
house. He was named aide on the staff of Governor Drayton on
December 15, and the next year was elected a trustee of South Carolina College, a rare compliment indeed for so young a man.[20]

The General Assembly of South Carolina followed more closely
than any other legislative body in America the traditions and practices of the British House of Commons. Members sat with their

hats on, removing them only to speak; and questions were decided by acclamation. It was an unwritten and unbroken law that adjournment should come in time to permit members to be at home by Christmas, which made the sessions surprisingly short. Calhoun's two sessions together amounted to only nine weeks. Much of importance was nevertheless accomplished, with a minimum of friction.

In the session of 1808 the choice of Presidential electors—who were instructed for Madison and Clinton, in spite of misgivings as to the latter—was the first order of business but the sectional compromise was first in importance. The compromise amendment was finally adopted by unanimous vote in both houses. Calhoun thus had the satisfaction of taking part in the final solution of the fifty-year-old quarrel between the upper and lower country in which his father had played so conspicuous a part.

7

Aggressive politician though he was at twenty-seven, Calhoun was woefully shy in matters of more personal concern. In the early summer of 1809 he entrusted his legal practice to his young partner, shed for the moment his new-found cares of state, and rode down from the hills through the scented pines and fragrant palmettos to Bonneau's Ferry; yet he saw Mrs. Calhoun and her brood depart for Newport, not only without confessing his devotion to Floride, but without being able to read in her manner any sign of encouragement or acquiescence, though his own ardor must have been all too evident. On the way home he fell in with a friend who was about to be married, and the meeting set him to brooding on his own prospects, which occupied the rest of the journey. When he found to his own astonishment and chagrin that his friends and neighbors were quite well aware of his intentions, he determined to get the matter cleared up at the earliest opportunity.[21]

Eternally serious by nature, and absorbed in the political scene, he considered himself superior to the normal agonies of young men in love; but as the days and weeks dragged on, he became thoroughly conscious of his merely human weakness. It was mid-July before a letter from Mrs. Calhoun put his mind at rest. "I can scarcely discribe my emotions," he wrote in reply, "when I saw your well known hand writing with the New Port post mark. But the contrariety of emotions it excited of hope and fear quickly subsided into the most agreeable feeling on perusing its contents." At this point he paused and made his confession. "This language does not correspond with my former opinion upon this subject. I formerly thought that it would be impossible for me to be strongly agitated in an affair of this kind; but that opinion now to me seems wholly unfounded, since, as it were in the very commencement, it can produce such effects." In fact, his agitation was so strong that he wondered if he should not write his proposal to Floride at once, but her mother persuaded him to wait until he could declare himself in person.

So the months passed, while Calhoun devoted his time to his practice and his thoughts to Floride. About November 20 he went to Columbia for his second session of the legislature, where he took part in abolishing the property qualification for voters. Mrs. Calhoun and her charming and disturbing daughter had returned meanwhile to Bonneau's Ferry; but it was Christmas, or possibly even later, before the infatuated young lawmaker could find time to go where his thoughts were already. Even then his shyness persisted until two days before he was obliged to leave to resume his practice. His proposal was made at last, however, sometime in January of 1810, and the response was all he could have wished.

At least once more before the family went to Newport for the summer of 1810, Calhoun was a visitor at Bonneau's Ferry, and thereafter he wrote faithfully to both mother and daughter. Gradually the rumors of his approaching marriage were officially confirmed, and he wondered if Newport in the fall would not do for time and place. Then Carolina in the winter was agreed upon, and he set out to find a suitable plantation which he might purchase as a home for his bride. He found one at last not far from the original Calhoun place, then occupied by his brother Patrick, and also near his brother William at Willington.

Late in the summer he attended, as he always did when possible, the commencement exercises of Dr. Waddel's academy close by. He was the idol of the boys and his career was the chosen prototype for theirs. Especially was he worshiped by George McDuffie and

Gus Longstreet, who roomed at William Calhoun's, and who went right on worshiping him all their lives. George, indeed, was a sort of protégé, who had been clerk for Calhoun and Wilson in Augusta, until the firm failed earlier that year. James had passed the lad along to William, so that he might go to school; and William, in due time, turned the finished product over to John. At the public exercises Calhoun sat on the platform along with Senator William H. Crawford, of Georgia, and Dr. William W. Bibb, member of the House of Representatives from the same state; but it was the young Carolinian who gave out the prizes, with appropriate words of praise for the winners.[22]

In September he expressed proper alarm at news of an accident suffered by Floride, and suitable joy at her recovery. And to Floride herself he wrote with an ardor that belied the outward coldness of his nature. ". . . my impatience daily increases. May heaven grant you a safe return. . . . My dearest one, may our love strengthen with each returning day, may it ripen and mellow with our years, and may it end in immortal joys. . . . When mere personal charms attract, the impression may be violent but cannot be lasting, and it requires the perpetual presence of the object to keep it alive; but when the beauty of mind, the soft and sweet disposition, the amiable and lovable character embellished with innocence and cheerfulness are united to the attractions of personal beauty, it bids defiance to time. . . ."[23]

The young couple were warmly congratulated by Floride's guardian, Henry W. De Saussure, now an equity judge, who also discussed with Calhoun the settlement of the property. On that score the prospective groom had ideas of his own, which he frankly expressed, indelicate or no. The fortune was Floride's, and he had not been influenced by it in his choice; but the choice being made, he opposed any form of marriage settlement. To him it implied distrust if the wife were unwilling to place her property along with her honor in her husband's hands.[24] His views prevailed, and instead of a settlement a partial partition of the property was made between Calhoun and his two brothers-in-law.[25]

Besides Bonneau's Ferry, which old Mrs. Calhoun retained for herself, there were more or less extensive land holdings along the Salkehatchie River in the southeastern part of the state, and in

Pendleton District in the Blue Ridge highlands. These lands were not as profitable as they might have been, nor as extensively cultivated, for Mrs. Calhoun had refused to permit the purchase of needed slaves when the African trade was open.[26] Deeply religious by nature, she was never really reconciled to slavery, and it is possible that this early distribution of her property was in some measure to free her own conscience from the burden of owning her fellow men.

8

While Calhoun was waiting impatiently for the return of his fiancée and applying his energies if not his enthusiasm to the law, his political future was being molded by party managers of the upper country and by his own abilities and ambition. His cousin, Colonel Joseph Calhoun, had represented Abbeville, Newberry and Laurens Counties in Congress for two terms, but now at sixty was ready to retire. Who better to succeed him than John Caldwell Calhoun, whose law practice had made him widely known throughout the district, and whose two terms in the state legislature had called him favorably to the attention of South Carolina Republican leaders?

The major issue was the continued violation by England of neutral rights, and the growing irritation over commercial restrictions and impressment. Calhoun was for war, which he had felt to be inevitable ever since the *Chesapeake* incident, and he made his position clear in a vigorous campaign, in the course of which he more than once debated with his opponent, General John A. Elmore of Laurens. In July he supposed there was no doubt of his election, and in September made plans to close out his legal practice before winter. As the day drew near, he thought his margin would be sizable; but when the votes were counted, it was overwhelming.[27]

9

The wedding took place on January 8, 1811, at Bonneau's Ferry. For days before the event guests were arriving—friends and relatives from all parts of the state, and perhaps some from other states as well.[28] South Carolina society in the early nineteenth century was as brilliant as any in the land, and this was a society affair. No doubt food was abundant and drink plentiful, for those were days of incredible meals and immoderate drinking; and conversation must have ranged, with the interests of the guests, from idle gossip to prospects for rice and cotton, to politics, and to the possibility of war with powerful and arrogant Great Britain.

The bride was small of stature beside her tall, loose-jointed husband. Her black hair was drawn down across the temples to emphasize the oval of her face, and her large, dark eyes were animated and gay, where his were grave. Successful lawyer, planter and Congressman-elect at twenty-eight, Calhoun was a man who dominated by the sheer power of his personality and mind every group of which he became a part. Floride, not quite nineteen, was graceful and poised, with gifts more social than intellectual, but strong of will and purpose.

After the ceremony and the festivities were over, the young couple remained for a time at Bonneau's Ferry, visiting Charleston and other parts of the state as the humor seized them. Their future home near Willington had been christened Bath, but no house had as yet been built. Floride's mother went as usual to New England for the summer, and her son-in-law took obvious satisfaction in reporting to her that his bride had been to the theater in Charleston and was "not at all pleased." Some matters of property were taken care of, relatives were visited and the ordinary affairs of the plantation were carried on; but actually the young Calhouns were marking time until November, when the Twelfth Congress was to meet.

CHAPTER IV

THE WAR HAWKS

1

CONGRESS had been called into session a month ahead of the usual time, and as the day approached, the sprawling, half-completed capital city bustled with activity and seethed with expectation. Since the repeal of the embargo, relations with Great Britain had steadily deteriorated until the plain people the country over knew that a crisis was at hand. Everywhere but in New England, men who temporized or favored negotiation were turned out of office and their places given to those like Calhoun who frankly stood for war: young, energetic, active men, preponderantly from the West and from the frontiers of the older sections. Inexperienced they might be in foreign affairs, but they were adroit at politics, were sure of themselves and supremely confident of their country's future.

Ambitious though he was to make a favorable first impression, Calhoun did not take his seat until November 6, two days after the session opened. He had delayed leaving his home until Floride was out of danger after the birth of their first child, a son whom they proudly christened Andrew Pickens in honor of the family's Revolutionary hero. Even then he remained uneasy lest his abrupt departure at such a time might injure his young wife's health, and his anxiety persisted until he heard at last that all was well.[1]

Calhoun had not yet arrived in Washington when the young Republican leaders gathered in private caucus to plan their own strategy the evening before Congress met, but he was with them in spirit. Fearing the conservatives of their own party more than they feared the greatly outnumbered Federalists, the War Hawks took things into their own capable hands and elected as Speaker one of themselves. The choice fell upon tall, magnetic Henry Clay of Kentucky, who was making his first appearance in the House. Virginia-born and trained in the law under the venerable Chancellor Wythe, Clay was already an almost legendary figure in the

West, and at thirty-four typified in his own person the boundless assurance, audacity and restless energy of young America, determined to break once and for all her ties of bondage to the European world.

The boardinghouse where many of the younger leaders stayed soon came to be called the War Mess, and it was there that Calhoun settled immediately upon his arrival in the city. With him lived his South Carolina colleagues, Langdon Cheves and William Lowndes, Dr. William Bibb of Georgia, Felix Grundy of Tennessee, and Clay. Cheves, who had just passed his thirty-fifth birthday, was the oldest among them, and with two months of experience in the House to his credit, he was also the veteran. A man of massive proportions and striking appearance, he was one of the brilliant lawyers of his day, with eight years in the legislature and a term as Attorney General of the state already behind him. Like Calhoun he was born in Abbeville District and had spent his childhood in the upper country. As a factor's apprentice in Charleston he had learned the ways of business before he studied law, and he stood pre-eminent among his fellows for his knowledge of the commercial world.

Lowndes, too, was a man not likely to be forgotten by any who had seen him. Standing more than six feet six inches tall, he was preternaturally thin, with bright golden hair and a too prominent nose. When he spoke it was in a voice so low that he could not be heard halfway across the chamber, yet there was no man in Congress whose words were more attentively followed by friend and foe alike. Curiously enough, the modest, soft-spoken Lowndes and the decisive and ambitious Calhoun, whose idyllic friendship was to survive even political rivalry, were not acquainted before they met in Congress, although both had been prominent figures in South Carolina affairs. An intimacy which was broken only by Lowndes's untimely death was quick to form. The day following their first meeting, Lowndes wrote to his wife that Calhoun was "well informed, easy in his manners, and I think amiable in his disposition. I like him already better than any member of our mess, and I give his politics the same preference."[2]

Calhoun and Lowndes, at twenty-nine, were the youngest of the group, but no member of the War Mess came within a dozen years of the average age of the House. Yet from the first day of its first session, they and their friends took command of Congress and drove it, in spite of bitter and sometimes treasonable opposition from commercial New England and the reluctance and vacillation of the Executive, into the declaration of war which the people of the back country, North, South and West alike, believed was necessary to vindicate the national honor. The national honor, they felt, was peculiarly within their keeping, for they were true "Americans": the first generation born after the Declaration of Independence to gain political power.

2

In the appointment of committees Clay assumed an undivided authority which gave the Speakership an importance second only to the Presidency itself. Seniority and experience were alike subordinated to energy and the will to war. The powerful Committee on Ways and Means, with its control over revenue measures, counted only one Federalist among its seven members; and the select Committees on Foreign Relations, Military Affairs, and Naval Affairs were almost as heavily weighted in favor of hostilities. Ezekiel Bacon from the Berkshire Hills of Massachusetts headed Ways and Means, and Peter B. Porter of western New York was chairman of Foreign Relations. Both were graduates of Yale and the Litchfield Law School. Calhoun was second to Porter, while two of his South Carolina colleagues, David R. Williams and Langdon Cheves, were chairmen respectively of Military and Naval Affairs.

The whole procedure in conservative eyes was "monstrous," but the result scarcely bore out the caustic charge of Josiah Quincy, Federalist leader of the House, that the War Hawks were only "young politicians, half hatched, the shell still on their heads, and their pin feathers not yet shed."[3] They knew what they wanted and how to get it as well as any veteran in Congress; and they declared their purpose before the session was a month old. The occasion was a report on foreign relations presented by Porter.

The report passed over the familiar list of grievances to go straight to the heart of the matter, and in its concise and often pungent phrasing the hand of John C. Calhoun was evident to all who knew him.[4] A brief review of events of the past five years served as an introduction. Under Napoleon's Berlin and Milan Decrees and Britain's retaliatory Orders in Council, both belligerents had pillaged American commerce wherever their navies could find it. To stop the depredations, trade advantages had been offered under the Nonimportation Act of 1810 to whichever of the two powers would first abandon the system. France accepted the offer (or so the devious diplomacy of Bonaparte wished the United States to believe) and revoked the decrees; but instead of withdrawing the Orders in Council, which no longer had any excuse for existence, Great Britain only demanded new concessions, continuing all the while to impress into her own service seamen forcibly taken from American vessels.

"To wrongs so daring in their character, and so disgraceful in their execution," the report concluded, "it is impossible that the people of the United States should remain indifferent. We must now tamely and quietly submit, or we must resist by those means which God has placed within our reach. . . . We have borne with injury until forbearance has ceased to be a virtue." Six resolutions were attached, designed to build up the Army and Navy to wartime strength and to authorize the use of militia and the arming of merchant vessels.

If the report left any doubts as to the intentions of the Committee on Foreign Relations, Porter quickly dispelled them when he opened debate on the resolutions a few days later. It was the determination of the committee, he declared, "to recommend open and decided war—a war as vigorous and effective as the resources of the country and the relative situation of ourselves and our enemy would enable us to prosecute." The resolutions were designed to bring about the proper state of preparedness.

The grievances against England were old and well understood, but the temper of the House was new, and significant. There was no cause for war that had not already existed for four or five years, and there was decidedly less reason for hostilities than there had been over the *Chesapeake* affair. Yet here was an unmistakable call to arms, and it came in the name of the majority. The situation had not changed but the men were different. They conceived themselves to have been elected to declare war on Britain, and that they proposed to do, whether the administration was ready or not.

3

While the War Hawks chafed under the slow processes of parliamentary democracy, Tecumseh led a band of Shawnees on the warpath far to the west. The savages were defeated by General William Henry Harrison in the bloody battle of Tippecanoe, but the loss in men was heavy and it left the frontier open. The West did not doubt that the hand of Britain was behind the Indian uprising, and the Western press called loudly for redress. News of the skirmish reached Washington about the time the report on foreign relations was presented; and the very day that Porter called on the House for active measures looking to war with England, the Secretary of State had supper with the War Mess. James Monroe, cautious and conservative but fully conscious of his responsibility, defended the administration against the charge that it lacked belligerent intent, and gave his word that the Executive would join with Congress in declaring war if the grievances were not redressed by May.[5]

That left at most six months in which to prepare for war with Great Britain. Six months to recruit, equip and train an effective military force in a nation so jealous of its liberties that it had even provided constitutional guarantees against standing armies and had never been able to put above 25,000 men in the field in any single year of the Revolution! Six months for preparation to engage a naval power so formidable that she had for years been treating every ship that sailed the sea as enemy or prize, even though it lay in its own harbor—and that by a nation whose few ships of war were rotting at the wharves and many of whose merchant seamen had been driven by commercial restrictions to seek employment under other flags!

The War Hawks knew full well the weakness of their country, but they also knew its strength, which was nowhere better exemplified than in their own audacity, and in the energy and ingenuity with which they set about to carry their program into action.

Six months! The first resolution, to fill the ranks of the regular

Army, was carried the same day that Porter spoke; and as soon as
the week-end holiday was over, Grundy called for discussion of the
second, which would raise an additional military force. John Randolph of Roanoke, brilliant to the limits of sanity and vindictive foe
of the administration and of war, was universally expected to take
from the Federalists the leadership of the opposition, and he did
not disappoint. The Republican leader of the House during Jefferson's first four years of office, Randolph had broken with his party
and now stood alone, a host within himself whom none could match
and few dared cross in argument. He was after Grundy as a cat
leaps on a mouse, demanding to know in explicit terms the purpose
for which this prospective army was intended.[6]

Grundy was the most celebrated criminal lawyer in the Southwest, but his success was based on a rare ability to sway the emotions of his jurors rather than on logic. His reply to Randolph
was eloquent and moving, but it was not a reasoned justification of
war so much as an appeal to the militant sentiment of the frontier.
The Virginian was on his feet again the next day, wandering about
the chamber on long, spindling legs, gesticulating with bony hands,
his tall, emaciated frame contrasting oddly with a face now amaz-
ingly boyish, now drawn as parchment and prematurely old. The
perfection of his English diction was marred by the high pitch of
his voice, the rapidity of his utterance and the venom of his words
as he blasted the glowing picture Grundy had painted. The country
was defenseless, to attack Canada quixotic, to accept the word of
Bonaparte childish. Britain, for all her faults, was fighting the
battle of civilization against the great destroyer of all human
liberty. Surely America's place was not on the side of the self-
styled emperor who held the lash over half. of Europe!

Richard M. Johnson of Kentucky was next to take up the cause
of war, but with no better success. Like Grundy he spoke for and
to the West, which needed no prompting. The War Hawks knew
that Randolph must be effectively answered, and Calhoun assumed
the task at which his friends had failed. So on December 12, hardly
more than a month after his first appearance in Congress, the young
South Carolinian rose to cross verbal swords with the veteran
whose oratorical gifts were acknowledged to be the best in the
House and whose tongue was merciless.

The lobby and galleries were crowded as they had been at every session since the debate began, but if Calhoun was aware of it, he showed no sign. Speaking as he always did, without flourishes or ornaments of rhetoric, but to the point, he quickly stripped Randolph's argument of its extraneous matter, and held the kernel up for all to see. He showed that the choice lay not between peace and war, nor yet between Bonaparte and Britain. The nation must defend or weakly yield the right to sail the ocean and to trade with all the world. If the country was unprepared, the more reason for raising an army. Men and money could be had if the violated rights were worth defending. To adopt any other course would be unworthy of a free people. "Protection and patriotism are reciprocal. This is the way which has led nations to greatness."

The impression Calhoun's speech made may be judged by the enthusiasm of Thomas Ritchie, whose Richmond *Enquirer* printed Randolph's harangue and Calhoun's answer side by side. He need not have pointed out the contrast between the long, discursive and indirect argument of the one and the concise, direct objectivity of the other. They were plain for all to see. And when Ritchie concluded his notice by hailing "this young South Carolinian as one of those master spirits, who stamp their name upon the age in which they live," he was expressing the almost universal satisfaction of the party that Randolph had at last met his match.[7]

More speeches were made, but there was no more to say; and after three days of argument the resolution was approved by the overwhelming vote of 110 to 22. Three of the four remaining resolutions were carried the same day, by even wider margins; and the sixth, which permitted the arming of merchant vessels, likewise passed before the week was out.

4

Yet there was truth in Randolph's argument and ample enough excuse for the attitude of phlegmatic unbelief with which the British regarded this sudden clamor for hostilities. Although the population of the United States was more than seven million, the Army numbered, exclusive of staff, exactly 2,765 officers and enlisted men, and the Navy consisted of just fifteen ships of war.[8] The

Army was the skeleton of an authorized regular force of ten thousand, and the Navy was all that remained of the fleet that had fought the power of France on equal terms a dozen years before. There were only five frigates (corresponding to the cruisers of today), which averaged forty guns, and there were no vessels at all in the class of Britain's great seventy-four-gun ships of the line. Yet with this trifling fleet of cockleshells, young America proposed to challenge the Mistress of the Seas, whose peacetime strength in American waters alone was six times that of the whole United States Navy.[9] With an Army scarcely larger than a corporal's guard to defend a million and a half square miles of thinly settled country, Calhoun and his colleagues called for war against one of the mightiest military powers on earth.

The prospect was too absurd to be taken seriously, especially when those who were most belligerent in Congress appeared so gay and lighthearted once they were outside the Capitol. They could usually be found at the weekly levees held at the President's "palace," where hundreds of guests came and went throughout the evening. On these occasions a band played in the great entrance foyer where wraps were left before passing on through the dining room, dominated by a life-sized portrait of Washington, to a smaller parlor, and thence into the immense magnificence of the oval drawing room. There tall, stately Dolly Madison and her grave, almost diminutive husband received their guests. Wine, punch and ices circulated freely, adding to the general bustle and confusion, while here and there knots of people gathered around some celebrity of the moment—perhaps handsome young Augustus Foster, the British Minister, or the radiantly beautiful Betsy Patterson, whose marriage to Jerome Bonaparte had caused an international sensation. The talk was excellent, but it conveyed no impression that the country was on the verge of war.

True, Calhoun was less often seen in society than were his colleagues of the War Mess, but that was only because he took less pleasure in such things. He declined an invitation to take Christmas dinner with the French Minister, but Lowndes went and saw no impropriety in it. All of them attended Foster's party on the birthday of his Queen, and a little later they went farther still, though some were willing to brand them traitors for it : they invited Foster to dine with them.[10] Their hostess was Mrs. Cheves, who spent the winter in Washington with her two small children.

If personal animosity played any part in their thinking, it was as well concealed as the nostalgia that some of them confessed to in the intimacy of private correspondence. Lowndes wrote wistfully to his wife of "a little boy of Mrs. Cheves's" who "comes into my room to hear stories and make boats";[11] and Calhoun was no less wistful when he wrote to Floride a little later in the winter that he had dreamed "all night the last night of being home with you; and nursing our dear son; and regreted when I awoke to find it a dream. I was in hopes that the morning's mail would bring me a letter from you; but was disappointed. . . ."[12]

These were the young men who had taken upon their own broad shoulders the destiny of a nation, and perhaps the fate of the world.

5

The President asked that the ranks of the regular Army be filled, and that an additional ten thousand troops be provided. The War Hawks gave him twenty-five thousand, and when a difference arose between Senate and House, they took the larger figure. They ought not, as Calhoun put it, to let a few thousand dollars stand in the way of a vigorous prosecution of war measures. But if the Army bill exceeded the scope of the administration's policy, the naval proposals went farther still from Madison's desires. Jefferson had believed, and from his far inland retreat at Monticello argued still, that a few gunboats which could be quickly built and which could operate within the shelter of the coast would serve the turn; but no such niggardly sentiments animated the glowing nationalism of the younger leaders. They were about to make war upon the world's most formidable fleet and would challenge power with power.

There must have been gasps of astonishment from more than one part of the House when Cheves, speaking for the Committee on Naval Affairs, abandoned with a sweep of the hand the traditional Republican naval policy in a bill to build twelve seventy-fours and twenty frigates. He spoke for the measure for the better part of two days, ably and intelligently, and buttressed every point with figures. The substance of his argument has been repeated in every debate on naval policy since: The United States is a maritime nation, and must therefore be a naval power. For a nation whose only potential foes are across an ocean, a navy is the cheapest, safest and best means of defense.[13]

Bold though it was, the measure wrought the first split in the ranks of the War Hawks and revealed, if only briefly, a fundamental divergence of aims. More farsighted or better aware of the need for unity than his Western colleagues, Clay supported the naval program, but the West would not follow his lead; nor would the South unite behind Cheves, Lowndes and Calhoun. After ten days of debate the bill was lost by the narrowest of margins, 62 to 59, and the traditional Republican policy was saved. The House voted half a million dollars to recondition five disused frigates, and twice that sum for harbor and coastal defenses, but beyond that it would not go. To the West and South a Navy was a sectional affair, designed only to protect and foster the commerce of the Eastern cities; and to the East the war and all the preparations for it were intended to destroy commerce and with it the political strength of New England.

6

Spring came and preparations for war were still chaotic. The proffered bounty of sixteen dollars and 160 acres of land for a five-year enlistment had tempted scarcely a thousand men, and the regular Army, whose strength had been increased on paper to 35,000, did not in fact yet amount to a tenth of that number. The revenue measures urged by Secretary of the Treasury Albert Gallatin had been passed up in favor of an $11,000,000 loan which the bankers of New England would not touch, though six percent was offered. In the face of these failures, the administration paid $50,000 for the letters of John Henry, a British agent lately active in Boston, in hopes of crystallizing public sentiment, but succeeded only in stiffening the opposition.

Neither was the road to war made easier by the obvious incompetence of the Secretaries of War and Navy, William Eustis of

Massachusetts and Paul Hamilton of South Carolina. The War Hawks demanded dismissal of both, and refused to authorize the appointment of two badly needed Assistant Secretaries of War lest their presence become an excuse for retaining Eustis.[14] Madison's resolve wavered, and the impetus of the drive toward war was visibly slowed. It took another flat refusal of the British Government to repeal the Orders in Council, delivered by Foster the last day of March, to get the wheels moving again. The answer was an embargo intended to allow time for ships at sea to reach port before war should make them lawful prize.

Following the embargo, interest lagged once more. The Senate voted to recess until June 8, and a similar vote was barely averted in the House. Members began going to their homes on leave, with the understanding that no business of importance would be taken up while they were away; and indeed there was little left for Congress to do but to declare war and get it over with. By the end of April debate had become mere bickering between members separated by rows of empty seats, while Calhoun and the young Republicans cursed the hesitancy of the Executive and the weakness of the military organization.[15]

Early in May a petition from eight hundred citizens of Albany praying repeal of the embargo precipitated another exchange between Randolph and Calhoun. The discussion turned not on the request of the petitioners but on the necessity or propriety of war with Britain: the ever-present ghost at every debate throughout the session—the real question which lay in the mind of every member present. Grundy's hope "that the sound of war would not again have been heard within these walls, until the main question was presented" remained mere rhetoric. Every question was the main question in disguise, for that question alone was of real interest to anyone. So against Randolph and the Albany merchants Calhoun defended the embargo on the ground that it was not a measure of commercial restriction but an instrument of war, and confidently proclaimed that "a war, just and necessary in its origin, wisely and vigorously carried on, and honorably terminated," would establish "the integrity and prosperity of our country for centuries."[16]

When the May elections returned Federalist legislatures in Massachusetts and New York, the War Hawks prepared to force the issue. They jammed through a resolution directing the Speaker to recall all absent members by the first of June, and Republican solidarity was once more established by the renomination of Madison in a party caucus. Unfavorable news from France gave the President another moment of hesitation, which he communicated to Jefferson along with the French dispatches; but the War Hawks soon had him at work again on a war message.[17] One final attempt was made by Randolph to stem the tide, but he was unceremoniously halted by Clay on a point of order raised by Calhoun. It was the first time in more than a dozen years in Congress that the irrepressible Virginian had been silenced.

7

Madison's war message was sent to Congress on June 1, 1812, and was read behind closed doors. It was just sixty days after the embargo had been imposed, and fulfilled to the letter Monroe's promise to the War Mess. It went as a matter of course to the Committee on Foreign Relations, of which Calhoun was now the Chairman, and the question of peace or war was fairly up to the young Carolinian. It was the climax toward which his career had pointed since his first public appearance at Abbeville five years before. He had demanded then that the *Chesapeake* be avenged, and vengeance was now in his hands.

Within forty-eight hours he presented a report which reviewed with admirable clarity and conciseness the whole course of British-American relations, concluding that only war could solve the outstanding difficulties.[18] First Quincy, then Randolph, moved to open the doors and debate the question in public. Calhoun and Clay had no objection, but the President wished secrecy to be preserved, and so the galleries remained cleared. The Federalist members then declined to contest the issue, which was just as well. No other question had in reality been discussed for the past six months, and surely nothing was left for either side to say that had not been said already over and over again. Without other preliminaries Calhoun introduced a bill formally declaring war with England. He had kept his pledge to his constituents and to himself, and he was satisfied.

The House adjourned to sleep on it, reassembling at eleven

o'clock on the morning of June 4. Before the question could be put for final passage, however, Madison's private secretary appeared, to ask that action be postponed until a communication from the President could be received. Suspecting no doubt that Madison had once more lost his nerve, Calhoun refused to take responsibility for delaying the vote until he knew the character of the message. The farthest he would go was to lay the facts before the House as he had received them.

The House agreed to wait, and after almost an hour, during which the members wandered about the hall, clustered in little knots, or moved aimlessly through the still unfinished building, the message finally arrived. Its purpose was to lay before Congress the correspondence of the past few days between the British Minister and the Secretary of State: a correspondence in which Foster, having finally discovered that the Federalists with whom he had been associating were wrong about the intentions of the administration, strove desperately to avert a war. He was handled by the suave and seasoned Monroe as a schoolmaster might handle a wayward child whom he is about to thrash after repeated warnings.[19]

Even after the House had passed the war bill, which it did as soon as the message had been read, the correspondence continued, ending only with Monroe's failure to answer Foster's letter of June 14. It was a petulant letter in which the minister expressed once more the deep attachment of His Majesty's Government to the interests of America, and the willingness of Britain to adjust the differences between the two countries by any means within her power—any means, that is, except to repeal the Orders in Council.

And even there she was ready to yield, had Foster but known it. For on May 11, as he entered the House of Commons, Prime Minister Spencer Perceval was assassinated, and the system he had so long and so blunderingly maintained came crashing down. The Orders in Council were repealed on the seventeenth of June.

On the evening of that same seventeenth of June, Foster attended a levee at the White House. He found President Madison "ghastly pale" but cordial.[20] Calhoun and Clay were there also, and they too were cordial, but they were not pale. To the young British Minister they must have seemed the very personification of all his troubles, as they moved easily from one to another of the President's guests, these tall, self-confident young men who, he had again and again been told by the best people, were only bluffing. Tonight they seemed triumphant as they towered above the tired little Madison, and Foster could hardly have been surprised when he reached home to find a message saying the war bill had passed the Senate.

The President signed it on June 18, and the members of the War Mess solemnly danced around the room in celebration.[21]

CHAPTER V

NEW ENGLAND OBJECTS

1

NEW ENGLAND did not want a war with Britain, then or at any future time. Unlike the South or West, or even the Middle States, New England had no products to export. Her ships and her sailors were engaged exclusively in a carrying trade, moving the raw materials of America to Europe and bringing back manufactured articles in return. It was a trade built up through twenty years during which the United States had been the only neutral in a world at war, and the New England merchant had come to regard it as his perquisite: the just reward of his own sagacity and skill. He cared nothing for duties or trade balances. He wanted only free passage for his ships, and this he made amply clear to the men who represented him in Congress.

Like his English prototype, the New England shipowner was troubled by few scruples. When the slave trade was open, he traded in slaves; and when his ports were closed by an embargo, he found secluded harbors where his goods could be moved without knowledge of the law. All this seemed eminently right to those who lived by it; and indeed it was no more than the merchant princes of Genoa and Venice and the Hanseatic towns had done before them—time-honored practice of the lords of trade. When the titanic struggle for empire between Napoleon and Great Britain made it seem wise to those in power to keep American ships out of European waters, New England and the whole merchant class saw in the move, and in all future restrictive measures, only a "Jacobin" attempt to pull down those whom their own spokesmen liked to call the wise, the rich and the good.

The grievances that brought about the war were never real to the commercial states. If a few American seamen were impressed, why, it no more than evened up. For the United States of the early 1800's, like that of a later day, was in truth a promised land, and

67

many a British sailor yielded to its lure when his ship was in an American port.[1] Britain was fighting for her life, against the mightiest military machine the world had yet produced, and her only hope lay in a war of attrition which would starve the continent into revolt. To starve the continent she had to impose an effective blockade, and the effectiveness of that blockade depended in the end not on her ships, of which she had abundance, but on her ability to keep them manned. So she replaced deserters by impressment, and perhaps got a few men ahead to make up in advance for those who would drop over the side the first time they found their vessel anchored in American waters.

All this was clear to the commercial interests, whose trade was largely with Great Britain and whose very ships had as often as not been built with money advanced by the British merchants with whom they dealt; and it was similarly clear to their Representatives in Congress. They did not share the grandiose dreams of dominion over the whole North American continent so dear to the men from the West and from the South; nor did they share the restless, surging energy that was to make the dream come true. They were practical, hardheaded businessmen who saw no virtue in sacrificing a thriving, prosperous trade for some visionary empire that would be impossible to defend, and would not pay dividends for generations, if at all.

The merchants and traders of the Northern and Eastern states, and those of the Southern ports like Charleston and Baltimore as well, were Federalists because that party had provided a strong government, capable of collecting debts and maintaining the rights of property. The prosperity and economy of Jefferson's administration had almost won them over when the embargo came to confirm their worst fears, and sent them scurrying back to the party whose leaders promised that their profits should be secure. Able though they were, and intelligent and capable as were the professional men who counseled them, who taught their sons and pleaded their cause in courts and legislatures, they were too comfortable in their present circumstances to perceive the portents of the future.

Perhaps the Southern and Western men did not see them all either, but they had the vision to believe in those they did see. The Western empire a crazy dream? Already, thanks to Whitney's

Yankee ingenuity, the cotton lands stretched beyond the Appalachians. New York had chartered and was soon to finance the Erie Canal. Steamboats plied the Hudson and the Delaware, and Roosevelt's packet *New Orleans* had recently appeared on the lower Mississippi. Oliver Evans had driven a clumsy vehicle through the streets of Philadelphia by steam; and young Sam Morse was already out of Yale.

The new America was in the making, and Calhoun and the young Republicans would test its metal in the furnace of war; would bring it unity, and confirm its courage and its faith by self-assertion. They would destroy once and for all the assumption of Europe that these states were still British colonies in revolt, by redressing grievances a decade old. If at the same time they should win new markets for their wheat and cotton, or challenge with the manufactured products of the Appalachian piedmont the long-held monopoly of England, so much the better.

All this the New England merchants could not see. If there were grievances against Britain, they maintained, they were grievances to the commercial states alone, yet it was the West and South that wanted war. Old Tim Pickering, who had served the Federalists in their day of power, professed to think that an attempt was to be made on Canada solely in order to give that province to Bonaparte, as the basis for a new French empire in America; and the Federalists generally came in time to believe that some secret understanding existed between Madison and the emperor. After the event, it was easy to see more than coincidence in the fact that the American declaration of war and Napoleon's Russian campaign came simultaneously, and many were convinced that the embargo too had been made in France.[2]

If they had read the Republican press, the most conservative among them must have noted an almost universal clamor for war with England; but they read only their own partisan sheets, which revealed no clue to public opinion outside the commercial cities. From the opening day of the first session of the Twelfth Congress, there was never any doubt that the young Republicans meant not only to propose a war, but to carry it through. The Federalists knew, because they resented it, that a dozen men in Congress, most of them in the House, were virtually in command of the affairs of the nation; and they must also have known, had they cared to, that all of these men had stood for war since 1807. Yet they remained so sure that Madison was bluffing, and that a real war would bring about his downfall, that many of them voted for the war measures as they were proposed in hopes of returning their own party to power in the fall of 1812.

When war was actually declared the leaders of the commercial states were at first incredulous, then violent in their opposition. Governor Strong of Massachusetts proclaimed a day of public fasting, while a special session of the Connecticut Legislature declared that state to be "free, sovereign and independent."[3] Madison's call for militia went unheeded. Republican Congressmen were hissed on the streets of Boston. The old grievances against the South and West, going back to Jefferson's first election, were revived and men of power and substance talked openly of a new confederacy of the northeastern states.[4]

2

Calhoun understood this opposition to the war and all that went with it perhaps better than most of his Republican colleagues. Thanks to his New England education and his visits in Newport and Boston, he knew that the mildly treasonable talk of the Federalists in and out of Congress was largely bombast; but he also knew that they were intensely sincere in their complaints. Of all of these the restrictive system stood as a symbol, and in the hurried closing days of the session he made a bold and determined effort to compromise what had become a sectional quarrel.

It must be remembered that the whole policy of the Republican Party under Jefferson was a policy of peace through economic pressure and that the instruments of this pressure were the embargo and the nonimportation acts. The policy rested on a belief that England could not operate her mills without American raw materials and would be forced to come to terms to relieve the distress of her own working class.

To this thesis Madison still clung when on June 19, 1812, Calhoun introduced a bill to repeal the embargo. It was promptly pigeonholed, but was immediately followed by a move from Cheves, now chairman of the Committee on Ways and Means, to permit certain imports on revenue grounds. As the discussion developed, an amendment was offered by one of the Massachusetts members calling for repeal of the embargo, and Calhoun spoke in support of this amendment. In so doing he was in effect repudiating the faith of his party, yet he did it so gently, so sincerely and so courageously that many others followed his lead. So many Republicans followed, in fact, that a Federalist motion for a committee to report a repealing bill brought a tie, and was defeated only by the administration vote of Speaker Clay.

Calhoun made it clear that his motive for seeking repeal of the embargo was not to avoid taxes. "We are at war. It is wisdom to make it efficient. . . ." He wished it because he thought the whole restrictive system, which amounted to class legislation, was wrong in principle. He did not deny that the embargo was an effective weapon. It was not for failure that he opposed it but because it deprived the merchants of their livelihood—because it bred disunion and led a large segment of the people to oppose their government.

So he was still to argue after twenty years, when the minority in whose behalf he now spoke had risen to power and had in their turn passed laws in the interest of a class.

The speech was effective for its calm sanity, its clarity of style and the compelling sincerity of its delivery. It was no less effective for its peroration: "We have had a peace like a war; in the name of Heaven let us not have the only thing that is worse, a war like a peace."[5]

Though his plea was lost, Calhoun's stature as a statesman rose. He had served notice that he would sacrifice no conviction for the sake of party regularity, whatever the reward might be. At the end of his first session in Congress he was a figure of national prominence, respected alike by friend and foe and assured of a high place in the councils of his party.

3

He was already acquiring, too, that hold upon the affections of South Carolina which was eventually to give him almost absolute authority within the state. So completely was his course in Congress approved by his constituents that no candidate appeared to run against him in the fall elections, and one veteran paid him the rare tribute of withdrawing in his favor. The reapportionment based on the census of 1810 gave South Carolina an additional seat, and in the regrouping of counties, Abbeville was combined with Edgefield instead of with Newberry and Laurens, as had previously been the case. The new arrangement brought Calhoun and his colleague, General William Butler of Edgefield, into the same district. Although Butler had served twelve years in Congress, he declined to contest the seat with his young rival, saying simply : "You can meet Randolph in debate—I cannot."[6]

A touch of irony was given the gesture by the defeat of Randolph at the hands of John W. Eppes, son-in-law and confidant of Thomas Jefferson, which was typical of the trend throughout the West and South. It was in the Northeastern states that the election told a very different story. There the Federalists made political capital of the almost immediate reverses suffered by the armies seeking to invade Canada, and of the Treasury's failure to dispose of its bonds. Unable to agree on a Presidential candidate of their own, the party leaders threw their strength to DeWitt Clinton, who had sought the Republican nomination in vain. In a bitter and hard-fought contest they swept New England and gained greatly in New York. Madison won his second term by the shaky margin of thirty-nine electoral votes, but Federalist strength in the next Congress would be doubled.

When they returned to Washington in November the War Hawks knew they would have to make the most of their majority before it grew dangerously small. They could risk no divisions among themselves, and so Calhoun declined the chairmanship of the Foreign Relations Committee, to which Porter's continued absence entitled him. His action was meant to avoid giving undue prominence to South Carolina, for Cheves remained at the head of Ways and Means and David R. Williams was still the Chairman of Military Affairs; but he was quickly overruled. The vacant post went to aged and genial John Smilie of Pennsylvania, who moved at the first meeting of the group that Calhoun be elected chairman, and so he was, unanimously, despite his own protest.[7]

The major business of the session was the more rigorous prosecution of the war, an end which Calhoun believed could be achieved only through the conciliation of New England. In this he was upheld by Cheves and Lowndes, and the three South Carolinians lost no opportunity to make overtures to the commercial interests. It had long been understood that repeal of the Orders in Council would bring an end to nonimportation, and American vessels had raced from England to be first with the luxuries so long denied. They arrived to find the nation at war, and their cargoes subject to forfeiture under laws of which their captains knew nothing. Despite the opposition of the Treasury and of a formidable administration phalanx led by the Speaker himself, the trio fought for and in the end secured release of the impounded cargoes and remission of all penalties levied against their owners. It meant passing up an opportunity to put fifteen million dollars into the empty Treasury and might well result in weakening the nonimportation laws, but these loomed as lesser evils to Calhoun and his colleagues than the alienation of the whole commercial class by whose wealth alone the credit of the country could be sustained.[8]

The three young South Carolina Congressmen were more than colleagues; they were friends. They no longer lived under the same roof, for the Cheveses had moved to more commodious quarters and Lowndes, too, had brought his wife to Washington and had set up housekeeping, but their social life continued to be spent largely together. Calhoun might generally be found of an evening at the home of one or the other, though it was to the Lowndes establishment in Georgetown that he went more frequently. There the talented Elizabeth Lowndes played hostess to the best society in the capital. In her drawing room even the Federalists felt at home, for she was of their own party and as stanch as her father, old General Thomas Pinckney himself.[9]

Evenings spent at the homes of his friends as often as not served for Calhoun a dual purpose. They provided neutral ground where political questions could be amicably discussed with those who sat on the other side of the House, and they gave him the companionship and relaxation which he sorely needed. Yet they only made him feel more keenly the absence of his own young wife and child. Before the session was three weeks old he was frankly homesick, and thinking more of Floride and of little Andrew than of the critical state of the nation. Since the days of his courtship and even before that his mother-in-law had been his principal confidant, and to her he confessed his loneliness. "If Floride bears my absence as badly as I do hers," he wrote, "she must occasionally be very impatient. I know you will not fail to keep her as cheerful as possible." It was still November, but already he was looking forward "with impatience" for the time of his return home.[10]

4

Although it produced one of the most thoughtful debates of the session, the disposal of the contraband cargoes was only a side issue so far as the main question before the country was concerned. The war was being lost because the ranks of the regular Army were only half filled, because the militia were not available when most needed and because too many ranking officers were incompetent.[11] While a new enlistment bill occupied the attention of Congress, Monroe toyed with the notion of assuming a military command on the northern frontier, but before he could make up his mind, William Eustis perceived with some prodding from the War Hawks that he did not belong in a wartime cabinet. He resigned early in December, and Monroe, without giving up the portfolio of State, assumed active charge of the War Department. Bills for improving the organization of the Army and increasing the military establishment were quickly laid before Congress, and the smoldering quarrel with New England flared up again.

The pay of the soldier had already been raised to eight dollars a month, and he had been exempted from arrest for debt. To get an additional twenty thousand men the new Secretary now proposed to increase the cash bounty to twenty-four dollars in addition to the usual quarter-section of land. Truculent Josiah Quincy led the Federalist onslaught. Was this new army to be used to invade Canada, or to suppress opposition to the war in New England? He re-examined all the old grounds on which sectional antagonism rested, and charged that an invasion of Canada was intended solely to give Monroe the glory of leading it, to elevate him to the Presidential chair, and thus perpetuate the servitude of the North to Virginia. In the course of his remarks Quincy alluded in uncomplimentary terms to the founder of the Republican Party, as well as to his successor in office.[12]

It was a challenge the War Hawks could not allow to pass, and an answer was delivered by Henry Clay with devastating effect, in the House. Fat and pompous Samuel Taggart branded the Speaker as "the most accomplished blackguard of the party" and thought his speech against Quincy was "in such a strain of low vulgar Billingsgate scurrility, as was better adapted to a barroom after the close of an angry town meeting when the disputants were pretty well heated with liquor, than to the hall of a national legislature."[13] Taggart seemed perhaps too well informed on the subject of barrooms for the New England minister he was, but Quincy apparently shared the general impression. He thought Clay was seeking to force him to accept a duel or disgrace, and thus destroy his usefulness to his party. He overestimated the esteem in which he was held by his opponents; but in this case, at least, he won part of his point. Monroe's prestige suffered so much as a result of Federalist attacks that he not only gave up the notion of commanding an army, he gave up the War Department as well. He was succeeded by John Armstrong of New York, lately a general in the Army, former Senator and envoy to France, and brother-in-law of Chancellor Robert Livingston.

But the rout of Monroe did not end the controversy over the Army bill, and again it was Calhoun who strove to end partisan dissension. Calling for national unity in the face of a foreign foe, he addressed himself to the Federalists.

"It behooves them, as they value the blessings of their freedom, not to permit themselves to be drawn into the vortex of party rage. For if, by such opposition, the firmest government should prove incompetent to maintain the rights of the nation against foreign aggression, they will realize too late the truth of the proposition, *that government is protection,* and that it cannot exist where it fails of this great and primary object. The authors of the weakness are commonly the first to take the advantage of it, and to turn it to the destruction of liberty."[14]

The measure was finally passed, but only because it had been made a question of confidence in the administration.[15]

The Navy found less opposition, which was perhaps only natural,

for the Navy had been winning victories. Public sentiment, at first
hostile to sea power, had swung over during the summer as the
deeds of Isaac Hull and Stephen Decatur fired the popular fancy.
In the first session of the war Congress, Cheves, Lowndes and
Calhoun had fought for a navy almost alone, save for the dubious
support of Quincy. Now the majority was of the same mind, and
four seventy-fours and six forty-four-gun frigates were authorized.
The effect was great, even though it would increase American naval
strength by no more than the number of capital ships Great Britain
then had in Chesapeake Bay. At the same time an abler Secretary
of the Navy in the person of William Jones, Philadelphia shipowner, promised to give new energy to the war at sea.

5

Calhoun thought the change of the "two fighting secretaries" for
the better,[16] but his major concern was still with the attitude of
New England toward the war, and he continued to oppose the
restrictive system at every opportunity. He and Lowndes were no
doubt informed in advance of a surprise move in that direction
which Cheves made in the closing weeks of the session. Under
guise of a revenue measure which fell within the province of his
committee, Cheves again proposed partial repeal of nonimportation, but he met with uncompromising opposition where he had
expected to find strong support.

It came from rugged Elisha Potter of Rhode Island, a former
blacksmith who was now the stanch Federalist Representative of
a seafaring constituency; and it showed that the restrictive system
had indeed divided the country, more deeply than Calhoun had
foreseen or was even yet aware of. For Potter denounced the
repeal of nonimportation as vehemently as he had once denounced
its passage, and in so doing gave a fleeting glimpse, to those who had
eyes to see, of the forces that were to dominate the century. Nonimportation and war had driven the merchants of Providence and
Pawtucket to manufacturing. To legalize shipping would not make
it possible for them to profit once more from commerce, because
their capital was no longer available for investment in trading ven-

tures. On the contrary, they would be ruined by the flood of foreign manufactures which would pour into the country as soon as the law admitted them.[17]

New England, in short, had begun the shift from a dominantly commercial to a dominantly manufacturing section; and the system that had once been anathema because it placed restrictions upon trade was now necessary because it afforded protection for industry. Although New England still refused militia and threatened to refuse taxes to the national Government, although she still proclaimed her sovereignty and her right to withdraw from the Union, the leaven that would turn her to nationalism and to centralization was already at work.

The best that could be done in the face of the changed attitude of the Federalists was to secure more rigid enforcement of non-importation, in the hope of increasing the pressure on the enemy; but that, too, was an illusion, if pressure meant keeping American goods from enemy hands. For New England merchants, even while they denounced the war and threatened secession, were conducting a thriving trade under license from the British Admiralty. War had scarcely been declared before these licenses began to appear, enabling the bearer to pass the blockade and sail for Portugal, which was under British control. Soon they were being bought and sold in the public exchanges. In 1813 a license with three months to run brought one thousand dollars and was worth it. Once past the coastal blockade, there was little chance of being stopped. A vessel might sail for Sweden as easily as Lisbon, and Sweden was then the gateway to the trade of Europe.

It was New England alone that profited by this trade, for it was only to her merchants that licenses were issued. Britain hoped thus to seduce the Northeastern states to separate from the Union. While New York and the whole Southern coast were blockaded, New England ports remained open until 1814, serving as outlets for an extensive commerce with the Canadian provinces. Much of the merchandise thus brought in from enemy territory was resold in other sections for gold or exportable produce, while exports, mainly food, went straight to the British armies in Canada, to Wellington's force in Spain and to England. Smuggling and privateering added to the total, until the real effect of the war, far from impoverishing the commercial states, was to enrich them enormously at the expense of the rest of the country.[18]

Yet because the New England merchants opposed the war that was making them rich, their wealth remained beyond the reach of the national government. The Treasury was so low by the time Congress adjourned in March that even military requisitions could not be met. The only means of securing funds in time to avert catastrophe was to borrow, and so a new sixteen-million-dollar loan was offered, but the New England banks would not touch it. Only four million was subscribed, and the loan would have fallen through entirely had not a personal friend of Secretary Gallatin, John Jacob Astor, stepped into the breach. The remaining bonds were bought by Astor himself, and through his influence by two Philadelphia bankers, German-born David Parish and French-born Stephen Girard. The Federalists never forgave these "foreigners" who had thus rescued their adopted country from the collapse so eagerly sought by some of its oldest families.

6

When Napoleon entered upon his disastrous Russian campaign, he gave Great Britain a new and powerful ally. It became at once to Russia's interest to put an end to Britain's war with the United States, so that all resources might be used to win the twenty-year-old struggle on the continent. In September of 1812 Czar Alexander asked the American Minister in St. Petersburg, John Quincy Adams, if the United States would consider a Russian offer of mediation; and Adams, on his own responsibility, answered with a qualified affirmative. The offer was formally transmitted to the Secretary of State by the Russian Minister in Washington on March 8, 1813, and was promptly accepted.

Madison hastened to name two commissioners to join Adams in St. Petersburg, even though the Senate was not in session to confirm the appointments. One place went to James A. Bayard of Delaware, veteran Federalist of the Senate, and the other was reluctantly given to Albert Gallatin at his own request. For Gallatin felt that his usefulness in the Treasury, at least for the time being, was at an end. He realized, perhaps better than anyone else, that the difficulties experienced in financing the war were in large part due to the failure of Congress in 1811 to recharter the Bank of the United States; and he knew also that the basis of that failure had been the personal hostility toward himself of a group of insurgent Senators. The fight for recharter had been led by William H. Crawford of Georgia, ablest Republican in the Senate, but Crawford's best effort produced only a tie which was broken by Vice President George Clinton with a vote against the administration.

So Gallatin withdrew, turning over the Treasury for the interim to Navy Secretary William Jones, and early in May he sailed with Bayard for the Russian capital. The two had been preceded by Crawford, who assumed the position of Minister to France made vacant by the death of Joel Barlow.

CHAPTER VI

THE STRATEGY OF OBSTRUCTION

1

THE situation was as critical as any in American history when the Thirteenth Congress came together in special session on May 24, 1813. A year of war on land had brought nothing but defeat. No more than twenty thousand men had been recruited to fill the ranks of an authorized army of three times that number; and the Treasury showed a deficit of five and a half million dollars, with no source of revenue in sight.

The already bitter opposition from the commercial states had been reinforced by new gains in the spring elections. Though the administration majority in the House was still substantial, standing at 114 to 68, the Federalist side was formidable indeed. Quincy was gone but his place was taken by battle-scarred Timothy Pickering, who had served in the Cabinets of Washington and Adams. The quondam editor of the hated *Federal Republican,* Alexander Hanson, joined the opposition forces from Baltimore, where he had achieved a species of martyrdom at the hands of an infuriated mob the preceding summer. From New York came Thomas P. Grosvenor, thought by the Republican chronicler of the session to be the "readiest debater and hardest hitter" of the party;[1] and swarthy, black-browed Daniel Webster made his first appearance on the political stage as a Representative from New Hampshire. The Federalists also held nine out of thirty-six seats in the Senate, where they joined forces with a small but powerful band of disaffected Republicans to reject the nomination of Albert Gallatin as one of the peace commissioners.

On the Republican side the only real gain was the absence of John Randolph, and there were not a few losses. William Butler of South Carolina was in the Army, after yielding his seat to Calhoun; and the Army had also claimed the services of such administration stalwarts as David R. Williams, Peter B. Porter and Richard M.

Johnson. Clay was again chosen as Speaker of the House and Calhoun once more headed the Committee on Foreign Relations; but Cheves, who was still absent when the appointments were made, was replaced by Eppes as Chairman of Ways and Means.

As soon as the necessary committee work could be completed Eppes offered a revenue program designed to make up the Treasury deficit, but the Federalists brushed it aside as they renewed with better marksmanship and heavier artillery their perennial attack on the war and all it involved. It was young Daniel Webster who rose to speak as soon as the money bills had been read. His diction was scholastic and his pronunciation old-fashioned and provincial, but his voice was resonant and clear.[2] He presented five resolutions, cleverly worded to reopen the question as to whether France had in fact revoked the Berlin and Milan Decrees, and to renew by innuendo the whole round of charges against the President. The debate began on June 16 and is notable as the first clash between Webster and Calhoun, young giants of a brave new world who had already taken the leadership of their respective parties from older but weaker hands. Their political battles were to dominate the next forty years of American history and their political ideas were long to outlive the golden tongues that proclaimed them to the world.

The debate was only one of an endless series in which the real question at issue was always the necessity, propriety and morality of the war. Federalist strategy sought to discredit the Republican party by discrediting the war, even at the cost of losing the struggle to Britain. No measure of military or financial import was allowed to pass without debating the issues once again, and when war measures did not come fast enough, resolutions and remonstrances served as vehicles for the same old argument. Not reasonableness and good will but self-interest and partisanship governed the debates. Arguments were addressed less to fellow members on the floor than to the people back home, who held the power of re-election or defeat for each individual Congressman. Speeches were made to the galleries, while opponents often enough wandered about the corridors well out of hearing; and votes were given not as judgments on evidence presented but in terms of economic convictions and political prejudices.

Webster, Pickering, Grosvenor and Hanson led the opposition, gambling, it sometimes seemed, with the very independence of their country in their bid for political power; and Calhoun on each occasion carried the main burden of defending the administration and of justifying the war. He spoke rapidly, with none of the sonorousness or emotional vibrance that characterized Webster's utterances, but with a rush of rhetoric that fairly overwhelmed his hearers. Yet there was magnetism in his manner and a sort of fascination in the way his eyes seemed to flash and deepen in color as he talked that carried conviction even where his words could not be followed nor his argument understood. He was never abusive, and even while he deplored the attitude of the Northeastern states, he sought at every opportunity to remove their grievances and to provide a sound basis for national unity.

2

Unity was never more urgent. Webster's resolutions were still under discussion toward the latter part of June when Madison was suddenly stricken with malaria. For more than a month his life hung in the balance, and only the alertness, discipline and unwearying labor of the party leaders averted catastrophe.

The President's successor, should he die in office, would be Elbridge Gerry, old and infirm, with a life expectancy scarcely better than that of the gravely stricken Madison; and after Gerry one of the most determined foes of the war might well gain the chief magistracy. For unbroken custom going back to the beginning of the Republic required the Vice President to withdraw a few days before the first session of each new Congress ended, to permit election by the Senate of a President pro tempore who became the legal heir to the vice presidential office. The strong opposition bloc in the Upper House prepared to take full advantage of the situation by naming one of their own number to take Gerry's place, and perhaps to succeed to the Presidency itself before the summer was over. So Gerry braved heat and pestilence and war to stick to his post, letting custom go by the board, and thereby prevented the choice of a successor by the Senate. His action left the Speaker of the House the next in line and assured the continuance of the war, whatever happened.[3]

Republican discipline was tightened under the lash of emergency, and the revenue legislation was driven through Congress with a minimum of debate. Only the direct tax drew strong Federalist opposition, which was the more unreasonable because they had themselves demanded such a tax in the previous Congress. Then when tempers were wearing thin under the oppressive heat of the Washington summer, Pickering offered a formal "Remonstrance of the Legislature of Massachusetts against the War," which went back over all the old ground and even challenged Louisiana's right to statehood. Calhoun called it a declaration of war by one state against another, but he refused to allow the administration forces to be drawn into the time-consuming argument which was Pickering's real purpose.

A few days later a detailed report in answer to Webster's resolutions came from the Secretary of State and was referred to the Committee on Foreign Relations. Calhoun responded by moving approval of the President's conduct, but Monroe's report was inherently weak and even the Republicans were not prepared to swallow it without a protest. The question was still pending on July 15, when Colonel Philip Stuart, a Revolutionary veteran representing a near-by Maryland district, hurried into the House chamber, and without pausing for breath moved that the galleries be cleared. He was a Federalist who seldom spoke, which made his request for secrecy the more ominous on this occasion. His business was briefly told. An enemy squadron of eight or ten ships of the line and frigates was on its way up the Potomac, and was already within sixty miles of the defenseless city.

Political quarrels were put aside and even the most bitter among the opposition members seemingly forgot their objections to the war in the general rush to save the Government and themselves from destruction. Some three thousand men were hastily recruited and armed under the personal leadership of the Secretaries of State, War and Navy, while business came to a standstill and all who could do so evacuated Washington.

Congress remained in session, though reports of its doings were meager. Both the editors of the *National Intelligencer,* who reported the debates in the two houses, were in the citizen army, as were seven of their printers. When the House considered the question of actively participating in the city's defense, the tumult was so great that even Clay, for all his parliamentary skill, his prestige and his authority of manner, could not keep order. "Gentlemen," he declared on one occasion, "if we do arm and take the field, I am sure we shall be beat, if there is not more order kept in the ranks than in this House."[4] The alarm continued for a week before the British dropped down the river again, after reaching Alexandria and destroying everything they could find in the way of commerce on the wharves and in the warehouses of that busy port.

3

Through it all the President remained in bed, but at the height of the invasion scare he passed the crisis. He was well enough by July 20 to send a confidential message to Congress. It was another appeal for a prohibition of exports to prevent illicit trade with the enemy, and it gave Calhoun one more opportunity to castigate the restrictive system. Speaking for the Foreign Relations Committee, he recommended that no action be taken; but the majority remained true to the ancient party faith. An embargo was drafted and passed, only to be defeated in the Senate as the session ended.

Madison renewed his request for an embargo as soon as the legislators returned to Washington in December, and this time it was a counsel of desperation. The war was fairly at a stalemate. The coast remained blockaded from New London south to Florida, and the only gains to be noted were gains in the volume of trade with the enemy and in the extent of American manufactures. Russian mediation had been refused by Great Britain, and the continued success of allied arms against Napoleon made the prospect for ultimate victory look grave indeed.

Again the embargo measure was introduced, and for days it was heatedly debated behind closed doors. Though it came from his committee, Calhoun refused to introduce the bill in the House, where Felix Grundy acted as its sponsor. As the contest developed, however, the question was adroitly turned into one of confidence in the administration. Fearing to risk party division at so critical a time, he reluctantly voted for it on the final roll call,[5] though Cheves and Lowndes remained consistent and voted as always against commercial restriction. This time the lines held firm, even in the

Senate, and foreign trade of all kinds once more became illegal.

Shortly after the President had signed the disputed bill a motion was made in the House to remove the injunction of secrecy from the embargo debates. Calhoun and Grundy opposed, but the motion was nevertheless carried. In the course of the discussion Thomas P. Grosvenor, always hotheaded and impetuous, accused the Carolinian of wishing to conceal his own inconsistency. Calhoun replied angrily, and the Speaker intervened when Grosvenor leaped to his feet to renew the attack. After a second attempt to speak was similarly overruled, the New York Representative appealed from the decision of the Chair, then changed his mind, since the matter "did not respect the House, but himself as an individual."[6] When the debate was over and Congressional privilege had been left behind, a challenge passed and an acceptance of it was received.

Calhoun's seconds were Henry Clay and Dr. William Bibb of Georgia, who had left the House for the Senate. Grosvenor was represented by Colonel Stuart and Rufus King of New York, another Federalist of the era of Washington and Adams. The encounter was fixed for one o'clock on Monday, December 27, and was to take place on the Virginia side of the Potomac.

At the last minute the affair was patched up "in a manner entirely honorable to both parties," through the good offices of Francis Scott Key, a young lawyer whose claim to immortality still lay ahead of him.[7] It was near noon, however, before the adjustment was made, and the House had already adjourned because of the absence of the Speaker. Grosvenor, unaware that negotiations were under way, had gone at an early hour to the dueling ground, where he was promptly arrested by a Virginia magistrate, but was released perforce because no duel had taken place.[8]

Although the adjustment was honorable to both parties, it could hardly have been satisfactory to either. Thereafter, while maintaining a scrupulous formality, there was an added sharpness to the frequent debates between them and a complete cessation of intercourse outside the House.[9]

4

Three days after the abortive duel, the British schooner *Bramble* put in at Annapolis under a flag of truce with a letter from Lord

Castlereagh to Monroe. The British Foreign Minister explained his refusal of Russian mediation and offered to negotiate directly, at London or at some neutral city. As though to emphasize the implications of the offer, newspapers carried on the same vessel brought word of Napoleon's defeat in the battle of Leipzig. Monroe read the newspapers and accepted.[10]

The "friends of peace, liberty and commerce," as the Federalists liked to call themselves, seized upon the British negotiation to renew their attack on the war and all who favored it. To resolutions already pending more were added, designed like all the others to provoke needless debate and to delay measures for the active continuance of hostilities. The war was depicted as the mere whim of a party rather than the cause of a people, and the argument was given added sting by news that Vermont's governor had ordered his militia to leave their posts with the Army and return home, where the militia of Massachusetts and Connecticut were already marking time.

In this strategy of obstruction, Daniel Webster continued to be the spokesman for the opposition, and Calhoun remained the principal defender of the administration and of the war. His skill as a speaker was steadily increasing and his speeches at this time reveal a full command of all the tricks of the orator, but he was at his best when he relied on the compelling power of reason alone. In his treatment of the Federalists he recurred again and again to one of the fundamental issues of democracy itself. To what lengths may opposition be safely carried before it ceases to be a right and becomes an abuse? Opposition which springs from mere difference of opinion, if united with patriotism and moderation, can do no harm and may lead to much good. But in combination "with faction and ambition, it bursts those limits, within which it may usefully act, and becomes the first of political evils . . . the fiercest and most ungovernable passions of our nature—ambition, pride, rivalry, and hate—enter into its dangerous composition; . . . attachment to a party becomes stronger than that to our country. . . . it is this moral treason . . . which has in all ages and countries, ever proved the most deadly foe to freedom. . . ."[11]

Despite persistent opposition new bonuses for recruits were authorized and the enlistment period was extended. Measures for tightening the enforcement of nonintercourse followed, and by 1814 New England began actually to feel some few of the hardships of which her merchants, through their spokesmen in Congress, had long complained. Freight once hauled by coastwise ships began to move slowly overland in covered wagons, while idle sailors and dock workers haunted the wharves or migrated with their families to the ever-beckoning West.[12] Coffee and sugar doubled in price, and the pinch of the British blockade extended northward to the coast of Maine.

Only the prospect of an early peace made the situation tolerable, and perhaps prevented actual dissolution of the Union. In his eagerness to speed the negotiations Madison was even willing to risk weakening his forces in Congress, naming Henry Clay to take the seat at the peace conference which had been denied to Gallatin. A new Speaker was chosen on January 19, 1814. The choice of the administration was understood to be Felix Grundy, who had steadfastly voted for the restrictive system, but the House preferred Langdon Cheves, who had never failed to support the cause of free trade. In the eyes of many Calhoun was the logical man for the place, but he declined to be a candidate for it against his older and more experienced colleague.[13]

5

Active partisan though he was, and the consistent champion of the war party in the House, Calhoun's thoughts for the moment centered elsewhere. He was thinking most frequently of his family, shortly to be increased, and waiting with impatience and anxiety for the letter that would tell him all was well. It came shortly after Cheves's elevation to the Speakership, and Calhoun hastened to express his relief and satisfaction.

"My dearest Floride," he began. "By Dr. Casey's letter of yesterday, I had the pleasure to hear of your safe delivery of a daughter; and that you had comparitively easy times. I had been waiting anxiously for mail day in expectation of such an event; and you may imagine the relief and joy it afforded me to hear not only of your safety, but the addition to our family. For both of your safety, I have all the fond wishes of a parent and an husband. I hope your mother till you are sufficiently recovered, will be punctual in writing every mail; as my anxiety will be increased to hear from you.

"As to the name, any one that you and your mother think proper will please me. It is a subject on which, I have no great choice; but my inclination would be to call her by the name which you and your mother bear. . . ."[14]

His inclination meant much to the young woman who was his wife, and this, their second child, was duly named Floride.

6

When the President received word that Gallatin was not on his way home but was determined to stay with his colleagues, commission or no, he once more sent in to the Senate the nomination of his erstwhile Secretary of the Treasury, this time to be one of the peace commissioners to negotiate with the British at Ghent in Holland. At the same time he yielded to the Senate's demand that Gallatin resign from the Treasury, nominating George Washington Campbell to succeed him in that position. Both appointments were confirmed.

Campbell was only another of Madison's unfortunate compromises. As Senator from Tennessee he had been a loyal administration supporter, but he had neither the ability nor the temperament to head the Treasury in such trying times. There was in fact only one man in America who had any real prospect of adequately filling Gallatin's shoes at that moment. He was Scotch-born Alexander J. Dallas of Philadelphia, independent, hardheaded and incorruptible, in no sense a party man, but an able and honest lawyer, versed in financial matters. Dallas was known to be Madison's preference for the post, but his name and all his works were anathema to Senator Laban of Pennsylvania, who warned the President in advance that Dallas would not be confirmed by the Senate.

Campbell assumed his duties as Secretary of the Treasury on February 9, 1814, and on the same day Chairman Eppes of the House Committee on Ways and Means introduced bills to raise twenty-five million dollars by borrowing and five million by an issue of Treasury notes. Washington wits were soon playing upon the new Secretary's initials, which might so conveniently stand for Government Wants Cash.[15]

The loan bill was the most controversial of the session and the most bitterly fought, taking nearly a month to pass the House and almost as long in the Senate. The Federalists did not deny that it was necessary to borrow money if the functions of government were to be carried on. They argued instead that the public credit was so low a loan could not be raised, and that since its purpose was to carry on an unjust war, it ought not to be voted even if it could be raised. The rest was all repetition and rebuttal.

It was not until Calhoun entered the debate late in the month that a new note was sounded. After perfunctory reference to the question at issue, he turned again to justification of the war, but there was in his argument a subtle shift of ground. He no longer dwelt upon the history of the Orders in Council and Napoleon's decrees, but placed his emphasis on impressment as the cause of hostilities.[16] Timothy Pickering spoke for the better part of two days in answer, first defending impressment in terms of British maritime history and then denying, on the basis of elaborate testimony from Massachusetts shipowners, that there was any impressment worth considering.

The argument was ingenious if not ingenuous, but Pickering was trapped. He could not explain away his own vigorous protests against impressment in his capacity as Secretary of State under Washington and Adams, nor those of his Federalist successor in that office, John Marshall. Failure to settle the impressment question had been the rock on which Jay's Treaty foundered, as it was the point on which Monroe and Pinkney failed. However mythical the repeal of Napoleon's decrees might be, impressment was real. Yet with magnificent disregard of public feeling, of the most obvious evidence and of plain common sense, the Federalists made Pickering's position their own, and by September of 1814 Robert Goodloe Harper was writing that impressment was "right in itself, and . . . not in the least dishonorable to the nation!"[17]

When the loan was finally authorized and the bonds were offered for sale, press and pulpit alike used every form of persuasion to keep New England from subscribing. Money was plentiful in Boston, and opportunities for safe and profitable investment were few;

but Boston and Philadelphia bankers, meeting privately in the Massachusetts city, voted not to take up the loan. The best they would agree to was to offer their financial aid to the Government if they could have assurances that satisfactory instructions had been given to the peace commissioners at Ghent.[18] The bankers were not allowed to dictate terms, and the loan failed. The specie which was concentrated in New England banks could not get back into circulation, and the grip of financial stringency tightened upon the whole country, while Bostonians bought British treasury notes at liberal discounts and exported coin to Canada to help pay the cost of the British fleet which was at that moment blockading their harbor.[19]

7

As the long European struggle neared an end, the restrictive system became less defensible than ever. The undercurrent of criticism increased in volume as the winter wore to a close. Early in March a move to suspend the embargo during peace negotiations was defeated by only three votes, and was followed by a move for outright repeal. Before the month was over, even Madison was ready to give it up, and on the last day of March he sent to Congress a message calling for opening of the ports. To protect the manufacturers he proposed to continue the wartime double duties for two years after the peace.

The message went, as usual, to the Committee on Foreign Relations, and on April 4 Calhoun presented a bill to repeal embargo and nonimportation alike.

The two were different things, as the representative of a manufacturing constituency was quick to point out. Embargoes kept American ships in port and destroyed all chance of trade, but nonimportation merely kept foreign goods from the market and served to protect home products against competition. The commercial states had opposed the former from the start, but the latter they had begun to regard with friendly eyes as their industrial ventures grew in size and profit. When an effort to split the bill failed, the manufacturing interests took another tack, and on motion of Samuel D. Ingham of Pennsylvania a resolution was unanimously adopted directing the Secretary of the Treasury to report at the next session "a general tariff of duties, conformably to the existing situation of the general and local interests of the United States."[20]

Calhoun disposed of the restrictive system he had so long opposed in a speech on April 6. The system, he declared, had sprung from an unusual combination of circumstances; it was a hope, however tenuous, of peace in a world at war, and it was meant to avoid war by the alternative of economic pressure. It should have ended when hostilities began, and that should have been earlier than it was. He concluded with some sympathetic words for industry:

"As to the manufacturing interest, in regard to which some fears have been expressed, the resolution voted by the House yesterday is a strong pledge, that it will not suffer the manufacturers to be unprotected, in case of a repeal of the restrictive system. I hope that at all times, and under every policy, they will be protected with due care. . . ."[21]

Webster followed Calhoun and pronounced a florid benediction over the restrictive system, not failing to seize this one final opportunity to tie it to the coattails of Bonaparte and make it seem as one with the "continental system" of the Little Corporal. He closed with a rounded declamation of the true isolationist principle. He would rejoice when he should see the Government "rely for maintenance of right and the redress of wrongs on the strength and resources of our own country, and break off all measures which tend, in any degree, to connect us with the fortunes of a foreign power."[22]

The repeal passed the House on April 7, 115 to 37, and received the approval of the Senate five days later. Party lines were curiously split on the final vote because Calhoun had insisted that embargo and nonimportation be included in a single bill. It is not without interest to note that opposition to repeal was led by Potter of Rhode Island, and that among the thirty-seven opposing votes in the House, nine were from Pennsylvania and four from Kentucky, both rising manufacturing states. Not a few of the Federalists were torn between traditional hostility to embargo and the new interest of their constituents in a prohibition of imports. Among these was Lewis Condict of New Jersey, whose uncle, Silas Condict, was secretary of an association of manufacturers of Essex County and was then planning a state-wide organization to lobby at the next session of Congress for a protective tariff.[23]

CHAPTER VII

PEACE WITHOUT VICTORY

1

THE news of Napoleon's abdication, which reached America early in the summer of 1814, filled Madison and his party with dismay, but in the strongholds of Federalism the triumph of British arms on the Continent was hailed with joy. Boston held a "Bourbon feast" in honor of the victory, though the Massachusetts coast from Gloucester to Cape Cod Bay was even then being ravaged by the victors; and in New York Gouverneur Morris paid the respects of his caste to democracy, that "child of squinting envy and self-tormenting spleen."[1]

Even as American fighting power declined, new British forces, released at last from European duty, were dispatched across the Atlantic. Warships multiplied in Chesapeake Bay, while seasoned troops moved up the broad tidewater valleys. Unable to give battle with his ridiculously outnumbered gunboats, Commodore Joshua Barney retreated up the Patuxent, then destroyed his flotilla and retired by land, taking with him only a few dismounted naval guns. The British pushed on behind him, reaching Bladensburg, five miles from Washington, on August 24. There they found Barney awaiting them, his handful of seamen and a larger group of hastily gathered militia disposed on a hillside overlooking the road. In the absence of the Secretary of War, Monroe assumed command, but while he quarreled with General Winder over the strategy of defense, the militia fled and Barney was routed. That evening the British entered the Capital, all but empty now of soldiers and civilians alike.

The Navy Yard had already been burned by its own defenders, but in the thirty-six hours they remained, the British completed the work of destruction. Then they moved on to Baltimore, which would have suffered the same fate but for the stubborn resistance of the little band who garrisoned Fort McHenry and inspired thereby our national anthem.

In September Castine on Penobscot Bay was occupied, and Governor Strong at last called out the Massachusetts militia, but even then he would not let them act under officers of the regular Army. Naturally enough President Madison saw no reason why this exclusively state force should be paid from the national treasury; so Strong talked darkly of taking "such measures for our safety as the times demand, and the principles of justice and the law of self-preservation will justify." The Federalist press proclaimed the Union as good as dissolved, and New England Republicans cried "Treason."[2]

The controversy was in full swing when Congress met September 19 in response to a Presidential proclamation. The Senate chamber and the Hall of Representatives were in ashes. The only public building spared by the invaders was Blodgett's Hotel, which housed the Patent Office, and that had escaped the torch only on the personal appeal of the Patent Commissioner, William Thornton. There Congress met, before the damp heat of summer had fully gone, to hear the President's message. Many of the members must have passed the blackened ruins of the Capitol or of the White House on the way to their temporary quarters, and if the sight produced depression of the spirit, the crowded room in which they presently found themselves did nothing to relieve it.

Neither was the annual message a cheerful document. MacDonough had won a hard-fought victory on Lake Champlain, and another rawboned Scot named Andrew Jackson had crushed the warlike Creeks in the West; but on other fronts the outlook was dismal. The negotiations at Ghent were in doubt; the country was on the verge of bankruptcy; the half-recruited army shifted from day to day as enlistment periods expired or militia companies disbanded, with or without permission; and Wellington's regulars and perhaps the Iron Duke himself were on the way to America.

When news finally arrived from the peace commissioners, it did nothing to lessen the general gloom. His Majesty's government had graciously consented to discuss ending hostilities with the United States; but the settlement must include a permanent Indian buffer state, under British protection, which was to take in parts of Ohio and Indiana, and all of Illinois, Wisconsin and Michigan; the United States must be excluded from all military or naval contact with the Great Lakes; Americans were no longer to be given access to the Atlantic fisheries; and that part of Maine lying between New Brunswick and Quebec was to be ceded to Canada.

The British terms had been rejected out of hand by the American commissioners, but Timothy Pickering, who spoke as a Federalist rather than as an American, thought them "moderate." They were published in the Boston papers on the same day that a committee of the Massachusetts Legislature called for a conference of the New England states "to lay the foundation for a radical reform in the National compact."

2

At his South Carolina home Calhoun heard news of the sack of Washington and the increasing disaffection of New England with deep anxiety. He was physically exhausted after the strenuous winter session, and it must have seemed to him that the cause for which he had worked so long and ardently was all but lost. Before he could regain his strength and buoyancy of temper he was taken ill with bilious fever, and it was a full month after the opening of the session before he was able to take his accustomed seat in the House.[3]

The President, his mind filled with the specter of revolt in New England, looked "miserably shattered and woebegone";[4] but new energy was conspicuous on both the military and financial fronts. Armstrong had been forced from office following his failure to defend the Capital and Monroe was back in the War Department, while the Treasury was at last in the capable hands of Alexander J. Dallas. Campbell had estimated the expenses for the rest of the year at twenty-five million dollars, and at twice that sum for 1815; but the Treasury was bare, the Government's bonds could not be sold and he had no sources of revenue to suggest. Confessing failure, he had resigned, and in the crisis the Senate withdrew its objections to Dallas. While the new Secretary familiarized himself with his task, Eppes proposed a revenue scheme which had been supplied him by Jefferson. Dallas disapproved it and substituted one of his own based on the creation of a national bank. Calhoun was chosen to steer the measure through Congress, and the whole plan was laid before him as soon as he made his belated appearance in Washington.[5]

The bank was to have a capital of fifty million dollars, of which six million would be gold and silver and the remainder Government stocks issued during the war. Forty percent of the total stock was to be subscribed by the Government; and the bank, which could not sell the Government stocks, was to lend the Treasury thirty million dollars as soon as it got into operation. To further insure Government control, the President was to be empowered to suspend specie payments at his discretion.

With no committee assignments to divide his attention, Calhoun began his own study of the measure and shortly concluded that he could not support it, regardless of the wishes of the administration. He thought the effect would simply be that the Government would "borrow back its own credit, and pay six percent per annum for what they had already paid eight or nine"—credit which might better be used directly in the form of Treasury notes, to be funded as part of the bank stock.

He refused to sponsor the administration's bill, and when debate began in the middle of November, he moved the first of a series of amendments avowedly designed to alter the whole character of the institution proposed. Fisk of New York, Forsyth of Georgia, and Ingham defended Dallas' plan, while Lowndes and Oakley of New York ably supported the South Carolinian. When a vote was taken after two days of heated argument, Calhoun's amendment was adopted by about sixty votes. The next day he continued his alteration of the administration's bill, again supported by Lowndes, and again successful. Section by section the process continued, until the bill was no longer the Treasury's but Calhoun's. When it was finally reported to the House from the Committee of the Whole, it was "so interleaved and interlined" as to be scarcely legible, even to the clerk.[6]

Calhoun's plan, like that of Dallas, called for a capital of fifty million dollars, of which six million would be precious metal, but the remainder was to be not war stocks but specie and Treasury notes, the latter issued for the occasion. He thought Dallas' scheme would give an undue advantage to those who had lent money to the Government during the war as against those who had not. Perhaps the Secretary so intended it, as a form of punishment for New England; but the fact that Dallas himself came from Philadelphia, where the bulk of the war stocks were held, put the matter in another light which the Federalists did not overlook.[7] Dallas, on the other hand, thought Calhoun's plan would give a disproportionate advantage to new creditors as against the old, and that the latter as well as capitalists generally could not fail to resent it.

The Federalists preferred Calhoun's plan to that of the Treasury, but many were opposed to any bank at all. Lowndes thought both plans called for too much capital; and it was this feature of the bank that brought about a deadlock which remained unbroken after a week of argument. A groundless suspicion that Calhoun's version had also originated in the Cabinet only complicated matters further,[8] and November 25 saw the bill recommitted. This time it went, not to Ways and Means, whose chairman was hostile to any bank, but to a special committee of which Lowndes was chairman and Calhoun a member. The others were Fisk, Ingham and Forsyth for the administration, and the Federalists Oakley and Gaston of North Carolina. Oakley favored Calhoun's plan, while Gaston opposed both versions. The committee was thus without a majority for either of the plans proposed; and after three days, unable to agree, they returned the bill as it was.

On the floor of the House once more, an amendment by Lowndes to reduce capital from fifty to thirty million was approved. Then Hanson moved to strike out the enacting clause, and a sharp debate with Calhoun followed, in the course of which both were more than once called to order for personalities. Grosvenor spoke in similar vein; and the triumphant Federalists were seemingly glorying in their country's bankruptcy when Colonel R. M. Johnson, back in the House after suffering crippling wounds in the war, called abruptly for the previous question. The bill was lost by as large a margin as that by which the Treasury's bill had been defeated.

3

In New England, meanwhile, the proposal of Massachusetts for an interstate conference had been accepted, and the meeting was

LANGDON CHEVES   HENRY CLAY

JAMES MADISON   JAMES MONROE

JOHN C. CALHOUN, ABOUT 1818
by John Wesley Jarvis

scheduled to take place in Hartford on December 15. In the press, in private correspondence and in the legislatures of the disaffected states the issue was debated to the virtual exclusion of everything else. Proposals ranged from formal remonstrance to the creation of a separate union of "all the states with which New England *ought* to wish any political connection."[9] Although propounded by Federalists, the argument followed lines identical with those laid down by Jefferson and Madison during the controversy of 1798 over the Alien and Sedition Laws. The states were "free, sovereign and independent nations" whose relation to the general government was "founded on express compact and treaty." As the "original parties to the compact," the states possessed "an inherent right to determine whether the terms of such compact have been violated, and its force destroyed."

As demands for a separate peace grew more insistent, conservatives saw their influence fading. Bolder men and sterner measures were required by public opinion, and in November Massachusetts substituted action for words. A secret envoy was sent to the British by way of Castine, empowered to discuss terms. The offer was relayed to London, and authority was conferred on officials in Canada to negotiate, aid being promised should the other states try to interfere.[10] Although unknown to the Government, the Union was already on the point of dissolution when Monroe proposed to fill the ranks of the authorized regular Army and to add forty thousand more by conscription.[11]

The storm of protest from New England Representatives shook the confidence of the boldest, and the House refused to act; but the Senate, whose members served longer terms, was less timorous. There a bill to draft eighty thousand militiamen into the regular Army was drawn up, and passed despite bitter opposition. When it reached the House, the Committee on Military Affairs refused it, because it was not the measure requested by the Secretary of War. It went instead to the Committee of the Whole, where Calhoun, sensing the stiffening temper of the opposition, announced himself in favor of it as a matter of policy. To press Monroe's project would be to lose all hope of passing any bill at all.

Webster and his New England colleagues led the attack, growing bolder in their avowal of frankly disunion sentiments as the date for the Hartford Convention drew near. The nation, if nation it might still be called, was bankrupt and visibly disintegrating. Of what further use could it be to conscript an army for the defense of what was for all practical purposes already lost? Under the continuous hammering of the Federalists, the House yielded, and the bill was vitiated by amendment before it passed on December 14.

On the following day representatives of the five New England states (it will be remembered that Maine was still a part of Massachusetts) assembled at Hartford to take measures for the defense of New England, whether against Great Britain or against the rest of the United States was not quite clear.

4

Back in Washington no official notice of the Hartford Convention was taken, but its shadow hung like a pall of doom over the Capital. Only money, and that without delay, could avert the end which seemed to be rapidly approaching. The House voted the heaviest taxes in the nation's brief and stormy history, but their value was negligible. New England alone had money to pay taxes, and no one could say whether she would still be a part of the Union when the time came to collect them. The bank remained the sole hope for financing a continuation of the war, and so it was the bank that absorbed the best energies of the Republicans and bore the brunt of Federalist hostility.

When the Senate's version of the Treasury plan was taken up in the lower chamber just before Christmas, Webster led the opposition, while Fisk and Ingham championed the administration. Both sides courted the support of Calhoun and Lowndes, who were acknowledged the foremost champions of a national bank but equally the leading foes of the Dallas scheme.

The debate reached a climax on December 29 in one of the stormiest sessions ever seen in the House,[12] which ended without action on Webster's motion to recommit. Then followed a brief interlude in which dissenting Republicans were whipped into line. On the second of January the bill was brought to a vote and carried, 81 to 80, with Lowndes voting for it and Calhoun against. The shout of triumph was quickly stilled, however, when Cheves rose to remind the House that he had not exercised his right to vote. He was unalterably opposed to the bank in that form and voted against it, producing a tie which meant defeat.

Upon those Republicans who had brought about the loss of the administration's bill rested a terrible responsibility, for it might well be that the nation itself was at stake. First among the dissidents was Calhoun, who now assumed as a matter of course the leadership of his party. The Hartford Convention still sat behind closed doors and for all he knew the Union might even then stand dissolved, but he did not believe it. Throughout the long sectional struggle he retained his faith that the men and women of New England were at bottom as patriotic and as devoted to their country as he was himself, and he made of the financial crisis a vehicle for proving it. In the sudden hush that followed Cheves's vote Calhoun strode across the chamber and boldly demanded Webster's assistance in the preparation of a new bank bill which all could support. Webster nodded his assent and the two young partisans clasped hands as the House adjourned in tumult.[13]

The following day a chastened group of Representatives, appalled by the glimpse of chaos their action had revealed, voted two to one to reconsider, and the Treasury bill was once more sent to a select committee. Neither Calhoun nor Webster was among its members, but when an amended bill was reported it looked strangely like Calhoun's original plan, save only that the capital was reduced to Lowndes's figure of thirty million dollars. Webster led the Federalists in its support, and the House approved it on January 7 by a vote of 120 to 38.

Into this atmosphere of better understanding came news that the Hartford Convention had adjourned after twenty days, and had indeed "bro't forth a mouse."[14] Conservatism had won the day and the solemnly chosen representatives of the New England states had done no more than propose amendments to the Constitution, which a committee of five would presently bring to Washington. They wanted the abolition of slave representation; the admission of new states to the Union only on concurrence of two-thirds in both Houses of Congress; the limitation of embargoes to sixty days' duration; the requirement of a two-thirds vote of both Houses for the passage of nonintercourse acts; a similar requirement for a declaration of war; a provision that no one thereafter naturalized should be eligible to any Federal office; and finally, an amendment forbidding any President to serve more than one term, or any state to furnish two successive Presidents.[15]

With the tension somewhat eased, the Senate yielded to administration pressure, amending the bank bill to approximate once more the Treasury plan, but the House was adamant and after ten days the Senate gave in. Dallas was made of sterner stuff, and the bill met with a curt Presidential veto, based on the objections the Treasury had originally advanced against Calhoun's scheme.

Bankruptcy and possible collapse not only of the war but of the Government itself again faced the administration, and a caucus was hastily called to draft a compromise bill. Fundamentally, however, the positions of Calhoun and Dallas were irreconcilable; and the Secretary, though he yielded much, could not concede all the South Carolinian demanded. The caucus broke up with the abrupt withdrawal of Calhoun, and the administration made a final effort to pass a modified bill without his aid.[16]

The new measure passed the Senate by a close 18 to 16 vote and was received in the lower house on February 13. Calhoun was on his feet at once. Members were being asked again to vote for a principle they had already rejected, on the sole ground that any bank was better than no bank. Let the emergency be withdrawn, and he thought the bill "would not receive the support of fifteen members." That evening word came from New York that a treaty was signed and would be in Washington the next day. Rumors were already afloat when the House met on the fourteenth, and the bill was tabled pending arrival of the mail. In the general rejoicing over the treaty, the whole question was forgotten, and three days later the bank issue was indefinitely postponed.

Another casualty of the peace was the Hartford Convention. The commissioners had started for Washington on February 3, carrying with them the terms on which New England could be reconciled to the Union. After various delays they reached Baltimore February 12, to be greeted by news of Jackson's victory at New Orleans. They knew then that they could no longer base their case on national calamity, and when they arrived in Washington on the fourteenth rumors of peace made their mission seem more hopeless still. The episode ended with prompt confirmation that a treaty had indeed been signed.

5

Relieved at last from the dangerous tension of the past months, weary Congressmen thought only of returning as quickly as possible to their homes. Calhoun left Washington as soon as the session ended on March 3, 1815, and was back in South Carolina in two weeks' time. He reached Bath on the twentieth and plunged at once into the active management of his plantation. During his absence his affairs had been largely carried on by his three brothers, for Floride, like her mother, was never skilled in the handling of slaves nor in matters of business.

The pleasure of reunion with his family was of brief duration. On April 7, almost without warning, his infant daughter died, and Floride was inconsolable. The young father, too, was deeply moved, and made no effort to conceal his grief behind the façade of detached reserve he was accustomed to show to the world.

"Bath 9th April 1815.

"My dear Mother, Floride wrote to you by Mr Shackleford that all were well. We at that time little calculated that in three days, we should experience the heaviest calamity that has ever occured to us. It is no less than the death of our interesting and dearest daughter. She was in the bloom of health on Wednesday morning the 6th inst. and was a corps the next day. She was taken with a vomiting and fever very suddenly about eleven o'clock and died about an hour by the sun the next morning. We suspected no danger till about midnight and even then except a wildness in her eyes the symtoms were not very distressing. We became much alarmed about day; and sent off a dispach for Dr Casey but he was gone to Augusta. Everything was done which we thought could be of service but in vain. Thus early was snatched from us in the bloom of life, our dear child whom providence seemed, but a few hours before, to destine to be our comfort and delight. So healthy, so cheerful, so stought; every prognostick of health and long life. She had just begun to talk and walk; and progressed so fast in both as to surprise every one. She could hardly step when I returned on the 20th of March and before her death she could run all over the house. But why should I dwell on these once flattering appearances? She is gone alas! from us forever; and has left behind nothing but our grief and tears. So fixed in sorrow is her distressed mother that every topick of consolation, which I attemp to offer but seems to grieve her the more. It is in vain I tell her it is the lot of humanity; that almost all parents have suffered equal calamity; that Providence may have intended it in kindness to her and ourselves, as no one can say what, had she lived, would have been her condition, whither it would have been happy or miserable; and above all we have the consolation to know that she is far more happy than she could be here with us. She thinks only of her dear child; and recalls to her mind every thing that made her interesting, thus furnishing additional food for her grief.

"We will expect you up as soon as your business will permit. Floride desires her love to you. Our respects to all friends."[17]

CHAPTER VIII

NATIONALISM TRIUMPHANT

1

ALTHOUGH in itself indecisive, the War of 1812 had far-reaching consequences for America and for the world. It brought the United States to the threshold of the industrial revolution; it hastened the destruction of the colonial economy which had formed the chief bond between the Old World and the New; and it began the forging of scattered cities and far-flung hinterland into the characteristic political unit of the modern world: a national state.

After 1815 Americans faced their own continent, eyes no longer on the sea and on the past but turned toward the vast plains and forests and mountains of the West. Thenceforward they were to depend upon no other land nor race but solely upon themselves. They were traders, speculators, gamblers, these people of young America—ready to take a chance, willing to work, eager to fight, insatiably curious, ingenious, imaginative. Largely untutored in any formal sense, they were free from the dead weight of tradition. Having never been taught any particular way to overcome the forces of nature, they were free to experiment, to make mistakes, to fail and to succeed in their own way. They were persistent, resolute, stubborn, immensely self-confident; and with all their latent power for good or for ill unleashed, they set themselves to the remaking of the world. All they needed was capital and technical skill, an adequate system of transportation, and some armor against the power and the jealousy of Europe. In short, they needed everything but raw materials and the will to rub Aladdin's lamp.

To provide for their needs was the task they imposed upon their Representatives in the National Legislature; and we shall presently see the tall, angular figure of John C. Calhoun moving tirelessly through committee rooms, executive offices and daylong meetings of the House, exerting every ounce of his great power of reasoning and his gift of speech to give young America all that she required. We shall see him wielding—through the superiority of his mind, the almost hypnotic fascination of his dark, flashing eyes, and the high character he bore in public and in private life— an influence greater than that of any other man in the Fourteenth Congress, to which his constituents had returned him again unopposed.

The body of men who met in December 1815 in the hastily erected temporary capitol was as able a group as any Congress in the nation's history. Calhoun was in Washington a week ahead of time, having made the last fifty miles of the trip by steamboat up the Potomac.[1] Most of the young war leaders were back, with added confidence and experience. Clay, Lowndes, Forsyth, Porter, Johnson and Ingham were among them; and new members included William Pinkney of Maryland, whose prowess at the bar was already legendary; Samuel Smith of Baltimore, veteran Senator of Jefferson's time, now first appearing in the House; John Sergeant of Pennsylvania; and Henry St. George Tucker, half brother of John Randolph, from Virginia. Randolph himself was back after a two-year absence and went as a matter of course into the opposition camp, where he was joined by such Federalist stalwarts as Timothy Pickering, Daniel Webster, Thomas P. Grosvenor and Alexander C. Hanson. Of the war leaders only Felix Grundy, a voluntary absentee, and Langdon Cheves, who had been replaced by Henry Middleton of Charleston, were missing.

Ability was badly needed. The country was rushing headlong into inflation. There was no reserve of precious metal, and paper depreciated in value day by day. The demands of the growing West could not begin to be supplied over the few primitive roads that crossed the mountains. British manufactures were beginning to flood the market at cutthroat prices, and commercial and industrial interests of all complexions were calling plaintively for Government aid. As the legislators buckled down to the business at hand, Henry Clay was again chosen Speaker of the House, and his most important appointments were those of William Lowndes to be chairman of Ways and Means, and Calhoun to head a select Committee on the National Currency. The major political controversies of the next twenty years revolved around the measures proposed by these two committees.

Financial problems absorbed Calhoun's attention for the first month of the session, and it was January before he took any part in the debates. When he spoke at last, it was to reveal how far he was from the humanistic, eighteenth-century concept of democracy. The belching chimneys and spawning machines of the age of invention demanded a belief in progress, and he could not reconcile that belief with the Jeffersonian faith in the equality of men. The excuse for his remarks was a bill for the establishment of three additional military academies, but the question became in his hands one of broad governmental policy—a glass through which he might examine those psychological forces upon which government and society itself are based.

Still stirred by the national spirit bred of war, he sought to avoid the old divisions and keep that spirit alive. The nation must be made secure and prosperous, not by sections or classes, but in all its parts, and there must be equal opportunity for all. A single academy would be filled with the sons of wealthy men, because they alone could afford to journey far from home to attend. Yet genius and talent were more likely to come from the middle and lower ranks of society, "not that these classes actually contain a greater portion of talent, but that they have stronger stimulants to its exertion. Rich men, being already at the top of the ladder, have no further motive to climb. It is that class of the community who find it necessary to strive for elevation, that furnishes you with officers. . . ."[2]

He believed, in short, that life was a competitive struggle in which weakness was more to be feared than strength: a struggle in which eminence would naturally be sought by all but would be achieved, through a process of natural selection, only by those whose talents and will were greatest. Upon these successful competitors in the struggle for place must rest the responsibility for leadership in the society.

Out of this finespun argument came a practical suggestion. A small but highly trained army would serve the needs of the nation better than a large but ill-disciplined body of militia. The common soldier could be trained with relative ease and speed, but officers were far more difficult to develop. Why not, then, an army of potential officers, capable of training and leading large bodies of citizen troops in time of war? Calhoun's discourse was lightly passed over by his colleagues, as was apt to be the case when he permitted himself the luxury of speculation, but he was soon to have an opportunity to discuss the subject of national defense in more concrete terms.

2

The occasion arose when Lowndes laid before the House a few days later a detailed revenue program which retained the principle of direct taxation and proposed to keep in effect approximately half of the wartime extraordinary duties until a new tariff schedule could be agreed upon.[3] The question of duties was delayed until the general tariff debate, which will be treated in another chapter; but the retention of the direct tax, reluctantly accepted by Congress only as a war measure, was immediately challenged.

More than a mere matter of taxes was at stake. Americans in 1816 were thoroughly conscious both of their destiny and of their isolation. They had just won a war with the mighty British Empire, but they had won it almost by default, when the enemy was too busy elsewhere to give the matter much attention. The United States in 1816 was the only considerable nation on earth committed to the free institutions of popular government, and thoughtful men had no doubt that the mere existence of such a nation was a threat to the continuance of class government and special privilege in other countries. More specifically, they had no doubt that America would offer a revolutionary example to the exploited masses of Europe, particularly of England, and that it was therefore obviously to England's interest to crush the United States as soon as she had sufficiently recovered herself to do so. American policy, in consequence, had to consider the probability of a renewal of the perennial struggle with Great Britain at a not too distant time, and to prepare to meet it. The United States must be made as strong as possible, not alone in military and naval affairs, but economically as well.

Supporters of the direct tax based their case on the necessity for maintaining strong defenses against any renewed aggression on the part of England or any other European power, and the measure was opposed by those who believed that America had more to fear from too strong a government at home than from distant transatlantic foes. The opposition came chiefly from the West, where the threat of foreign invasion never seemed real, and from New England, where Federalist opposition had become a habit; but its leader was John Randolph, the lone wolf who spoke only for himself and for a future not yet clear to men of less prophetic gaze.

When Calhoun took part in the debate, it was to answer Randolph. He thought his peace-loving, profit-taking countrymen were more likely to let their government sink into impotence than they were to suffer the rise of military despotism. The seeming remoteness of foreign enemies and the unwillingness of a commercial people to face the disruption of business consequent on war were sources of weakness, which threatened to leave the country unprepared in the hour of crisis.

"England is the most formidable power in the world: she has the most numerous army and navy at her command. We, on the other hand, are the most growing nation on earth: most rapidly improving in those very particulars in which she excels. . . . Will Great Britain permit us to go on in an uninterrupted march to the height of national greatness and prosperity? I fear not. . . . You will have to encounter British jealousy and hostility in every shape; not immediately manifested by open force or violence, perhaps, but by indirect attempts to check your growth and prosperity. . . ."

There was nothing in the history of Anglo-American relations to make this view seem overdrawn, nor was there anything far-fetched about Calhoun's conclusion that the only safe policy for the United States must be a policy designed to repel future aggression on the part of Britain. We must have an adequate navy, a standing army large enough to man an improved chain of fortifications, and a militia adequately trained. In time of war an expanded force should be recruited by draft from the whole citizen body. The last proposal was revolutionary, and he felt called upon to defend it against those who wished to enjoy liberty without working for it. Improved communications in the form of roads and canals were also included in Calhoun's defense program, and he would have the country independent of foreign sources for basic manufactures, even at the cost of subsidy.

His final point was that a system of revenue equal to the strain of war could not be created after war had begun, but must have permanent existence during peace. Taxes are not oppressive if they are necessary, and what could be more necessary than to provide for defense of the country?[4] If the speech showed a leaning toward abstract thought, it revealed also an unusual breadth of background, and it left no doubt as to his acute awareness of the changing economic structure of America. When Randolph replied, it was first of all to say that the respect he already had for the young South Carolinian's talents had been increased in no small degree by his performance.

Randolph's answer was one which Calhoun passed over at the time, but to which he paid tribute many years later. It was simply that however patriotic the motive might be, the direct taxes, the large navy, the well-drilled army, the roads and canals and subsidized industry all tended to consolidate and strengthen the National Government at the expense of the states; but despite the eccentric Virginian's warning that in the nature of men and nations the road to power is the road to tyranny, the direct tax was accepted.

3

As soon as the question of taxation was settled, the House took up a bill offered by Calhoun to incorporate the subscribers of a Bank of the United States.[5] With Government borrowing no longer a factor and resumption of specie payments admittedly the most important bank function, it was now possible for Dallas to approve Calhoun's plan, though it differed little from the scheme he had rejected a year earlier. Neither did it vary materially from the pattern set by the original Bank of the United States, which Hamilton had conceived and the Federalists had chartered in their heyday of power.

It was to have a capital of thirty-five million dollars which Congress might later increase to fifty million. One-fifth of the total was to be paid by the Federal Government, in the form of coin, Treasury notes or Government stocks, while bank stock representing the remainder was to be offered for public sale. At least one-quarter of the latter was to be paid for in gold or silver coin, but funded debts of the United States would be accepted in payment for the other three-quarters. The bank was to be located in Philadelphia, but might have branches in other cities. The parent bank would have twenty-five directors, of whom five were to be appointed by the President of the United States, and twenty elected by the resident citizen stockholders. These directors were to choose governing boards of thirteen members each for branch banks and were to select their own president, who must, however, be one of the five Governmental appointees. The bank was to have an exclusive charter for twenty-one years, and its notes were to be legal tender, in return for which privileges it was to transact certain public business free of charge and was to pay to the Treasury a bonus of $1,500,000 in three instalments, over a four-year period. Congress was to have power to suspend or refuse to suspend specie payments.

In opening the discussion when the bill reached the floor late in February, Calhoun sought first of all to limit the scope of debate. The constitutional power of Congress to establish a bank had often been debated, and members had long since made up their minds on the point. Neither was anything to be gained by arguing the relation of banks to public liberty and prosperity, for they were already too closely bound up with the commerce and industry of the nation to be uprooted. The favorable effect of a national bank on the administration of Government finances was no longer open to question. Waiving for the time being the details of the particular institution proposed, the question to be decided was whether or not inflation could be checked by the establishment of a national bank.

To answer that question he reviewed the financial history of the preceding twenty-five years. The Constitution gave to Congress an exclusive power to regulate the currency, and forbade the states to issue bills of credit; yet the states were permitted to create banks which could do what the states themselves could not. At the time the Constitution was written, there was just one bank in the United States, and its capital was only $400,000. In the intervening quarter of a century, 260 banks had come into existence, with a total capital of $80,000,000. The notes of these banks were the nation's currency, and since the banks had little or no precious metal with which to redeem them, their value was only what they would bring in exchange, varying from place to place and from day to day, and steadily decreasing as the volume of bank notes rose.

As long as this state of things continued, Congress had no control whatever over the currency. It could fulfil its constitutional obligation only by forcing the banks to carry out their contracts: by compelling them to surrender the illegal power they had acquired through issuing paper in excess of their ability to redeem it. The banks were not insolvent and could return to a metallic basis in a comparatively short time if they would all act together in a policy of gradual retrenchment, but this they would not do. The existing freedom from Government regulation was greatly to their profit—so much so that stockholders had been receiving from twelve to twenty percent, and it was idle to believe that this profit would voluntarily be foregone. They would return to specie payments only when it was to their interest to do so.

The existing situation meant that people in different sections of the Union were unequally taxed, but they could not make their wishes effectively known because of the control exerted over the press by the banks. It was up to Congress alone to apply the remedy. The establishment of a national bank, itself paying specie and refusing the notes of all banks that did not do so, would soon make it to the interest of all banks to get back on the gold standard. Further weight could be added by requiring that taxes be paid in specie or in the notes of specie-paying banks, and by confining Government business to the same institutions.[6]

The limits which Calhoun had fixed for the debate were tacitly accepted by the House, as was also his analysis of the existing currency situation. The opposition took two principal forms. One group, led by Randolph, argued that the evil could be remedied without any kind of national bank; the other group, for which Webster was foremost spokesman, did not favor the particular bank proposed. The question consumed most of the time of the House for more than two weeks, but on March 14 the bill was passed by a vote of 80 to 71. Among those opposing the bank were John Sergeant, who became one of its first directors, and Daniel Webster, who became its attorney.

All in all, it was an example of skillful management on Calhoun's part. From the beginning he conducted the campaign, personally entering the discussion again and again, trying always to smooth over the points of difference, yielding or accepting modifications in detail when it was necessary to do so to save a basic principle. He received occasional support from Federalist members, but he had also to accept the defection of Western Republicans who wanted cheap money. At every point he was prepared with an answer and was by all odds the best-informed man in the House on the subject under consideration. He took full advantage of the divided sentiments of the Federalists and utilized every argument and every parliamentary device he could command, both in the House and outside it, to carry the bill.

The opposition sought first to reduce the capital from thirty-five million dollars to twenty million, but succeeded only in striking out the clause that gave Congress power at some future time to increase the amount. An attempt to forbid the Government to hold stock in the bank was decisively beaten, and a determined effort to prevent Presidential appointment of five directors resulted only in an amendment annulling the rule that the bank's president must be one of the five. The only other modifications were an amendment which forbade Congress to suspend specie payments and one which withdrew the Government's right to use Treasury notes in payment for bank stock. Amendments that failed were one to prevent establishment of more than one branch of the bank in any single state and another that would have excluded any but native-born citizens from the board of directors. The latter was aimed at Dallas, who, it was widely thought, was to be the bank's first president.

Early in April the measure passed in the Senate, and it remained only to fix a date for the resumption of specie payments. Dallas suggested January 1, 1817, and a bill to that effect was introduced by Calhoun. It was eventually defeated by a single vote, but the same purpose was accomplished by the adoption of a resolution requiring payment of all Government revenues in legal tender after February 20, 1817.[7]

4

During the progress of the bank bill through the House there was only one interruption, when Colonel Richard M. Johnson of Kentucky claimed the floor. Hero of the Battle of the Thames who had slain the dreaded Indian warrior Tecumseh in single combat, Johnson was probably the most popular man in Congress.[8] His manner was bluff and hearty, his features large and good-humored, and his figure, habitually adorned by a scarlet waistcoat, was rather on the dumpy side. He was listened to with attention as he complained of the long delays attending the transaction of the public business, which he attributed to the fact that members of Congress were paid by the day and so were tempted to remain in session longer than was necessary. Without opposition the matter was turned over to a special committee headed by Johnson, with Webster and Grosvenor among its members.[9]

After two days a bill to change the compensation of Congressmen from six dollars a day to fifteen hundred dollars a year was brought in and briefly debated. Except for a few who had constitutional scruples, there was no real objection save that the sum proposed was too small. All recognized the abuse it was meant to cure. No one disputed Randolph's charge that members had to be waked up to vote, or that they kept the House from adjourning "because they have not finished a letter, or sent off the latest newspaper."[10] The only serious discussion centered around an amendment offered by Randolph which would make the new compensation effective only after March 4, 1817. It was intended to place above suspicion the motives of those who passed the bill, but it was badly beaten.

On March 8 Calhoun spoke for the measure and gave it, by so doing, a semblance of administration support. He agreed with Randolph and others that the sum should have been fixed at twenty-five hundred dollars instead of fifteen hundred, but his argument was not in terms of the cost of living or of the speedy dispatch of the public business. It was an analysis of political power.

If the constitutional power of the President, with his veto and his control of patronage, was, as some feared, dangerously great, the remedy lay not in weakening the Executive but in strengthening the Legislature. Against the power of the President Calhoun proposed to balance the "character, experience, and intelligence" of the House; and to this end he favored the increased pay in the hope that it would draw men of greater ability to Congress and keep them there, instead of forcing them to return to private life to provide for their families just as they acquired the experience that would make them most useful to the nation. "If we are wise, we will . . . attract and secure ability and integrity in the public service." These belong to the nation, "and any people, as they use or neglect them, flourish or decay."[11]

There was some further discussion, almost casual in nature, and the bill was passed, the vote being 81 to 67. Even of those who voted against it, few really disapproved, but opposed on some other ground such as the indelicacy of making the increased pay applicable to themselves. Then they returned to the more important matter of the bank, and after it the tariff, while news of how they had voted themselves a yearly salary filtered back to their constituents and storm clouds began to gather on the political horizon.

CHAPTER IX

SUBSIDIZED INDUSTRY

1

A PRESIDENT of the United States was to be elected in the fall of 1816, but the actual choice, as everybody knew, would be made by a caucus of Republican Congressmen some time before the spring adjournment. The candidates were Governor Daniel D. Tompkins of New York; William H. Crawford, former Senator from Georgia, envoy to France, and since August of 1815 Secretary of War; and James Monroe, last of Virginia's elder statesmen. Monroe had sought the nomination in 1808 and was generally understood to have received a pledge of support for 1816 when he entered Madison's cabinet. Crawford had been Presidential timber since his masterly but losing fight to save the first Bank of the United States in 1811. Tompkins lacked a national reputation, and his only strength lay in his being a Northern man.[1]

Calhoun was well acquainted personally with the two leading candidates. Crawford's home was just across the Savannah River from Bath, and like Calhoun he had attended Moses Waddel's academy. The two men may indeed have known each other since their student days, for Crawford, though the elder by ten years, was probably still at the school when Calhoun briefly attended it in 1796.[2] With Monroe the young Carolinian had been thrown into close association by his chairmanship of the Foreign Relations Committee during the war. Between the two, he preferred the Virginian and was active in his support, but without personal animus. He remained, at least, on terms of intimacy with Dr. Bibb and with Charles Tait, the Georgia Senators who were Crawford's managers.

Monroe was not particularly popular, and there was strong opposition in many quarters to another Virginia President under any circumstances. With administration support, however, his

114

strength increased as time went on, and the strategy of his supporters accordingly was to delay the caucus as long as possible. It
was March 10 before an anonymous notice prominently displayed in the temporary capitol invited Republican Congressmen
to meet in the hall of Representatives on the twelfth "to take
into consideration the propriety of nominating persons as candidates for President and Vice-President of the United States."[3]
The caucus system was rapidly coming into popular disfavor, and
the expediency of making nominations at all was questioned by
many, among them Lowndes and Clay. This feeling doubtless had
much to do with the fact that only 58 out of 141 Republican members attended the meeting. In the circumstances a better showing was imperative, and a second notice was posted. This time it
was signed by Jeremiah Morrow of Ohio and fixed the time for the
caucus as the evening of March 16.

The second attempt brought out 119 members, including Clay,
who moved without success the adoption of a resolution declaring
nominations inexpedient. Among the absentees were Bibb and
Tait. At the last minute they had withdrawn Crawford's candidacy, in accordance with his instructions; but they failed to carry
out the rest of the plan, whereby they were to attend the caucus,
vote for Monroe, and explain their action in a joint letter to the editors of the *National Intelligencer*.[4] The maneuver was intended to
give the Georgian, who was only forty-four, a long head start in
the succeeding Presidential contest; but it was so unskillfully managed as to leave a bad impression. Crawford's name was duly
presented to the caucus, where he received 54 votes to Monroe's 65.
Governor Tompkins did not figure in the race, but received 85 votes
for the Vice Presidency, where his political career ended.

Monroe's margin of victory was in no small degree attributable
to the efforts of Calhoun, a point which the unsuccessful con-
testant was not likely to overlook. The caucus marked also the
first rift between Calhoun and Clay.[5]

2

The next business on the House calendar was a new tariff schedule proposed by the Treasury, with duties designed less for revenue

than for the protection of manufactures. The question had become acute following the diversion of large amounts of capital
from commerce to industry during the period of restriction and
war; but the pressures which finally brought the "American System" into being were as old as the Government itself. Even before
Washington had taken office in 1789, petitions began to reach Congress from manufacturing groups, praying for a tariff on some
finished product or for a remission of duty on some raw material,
or both. By 1816 there was not an industry in America that had
not asked again and again for protection, and the demands increased in vehemence and urgency as financial strength and potential profit grew.

The variety and extent of American manufacturing ventures
before 1816 is no less significant than the complete unanimity with
which their sponsors, one and all, appealed as a matter of course to
Government for legislation calculated to increase their wealth.
Before 1800 there were requests for protection from cordwainers
and candle makers, manufacturers of hats, of paint, of glass, of
leather, of soap and of chocolate, scattered over the New England
and Middle States; from coal operators in Virginia; and from
groups of manufacturers, mechanics and merchants from Baltimore to Boston. Jefferson had no sooner taken office than demands
for protection increased in volume and variety, including makers
of paper, of gunpowder, of brushes and umbrellas, in half a dozen
states. There were ironmongers and gunsmiths in New Jersey
and Pennsylvania, sugar refiners in Baltimore, ropemakers and
sailmakers in Kentucky, printers, type founders, cork cutters,
manufacturers of copper utensils; and there were petitions by the
dozen in behalf of industry in general from local associations of
merchants, manufacturers and tradesmen.[6]

The era of commercial restriction which began with the embargo
in 1808 hastened the investment of American capital in industrial
enterprises, and the wartime double duties contributed to the same
end. The close of the war found few indeed to question the
wisdom of fostering manufactures. Even that stanch agrarian
Thomas Jefferson was at last convinced that industrial independence from the Old World was a military necessity, and the younger
men were ready to concede that manufactures would contribute

both to material comfort and to national wealth. The whole social and cultural fabric of America was in ferment and men could perhaps be forgiven if in their enthusiasm they failed to perceive or to heed that evil as well as good lay hidden in the forces they unloosed. They rode the crest of a vast social movement, which they could no more have stemmed or turned from its course than Canute could still the waves. Wherever one looked lay freedom and opportunity in this great promised land which the gods of democracy had set aside for their chosen people.

3

Alexander Hamilton's celebrated *Report on Manufactures* in 1791 had demonstrated that industry could not be established without Government subsidy and had satisfactorily shown that, although the initial price of manufactured goods would be somewhat higher because of the subsidy, internal competition and lower transportation costs would inevitably bring about an ultimate price lower than would ever be possible on imported goods. The logic was persuasive, and by 1816 those Americans who believed in manufactures at all believed as a matter of course in protection, which meant a tariff on imported goods sufficiently high to counterbalance the lower production costs of older and better established foreign competitors. The only real arguments were whether manufacturing was desirable at all and, if so, how high a tariff was needed to produce the proper differential in favor of the home product.

Dallas' report might have been written by Hamilton himself. It divided manufactures into three classes. The first class included those already firmly established and able to supply all or nearly all domestic needs. On these a prohibitive duty was recommended. To the second class belonged those manufactures recently or partially established, capable in time of supplying the entire domestic demand but not yet able to do so. Adjusting the tariff on this class of goods was most difficult, because the rate ought to be high enough to afford adequate protection but low enough to permit entry of imports in quantity sufficient to meet that part of the demand which could not yet be domestically supplied. The third class comprised products for which dependence on foreign sources of supply was necessary, and these were to be admitted free of duty.

The Secretary's report was accompanied by a complete tariff schedule and was buttressed by an elaborate analysis, simultaneously presented by the Committee on Commerce and Manufactures of the House, of the status and needs of domestic cotton manufacturing.[7]

A bill following the general lines proposed by Dallas was drafted in the Committee on Ways and Means and was defended by Lowndes when it reached the floor on March 20, 1816. The Treasury schedule called for a duty of thirty-three and one-third percent on cotton products and twenty-eight percent on woolens, but the committee had reduced both to twenty-five percent. A Representative from Massachusetts, where the forty-million-dollar cotton textile industry centered, immediately moved to restore the higher schedule. Lowndes answered, and the fight was on. It was quickly obvious that on this question political friends of long standing were at odds if the economic interests of their respective states happened to differ. Even colleagues from the same state, if her interests were divided, might be on opposite sides.

As the debate moved on through the rest of the month, many voices were heard, with each speaker advocating increased duties on some particular article produced in the section from which he came. Smith of Maryland wanted higher duties on sheet iron, rod iron and bolts. Robertson of Louisiana wanted full protection for sugar. Ingham joined Southard of New Jersey in asking higher duties on gunpowder. Hopkinson of Pennsylvania sought to increase the tariff on lead bars, and Clay wanted an increase for lead ground in oil. Irving of New York thought clocks and clock parts should be protected but strenuously opposed the motion of Pleasants of Virginia to raise the tariff on coal. John Reed of Yarmouth wanted olive oil taxed to encourage the use of whale oil as a substitute. In short, the Government was about to pay a subsidy to selected private interests, and it was up to each member of Congress to get as much as he could for the particular interests he represented, at the same time being careful to make no move that would injure his constituents by raising the price of articles they consumed.

Webster, who still represented seafaring Portsmouth, New Hampshire, brought the discussion back to cotton on March 25 with a motion to make the duty thirty percent for two years, twenty-five percent for two years, and thereafter twenty percent. Clay objected that a longer period of subsidy might be required before domestic production costs could be brought down to the level of those abroad, but Webster replied that he understood the manufacturers would be satisfied with thirty percent for only one year. This was vigorously denied by a Massachusetts member. Calhoun supported Webster's position, affirming his belief that the "policy of the country required protection of our manufacturing establishments," but expressing a personal conviction that the permanent duty of twenty percent was ample.[8]

By April the debate had become acrimonious, and Wright of Maryland moved to exclude from a vote on cotton duties all members holding shares in the industry. A quick adjournment cut off debate; and the next day, after an unreported speech by his colleague, Samuel Smith, Wright withdrew the motion. Then the Committee of the Whole reported an amended bill, and one by one the amendments were adopted by the House. One of these granting special concessions to importers of India cottons was warmly supported by Webster as "an act of strict justice," but Telfair of Georgia sharply protested against "taxing the community one day to foster the interest of the manufacturers, and on the next to secure to the mercantile class a high profit. . . ."[9]

It was another by-product of the India trade that precipitated the last major clash of the tariff debate and brought from Calhoun the only speech he made on the question. The Treasury report had contained a clause valuing at twenty-five cents per square yard for tariff purposes all cotton goods whose original cost was less than that figure, and the provision had been retained as the bill came from the Committee on Ways and Means and as it made its tortuous way through the House. This was the much-reprobated minimum principle, which was expected to afford protection against the fantastically cheap labor of India, and which would at the same time permit hand-woven American cloths to compete with the product of England's power looms. The provision was deemed necessary because the bulk of the American cotton industry was confined to spinning, the weaving being carried on in the home. The minimum principle was devised, however, not by the less efficient members of the industry but by Francis Cabot Lowell, whose Boston Manufacturing Company was equipped with power looms and could weave as cheaply as the British.[10]

On April 4, shortly before the tariff was due to be called up for a final vote, Randolph moved to strike out the minimum clause, and in a long but unreported speech attacked the whole protective system. To his preternaturally acute mind, a tariff that went beyond mere revenue needs could be regarded only as "an immense tax on one portion of the community to put money into the pockets of another."

4

Up to this point Calhoun had taken little part in the debate, and he had not given any special study to the details of the bill. The bank had engrossed his attention since the beginning of the session, and until its final passage he felt that to be his major responsibility. Randolph's remarks were made on the very day that the bank bill came back from the Senate with minor amendments, and he was writing at his desk when Ingham approached him. The Pennsylvania Representative thought the House was becoming restive and confused, and he wanted Calhoun, whose influence was greater than that of any other member, to try to stem the apparent break and rally the party forces.[11]

The speech he delivered was unpremeditated and not in reply to anyone in particular. It was rather an effort to bring the House back from the far-away places to which Randolph invariably led it, and so he went back to the minimum principle which had been the Virginian's point of departure. To deny that principle, he argued, was in effect to deny that manufactures should be protected at all, whereas the debate had theretofore been concerned only with the extent of protection needed. He referred briefly to the agrarian nature of his own constituency in support of his disinterestedness and then proceeded to justify encouragement of manufactures on the ground he had already assumed in connection with the direct tax: national defense.

He repeated his conviction that the country must ultimately face another war with England, and that to wage successful war a balanced economy would be essential. "Neither agriculture, manufactures, nor commerce, taken separately, is the cause of wealth; it flows from the three combined, and cannot exist without each. . . . Without commerce, industry would have no stimulus; without manufactures, it would be without the means of production; and without agriculture neither of the others can subsist. When separated entirely and permanently, they perish," and war "produces, to a great extent, that effect . . ."

Until American naval power should be great enough to challenge that of Britain, he saw no alternative to the development of a balanced economy independent of any foreign source of supplies, for the first act of war would inevitably bring a blockade which would throw the country entirely on its own resources. It was in these terms, and these alone, that he justified the protective tariff. "Had we the means of attaining an immediate naval ascendency . . . the policy recommended by this bill would be very questionable. . . ." It was because the United States could not hope to keep the sea lanes open against the British fleet that self-sufficiency remained the only road to national salvation.

The remainder of the speech was a refutation of the various arguments advanced against the tariff. He denied that the country was unprepared for the introduction of manufacturing. Resources were abundant and great accumulations of capital, derived from a commerce that grew out of European conditions no longer in effect, were available for investment. "What channel can it take but that of manufactures?" The textile industry was already established and offered proof enough in itself that the United States was ready for such undertakings. He did not believe the bill would seriously injure the shipping interests, for though foreign trade might fall off, the coasting trade, already a third of the total, must increase with an expanding domestic market. Neither would he concede that manufacturing was detrimental to the moral or physical power of a people, preferring to attribute the widespread pauperism of England to bad laws and excessive taxes.

The only objection he would admit was that "capital employed in manufacturing produced a greater dependence on the part of the employed, than in commerce, navigation, or agriculture." This objection, however, he did not think decisive. He thought it outweighed by the creation of a wholly American interest comparable to agriculture and not tied to foreign nations, like commerce and navigation. He thought the industrial system would increase mutual dependence of the parts of the Union and thus promote internal improvements as a consequence of expanding intercourse.[12]

The speech revealed the same kind of thinking that had preoccupied him all through the session. He was not satisfied that the war was over; and reviewing the twenty-year history of the Napoleonic conflict he was perhaps right in believing the cessation of hostilities was an armistice rather than a peace. So far as England was concerned, the object of the war had not been accomplished; and she had shown herself singularly stubborn in returning to complete unfinished business. Nor is that all. Underlying his every speech and act in the Fourteenth Congress is the fully developed concept of the national state, diverse in its own interests but presenting a united front to the world.

Randolph made another effort a few days later to defeat the bill, this time by postponement, but though he spoke for three hours, he made no converts. Calhoun rose briefly to deny an insinuation that the tariff was in some mysterious way connected with the bank; a few more charges and countercharges were made, and the bill was carried, 88 to 54.

The day after the House had passed the tariff of 1816, although quite unknown to Calhoun and his colleagues, Lord Brougham was explaining to Parliament, in connection with recent heavy exports to America, that it was "well worth while to incur a loss upon the first exportation, in order, by the glut, to stifle in the cradle those rising manufactures in the United States, which war had forced into existence, contrary to the natural course of things."[13]

Surely Calhoun was justified in doubting the durability of peace with England; and Randolph, too, was right in forecasting that military peace would bring economic war.

5

It was easy enough for Calhoun to deny in 1833 that the tariff of 1816 had been a protective measure, for the duties imposed by it, save only those on coarse cottons under the minimum principle, were far short of enough to enable American industry to compete with that of Britain. They were in fact substantial reductions from the double duties they replaced, and in all but trifling instances were considerably lowered by Congress from those proposed by the Treasury. The fact remains, however, that the tariff was passed in response to a request from the President for legislation to protect American manufactures. Representatives of industry hovered about Washington, conferring with Congressmen and appearing before committees; and members were careful to consult the wishes of those manufacturers who were among their constituents. Throughout the debate the bill was defended or attacked as a protective measure, and few if any doubted that it was such at the time. Calhoun had himself accepted protection fully two years earlier than this[14] and had not wavered in his belief nor in his reasons for it. He simply thought, in 1816, that duties of twenty percent were protective, whereas he had learned by 1833 how naïve had been his younger self.

More significant than the question of whether the tariff was or was not protective is the commentary it offers on the nature of representative government. The members of Congress who passed judgment on the bill did so in terms of the effect they believed it would have upon the fortunes of those whom they conceived themselves to represent. By common consent, four major interests were recognized: agriculture, commerce, navigation and manufacturing; and it was these interests and their subdivisions that found actual representation on the floor. It was localism and not nationalism that swayed the voting on both sides, in all but a handful of cases.

Neither state nor party divisions played any significant part. The Republicans gave the bill 63 votes to 31 against it, while the Federalists cast 25 votes in its favor and 23 opposed. The dominantly manufacturing states of Kentucky, New Jersey, Pennsylvania and Rhode Island were overwhelmingly in favor of the tariff, as was New York, already anticipating a rich traffic with the West by way of the Erie Canal. Ohio and Vermont favored protection, but North Carolina, New Hampshire and the lone Representative from Louisiana opposed. Virginia and Maryland were two to one against it. Massachusetts, where merchant and manufacturer alike claimed allegiance, showed great uncertainty. Seven of her

Representatives voted in favor of it and four against it, but eight did not vote at all. Other states, including South Carolina, were very nearly evenly divided. Pennsylvania and New York between them cast enough votes for the tariff to more than make up the margin by which the measure passed.[15]

The cotton manufacturers, for whose benefit the policy was admittedly proposed, actually lost by it—all, that is, except Lowell. For in its final form the duties on cottons other than those subject to the minimum were lower than those under which the industry was already unable to compete. They were limited in time; and the only gain, the minimum, did not go into full operation for a year. Yet a beginning had been made and a precedent set which could not fail to bear further fruit.

The country generally supported the sweeping program of economic reconstruction of which the tariff and the bank were the major instruments; and because of their agency in bringing it about, Calhoun and Lowndes were seriously considered for the Treasury when Dallas expressed his desire to withdraw.[16] It was William H. Crawford, however, who finally accepted the post, though he did not assume its duties until late in October, after Clay and Lowndes had both refused the War portfolio and Madison had finally decided to leave that department in the hands of George Graham, its chief clerk.

6

Calhoun returned home after Congress adjourned to find that the immense popularity he had hitherto enjoyed in his district had suddenly vanished. The same constituents who had unanimously re-elected him two years before were now bent upon removing him forthwith from public life, should he have the ill grace not to remove himself. The popular reaction to the "salary grab bill" was as thoroughgoing as it was irrational, and in the end it effectively broke up the galaxy of political talents that made up the Fourteenth Congress.

Even those who had once been his warmest supporters Calhoun now found in violent opposition to him, including among their number Colonel Joseph Calhoun, the cousin who had withdrawn in his favor on the occasion of his first election to Congress, and General William Butler, his recent colleague. So incensed was the latter that he announced himself a candidate to reclaim the seat he had yielded in the fall of 1812. Two other candidates also appeared, now that it seemed an easy matter to defeat the tall, shaggy-headed young Scot who had always before been unbeatable.

The friends who remained loyal advised him "to appeal to the kind feelings of his constituents, and apologize for his course," but this he refused to do. When he voted for the compensation bill, he believed it to be right, and he still held to that opinion. He arranged instead for two mass meetings, one at each of the two principal towns in his district, Abbeville and Edgefield. At these two meetings he explained with perfect candor why he had voted as he did.[17]

When the election was held on October 14 and 15, Calhoun was re-elected by a large majority; but few indeed of his colleagues fared as well. Some resigned when they saw the disapproval of their constituents; others declined to stand for re-election; and still others were defeated at the polls. Altogether, half of the members of the Senate and two-thirds of the House were replaced. The turnover was even more complete than that which brought the young War Hawks to power in 1811; yet the cause was trivial, where that had been the gravest crisis yet faced by the American nation. In their anger the sovereign people did not distinguish clearly between friend and foe, for half of those who voted "nay" on the hated measure were turned out, together with four-fifths of those who voted "aye." Many among the most popular members of the House, such as Henry Clay and Richard M. Johnson, were re-elected only by abasing themselves to their constituents and publicly acknowledging their error; while others equally popular in their own districts, such as Randolph and Pickering, were defeated.

The America which thus turned out of office almost en masse the most able group of Representatives ever assembled under the Constitution was no longer the aristocratic republic of Washington nor the idealistic democracy of Jefferson, but something derived in part from both, by reaction and extension. This was the proletarian America that would soon choose for its leader the self-taught

Hero of New Orleans, and would come in time to value political shrewdness above intelligence.

In sharp contrast to the rough going experienced by candidates for Congressional seats, Monroe's path to the Presidency was smooth and easy. In Ohio and in all the states south of Maryland he was unopposed, and only in Massachusetts, Connecticut and Delaware was he defeated. Monroe received 183 electoral votes, while only 34 Federalist electors, uninstructed for any particular candidate, were chosen. When they cast their votes, by courtesy, for Rufus King, they performed the last political act of their party, which did not again contest a national election.

CHAPTER X

BINDING THE REPUBLIC TOGETHER

1

IT WAS an unusually grave and thoughtful group of Congressmen who gathered in Washington for the opening of the short session on December 2, 1816. They listened half-heartedly as the clerk read the President's message, and hurried through the routine business of organizing the House. Then Colonel Richard M. Johnson, who had introduced the Compensation Act in the previous session, secured the floor to describe in vivid terms the reaction of Kentucky to the law he had fathered: how a creditor had been refused payment of a just debt because he favored the law; how promotion in the public service had been made conditional upon denunciation of the Congress that passed it; and how opposition to it had been made a *sine qua non* for all candidates for office. He still believed the objectionable statute to be proper and just, but he regarded himself as bound by the expressed will of his constituents.

A committee was duly named, with Johnson as its chairman, to consider repeal of the obnoxious act; and after a lapse of two weeks, a dignified and unrepentant report, drafted by Webster, was presented.[1] It conceded nothing except the undoubted right of the people to instruct their Representatives in Congress and the duty of the latter to obey. The law was defended and its principle reaffirmed; but in deference to the popular wish, it recommended that compensation on the old per diem basis be restored, leaving the amount to be determined by the House. To avoid suspicion of indecorous haste, consideration of the accompanying bill was postponed until the middle of January.

The subdued spirit in which the debate began contrasted oddly with the air of offhand routine that had ushered the first bill into the world. The discussion was featured by an exchange between Henry Clay, who had been re-elected by humbling himself to his constituents, and John Randolph, who knew not the meaning of humility and had been in consequence returned to private life. Clay based his case upon the binding nature of instructions from the people, and Randolph answered in terms deliberately calculated to be irritating. As the days wore on, humility was less in evidence and temper more so; but the majority of the members recalled too clearly the unpleasant summer at home to be diverted from their purpose by mere personalities. When the bill was reported to the House from the Committee of the Whole, it called for the old compensation of six dollars a day and six dollars for each twenty miles traveled to and from the sessions.

The question was put by the Speaker on the seventeenth, and Calhoun rose in opposition. He was perhaps the only man in the House who could do so with a clear conscience; but the remarks he made were too characteristic to have been influenced in any way by the personal justification he had wrung from hostile voters of Abbeville and Edgefield.

As he so often did, he brushed aside lesser considerations to strike at the root of the whole matter: the nature of a lawmaker's responsibility to his constituents and to his conscience. The speech was in many respects his most brilliant performance up to that time. It exhibited at once the great range and extent of his knowledge, his logical clarity of expression, and his power to compress his ideas into brief and pointed compass. His mind has been likened to a lens for its power to bring to a focus diverging rays of light,[2] and in none of his early speeches is the simile better justified than in this on the second compensation bill.

Among all the branches of the general Government, he saw the House of Representatives as of necessity the ultimate guardian of liberty, because only its members were directly in contact with the source of political power.[3] It was therefore by the House that corruption and extravagance in the other departments were to be sought out and brought to the attention of the people. Yet "the President holds offices in his gift, which, as regards honor or profit, are more desirable than a seat in this House. . . ."

Calhoun stopped abruptly with a gesture of apology.

"I find myself committing an unpardonable error, in presenting arguments to this body. The ear of this House, on this subject, is closed to truth and reason. What has produced this magic spell?

ANDREW JACKSON
by Thomas Sully

WILLIAM HARRIS CRAWFORD
by John Wesley Jarvis

Instructions! Well, then, has it come to this? Have the people of this country snatched the power of deliberation from this body? Have they resolved the Government into its original elements, and resumed their primitive power of legislation? Are we, then, a body of individual agents, and not a deliberative one, without the power, but possessing the form of legislation?"

No, the truth of the matter was that a law had proved unpopular, and so Congress felt bound to repeal it though reason and conscience told them the law was right and the people were wrong. He refused to recognize any doctrine of implied instruction. The only instructions he would follow would be those that came from a formal assemblage met for that purpose, those that were contained in the Constitution, and those offered by his own conscience. The next Congress would reflect the constitutional expression of public sentiment on the question before them. Let them take whatever action they felt bound to take. The existing Congress had already made its position clear and could not without loss of character reverse itself. The state of public feeling on any given question was, surely, a fact to be reckoned with; but for his own part he preferred "that erectness of mind which, in all cases, is disposed to embrace what is, in itself, just and wise."

After this digression, Calhoun returned to the argument he had interrupted. He thought the deep wellsprings of human action were a love of gain and a love of distinction. It was unreasonable to suppose that men would long remain in the only national office to which the people might send them when there were in the power of the President to bestow "a multitude of offices more profitable, and many both more profitable and honorable, in public estimation," than a seat in the House. Thus would patronage and the honors and emoluments of office tend to draw the more able and ambitious from the direct service of the people, and weaken in proportion the power of Congress to guard their liberty.

"Make a seat in Congress what it ought to be—the first post in the community next to the Presidency, and men of the greatest distinction in every part of the country will seek it. The post, then, of honor and distinction being in the people, and not in the President, will be open to all parties, in proportion to their ascendency in the Union. That entire monopoly of honor and public profit by the majority will not be experienced, which must be felt, when the honors of the country are principally in the hands of the Chief Magistrate. Those who best understand our nature, can the most fully appreciate the consequences. Although it may not abate the heat of party, it will greatly affect its feelings towards our happy political institutions."[4]

Before Congress rose that day, the report of the Committee of the Whole had been rejected, and the House faced anew the blanks where the report had inserted "six dollars."

The next afternoon a new member from Virginia, twenty-six-year-old John Tyler, made his maiden speech; and it was Calhoun with whom he chose to break his initial lance. He proclaimed the true Jeffersonian doctrine when he avowed himself the agent of those who had elected him and insisted that it was not for him to question the correctness of their will, but only to know it and obey.

Tyler finished at four o'clock, and Grosvenor rose with an apology. He thought the law had been triumphantly vindicated already by several speakers, among whom he had "heard with peculiar satisfaction the able, manly, and constitutional speech of the honorable gentleman from South Carolina." He paused, recalling his near duel with Calhoun of three years before, and then resumed impulsively: "Mr. Speaker, I will not be restrained, no barriers shall exist which I will not leap over for the purpose of offering to that gentleman my thanks for the judicious, independent, and national course, which he has pursued in this House for the last two years, and particularly on the subject now before us. Let the honorable gentleman continue with the same manly independence, aloof from party views, and local prejudices, to pursue the great interests of his country—and fulfil the high destiny for which it is manifest he was born. The buzz of popular applause may not cheer him on his way, but he will inevitably arrive at a high and happy elevation in the view of his country and the world. . . ."[5]

It was almost a week later, after efforts to postpone and recommit had failed, that an acceptable bill was passed. It left the law untouched as it affected the existing Congress, but repealed it as of March 4, 1817, without reviving the old law which it replaced. Thus the incoming Congress would be forced to answer the question for itself; but even this compromise solution did not satisfy Calhoun, who voted nay.

2

Having acknowledged its fealty to the popular will, the House resumed the course it had pursued for five years, as unconcernedly as though a majority of its members had not just been rejected at the polls. It was a course that led to national self-sufficiency and to world power, not disdaining to use foreign commerce as an instrument of policy, nor fearing to tax freely and spend with a lavish hand. It has probably never been possible in any age or country to separate the economic from the political functions of government. Whether it be aristocratic or republican in its philosophy, whether it favors a landowning, a mercantile, a capitalist or a laboring class, every government must and does affect to greater or less degree the creation and distribution of wealth in the society of which it is a part. Its influence may be felt in legislation or through failure to legislate; it may be felt in the administration of the law or in the adjudication of claims by the courts; but felt it will be, in positive or negative form. Whether the influence be for good or ill depends upon the values accepted by the times.

The Fourteenth Congress, coming as it did immediately after a war which strained the economy of the nation almost to the breaking point, was peculiarly aware of its economic responsibilities; and its activities were heavily weighted on the side of encouragement to private enterprise. The self-sufficient nationalism that was its goal required that, as the ties that bound America to Europe were consciously severed, the potentialities of the United States should be developed to make good the loss. The chief instruments of this development were the tariff and internal improvements; and of these what came to be known as the American System was compounded. Commercial restrictions were replaced by a policy of subsidization, and it would be surprising indeed if no group had magnified its needs or sought to reach too deeply into the public purse; for it is in the nature of man to believe that the body politic is sound when he is prosperous.

Internal improvements meant simply transportation: roads, canals and deepened river channels by means of which the raw materials of the West and South could reach the growing factories of the East, and over which in return might flow a steady stream of manufactured goods. The need for adequate transportation was as old as the Union, and upon its fulfilment the future extent and even the existence of the Union in large measure depended. On this score there was little argument. The question of jurisdiction was a different matter.

The old Federalist doctrine had recognized a national interest in transportation, and even Jefferson had been forced to accept the extension of national power represented by the Cumberland Road. The Republican attitude thereafter, however, remained one of doubt, and Gallatin's masterly plan of 1808 was shelved.[6] Petitions for Federal aid in the construction of roads and canals nevertheless continued to pour in upon Congress and to be referred to committees, where they languished year after year. Some of the projects covered by these petitions, like the Chesapeake and Delaware Canal and the Erie Canal, were powerfully backed, both politically and economically; and as the same requests were made of successive Congresses, they became harder and harder to refuse.

So great was the pressure by 1815 that Madison, although he shared Jefferson's constitutional misgivings, called the attention of Congress to the "great importance of establishing throughout our country the roads and canals which can be best executed, under the national authority." His own doubts he resolved by the "happy reflection, that any defect of Constitutional authority, which may be encountered, can be supplied in a mode which the Constitution itself has providently pointed out."[7]

Calhoun had no such doubts, and he seized the first opportunity that presented itself to carry into effect what he understood to be the President's wish. Neither the opportunity nor the means occurred during the first session; but on December 16, 1816, he moved for the appointment of a committee "to inquire into the expediency of setting apart the bonus and the net annual proceeds of the National Bank, as a permanent fund for internal improvement." The resolution was agreed to without opposition and a committee appointed, including Calhoun, Grosvenor and Ingham among its members. A week later a bill was introduced, was twice read, and was committed until more urgent matters could be cleared out of the way.[8]

Not until February 4, 1817, just a month before the session ended, was the bill called up in Committee of the Whole, and the long delay led Calhoun to fear for its ultimate success. He proceeded nevertheless to explain in crisp, pungent phrases why internal improvements were necessary and on what grounds he thought they could be constitutionally carried out by the general Government.

To the argument that all branches of economic enterprise—agriculture, manufactures and commerce—would profit immeasurably by a better transportation system there could be no answer, and so he chose that for a starting point, moving from there to his favorite argument: military necessity. If the only advantage of improved transportation were pecuniary, it might be possible to argue that it should be supplied by private enterprise; but the recent war had shown that the nation's greatest weakness was the magnitude of its territory in comparison to its population. Only a system of roads and canals would make possible concentration of strength at any threatened point in time of war; and the same highways, as arteries of commerce, would serve when war was over to redistribute the financial resources which must inevitably be concentrated near the point of conflict.

Roads and canals, in short, were to be the sinews of that American prosperity for which the bank and the protective system were to provide the substance. More than that, they were to be the ties that would bind into a single nation states and sections far apart in space and farther still in interests and ideals.

"We are great, and rapidly—I was about to say fearfully—growing. This is our pride and our danger; our weakness and our strength. Little does he deserve to be intrusted with the liberties of this people, who does not raise his mind to these truths. We are under the most imperious obligation to counteract every tendency to disunion. The strongest of all cements is, undoubtedly, the wisdom, justice, and above all, the moderation of this House; yet the great subject on which we are now deliberating, in this respect deserves the most serious consideration. Whatever impedes the intercourse of the extremes with this, the centre of the republic, weakens the union. The more enlarged the sphere of commercial circulation —the more extended that of social intercourse—the more strongly are we bound together—the more inseparable are our destinies. Those who understand the human heart best know how powerfully distance tends to break the sympathies of our nature. Nothing— not even dissimilarity of language—tends more to estrange man from man. Let us, then, bind the republic together with a perfect system of roads and canals. Let us conquer space."

The railroad and the telegraph were still to come, yet one could ask no clearer statement of the unifying power of transportation. That it could also be a disintegrating force Calhoun was not yet fully aware, though he knew that "in a country so extensive, and so various in its interests, what is necessary for the common good may apparently be opposed to the interest of particular sections."

In this speech, at least, he was close to grasping the essential condition in terms of which alone industrialism could succeed. For the secret of the industrial revolution is the exploitation of the machine; and the machine can be put to profitable use only for large-scale, or mass, production, which requires in turn a vastly extended market easily and cheaply reached. Britain had become the first modern industrial state because her market was the world, and her road thither followed ocean lanes which cost her nothing. The United States, when she deliberately closed her doors to British goods, assumed responsibility for supplying the growing needs of her own people; and that responsibility inevitably carried with it an obligation to provide means by which those people could be reached.

Having made out an all but untouchable case for internal improvements, Calhoun moved on to the constitutional argument. He understood there were two objections: first, that Congress had no power to cut a road or canal through any state without that state's consent; and second, that money could be appropriated only to give effect to the powers enumerated in the Constitution. The first objection he dismissed out of hand. The bill under discussion did not authorize any particular road or canal, so that the question of consent did not arise. When it should come up, he had no doubt the states would grant it. As for the second objection, he professed himself "no advocate for refined arguments on the constitution. The instrument was not intended as a thesis for the logician to exercise his ingenuity on. It ought to be construed with plain, good sense. . . ." A system of roads and canals could not fail to aid the common defense or promote the general welfare, and on that power he rested his case.

The rest of his speech was devoted to outlining the transportation system he hoped might grow in part out of the fund that would be created by his bill: a fund which he estimated at about $650,000 a year. Like Gallatin, he would connect the Atlantic cities with the West, and the Hudson with the Great Lakes, while the principal artery of the whole system would link Maine and Louisiana, at the extremities of the Union.[9] It was the high-water mark of Calhoun's career in the House of Representatives. As always, he was master of his subject and of his situation, impressing all who heard him with his breadth of view, his sincerity and his knowledge. He spoke with a rapidity that sometimes left his hearers breathless, and his arguments were often abstract and overdrawn; but his simplicity of style and intensity of manner carried conviction even to those who could not follow his points.[10]

The opposition to the bill was expressed almost exclusively in constitutional terms, but before a vote was taken the major objections were met by amendments. One of these, moved by Pickering, derived the power to build roads and canals from the commerce clause; another required the consent of the states to any improvements undertaken within their limits; and a third made the expenditure within each state proportional to its representation in the lower House of Congress, except as the states themselves might determine otherwise. The usefulness of the bill was not seriously impaired, however, and Calhoun could be justly proud of the result when it passed after a week of debate by the slender margin of 86 to 84. He had fought the opposition every step of the way, almost alone, and he had won his point. On the opening day of the debate he was powerfully supported by Henry Clay; but thereafter the weight of eloquence was all on the other side, where Smith of Maryland and John Randolph led the constitutional attack.

An examination of the voting is of considerable interest. New England Representatives were almost solidly opposed; the South was nearly evenly divided, but went against the measure 25 to 23; the West favored internal improvements, but by a very much smaller margin than might have been expected; and the three Middle States of Delaware, Maryland and New Jersey were more than two to one against the bill. Just as in the case of the tariff, it was the overwhelming support of New York and Pennsylvania that carried the day.[11] The former hoped for financial aid from the Federal Government in the building of the Erie Canal. The latter, herself divided by the mountain rampart of the Alleghenies, sought internal unity and cheaper trade routes for her two great industrial cities: for Philadelphia a gateway to the South through the Chesapeake and Delaware Canal, and for Pittsburgh the growing trade of the West by making navigable the falls of the Ohio.

It becomes clear from these votes that the American System, although it has come to be indelibly associated in our minds with Henry Clay, and although Calhoun was certainly among its original sponsors, was the offspring of neither West nor South. It sprang from the commercial needs and industrial aspirations of New York and Pennsylvania, and its aftermath was the growth within those states of an economic power so vast that a century was required for its assimilation by the slow processes of democracy.

3

The last important business of the session resulted from an attempt to repeal the internal taxes, which had produced six million dollars in revenue for 1815. The move originated in the West and was aimed primarily at the whisky tax. It was brought up, however, by Lewis Williams of North Carolina, who defended it on the ground that the receipts from customs would be greater than the Treasury estimate, and that expenditures, particularly those for the military establishment, ought to be reduced. The matter was finally dropped, but not until Calhoun had antagonized Williams, with serious consequences for his own future career.

He stored up trouble for himself in another quarter at about the same time when he severely criticized the War Department in the course of a debate on the military appropriation bill. His plea for more careful accounting and for detailed annual reports from the Executive Departments was reasonable enough; but his strictures upon the loose handling of War Department funds implied a censure of Crawford which was not forgotten.

These personal clashes in no way weakened his power in the House, however; and he effectually blocked a final effort to defeat the internal improvement bill when it came from the Senate with minor amendments on March 1.

His close but well-merited victory was still uppermost in his mind when he called next day at the Octagon House where the Madisons were still living. Both good politics and good manners required ambitious legislators to pay their respects and offer their congratulations to a retiring President, and such was the object of Calhoun's visit. He had already taken his leave and was on his way to the door, when Madison called him back. The President had before him the internal improvement bill and explained to its tri-umphant author that on constitutional grounds he could not ap-prove it. Calhoun was taken completely by surprise. He had supposed the bill merely carried out the President's wishes, and he would certainly never have subjected himself to the implied censure of a veto had he known in time that the administration disapproved. His arguments, however, were of no avail; and he could only swallow his mortification and wait for the veto message.[12]

It came on Monday, March 3, President Madison's last day in office. Neither the commerce clause nor the general welfare clause of the Constitution could legitimately be made to justify any power not among those enumerated in section 8 of article I. Thus Cal-houn saw his own liberal construction argument completely de-stroyed, on the authority of the one man above all others who might be said to understand the Constitution best. It was a heavy blow, which was only partially lightened by the gallant gesture of Henry Clay in his support. The Speaker asserted his right to vote, and his name is recorded first among those who would sustain the bill. The final count, however, was only 60 to 56, far short of the necessary two-thirds.

To New York and the West the veto was only a temporary setback, but to the South it was a disaster. The Erie Canal was built in ten years' time without Federal assistance, and the West

continued to send its produce to New Orleans over the broad highway of the Mississippi; but there was no hope of internal improvements in the South without assistance from Washington.

4

As the Fourteenth Congress neared its final adjournment, the
solid fruits of its labor began to ripen. The second Bank of the
United States opened its doors in January 1817; and on February
20 specie payments were resumed. The premium of two and a half
percent paid for specie at New York as late as the very morning
of the twentieth immediately vanished, and although the nation
had a funded debt of $130,000,000, the financial stringency of the
war period was over.[13] The balance of trade had already turned
in favor of the United States, and gold was flowing into the country from England in a steady stream.

Even the physical memories of the war were rapidly passing as
a new and more graceful Capitol rose under the skillful hands of
Benjamin Latrobe and the damaged White House was rebuilt.
Everywhere signs of prosperity were apparent, and even New England was beginning to emerge from her immediate postwar depression. Although it had been overwhelmingly repudiated by the
voters, the policies of the Congress were vindicated, and the Era
of Good Feeling was at hand.

Monroe sought to encourage this new-found harmony in the
selection of his advisers, intending that each section of the country
should be represented. His first choice was that of John Quincy
Adams for Secretary of State. It was motivated by a sincere wish
to conciliate New England and to allay if possible her jealousy of
Virginia, but there was another reason also. The first post in the
Cabinet had become in the popular mind an almost infallible step-
ping stone to the Presidency. So it had proved for Jefferson,
Madison and Monroe himself; and he was well aware that if he
named to that office a known aspirant for the succession, it would
be taken as a promise. So Crawford and Clay, both of whom
wanted the place, were passed over, lest the choice of either arouse
the hostility of the other.[14] Crawford was asked instead to remain
at the Treasury, and Clay was offered the War Department, which

he refused. Benjamin Crowninshield of Massachusetts remained as Secretary of the Navy, and Madison's Attorney General, Richard Rush, was not replaced by William Wirt of Virginia until November.

Clay's refusal of the War Department left that position open and left the Cabinet without any representative of the West. Andrew Jackson strongly urged the appointment of William Drayton, a South Carolina Federalist, arguing cogently against partisanship in the distribution of offices.[15] Jackson himself was thought of, but Monroe was probably relieved to learn that the arbitrary and strong-willed general did not want the place.[16] Inauguration day came and passed, and still the Cabinet was not complete.

On the solicitation of R. M. Johnson and others,[17] Governor Isaac Shelby of Kentucky was finally appointed to the vacant department, but he was not to be coaxed from the retirement he had earned. It was next tendered to Lowndes, who had declined a similar offer from Madison and refused Monroe's with equal promptness. General Harrison was understood to want the place but was not favorably regarded; and David R. Williams of South Carolina may also have been considered.[18] As a last resort the War Department was offered to Calhoun by letter of October 10, 1817, and was accepted three weeks later.

Calhoun's biographers have generally argued that he was in fact Monroe's first choice to be Secretary of War, that he had already been sounded out, and that the preceding offers were made only for political purposes, with the knowledge that they would be refused.[19] There is little justification for such a view. Had Calhoun been approached on the question before Monroe's earlier offers were made, he would have been more circumspect in his criticism of the military appropriation in the closing weeks of the Congress, and he would have had no reason for hesitation when his turn came. Monroe's later explanation was that after Shelby's refusal he felt free to draw from any part of the country and decided at once on Lowndes or Calhoun.[20] Yet it was known as early as July that Lowndes would not take it,[21] while Calhoun was not approached until October. It is true that Monroe was traveling during this interval; but if his mind had been made up, he would hardly have waited so long in view of the known disorder in the department, already without a head since October 1816. It may perhaps be significant that in the course of a journey through the Northern states during the summer of 1817 the President inspected various Army posts, where he found Calhoun well regarded by the officers.

Despite his political obligations, Monroe seemed reluctant rather than eager to have the young Carolinian in his Cabinet, and it is conceivable that he did not relish the prospect of including in his official family a man of Calhoun's positive views and wide popularity. Indeed, it may be argued that Monroe's original intention was to surround himself with respected but inactive advisers, who would not be politically troublesome and would offer no bar to the party and sectional harmony that seemed developing. Adams and even Crawford might be fitted into such a design. The President had enjoyed little personal contact with Adams and might well have been deceived as to the strength of his character and the extent of his ambition. Clay was deliberately sidetracked, and at least one observer thought Crawford was being retained through no wish of Monroe's, but because he desired to stay and was too powerful to be ejected.[22]

Calhoun, for his part, hesitated to accept the proffered seat, and delayed so long that his answer had not even been written at the time Monroe was daily expecting to receive it in Washington.[23] He had, in the space of six short years, achieved a position of power and influence in the House of Representatives and had already been re-elected, in spite of the storm over the compensation bill. His skill as a speaker had increased greatly, and he had displayed rare ability also as a legislative manager and on committee assignments. For administrative work, on the other hand, his qualities were quite unknown, even to himself. He stood, in fact, to lose rather than to gain by the shift; and his closest political friends, particularly Lowndes, advised against his taking the post. Had he not himself argued that the country lost in the long run by the transfer of her most able men through the lure of place, from the legislature to the executive offices?

His ultimate decision to accept the War Department was perhaps the measure of his ambition and of his self-discipline; for no man had yet held the Presidency, nor was likely to for many years to come, who had not proved his worth in some executive capacity.

Before he could aspire with any hope of success to the highest office in the land, he knew that he must show ability to administer as well as to make laws. The mere theorist, the metaphysician, the disembodied intellect can never hope to win the confidence of "practical" men until he has shown them that he too has his feet upon the earth; and even then, although Calhoun was not yet aware of it, they will secretly distrust a character they cannot understand. That his chief abilities lay in the field of thought rather than that of action was very generally believed in 1817; and it was primarily to disprove this estimate of himself that Calhoun agreed to become Secretary of War.[24]

CHAPTER XI

THE WAR DEPARTMENT

1

THE first week of November 1817 was a hectic one at Bath. Calhoun had delayed overlong his acceptance of a Cabinet post, but now that the decision was made he was eager to get to work. So while he rambled over his fields, giving directions and bidding good-by to the slaves, Floride prepared the children for the trip to Washington. There were two of them now: Andrew, a sturdy youngster of six who still showed traces of a recent fever, and Anna Maria, not quite nine months old. Again and again, no doubt, they were interrupted by calls from friends and neighbors, come to congratulate the young Secretary and to wish him well; for the house was always open and Calhoun was still the favorite of all the district, as he had been when a lad.

When at last all was in readiness, the management of the plantation was turned over to William Calhoun, who was already as familiar with the business as was John himself; and supervision of the low-country property was placed in the hands of John Ewing, who was also no stranger to his brother-in-law's affairs. Traveling in their own carriage, the Calhouns followed the announcement of their coming by less than ten days. Hector, the squat Negro coachman, belied his sleepy appearance by covering thirty miles a day, and they reached the Capital on December 2, after a fast and uneventful trip.[1] Until other arrangements could be made, they established themselves in the home of William Lowndes.

Calhoun called upon the President shortly after his arrival to discuss the duties of his new office, and on December 8 he took the oath as Secretary of War.

2

More by accident than by design, Monroe's Cabinet was one of the strongest any President has been able to boast, though it made no pretense of conforming to his originally expressed wish for sectional balance. Three of the five department heads were from the South and the remaining two from Massachusetts, nor was the balance notably improved when Crowninshield gave way late in 1818 to Smith Thompson of New York. The only Western man even close to the administration councils was the Postmaster General, Return J. Meigs of Ohio, and he was not at that time considered a member of the Cabinet.

In physical appearance, mental qualities, and character, Monroe's advisers were as ill-assorted as they were able. First came John Quincy Adams, short, fat and bald, with blinking watery eyes that looked out suspiciously upon a hostile world. Scholar, puritan and seasoned diplomat, Adams was a tireless worker who spared neither himself nor those around him. His dress was careless, almost slovenly; his speech was blunt and caustic, but so fluent that he often overwhelmed opponents in argument by sheer verbosity; and his egotism was boundless. Into his diary he poured, day after day, his judgments upon men and measures as long as his cramped fingers could grip the pen, until his hand grew permanently lame. Even those few he called his friends, could they have read the candid and too often venomous record he was preparing for posterity, would have turned from him in anger and disgust. Yet Adams' ability was great and his patriotism beyond question. He had been a member of the Republican Party only since 1808, and many thought him a Federalist still; but he had, or appeared to have, all the qualifications Monroe could require in a Secretary of State.

It was soon evident that Adams and his followers saw in the appointment precisely what Monroe least wished them to see. The President was seemingly unaware that a quiet Adams boom had been started as early as 1815 and was still slowly gathering momentum among tight-lipped New Englanders, but the publication of McKean's letters to old John Adams in *Niles' Register* in July 1817 left no doubt of the matter. Crawford had long been aware of it, and predicted shortly after Monroe's inauguration that the Presidential succession would be fiercely contested between North and West, with Adams and Clay the protagonists.[2] He did not mean by that, however, to exclude himself.

William H. Crawford was as unlike John Quincy Adams as the limits of nature allowed. A man of huge stature and enormous strength, his clear and logical mind was not overstuffed with educational niceties. Born in Virginia of Scotch-Irish parents, he had moved first to Edgefield District, South Carolina, and then across the Savannah into Georgia while still a child. There he grew to manhood, received his schooling from Moses Waddel, read law in the office of Charles Tait and was admitted to the bar. He first entered politics to expose the Yazoo land frauds, rising steadily thereafter until he was in 1817 perhaps the most powerful single force in public life. Like Adams, he wanted to be President. He had stepped aside for Monroe, but he did not mean to step aside again.

Calhoun said of him a few years later that no man had ever risen so high upon so little basis,[3] but the remark was made during the bitterness of a Presidential campaign after he had suffered severely and unnecessarily at Crawford's hands. The Georgian's abilities were very real and his political acumen was great. He was simply of a mold as yet unfamiliar to Calhoun and with which he never learned successfully to cope: the lifelong professional politician whose method was the manipulation of votes and whose tool was patronage. Where Calhoun appealed to the intellect and rested his case on logical proof, Crawford appealed to self-interest and depended for results upon organization. To say so much is not in any sense to cast doubt upon his integrity or his morals. Gracious and affable, with keen mind, commanding presence and sure intuition, his interest was in men rather than in ideas, for he knew that men were the bricks of which the political structure was built.

Third-ranking member of the Cabinet was Calhoun himself, his tall, angular figure, sparkling eyes and overabundant hair making him the very antithesis of Adams, with whom he soon became intimate. At thirty-five he was just reaching maturity but lacked nothing in self-confidence. Sure of himself and of his reputation in the field of legislation, he was all too eager to challenge the more tangible difficulties of administration; and there were those who placed him, for intellect and ability, first among the President's official family.[4] Though as ambitious as his senior colleagues, Calhoun was not yet a Presidential candidate. He was therefore not a rival and might prove a powerful ally of either Adams or Crawford.

The fourth member of the administration was the Attorney General, William Wirt of Virginia, whose pioneer biography of Patrick Henry had only just come from the press and was the subject of animated controversy among Revolutionary veterans from Maine to Georgia. Wirt, too, was a big man, standing above six feet in height, and built in face and figure in the massive proportions inherited from Teutonic parents. His blue eyes and thick lips smiled easily. He was genial, cheerful, gay and lovable; and being utterly without political ambition, he was in no man's way, free to observe and judge in silence the race for power that was soon to reveal itself among his colleagues. Wirt had only two passions: the law and literature. In both callings he had achieved assured success, with which he professed to be, and was, content.

Benjamin Crowninshield, Monroe's first Secretary of the Navy, remained from Madison's Cabinet, but did not remain long enough to be considered a full-fledged member of the group. His successor, Smith Thompson, had not ceased to be an active figure in New York politics when he became Chief Justice of the State Supreme Court, a position which he owed in large measure to the rising power of Martin Van Buren. He was so direct in his methods as occasionally to appear naïve, but he possessed great political shrewdness and an ambition as boundless as that of Adams and Crawford.

Though his Cabinet was made up of men who would mold the future, James Monroe represented primarily the past. A stocky, loose-jointed six-footer, the President dwelt in the world of the Revolutionary fathers, of whom he was himself the last. He clung to smallclothes and cocked hat, and on occasions of ceremony often wore the buff and blue uniform of a Continental officer. He gave unsparingly of his energy and time, seeming always conscious of the honor and dignity of his office, which he, like Washington, conceived to be above all partisanship. Slow but tenacious once his judgment was given, he was under constant pressure from Jefferson and his Virginia friends on one side and from the members of his council on the other, a lonely and sometimes bewildered figure, irresolute between two worlds.

The administration began with every evidence of harmony. Adams and Crawford, to be sure, were measuring each other for the Presidential contest still seven years away, and Crawford had not forgiven Calhoun for his support of Monroe in the caucus fight of 1816; but these were considerations apart from the business of the Cabinet, and for a time they so remained, creeping now and again into the pages of Adams' diary but otherwise ignored. The President took no important step without consulting his advisers and meetings accordingly were frequent. Messages were submitted for criticism, and in like manner the reports and dispatches of the department heads were freely discussed before they were finally approved. The method was one ideally suited to produce Presidential candidates, since each member of the council was thus literally forced to familiarize himself with the business of the entire Executive establishment. It was a method, too, that gave Calhoun's particular qualities of mind their widest scope; and young though he was, he was almost from the start the intellectual leader of the group, suggesting doubts and difficulties in true Socratic style, and illuminating every question upon which he touched.

3

When the new Congress met in December, Henry Clay was returned to the Speakership by an overwhelming vote, but it was soon apparent that the places of those who were missing had not been filled by their successors.[5] This was the Congress that had been chosen on a wave of resentment against what the public chose to regard as a "salary grab," and its members were keenly aware of the power and temper of the electorate. Though such veterans as Lowndes and Ingham were back, the majority were new and owed their places to the diligence and skill with which they had appealed to popular prejudice. It was inevitable that popularity would be their guiding principle and that the Legislature would shortly be divided into factions based on local interests and individual ambitions.

Shrewd political observer that he was, Crawford had anticipated the situation and was prepared to turn it to his own account. He saw that unless a firm stand was taken against it, money would be voted by such a Congress with a lavish hand while the sources of revenue would be diminished, but he did not see fit to stiffen the President's spine. Monroe's first message to Congress recommended an extension of the pension list and, at the suggestion of the Treasury, repeal of the internal taxes.[6]

On other questions, however, the President's stand was less popular, as he was promptly to learn. He professed complete neutrality in the struggle between Spain and her erstwhile South American colonies; he was noncommittal about protection for manufactures; and in the matter of internal improvements he expressed his belief that only a constitutional amendment would make them possible, which was the same as saying that he would veto any bill Congress might pass. By the time Calhoun had officially assumed his new duties, the House was already in revolt. The nationalism of the war period had begun to crumble under the assault of selfish interests and personal ambitions.

Monroe tried, though ineptly, to pacify those whom his appointments had offended, but in his eagerness to stay the disintegration of his party, he failed to appreciate the fact that political succession goes of necessity either to the heir apparent of the faction in power or to the leader of a rival group. When he failed to name Clay to the State Department, Monroe automatically forced the Kentuckian into opposition; and though he did not yet know it, Crawford also was at work building an anti-administration party for the same reason. Adams was content for the moment with the prestige his position gave him, though he, too, had spread his net; and the Jackson managers were quietly awaiting developments. Surfeited with power, the Republican organization could no longer be held together by hands as weak as Monroe's.

First to attack the administration openly was Clay, who demanded that the independence of Spanish America be recognized and answered Monroe's stand on internal improvements with a resolution declaring the authority of Congress paramount to that of the Executive in matters of constitutional interpretation.[7] The press on both sides took up the quarrel and the President began to lose ground, while more and more power passed into the hands of men who sought not the honors but the profits of office: men who professed to speak for the common people but who were at the same time cogs in one or another political machine.[8] From the very beginning a disposition was manifest to harass the Executive with calls for information and trivial inquiries, which Monroe found "oppressive" and "querulous."[9]

To make matters worse, Mrs. Monroe proved a cold and formal hostess after the sparkling Dolly Madison, and all too many wives of the potentially well-disposed chose to take offense where none was meant. The levees were continued on alternate weeks, but they were stiff and dull; and the First Lady declined either to pay or to return calls. The President's Friday dinners brought members of Congress together in tactless array that did violence to political associations and personal friendships; and there were sneers and whispers about unrepublican luxury and reserve.[10]

During Monroe's eight years as President the major issues of the next half century emerged, and on the basis of these issues, symbolized by men, new party lines were drawn. Crawford stood for the old Virginia State Rights school, but to the principles of Jefferson he had engrafted the methods of Burr. He was a machine politician. Clay had identified himself with internal improvements, the tariff and the natural desire of the West for a President. Adams had shrewdly gauged the sentiment of the North, had watched the old Northwest Territory fill with men of New England stock, and took his stand on his Northern birth and all it represented. DeWitt Clinton's power waxed and waned with the fortunes of the Erie Canal; and still another wing of the old Jeffersonian party built its hopes on Andrew Jackson.

In Congress men soon came to be known as the friends of this or that potential candidate, but the President seemed to have no friends at all. Too much a nationalist for the Virginia school he represented, too much a Virginian for the North, Monroe was doomed to ineffectiveness from the start; and as the rivalry between Crawford and Adams grew more intense, he relied more and more heavily upon the advice and assistance of Calhoun.

4

Only a man as young, as confident and as inexperienced as Calhoun was in the fall of 1817 would have risked his reputation at the head of the War Department at such a time. There were unsettled accounts amounting to more than $45,000,000, a staggering sum for those days.[11] There was no military policy worth mentioning; the Indian policy was under fire from settlers and traders alike; the Army itself was without unity of command or any generally accepted regulations or disciplinary procedure.

The strength of the Army had been fixed following the war at a little over twelve thousand men, including officers and engineers, but only eight thousand were actually in service. These were distributed between the Northern and Southern Divisions in a ratio of approximately four to three, the Northern sector being commanded by Major General Jacob Brown and the Southern by Andrew Jackson. The two generals were co-ordinate and each was supreme in his own territory, their only common allegiance being to the President, represented by the Secretary o˙ War. The coastal fortifications envisioned by Monroe and championed by Calhoun on the floor of the House had not been built, nor even adequately planned; the system of supply was in the hands of private contractors not responsible to commanders of the Army units they were supposed to serve; and appropriations had been shifted from one item to another without clear authorization until the accounts of the department were in a state of chaos.

Even this list does not exhaust the difficulties of the position in which the new Secretary found himself, for in addition to its purely military concerns the War Department was also responsible for relations with the Indian tribes. These were governed by treaties, under which a precarious peace was maintained by gifts and annuities, with military outposts ready to use coercion if conciliation failed. Tribes goaded by the British to take the warpath must be pacified, and hostile chiefs must be convinced that friendship and trade promised more than war. Responsibility for carrying out Indian policy was divided among three separate agencies, often sharing the same field headquarters but not under a unified command: the Indian agents, who were directly subject to the War Department or to the Territorial Governors; the actual military posts on the frontier; and the Government-operated trading houses or factories.

The factory system, as it was called, was a source of no little annoyance to the private traders who could operate only under license and who were forced by the competition to deal somewhat more honestly with the savages than their own instincts prompted. But the profits were too great to be curtailed for long by mere humanitarianism, and in the end the entire field was to be secured for private enterprise. The struggle brought Calhoun, who defended the factory system, into eventual conflict with John Jacob Astor and with the powerful Congressional spokesmen for Astor's American Fur Company.

5

It was none of these things, however, but a question of precedence that required Calhoun's immediate attention. The origin of the trouble went back to 1816 when Jackson, fearing an Indian rising along the Mississippi, sent Major Stephen Long of the Topographical Engineers to survey the country in which the fighting might be expected to occur. About the time Long's survey was completed, but before any report to Jackson had been made, he received orders from the War Department sending him to New York, where he prepared and published the results of his Mississippi reconnaissance.

General Jackson, either because he had not been notified or because the notification had miscarried, knew nothing about the change in Long's whereabouts until he received a copy of the published report early in January 1817. Thereupon, in typical Jackson fashion, he fell into a towering rage and wrote a blunt and uncourteous letter to the Acting Secretary. Graham answered coldly that War Department orders superseded those of Division Commanders and dropped the matter, but Jackson did not yield easily. He waited only until March 4, when a new President came into office. Then he wrote a long letter to his new Commander in Chief, beginning with detailed advice on how the administration should be conducted and ending with a repetition of his protest against War Department interference with the affairs of the Southern Division of the Army.[12]

Monroe delayed answering, and on April 22 Jackson took matters into his own too-capable hands, directing that no orders were to be obeyed that were not transmitted through the appropriate military command.[13] In the course of the summer Monroe made up his mind to treat the affair as a misunderstanding, and wrote the General to that effect in August. "The principle is clear, that every order from the dept. of war, to whomever directed, must be obeyed. I cannot think that you are of a different opinion. . . ."[14] Jackson's order stood, none the less; and when General Ripley at New Orleans refused in consequence to obey instructions from Washington because they had not come through his own commander, Jackson took full responsibility upon himself and wrote again to Monroe to justify the refusal.[15]

This letter was answered December 29 by Calhoun, who confirmed the major principle for which Jackson contended, that War Department orders should be transmitted through the appropriate military channels, but maintained the right of the department to make exceptions in cases of absolute necessity. With this the General was satisfied, and his opinion of the young Secretary of War was greatly influenced by it.[16]

Simultaneously came orders to proceed against the Seminoles, and Jackson forgot all lesser matters in the joy of action, while Calhoun set himself to unravel the tangled skein of War Department affairs.

6

Working regularly fourteen or fifteen hours a day, studying records and seeking advice from military officers and civilian experts alike, the ambitious Carolinian soon acquired a practical mastery of his new duties and an appreciation of the problems with which he had to deal.[17] First among them came the reorganization of the Army. A General Staff had been created in 1816, but its personnel was drawn indiscriminately from the line and from civil life. Officers were without adequate technical knowledge or clearly defined duties, while important staff functions were omitted entirely. Alterations in the law were suggested to Calhoun by his Chief Clerk, Major Christopher Van Deventer, former Deputy Quartermaster General for the Southern Division. These were discussed with Senator John Williams of Tennessee, chairman of the Military Affairs Committee, as well as with General Brown and other high-ranking officers, until a complete plan was evolved. A bill embodying the scheme was then drafted by the Secretary, who continued to alter it in various particulars as it made its way through Congress until it became law on April 14.[18]

Under the new arrangement a Surgeon General and a Judge Advocate General were added to the staff, which already included an Adjutant and Inspector General, a Quartermaster General, and a Commissary General. Each of these officers was placed in charge of a department, located in Washington. This marked the first appearance under the Federal Government of the bureau or functional type of organization, which was presently extended to include, in addition to the departments of the Army, a Land Warrant Bureau and a Pension Bureau.

It was the Pension Bureau that carried the heaviest load and probably represented Calhoun's most important administrative achievement, for Congress did not disappoint those who had predicted liberal spending. New pensions were freely voted, and it was left to the War Department to distribute the funds after determining what veterans qualified under the law. Rules and procedures had to be devised, fraudulent claims detected, and political pressures withstood, though personnel and office space were alike inadequate. Yet close to thirty thousand applications were handled during the first year, of which forty percent were turned down.[19]

7

The burden upon Calhoun, both physically and financially, was excessive. He had not been a month in the Capital with his family before he realized that living would be a great deal more expensive than he had calculated. Cabinet officers were expected to entertain liberally, and he shared all the instincts and traditions of the hospitable South in this respect. Floride was a gracious hostess and

he himself was a fascinating and willing talker. It is hardly surprising that the $4500 salary paid to the Secretary of War could
not be stretched to cover the necessary dinners, parties, "drawing
rooms," and "at homes," when we remember that the number of
guests was often so great that introductions were dispensed with,
while affairs were so frequent that Attorney General Wirt found
himself forty-three calls in arrears within two months.[20]

Least of all could Calhoun's official salary be made to cover the
purchase of a house and furniture, and to make matters worse the
cotton crop was only half of normal. Since he could not stay on
indefinitely with Lowndes, he proposed to return to South Carolina
as soon as possible to raise the necessary funds, meanwhile authorizing his brother-in-law to sell a portion of his low-country holdings
if a satisfactory offer could be had.[21]

The opportunity came near the end of May when Calhoun was
asked to accompany the President and the Secretary of the Navy on
a tour of the defenses in the Chesapeake Bay area. The trip had
long been planned, having been intended to follow immediately
after Monroe's northern tour of the previous summer, but circumstances had forced postponement until now. The party arrived at
Annapolis early on the evening of the twenty-eighth and inspected
the harbor from the water the next day, one of the objects of the
trip being to determine the site for a naval depot.[22]

From Annapolis they proceeded down the bay to Norfolk, where
they were met by Brigadier General Joseph G. Swift, Chief of the
Army Engineers, and a group of officers in charge of constructing
the fortifications. In the course of the next few days they visited
Old Point Comfort, where the ground was being cleared preparatory to construction of Fortress Monroe, and the Rip Rap Shoal a
mile away in Hampton Roads, upon which the Engineers proposed
to erect Fort Calhoun. The farthest point of the trip was Elizabeth
City, North Carolina, which was reached by way of the still uncompleted Dismal Swamp Canal. There Calhoun left the party for
his home, while Monroe returned to Washington. Crowninshield
went on to Massachusetts and shortly afterward tendered his resignation without again resuming the duties of the Navy Department.

Calhoun reached Raleigh on June 15, where he professed ignorance of the site to be chosen for the naval depot, but spoke in glow-

ing terms of his plans for a chain of impregnable fortifications that would completely block the mouth of the Chesapeake to any invading force. In another week he reached Bath, where he surveyed the parched and withered remnants of a crop destroyed by drought—his second cotton failure in as many years.[23]

During the nine days he spent at home, the papers all over the South were playing up stories of the execution of two British subjects in Florida by General Jackson; and before he set out for Washington again, Calhoun must have known also that the Spanish city of Pensacola had been taken, though on what authority he was yet to learn.

CHAPTER XII

JACKSON DISREGARDS ORDERS

1

TROUBLE with the Seminoles in lower Georgia broke out early in 1817 and continued for months as a series of sporadic raids and border clashes, negotiations, thefts, murders and more clashes with planters or with frontier patrols. After each foray the Indians retreated into Florida and safety beneath the Spanish flag. The forces in the vicinity were strengthened but without materially altering the situation. The Indians refused to make reparation of any sort, and the Spanish authorities were un-co-operative in the extreme. The Acting Secretary of War hoped only that no action would be necessary before he could get out of his uncomfortable office, and Monroe followed his usual policy of doing nothing.

By the time Calhoun assumed command, settlement of the trouble had become a matter of necessity, not only to preserve the property and the loyalty of half of Georgia, but to avoid disastrous loss of prestige both among the Indians and with foreign powers. Calhoun was quick to recognize the imperative nature of the case, and before he had been at the head of the War Department a full week new orders were dispatched to General Edmund Pendleton Gaines, in immediate command in Georgia:

"On receipt of this letter, should the Seminole Indians still refuse to make reparation for their outrages and depredations on the citizens of the United States, it is the wish of the President [Calhoun had convinced him that it was his wish] that you consider yourself at liberty to march across the Florida line, and to attack them within its limits, should it be found necessary, unless they should shelter themselves under a Spanish post. In the last event, you will immediately notify this Department."[1]

The day after Christmas, with news from the South still unfavorable, the situation was discussed at a meeting of the Cabinet, and it was agreed that Jackson himself should be directed to take

155

command. He succeeded to the orders previously given to Gaines.[2]

Jackson saw in the final sentence of the order only an unnecessary impediment to military efficiency, and wrote at once to Monroe—not to Calhoun—to point out what seemed to him the danger to an American force of waiting helplessly outside a Spanish fort for new orders from Washington. From a military point of view he was entirely correct, but he quite failed to appreciate the distinction between an Indian campaign and a war that might involve the Holy Alliance. He thought, in fact, that his orders to end the conflict could best be carried out by capturing all of East Florida and offered to do it without compromising the administration if Monroe would say the word. "Let it be signified to me through any channel, (say Mr. J. Rhea) that the possession of the Floridas would be desirable to the United States, and in sixty days it will be accomplished."[3] John Rhea was a member of Congress from Tennessee, a Revolutionary veteran advanced in years and wholly devoted to the service of Andrew Jackson.

It is worthy of note, perhaps, that in a letter written a few days later to Calhoun[4] there is no hint of this grandiose scheme to reduce Florida, or even of any objection to the order for the campaign. Though he insisted upon orders to his own subordinates clearing through him, Jackson himself preferred to deal with the Commander in Chief rather than with his own immediate superior.

Monroe was ill when Jackson's highly unethical proposition reached him and he probably temporized. At least he did not answer, through Rhea or anyone else; and when the whole affair was a subject of bitter controversy in 1831, he endorsed the letter with a flat denial, confirmed by Rhea. Jackson was equally emphatic at the later date that he had received and was following secret orders from the President. At his camp in the Seminole country he did indeed receive a cryptic and ambiguous note from Rhea, which referred in fact to the controversy over Major Long's orders; but a glance at its date should have shown him that it must certainly have been written before Monroe could have received his letter. It is true that he was not given to that kind of analysis, and it may be argued, as Jackson's apologists are prone to contend, that he took Rhea's note to be the approval he expected. There is no evidence in his correspondence through 1818, however, that he then regarded him-

self as following secret orders, and he even went to some lengths
to justify his course on the basis of his public ones.[5] It is curious
also that it was not until August of 1818, seven months after his
offer to take the Floridas in sixty days, that Jackson directed
Gaines to invest and capture St. Augustine, an operation that was
halted by the Secretary of War as soon as he heard of it.[6]

But this controversy belongs to a later period. So far as Calhoun knew at the time, Jackson pursued the Seminoles into Spanish
territory on War Department orders and would be bound by those
orders throughout the campaign.

2

Amelia Island off the south Georgia coast became meanwhile the
scene of a parallel and, as it proved, not unrelated series of events.
During the summer of 1817 the island was occupied by pirates
whose ships for convenience' sake flew Mexican and Venezuelan
flags. While the Spanish sovereignty protected their island base,
they preyed on sea-borne commerce just as the Seminoles robbed
on land, and found sanctuary in the territory of a friendly power.
The interests whose vessels and rich India cargoes fell prizes to the
pirates were more articulate than the south Georgia planters, however, and in mid-November joint orders went out to Army and
Navy commands to occupy Amelia Island. Calhoun had no hand
in the decision but fell heir to the result, as the American flag was
raised at Fernandina, capital city of the island, on December 23.

The able and watchful Luis de Onis, Minister from Spain, protested the seizure even before it happened; and Monroe, unwilling
to risk a major war, proposed to his Cabinet early in January that
the troops should be withdrawn. With this opinion Crawford,
Crowninshield and Wirt agreed, but Calhoun argued that the island
should be held pending negotiations with Spain. His efforts on this
occasion led John Quincy Adams to write in his diary that night:
"Calhoun thinks for himself, independently of all the rest, with
sound judgment, quick discrimination, and keen observation. He
supports his opinions, too, with powerful eloquence."[7]

More important than the impression he made on Adams was
the effect of Calhoun's arguments upon Monroe, who began once

more to waver. The discussion was renewed periodically without decision until near the end of January, when the British Government offered to mediate between the United States and Spain. On this point the members of the Cabinet agreed and the offer was unanimously rejected. The island was retained while Jackson pursued the Seminoles into Florida, and the diplomatic correspondence between Adams and De Onis became undiplomatically tart.

Among those who urged the President not to withdraw the troops from Amelia Island, lest it become once again a base for pirates to prey on returning Indiamen, was one of America's most powerful businessmen, John Jacob Astor.[8]

3

Dispatches came slowly from the trackless swamps of Florida; but the Seminole campaign, after Jackson took personal direction of it, moved with rapidity and decision. By the end of March the Indians, with their motley band of runaway slaves, had been driven across the neck of West Florida to the Spanish fort of St. Marks. As the American commander well knew, the post was only weakly garrisoned and would be unable to hold out should the Indians seek to take it. He suspected, too, that the Spaniards were actually supplying the marauders, if they had not in fact instigated the whole affair. Finding that the Indians had already demanded the surrender of St. Marks, he forestalled them by taking the fortress himself, and it became thereafter his supply base for the Florida war. Among the prisoners was a Scotch trader named Arbuthnot, and a few days later another white man was captured, this time a former lieutenant of British marines named Ambrister. Between the two of them, Jackson shortly convinced himself that he had secured the persons of those responsible for the uprising.[9]

News of the capture of St. Marks reached the War Department in May, but no serious question as to the morality of the act appears to have been raised. It was assumed by Calhoun, as it had been by Jackson, that without the prompt intervention of the latter the fort would have been surrendered to the Indians, which would have made it necessary to take the place by storm. It was agreed that for the present neither Amelia Island nor those portions of Florida under occupation should be evacuated, and Calhoun so assured the worried Governor of Alabama Territory, his old friend Dr. Bibb.[10]

Jackson, however, was by no means ready to call his task completed. The Indians had fled toward the Apalachicola River and presently were reported to be sheltering in Pensacola itself, under the nose if not the protection of the Spanish governor of the province. So to Pensacola Jackson proposed to follow, announcing in a letter to Calhoun written on May 5 his intention of taking that city as he had taken St. Marks, if the Indians were not surrendered. He stayed the pursuit only long enough to court-martial and execute the two British prisoners, on the basis of evidence supplied by a confederate. Papers found on Arbuthnot's trading schooner revealed a connection with the Amelia Island pirates and implicated the Government of Great Britain.

The official report of the court-martial did not reach the War Department before Calhoun left the city, and he had no inkling of the affair when he set off with Monroe and Crowninshield for Annapolis. He could have done nothing, even had he known the facts; for Jackson, having forgotten or chosen to disregard his orders, which specifically enjoined him to communicate with the War Department should the Indians seek refuge in a Spanish fort, had already accomplished the object of his campaign. He had entered Pensacola on May 21 and on the twenty-fifth had invested Fort Barancas, where the Spanish Governor and garrison surrendered to him after two days of alternate resistance and parleying.

4

Adams and Crawford were representing the administration in Washington when varying accounts of the trial and execution of Arbuthnot and Ambrister began to appear in the press. The British Envoy lost no time in protesting this summary execution of his fellow subjects, and expressed his hurt amazement at the charge of more than one editor that perfidy on the part of his Government lay at the bottom of the recent events in Florida. In the absence of any official report from Jackson, however, Adams could explain nothing and contented himself by indicating his suspicion that perfidy was entirely compatible with the character of British institutions.[11] By the time Monroe returned to Washington, news of the capture of Pensacola had all but driven the unfortunate victims of Jackson's court-martial from the papers, but still no official report had been received. The President nevertheless expressed his opinion that the business was contrary to Jackson's orders, and went so far as to assure the British Minister that this latest exploit of the Hero of New Orleans was unauthorized and unexpected.

When Jackson's report at last arrived early in July, Monroe had retired to his Loudoun County estate. There the report followed him, leaving Adams to face the protesting diplomats without any real knowledge as to what had happened, or why. He nevertheless refused flatly to disavow anything Jackson had done, and was still refusing when Calhoun returned from his hurried Southern visit on the eighth or ninth of the month.

A few days later the President also reached the Capital, and the Cabinet went hastily into session. The first dispatches from Jackson were incomplete, but Monroe was too perturbed to give more than a passing thought to any other business. He was not yet aware that Jackson considered himself to be following Presidential orders, in contradiction to those of the War Department.

The immediate reaction of the members of the administration, with the single exception of the Secretary of State, was that Jackson had deliberately disregarded his instructions and had committed an act of war against Spain, an act which must be promptly disavowed if the confidence of the country was to be retained. Adams, on the other hand, contended that everything Jackson had done was implicit in his orders, even though not expressed in so many words.

As the discussion proceeded through succeeding days, it resolved itself into an argument between Calhoun and Adams, with the President and the other members of the council siding with the Secretary of War. The capture of St. Marks was very probably a matter of necessity. The court-martial of the two Englishmen could not be reviewed until the complete record was received. But about the siege of Fort Barancas at the mouth of Pensacola Bay there seemed to be no doubt. Neither the occupation of the city nor the capture of the fort was necessary to Jackson's safety. The General had, furthermore, announced in advance his intention to take Pensacola, which made the action a premeditated violation of specific orders. This Adams did not deny, but insisted that the city could be restored to Spain without repudiating Jackson.

It was on this basis that a compromise acceptable to all was eventually worked out. The return of the captured forts was pledged, but the captures themselves were not disavowed, and the Spanish officials who had aided the Seminoles were charged in their turn with treaty violation.

5

More important, perhaps, than the Cabinet discussions were the reasons for the opinions held. Calhoun was the most directly concerned, for he was Jackson's immediate superior. To him it was only a question of whether orders had or had not been violated. The whole military establishment was necessarily based on unquestioning obedience. It was a principle Jackson would have been first to insist upon, and one the relaxation of which would immeasurably increase the very chaos Calhoun had been for six months striving to overcome in his department. He was, moreover, fundamentally a conservative, whose disposition was to proceed cautiously but always to proceed by rule. It was inevitable that to his orderly mind Jackson and at times Adams should appear erratic and inconsistent. Crawford and Monroe, each of whom had been Secretary of War and understood the disciplinary problem, accepted Calhoun's view, as did Wirt, who saw the matter perhaps more objectively than the others.

To Adams, however, the whole problem appeared in an altogether different light. He was certainly too intelligent to believe he could justify Jackson's actions on grounds of international law, unless he could make it appear that the General had been attacked or was in imminent and proved danger of attack by the Spanish garrisons, but for his purposes mere legality was unimportant. He knew from his long residence abroad and his familiarity with the diplomatic process that, right or wrong, what Jackson had done was precisely the sort of thing European courts would respect; and he would not weaken its effect by a disavowal or a reprimand. Calhoun was thinking of the consequences to his own department, should insubordination by the second ranking officer in the Army be allowed to pass. Adams was thinking of the treaty he was trying to negotiate with Spain for the cession of Florida; and he shrewdly guessed the task would be less difficult if Spain were made aware how easily the territory could be taken by force and that the administration saw no breach of faith in such a course.

There was another element in Adams' thinking, too, which he partially avowed on the second day of the Cabinet discussion. He contended, with much justice, that to disavow the attack on Pensacola would be to place all the blame upon Jackson, who would promptly resign his commission and attack the administration, carrying with him, Adams thought, a large share of popular sentiment. The rotund and aloof New Englander had perceived more quickly than his colleagues the political potency of Jackson's popularity, and he already planned (though this he kept to himself) to turn it to his own account. Jackson he knew to be well disposed toward him personally, because the General had written as much to Monroe shortly after the President's inauguration.[12] Why then should not Jackson be the Vice Presidential candidate in 1824 on a ticket headed by Adams? He was so taken with the idea that he did not give it up, as we shall see, until the very eve of the election itself.

6

For the often repeated charge that Calhoun concealed his opinion of Jackson's conduct during the Florida campaign to avoid antagonizing the General there seems scant justification. After the Cabinet decision, in which all concurred, to restore the Spanish forts but to avoid reprimanding Jackson, the Secretary of War still freely expressed his original opinion that the capture of Pensacola was without authorization.[13] Crawford, moreover, let it be known among his political friends what the Cabinet division had been, and it is certain Jackson was aware of Calhoun's opinion in the matter by 1819 at the latest.[14]

The young Carolinian was not yet a candidate for the Presidency, nor did he have any idea that he would be in the near future; and even if he had anticipated the circumstances that brought him into the contest in 1821, he could not possibly have foreseen the part that Jackson would play in the campaign. As things stood, his own obvious interest lay in letting the headstrong Commander of the Southern Division understand that orders from the War Department were to be obeyed, even by Andrew Jackson; and he did in fact tell the General precisely that in so many words in connection with another infraction the following summer.[15]

Even while he acceded to the Cabinet compromise on the handling of the Florida crisis, Calhoun doubted its wisdom and feared an unfavorable public reaction.[16] He did not gauge public opinion well, perhaps because he expected the public to be intelligent. It was a weakness of Southern statesmen that they did not have any means of knowing what the common man—the proletariat, if you will—thought about anything, because in the South there were no common men. Labor was performed by slaves, who could have no opinions that mattered; and because the mere presence of the Negro gave to all Southerners, planter and poor white alike, a common bond based on a common danger, the thinking of the South came more and more to follow a single pattern. When Calhoun estimated the probable reaction to a measure or a policy, it was in middle-class terms that he thought. He knew, of course, that small farmers dotted the free states and that the cities of the North and East sheltered a growing body of factory workers, but he had no personal knowledge of these types or of how they thought. He expected them to be rational and was often amazed when they were not.

CHAPTER XIII

MILITARY POLICY

1

WHILE public attention was centered on the more spectacular Florida campaign, the far-ranging complex of War Department activities was slowly being molded into a broad military program. Plans were made for the fortification of strategic points along the Great Lakes, the Atlantic coast and the Gulf of Mexico, which were to be connected with each other and with important industrial and food-producing centers by a network of roads and canals. The military frontier was pushed hundreds of miles farther to the West, and with it the fringe of settlements. Relations with the Indians were recast in the light of a policy of humanitarianism and fair dealing. A new efficiency was brought into the organization and administration of the Army, while scientific research and exploration were added to its functions.

It was such a program as only a man with youth, daring and superb self-confidence could have contemplated, and such as no man could have carried through without arousing the hostility of powerful political and economic interests.

Under General Swift and General Simon Bernard, a former Napoleonic officer, preliminary surveys for the coastal forts were already in progress when Calhoun took over the War Department. By the fall of 1818 the reconnaissance was completed and detailed plans were laid before Congress with the budget for 1819. The actual construction was to be done under contract with private builders, but the work would be supervised by the Corps of Engineers which was accountable for all money spent and was responsible for the quality of the product. The staff reorganization brought General Swift to Washington, where he was placed in direct charge of the whole fortifications program, with authority to let contracts and proceed with the building as rapidly as funds became available.[1]

To supplement these harbor defenses Calhoun proposed a complete trunk system of land and water communication which would permit rapid concentration of troops and supplies at any threatened point.[2] A canal joining Lake Michigan with the Illinois River would provide a primary artery for north and south traffic by way of the Mississippi, the mouth of which was to be protected by permanent fortifications. The existing Atlantic coast highway was to be extended and improved to link Maine and Louisiana by a "durable and well-finished road," while rivers and bays were to be connected to form an inland waterway between Boston and Savannah. By shortening distances, such an interior channel would give to an American fleet greater mobility than would be possessed by any attacking force, while fixed batteries guarding outlets to the sea would give it additional protection.

For communication between the Atlantic cities and the West the strategic routes lay between Albany and the Lakes, where the Erie Canal was under construction; between the Chesapeake Bay area and the Ohio River, already served in part by the Cumberland Road; and between the Charleston-Augusta region and the Tennessee. All three of these were being developed by the states and communities most concerned, but in view of their military importance Calhoun urged a proportionate Federal expenditure.

For the Northern frontier, he thought the needed communication lines, in addition to such of those already mentioned as might serve a Northern army, were waterways to link Albany with Lake George and Lake Ontario, both already begun by New York State, and a similar water connection between Pittsburgh and Lake Erie. Farther to the West he would complete the road then under construction from Detroit to Ohio, and in the South a military highway was to connect New Orleans with the Tennessee River, while inland water channels would link the Louisiana metropolis with Mobile Bay.

2

No less important was the frontier policy, for the tide of settlement was pushing west into the hunting grounds of Indian tribes who knew the white man only as an unscrupulous trader or as a bloody and relentless foe. The westward expansion could not under any pretence be halted, nor could the fur trade be stopped. The only possible course was to extend protection to settlers and traders alike, and if these were to live in peace, to extend it also to the Indians.

So Calhoun planned to push the line of military posts far into the Indian country, whither they would be followed by the Government trading houses and by settlers. The coastal fortifications could be manned by comparatively small garrisons, which with co-operation from the Navy would be adequate to protect the maritime states until reinforcements could be raised, thus relieving the bulk of the Army for duty in the Northwest. On the southern part of the frontier the Indians were either inconsiderable in numbers or were too completely surrounded by the whites to be dangerous, but in the North the advancing settlements were coming into contact with powerful and warlike tribes, who were also subject to British influence. The new line of posts was to form a wedge, driven between the British and the Indians, and was to be garrisoned with ample force to overawe the tribes.

At the beginning of 1818 the Northern military frontier was marked by Fort Howard at Green Bay, Fort Crawford at Prairie du Chien and Fort Armstrong at Rock Island; yet the settlements had already moved across the Mississippi, and the fur traders ranged clear to the Rockies and beyond. The plan Calhoun advanced was to push new posts eighteen hundred miles up the Missouri River to the Yellowstone; to establish a post at the mouth of the St. Peter's (now the Minnesota) River, which was as far as boats could ascend the Mississippi; and to occupy a site near the falls of the St. Mary's, between Lake Huron and Lake Superior, which would command the channel between the two lakes. Intermediate posts on the Missouri were to be at Council Bluffs and at the Mandan Village, near the present city of ·Bismarck, North Dakota, where Lewis and Clark had wintered in 1804-1805. The strategic importance of the latter was that it approached the nearest of any point on the Missouri to the Hudson's Bay Company's outpost on the Red River of the North.[3]

Once plans for the Missouri expedition were completed, Calhoun set himself with characteristic enthusiasm and self-assurance to turn them into action. Additional troops were ordered to St. Louis; supply and transportation contracts were let; and General Thomas A. Smith, within whose military department the territory lay, was instructed to send a detachment up the river as promptly as possible. It was March when the orders went out from Washington, already too late for any hope of reaching the Yellowstone that year, but the young Secretary thought that the expedition might winter at the Mandan Village, where crops could be put in to help with the next year's supplies. General Smith was less optimistic. He, too, hoped the Mandan Village might be reached, but a British agent had already been captured in the act of inciting the Indians to resistance, and there was evidence that private traders were similarly engaged. He knew too, as Calhoun did not, the immense inertia of the whole military organization. The moving of troops and supplies to distant points was slow and costly, and too often beyond the control of the officers responsible.[4]

The contracts for supplies and transportation were eagerly solicited by James Johnson of Kentucky, who had been furnishing subsistence to troops at Western posts since the war. In the darkest days of the conflict he had even used his own credit when that of the Government failed. He was a brother of Calhoun's old friend Colonel Richard M. Johnson, now chairman of the House Committee on Military Affairs; and it was with the latter, acting as attorney for his brother, that the arrangements were finally made, after a great deal of hesitation on the part of the Quartermaster General.

The customary advances were given by the War Department when the contracts were signed; but almost immediately a second advance was requested, on the ground that the failure of a debtor had temporarily deprived the Johnsons of "large funds." In May General Smith directed the contractor to deposit sixteen months' rations for three hundred men at Belle Fontaine, near the mouth of the Missouri, and again Johnson sought an advance, this time actually drawing upon the War Department for twelve thousand dollars in order to pay a debt to the United States Bank and thereby preserve his own credit. Despite the irregularity of the procedure, Calhoun had no choice but to honor the draft. Johnson's security was ample, his record as an Army contractor excellent, and his brother politically powerful.[5]

The Johnson brothers next wrote of their desire to use steamboats for transporting the supplies and soldiers. It was true that no steamboat had yet breasted the treacherous Missouri current, but they were confident it could be done and would add speed and prestige to the expedition. Calhoun referred the question to General Smith, who agreed; but it soon developed that the steamboats were not yet built. It was late in August before Colonel Talbot Chambers got away from Belle Fontaine with six keelboats and a tender to establish winter quarters, not at the Mandan Village or even at Council Bluffs, but at Cow Island only four hundred miles up the river.

No more could be done before spring, but to avoid any misunderstanding Monroe outlined the entire project in his annual message when Congress met in November.

3

The purpose of the new Western posts was first of all to extend and protect the Indian trade, but there was fundamental disagreement as to how and by whom that trade was to be carried on. In 1816 John Jacob Astor had prevailed upon Congress to restrict issuance of trading licenses to Americans, thereby effectually eliminating the British Hudson's Bay Company.[6] The Government factories, however, remained competitors, and a determined fight to abolish them was soon under way.

Astor himself fired the opening gun with a letter to Calhoun in March 1818 asking the intentions of the department with respect to private traders. He professed to have lost heavily by Government activities in the past, "so much so that it would indeed be ruinous to continue to trade under such circumstances."[7] The letter was delivered by Ramsay Crooks, trusted agent of the American Fur Company and Astor's successor as its president, who elaborated upon the complaints of the private traders against the factory system.

At the same time delegates from the fur-producing territories raised the issue in Congress, and Calhoun was soon forced to take a stand. The law under which the factories existed was due to expire March 1, 1819, and he must decide what legislation he wanted in its stead. The case for the private traders as Astor and Crooks presented it was impressive, but Thomas L. McKenney, the Superintendent of Indian Trade,[8] argued just as ably for the Government-sponsored factors. Letters to the Territorial Governors revealed that Lewis Cass of Michigan and Ninian Edwards of Illinois sided with the traders; but William Clark of Missouri, who since the famous expedition with Meriwether Lewis had stood pre-eminent among Americans for his knowledge of the Indians, favored keeping the trade in Government hands.

Even as he studied the problem, Calhoun infused new life into the Indian system, sending commissioners with presents of merchandise, ornaments and tools to treat with the different tribes, and offering annuities and new lands to those who would move beyond the Mississippi. But the question of profit and loss in pelts seemed less important to him than the future relations of the white and red races, and when he reported to Congress late in 1818 it was to call for a new Indian policy to meet new conditions.[9]

Those of the tribes that had been long in contact with civilization had largely lost their ancient skills, and with them their independence. They were no longer free nations and should not be so considered. The only hope for their survival lay in an ultimate merging with the culture of the dominant race, and toward this end the policy of the Government should be directed.

All relations with the Indians Calhoun proposed to center in a Superintendent of Indian Affairs responsible to the Secretary of War. Indian trade would be carried on under license from this officer. A fee of one hundred to five hundred dollars was to be charged for a license, and the penalty for trading without one was to be stiff enough to discourage violations. Alcohol was to be strictly forbidden. The trading houses were likewise to be licensed, and books showing prices of goods bought and sold were to be kept at each establishment, subject to inspection by an authorized agent. The proposed license was costly for those days, but it was meant to be, for the whole arrangement as Calhoun envisioned it was intended to restrict the Indian trade to firms of large capital. He believed that only those who would suffer heavy losses by suspension of their trading activities could be effectively controlled, and he regarded the money invested in the trade as a bond to insure honest dealing.

The Government-operated trading houses were to serve as instruments of civilization, becoming the centers around which the tribes would tend to settle and take to agricultural pursuits as the furs grew less abundant. To hasten the process Calhoun proposed to establish the Indians on lands of their own, with the distinct understanding that no more demands for territory would be made upon them. He would imbue in them the idea of individual property in the soil, using the annuities paid them under existing treaties to educate their children; and when they were ready, he would admit them to citizenship with full political rights.

To deal with the wild, semimigratory tribes of the Rockies and the Pacific slope Calhoun recommended a plan earlier suggested by Governor Clark. He called for a thirty-year transition period, during which the Indians would be protected from the intrigues of foreign powers and the cupidity of rival traders by a Government monopoly of the fur trade. Then, when they had learned the ways of civilization, they too were to be given land, education and eventual citizenship.

It was a far-seeing policy which might have saved a vast deal of bloodshed had it been adopted; but it was more than fifty years before any part of it became law, and well over a century before it was finally put into practice. The real meat of the report left Congress untouched; but the factory system, at least, was allowed to stand, and in 1819 Calhoun succeeded in tightening the license regulations. His attitude brought upon him the determined hostility of the fur-trading interests. Indian policy became a political issue, and the opposition soon came to embrace the whole frontier and military policy.

4

Engrossed as he was in the administration of his office, Calhoun did not sense for some time this undercurrent of opposition. He had accepted the War portfolio in the first place to prove to himself and to the country that he was a practical executive as well as a skilled dialectician. As he became more sure of himself and more familiar with the workings and functions of his department, order and system replaced chaos and he was satisfied. With equal tact and skill he dealt with questions of policy that looked far into the future and with the small and immediate details of everyday administration.

Even the knotty and difficult problems of discipline and military precedence the young Secretary faced squarely, though he did not always find an adequate solution. An old dispute over rank between Generals Bernard and Swift led to the latter's resignation late in 1818, but Calhoun managed to keep Swift's good will and even in part his services, finding him a place as Surveyor of the Port of New York.[10] More serious, however, was the case of Andrew Jackson, who continued even after the Seminole campaign to regard himself as independent of the War Department. The reorganization act of April 1818 made deputy commissaries responsible only to the Commissary General, but Jackson chose to disregard the act and court-martialed a supply officer for not following his own orders. Calhoun canceled the proceedings and reproved the General, but without effect. In the spring of 1819 it was General Alexander Macomb who drew a rebuke for "extravagance and irregularity in making disbursements"; and by summer Jackson was again ignoring orders.[11]

At about this same time Jackson was freely displaying copies of certain incredibly bombastic letters addressed by him to General Winfield Scott, who had privately disapproved of Jackson's controversy with the War Department over the manner in which orders were to be issued. In some roundabout way Jackson learned of Scott's attitude, called him to account for it, and though the two men were personally unknown to each other, a sharp controversy was carried on between them for a year or more.[12] It was hardly important enough to justify direct interference but the publicity was bad, so Calhoun prohibited newspaper publication of quarrels between officers.

Not long afterward he received a letter from Scott who charged that Jackson, by passing around manuscript copies of half the correspondence, was violating the order, and announced his intention of correcting any misapprehension that might have arisen by publishing both sides of the controversy. Calhoun's reply was typical. "Whether Genl. Jackson has done any act in violation of the order in this case," he wrote, "I am not apprized but admitting he has the Department would find in such violation a reason for enforcing and not for rescinding or relaxing the order."[13] Scott promptly went over the Secretary's head to Monroe, who tried persuasion when he should have been firm. The correspondence was published in pamphlet form and copied in the newspapers. Calhoun discreetly let the matter drop and the two generals did likewise.

In other departments his orders met with greater co-operation. The supply services of the Army were made subject to military law and responsibility under a system of direct purchase by the Commissary General which went into effect June 1, 1819. The old contract system had protected the Treasury by the forfeit of bond, but the new one provided food for the Army. It was better food than ever before, too. After a study by the newly appointed Surgeon General, Dr. Joseph Lovell, vegetables were added to the ration, and twice a week fresh meat replaced dried beef and salt pork. Orders were issued to cultivate vegetables at the permanent posts, and in the more remote regions garrisons were expected to produce their own corn and meat as well.[14]

Undismayed by the unsettled accounts of the department, Calhoun regularly included in his annual budget a sum for reducing the arrears. He put General Scott to work on the preparation of a manual of infantry tactics, which was completed late in 1818 and was eventually sanctioned by Congress. Somehow he found time to review the instruction given and the results obtained at West Point; and in order to provide a reserve of trained men to command the militia and officer an expanded wartime army, he recommended establishment of a second military academy, located to serve the West and South. He proposed also a "school of practice" for men in service—a proposal out of which grew the Artillery School at Fortress Monroe, and in time the Army War College.[15]

Most important of all, perhaps, if we think in terms of centuries rather than of years or decades, was an order to the surgeons of the Army to keep detailed day-to-day weather records at all posts. Compiled after twenty years, these records constituted the basic data for the first scientific study of meteorology in the United

States. Nowhere in the world up to that time had simultaneous observations been taken at so many points over so extended a period.[16] Calhoun was among the original subscribers to Benjamin Silliman's *Journal of Science,* which made its appearance in 1818, and he gave additional evidence of his interest in precise knowledge when he attached a scientific corps under Major Stephen Long to the Missouri expedition.

5

Aside from delay in getting the Missouri expedition started and the chronic insubordination of headstrong generals, Calhoun's success as an executive was marked. He brought to the War Department the same youth, energy and intelligence that Alexander Hamilton had given to the Treasury twenty years before, with results so evident that William Lowndes, on a visit to England in the spring of 1819, could not avoid measuring his friend against the British War Minister, Lord Palmerston, in terms not flattering to the latter.[17]

No less striking was the position achieved by the Calhouns in the social life of Washington. In the fall of 1818 they bought a house, where they were soon entertaining in the best Southern tradition. In the very heart of the Washington of that day, the new home was on the south side of E Street between Sixth and Seventh, northwest of the Capitol. The nine-thousand-dollar investment left Calhoun "in great need of money," but that was a condition fast becoming chronic and does not appear to have had the least effect on the young Secretary's spirits or on those of his lady. Though she was just recovered from a dangerous illness, Floride impressed with her cheerfulness and charm all who came in contact with her, and her husband proved as captivating in private as he was compelling on the public stage.[18]

Things were running far too smoothly, considering the natural inertia of the human species. Calhoun had undertaken to change too much in too short a time, and he was to suffer the perhaps inevitable fate of the reformer who sets about giving his fellows the things they should have without considering what they want. In the West men believed they had a divine right to fill Indians with whisky preparatory to bargaining for their furs, and to kill a suitable number of braves every now and then as proof of the inherent superiority of the white man; while the commercial East saw in the whole frontier program only another proof of the rising power of the West. The tide of postwar depression presently engulfed the land, retrenchment became the order of the day, and a nationalistic military policy became, in the eyes of many, a costly and dangerous experiment.

CHAPTER XIV

DEPRESSION AND REACTION

1

As SOON as the restraining hand of war had been lifted, trade and industry began a furious expansion in keeping with the confidence of America in her future greatness. The business of supplying capital for this growing enterprise fell to the Bank of the United States, and the bank made the most of its opportunity. From the very beginning it lent money far too freely, with the branch banks in the South and West outdoing the parent institution. In some instances outright dishonesty was added to ignorance and indifference, until by the end of 1817 the situation had become critical. The crisis came six months later, when the specie reserve of the bank had fallen to less than five percent of its outstanding loans. In August of 1818 a sharp retrenchment was begun, and economic depression settled over the land.

Soon hard-pressed and broken families in the East and South were moving in long caravans Westward along the Cumberland Road, the old Wilderness Trail and the Genesee Path, hoping to make a new start in a new country. Throughout the winter the depression deepened until perhaps three million people, or a third of the population, were affected by it. Soup kitchens were set up in the Eastern cities and thousands received public relief, while land values dropped to half, to a third and sometimes to only a tenth of their former rate.[1]

The West suffered most, for there speculation had been least restrained. In Kentucky and Ohio and Tennessee vast sums had been borrowed on faith alone to be invested in permanent improvements. The borrowers had never intended to repay the loans when due, but merely to renew year after year. Western banking practices had long permitted such unorthodox methods, for they served to manufacture the capital so desperately needed. It is true this capital was only paper, but it had value in the West because western men had faith in their future. The bubble burst when the United States Bank called upon its western branches to collect. The debtors had neither specie nor bank notes, and the East would not accept their prospects in lieu of coin. When protest proved unavailing, all the resentment of the dispossessed turned into political channels. State legislatures passed bankruptcy laws to relieve the debtors and set about to tax the bank and its branches out of existence.

Early in 1819 William Jones resigned his presidency of the bank, following a sharply critical Congressional inquiry, and shortly thereafter it became known that the Baltimore and Philadelphia branches had been systematically looted by some of their officers. The effect was merely to confirm the popular impression that corruption and intrigue were at the bottom of all the trouble. An abiding distrust of all banks, and particularly of the Bank of the United States, spread over the country, carrying with it loss of prestige for all public men who had ever championed that institution. Calhoun suffered with the others, but used all his influence to save the charter he had originally drawn.

For a time the bank appeared doomed, but reorganization won the day against dissolution. In March Langdon Cheves succeeded the ineffectual Jones. Dividends were suspended until the impaired capital should be restored. The Western and Southern branches were ordered to stop issuing notes, while the parent bank stopped buying or collecting exchange on the West and South. The policy restored solvency in six weeks' time but it brought violent protest from local banks and businesses, and the general impression grew that the bank had been saved at the expense of the people.[2]

Time and place are unimportant when people see their property shrink and vanish, their employment become insecure, and their families faced with hunger and privation. It is then that men put their faith in panaceas, fix blame and hatred upon existing institutions, and follow as a messiah anyone who offers them action instead of the mere words they do not understand and have learned to distrust, for action alone is the salvation of the dispossessed.

In the winter of 1818-1819 all the necessary elements were present. The bank represented the devil; the tariff, which was presently linked with internal improvements and abolition, was offered as the panacea; and Andrew Jackson, whose conduct in Florida shared the attention of Congress with the bank crisis, became the messiah—the man of action who cut red tape with the sword, who hanged traitors first and asked questions afterward, who was direct, forthright, resolute and every inch a leader of men.

2

The Seminole affair was soon a partisan issue. When the House Committee on Military Affairs reported a caustic disapproval of the proceedings against Arbuthnot and Ambrister, Richard M. Johnson, the committee's chairman, took issue with his colleagues and defended the General in an able minority report. Thomas W. Cobb of Georgia, Crawford's leader in the House, replied when the question reached the floor about the middle of January. He arraigned the whole Florida campaign, condemned the seizure of St. Marks and Pensacola "contrary to orders, and in violation of the Constitution," and censured the administration for its failure to call Jackson to account for his breach of discipline.[3] Adams' supporters made common cause with Johnson to defend the Hero, and were presently joined by the Clintonians, while Clay took over the leadership of the anti-Jackson forces.[4]

Clay's was, as befitted his talents, the major speech on the subject. It was thoroughly publicized in advance, and the rules of the House were relaxed to take care of the large audience, which overflowed the low galleries and swarmed out onto the floor itself. Margaret Bayard Smith, whose letters give so vivid a picture of Washington society, came in from her country home and stayed overnight with the Calhouns in order to be on hand. In the crush of visitors she was unable to join Floride and Elizabeth Lowndes in the gallery and had perforce to watch the proceedings from the floor, where one of the members gallantly gave her a seat. The Senate adjourned to hear the brilliant Kentuckian, and the diplomatic corps was there in force.

Clay was eloquent and amusing, but he directed his remarks at General Jackson rather than to President Monroe. He seemed half apologetic because he found himself again in opposition to the administration and confined his attentions to the General and to those who had spoken on the other side. Colonel Johnson rose at once to reply, but could not secure the attention of the House. The spell of Clay's wizardry broke in a general hubbub. Gentlemen passed oranges, tied in handkerchiefs and appropriately labeled, up to the ladies in the gallery, and the buzz of conversation and of laughter echoed from the corridors and from the floor itself. Johnson abandoned the attempt until another day; the House adjourned.

Mrs. Smith provided Calhoun with a detailed account of the speech at dinner, and the conversation lasted without interruption until nine o'clock.[5] J. Q. Adams received his report from Joseph Hopkinson, Federalist Representative of a Philadelphia district and author of the popular "Hail Columbia."[6]

Johnson resumed his interrupted reply to Clay on January twenty-first, in a speech of unusual merit, rich in citations from both well-known and obscure works on international law. The material had been supplied him three days before by the one man in Washington who knew such subjects best, the Secretary of State, who had also taken pains that Jackson should hear of his interest.

Jackson himself, meanwhile, was on his way to the Capital, where his advisers felt that his presence was desirable. At a dinner in Winchester he toasted Calhoun, and in Washington the only invitation he would accept was one from the Secretary of War to dine with various military men. Calhoun, for his part, did all in his power to smooth the fiery General's path. He had not changed his views as to the Florida campaign, but he was convinced that Jackson's purposes throughout had been honest and patriotic, and he saw nothing to be gained by a Congressional censure that might reflect discredit on the War Department as well as on the General. He went so far as to urge Abner Lacock, chairman of the committee investigating the affair in the Senate, to accept the administration's view, and in sending papers to the committee was careful to include only those specifically called for.[7]

It was not Calhoun, however, but Adams whom Jackson regarded as his special champion. With the Secretary of State he talked at length of politics, charging that Clay and Crawford had entered into an alliance, and blaming the latter for the present Congressional investigation of himself. The disputed order of 1817 he attributed to the hostility of Crawford, and when the Lacock committee presented an unfavorable report he laid that too at Craw-

ford's door.[8] To Adams it all meant that Jackson was on his side
in the still distant Presidential contest, and his hopes were high.

A week after his appearance in Washington, Jackson attended
a Presidential levee, where his enormous personal popularity was
reaffirmed; and a few days later the House voted an overwhelming
vindication of the Hero: a result which the political partisans of
John Quincy Adams aided materially in bringing about.

The reaction was an immediate call for reduction of the Army.
If generals could not be held accountable, they could at least be
given so little power that they would constitute no menace to free
institutions. A resolution calling upon the Military Affairs Committee of the House "to inquire into the expedience of reducing the
Army of the United States" had been proposed early in December
1818, well before the Seminole discussion began, but had been laid
on the table for the time being at the request of its author, Lewis
Williams of North Carolina. Williams, it will be recalled, was not
well disposed toward the Secretary of War, but was even less
partial to Andrew Jackson; and his brother, Senator John Williams
of Tennessee, was Jackson's principal political rival in that state.
Both the brothers were partisans of Crawford, whose prestige as a
candidate would suffer unless the importance of Jackson's vindication could somehow be minimized. So, with the aid of Henry Clay,
who had also lost face, the forgotten Williams resolution was called
up and passed the very day after Jackson's triumph.

The resolution served a double purpose. It renewed by indirection the attack on Jackson, and in time of great financial stringency
it called sharply to public notice the disproportionately large cost
of the military establishment. It marked, too, the beginning of a
breach between Calhoun and Crawford; for the latter's candidacy
required that the books of the Treasury, under his administration
of the finances, should come somewhere near to a balance, and the
obvious place to cut expenses was the War Department.[9]

3

Calhoun's own primary concern still lay in carrying out the ambitious defense program he had conceived and set in motion, and in
the face of threatening relations with Spain and Great Britain, he
could not believe that a serious opposition to it would develop. As

parties formed around the personal leadership of the various aspirants to the Presidency, he remained uncommitted and apparently indifferent. Adams, however, noted what seemed to him an excess of patronage going to the Treasury Department, and he recalled that Calhoun and Crawford had taken the same side during the Cabinet discussion of the Seminole campaign. He began to wonder just where his colleague stood, and he voiced his doubts in the course of a lengthy discussion with Henry Middleton, until recently a member of Congress from Charleston. Middleton assured the New Englander that "as a Southern man, Calhoun must have views of his own, which could not be advanced by Crawford's election as President," but he promised to "ascertain something more as to his dispositions."[10]

It was an unnecessary precaution. Monroe believed in showing himself to the people, for all the sly gibes at the unrepublican elegance of his household, and he proposed to spend the spring and summer of 1819 traveling through the South and West. Calhoun was to accompany the President as far as his South Carolina home, and when he left Washington late in March it was to Adams that he turned over the management of War Department affairs, although Crawford was certainly more familiar with the duties and had filled in during a similar absence the preceding summer. The implications of the move could hardly have been misunderstood by Crawford. Certainly they were not misunderstood by Adams.[11]

The President's party included Floride and her two children as well as Calhoun. Another child was expected in the fall, and like the others it was to be born in Carolina. So for Floride it was the beginning of a long holiday at home. For her husband it was official business, but he hoped to rejoin her later in the year.

The party reached Norfolk by steamboat late in the afternoon on the last day of March, and the next few days were spent inspecting sites for forts and bases: Old Point Comfort where Fortress Monroe would stand; the Rip Rap Shoal from which Fort Calhoun would dominate Hampton Roads; and finally Burril's Bay where the proposed Naval Depot was to be built. Then followed a public dinner on Saturday, April 3, and the next day found the party threading the narrow passage of the Dismal Swamp Canal. The same evening they were in Edenton, North Carolina.[12]

For the better part of a week President Monroe and his Secretary of War steamed up and down Albemarle and Pamlico Sounds, examining inlets and coves while they talked no doubt of the long chain of coastal forts that would forever prevent any future landing by hostile troops, and of the intracoastal waterway through which the still small but competent American Navy could be concentrated against larger forces. On April 9 they moved up the Pamlico River to the town of Washington, and the following day set up headquarters at New Bern, where the cycle of receptions followed by the inevitable public dinner was repeated. The fifteenth found them in Wilmington, where Floride and her brood held their own court while Monroe and Calhoun spent another four days inspecting forts and sites for forts from Oak Island to Cape Fear.

The next stage of the journey brought them into Calhoun's native South Carolina, where their first halt was at Georgetown on April 21. This time public hospitality gave way to private, and the whole entourage—Monroe, the Calhouns, Samuel Gouverneur, the President's secretary and future son-in-law, and various and sundry military, naval and civilian attaches—were carried in triumph to Prospect Hill, the plantation home of Benjamin Huger. Georgetown gave them a dinner the next day, to which they were brought in Colonel Alston's "elegant New York barge."

But the enthusiasm everywhere encountered so far was nothing beside the welcome they received in Charleston when they reached that city the afternoon of the twenty-sixth. There the inspection of land and water defenses was supplemented by military pageantry. The President rode in the Governor's barouche, and a troop of cavalry served as escort. There were dinners and speeches too, with the eternal round of toasts, and a theater party with *Julius Caesar* as the offering.

It was early May before the Southern journey was resumed by way of Beaufort and Savannah, augmented now by General Gaines and his family. The first night en route was spent at the beautiful home of Henry Middleton just outside Charleston, and we may presume that Middleton fulfilled his promise to J. Q. Adams. An evening was also passed with Charles Cotesworth Pinckney before they were noisily welcomed on May 8 by the citizens of Savannah.

This time General Gaines, who commanded the southeastern military department, accompanied the President and the Secretary of War on the tour of fortifications, while the ladies of the party enjoyed the hospitality of the city.

The next stop was the bustling river city of Augusta, shipping point for countless bales of Southern cotton; and on the nineteenth of May they rode into Washington, Georgia. Thence Monroe and Gaines moved on toward Lexington and Athens on the road to Nashville, while Calhoun and his family crossed the near-by Savannah River into their own home district. The citizens of Abbeville turned out to do them honor, and a public dinner was quickly planned to celebrate the return of their first citizen. While Floride and her children rested on the plantation at Willington (women did not attend public dinners in those days), Calhoun received the well-merited acclaim of those who had known him since childhood, and none among them doubted that he would someday rise "to that political elevation to which Providence seems to have destined him."

4

Awaiting the young Secretary's arrival in South Carolina was a sheaf of mail forwarded from Washington, and most of it seemed to be from Colonel Richard M. Johnson.[13] The letters were written in an extravagant and bombastic style compounded of wheedling and bullying, flattery and covert threats. The launching of the steamer *Calhoun* at Leestown was fulsomely described, and much was made of the great popularity of the Missouri expedition in the West. But the times were hard and money scarce. The Johnsons must have another fifty-thousand-dollar advance or they could not get provisions to Belle Fontaine in time for an early start.

The next letter told how the steamboats *Johnson, Jefferson* and *Expedition* would be off for Missouri in a week, each commanded by a brother of the Johnsons, while James Johnson himself and Quartermaster General Jesup would be aboard the *Calhoun*. Interest and enthusiasm remained high, but credit was low. It was impossible to secure private capital in the West, and only fifty thousand dollars before June 1 could keep the contractor from bankruptcy. The War Department, furthermore, was expected to pay for the steamboats. The value of the security was emphasized, and the number of brothers personally involved was adduced as evidence of good faith.

The story continued with the arrival of the contractor in St. Louis, where he found a judgment against him in possession of the Bank of Missouri, and the boats threatened with attachment. This was followed by the appointment of a new board of directors for the branch bank at Lexington: "notorious federalists," who would not extend further credit even though the Johnsons held Government contracts. To rescue the expedition and save the money already invested, more must be paid over, and that without delay.

Calhoun thought Johnson must be in error as to the amount of his contracts. He had already received by way of advances almost the entire sum of his transportation account, yet he called imperiously for more and offered evidence to prove that moving supplies up the Missouri would cost more than had been estimated. The Secretary wrote to Commissary General Gibson with instructions to advance thirty-five thousand dollars if it appeared absolutely necessary to save the expedition, but to await his return to Washington if the situation permitted.[14]

Three of the four steamboats, meanwhile, had arrived opposite Belle Fontaine, but they dared not land their cargoes for inspection lest they be attached by the Missouri authorities. Colonel Henry Atkinson, who was to command the expedition, refused to accept the supplies without inspection. Johnson was inclined to resent this slur upon his integrity, but after much delay and no little friction the cargoes were landed on Illinois soil and examined. The quality of the provisions was poor and the quantity short. The boats were without proper accommodation for troops, the engines were weak and the crews were inexperienced; but Atkinson was too eager to get started to brook further delay. The Sixth Regiment had long since reached St. Louis from Plattsburg after a trek of nearly three months. He resolved to wait no longer for the missing steamboat, and set out on July 4.

Calhoun had not been back at his desk in the War Department for more than a few days when he received a letter from Monroe

The President was then in Kentucky where he was impressed with the obvious popularity of the Missouri expedition and with the patriotism of the Johnson brothers in the face of misfortunes beyond their control, and he directed the Secretary to advance $85,000 on the various contracts held by them, together with another $57,500 on receipt of title to the four steamboats. Accompanying Monroe's letter was another praising the expedition and the Johnsons in the highest terms, and urging that every accommodation be given them. It was signed by eight of the first citizens of the West, including Isaac Shelby, Andrew Jackson, Senator William A. Trimble of Ohio and William T. Barry. A letter from R. M. Johnson completed the cycle. "I shall never be done acknowledging my gratitude to the President & yourself," he wrote. "I have never meet with men so much entitled to my gratitude & friendship, although the support rendered is nothing but what corresponds with justice, liberality, policy & public duty. . . ."[15]

He had already drawn against the advances ordered by Monroe to the extent of $107,500.

Calhoun was stunned. The advances on the Johnson contracts already amounted to more than $100,000 without this, and the appropriation for the quartermaster's department was almost exhausted with only half of the fiscal year gone.[16] He wrote to beg Johnson to make no further drafts, lest he be forced through sheer want of funds to refuse payment. Advances and outstanding drafts already amounted to within $30,000 of the entire sum that would be due when all the contracts were fully performed.[17] The letter crossed one from Johnson on the way. The $35,000 advance Calhoun had left to the discretion of the Commissary General had been withheld, but bills had been drawn in anticipation of it. And a few days later came word that Johnson's notes had been protested by the Lexington branch of the United States Bank. To avoid suit he had drawn once more upon the War Department. The letters were filled with extravagant praise of Calhoun, of Colonel Atkinson, of General Jesup and of James Johnson, and insinuated that all his difficulties were due to the jealousy of the people of Missouri and the hostility of the Lexington bank.[18]

At this point Monroe returned to Washington and agreed that a halt must be called, but Johnson himself followed hard upon the

President's heels, and got yet another substantial advance before he departed again for the West early in September.

The Johnson steamboats had already proved worthless for the purpose intended. The *Calhoun* never reached St. Louis at all, and the others, even with only partial loads, could not make headway in the swift, mud-saturated Missouri. One after another they were abandoned for keelboats. It was the end of September before the troops were landed at Council Bluffs, where they found an encampment already made and a grotesque wooden sea serpent moored to the farther shore. The encampment was that of Major Long and his scientific corps, and the serpent was the steamboat *Western Engineer,* so built to overawe the Indians. She had been launched in Pittsburgh late in March and had passed St. Louis while Atkinson and the Missouri authorities were wrangling over the supplies.[19]

Despite her clumsy appearance, the *Western Engineer* had made the five-hundred-mile trip against the treacherous Missouri current without incident or mishap, thereby vindicating the choice of steamboats. It was already too late. The whole expedition was under savage attack in the St. Louis *Enquirer,* published by Thomas Hart Benton, who was also interested in the Bank of Missouri and was not altogether innocent of connection with the fur trade.

5

Middleton's report to Adams must have been satisfactory, for the Secretary of State was unusually cordial and attentive to his younger colleague. When Monroe returned to the Capital early in August, the two Secretaries paid him an evening call together, and after an hour's talk the plump New Englander drove the lanky Carolinian home in his carriage. Again, after a Cabinet session which ended with dinner at the White House, Adams and Calhoun left together and took a "long evening ramble."[20] But the Presidential succession which engrossed Adams' thoughts was not yet uppermost in Calhoun's mind. All his attention and abilities were needed to carry into full effect the wide-ranging policy to which he was committed.

Aside from the Missouri expedition, which was complicated by the demands and the failures of the Johnsons, the program was running smoothly. Colonel Leavenworth reached the head of navigation on the Mississippi without incident, and Congress accepted the policy of civilizing the Indians to the extent of providing an annual sum of ten thousand dollars to guard "against the further decline and final extinction" of the tribes. Calhoun arranged for administration of the fund by the various missionary groups that had interested themselves in procuring it. Applications for funds were to include a plan of education that "in addition to reading, writing, and arithmetic, should, in the instruction of the boys, extend to the practical knowledge of the mode of agriculture, and of such of the mechanic arts as are suited to the condition of the Indians; and in that of the girls, to spinning, weaving, and sewing."[21] He made it, in the terminology of today, a conditional grant for vocational education; and had he had his way, the annuities paid various of the Indian tribes would have been used in the same manner. It was out of this fund that the detailed survey of conditions among the Indians made by the Reverend Jedidiah Morse in 1820-1821 was financed.

Late in September Calhoun turned the affairs of his department over to Van Deventer and McKenney and hurried south in order to be with Floride when their fourth child was born. Old Mrs. Calhoun had recently acquired a summer home at Pendleton, high in the Blue Ridge foothills and some fifty miles northwest of Abbeville. The estate was known as Clergy Hall, and it was there that Floride had gone for her confinement.[22] The dry air of the mountains was bracing, and the sweep of the hills with their ever-changing shadows a constant delight to the eye, but Calhoun would not yield to the temptation to linger. Again the child was a girl, this time christened Elizabeth, and as soon as mother and daughter were able to travel they set out for Washington. With them went Floride's mother, who proposed to spend the winter in the Capital.

It was as well that his family was with him, for the strain of two southern trips within so short a time, combined with the long hours he had spent at his desk and worry over the Johnson contracts, had weakened Calhoun's resistance. In Rockingham County, North Carolina, just south of the Virginia border, he was struck down by **fever** and could go no farther. It was on November 9 that he became ill, and ten days later the news reached the Capital. For more than a week he battled silently for his life while official Washington shared the concern of friends and relatives. Lowndes, who had just returned from Europe, wrote with great feeling to Cheves of the "alarming illness" of their friend,[23] and a general gloom spread over the city. The case was diagnosed as bilious fever—the same disease from which he had suffered in the fall of 1814; but soon, according to an unnamed friend who reached his bedside on the sixteenth, "sunk down to a typhus type ... which has raged with extraordinary violence."[24]

It was not until the nineteenth that he was reported out of danger. Thereafter he improved slowly but steadily, and as soon as he could move he insisted on resuming his journey. Still weak and shaken, but confident as ever, he reached Washington December 3, in time for the opening of Congress, and by January was his old self again.[25]

CHAPTER XV

A FIRE BELL IN THE NIGHT

1

THE justification of Jackson's conduct in Florida and the rise of an economy bloc in Congress under the leadership of the Secretary of the Treasury were only two elements in a many-sided reaction to a complex situation, which affected different classes of the population in varying ways. Among the victims of hard times were the war-fostered American industries, already bitter against British dumping and evasion of customs laws; and their spokesmen soon discovered that popular distress could be turned to profitable account. So the self-styled "friends of American manufactures" preached the gospel of protection, using every means the times afforded for spreading information and argument. Rallies and speeches, petitions, memorials and associations, newspapers, handbills, broadsides, pamphlets and books were all used to prove that a subsidized industry alone could pull the country from the morass into which it had fallen.

The leading spirit was Mathew Carey, Philadelphia editor and publisher. Though he had no personal stake in industry and the manufacturers seemed at times to show small gratitude for the service he did them, Carey propagandized for the tariff from 1818 on to the end of his life.[1] He was soon ably abetted by Hezekiah Niles whose *Weekly Register* circulated all over the United States. Papers like the *Patron of Industry* and the *Manufacturers Journal* sprang up to carry on the cause, and conservative but shrewd New Englanders began shifting their capital from commerce to manufacturing ventures.

Under constant and growing pressure, Congressmen from the states where the new cult had taken hold one after another bowed down before this glittering will-o'-the-wisp that promised a sure road to lasting prosperity, and the protectionists recorded their first real triumph in mid-April of 1818. The existing tariff pro-

188

visions which had only a year more to run were extended to 1826, and minor increases were granted in some few of the duties then in force. Economic conditions, nevertheless, grew steadily worse through 1819; and the protectionists called loudly for an early session of the new Congress in the fall, the purpose of which would be, of course, to raise the tariff. They did not succeed at once, but again they gained; for though Congress did not meet until the usual time, a standing Committee on Manufactures was created in the House under the chairmanship of Henry Baldwin from industrial Pittsburgh.

These tariff moves were immediately countered by leaders in the agricultural states. Their means of livelihood had also suffered, and they saw in further restriction of imports only an inevitable further curtailment of their foreign markets. The argument against the tariff took the obvious form of denying the right of Congress to pass such legislation, and the whole question was presently merged with widespread opposition to centralization for which the Supreme Court furnished the text.

2

Basically the quarrel went back to 1803, when Chief Justice Marshall had made of the famous case of Marbury vs. Madison a vehicle for asserting the power of the court to declare acts of Congress void. Jefferson and the Virginia State Rights school of which he was the leader had bitterly resented the decision, and Marshall had been denounced so savagely that even he was alarmed. When the impeachment trial of Judge Chase failed, however, the storm died down; and for a time the issue between state sovereignty and national power remained in abeyance. Then in 1810 came Fletcher vs. Peck, a trumped-up case which gave the court an opportunity to uphold the admittedly corrupt sale of the Yazoo lands by the Georgia Legislature on the ground of the inviolability of contract, and in which John Quincy Adams was one of the attorneys for the winning side. It was a long step forward for those who believed that "in the absence of military force, political power naturally and necessarily goes into the hands which hold the property."[2]

It was in the February term of 1819, however, that the Supreme Court unfolded in three major cases the philosophy of centralized power in the hands of the economically well-to-do which has played so important, and sometimes so tragic, a role in the industrial development of America. The cases were the Dartmouth College case, decided February 2; Sturges vs. Crowninshield, which followed two weeks later; and M'Culloch vs. Maryland on March 6, 1819—the day that Langdon Cheves became president of the bank. Two of the cases grew directly out of the economic crisis, and the third was closely related in its results.

This is not the place to enter at length into the details of these cases. Let it suffice to say that in Sturges vs. Crowninshield, a New York bankruptcy law designed to relieve impoverished debtors was declared unconstitutional, the successful attorneys being David Daggett, former Federalist Senator from Connecticut, and Joseph Hopkinson. In M'Culloch vs. Maryland, the court denied the right of a state to tax the United States Bank, since the bank was a creature of the National Government. Webster, arguing for the bank, had shown that the power to tax is the power to destroy; and in denying it to the states where a national institution was concerned, the court in effect affirmed the supremacy of the National Legislature. First in point of time, the Dartmouth College case was perhaps most far-reaching of all in the implications of its decision; for here the court held that a charter of incorporation was a contract, and like other contracts was inviolable. Again it was Webster who carried off the honors.

These historic decisions had two immediate effects. They gave renewed impetus to the development and spread of the corporate form of business organization, thereby concentrating already powerful economic forces and aligning these forces on the side of a strong central government; and they precipitated a sharp reaction from those interests that, from their distribution, could not hope to control a majority in the National Legislature. For the theory of government thus made a part of the Constitution was a theory under which minority interests could not hope to survive, and those who spoke for them were therefore compelled to seek salvation in the opposing theory of State Rights.

Virginia, with the aged Thomas Jefferson himself still in command, took the lead; and no more able group of men ever united behind a cause than those who tried unsuccessfully to upset the most vulnerable of the court's decisions—that in M'Culloch vs. Maryland. The constellation included Spencer Roane, Chief Justice of the Virginia Court of Appeals, and the man whom Jefferson had intended for the place occupied by John Marshall; the Father of the Constitution, ex-President James Madison; John Taylor of Hazelwood in Caroline County, most profound political thinker of his time, who is best known as John Taylor of Caroline; young Thomas Ritchie, whose Richmond *Enquirer* was a power to be reckoned with; and such rising stars as James and Philip Barbour, John Floyd and John Tyler. John Randolph of Roanoke also aided powerfully in the fight but played his hand, as usual, alone.

Into the midst of this State Rights controversy the slavery question was injected without warning, and served to fix irrevocably the sectional lines already indicated by the opposing interests of industry and agriculture. For the ownership of slaves was one of the minority interests whose doom was sure, once complete sovereignty was conceded to a majority in Congress. To the Northern States, the extinction of slavery merely meant the carrying out of the intention of the Constitution. To the South, it meant losing an enormous capital investment, impairing if not destroying the whole of Southern agriculture, and exposing homes and families to the whims of a large and semibarbarous population all too likely to use new freedom to wreak vengeance for past servitude. The Reconstruction of half a century later showed how well grounded the fear had been.

3

While the friends of domestic industry were keeping the printers busy and the Army was preparing to occupy new military posts in the West, the citizens of the Missouri Territory were bombarding Congress with petitions asking to be admitted as a state into the Union. After many delays, a bill to gratify them reached the floor of the House on February 13, 1819, a few days after the apotheosis of Jackson. James Tallmadge of New York, a future president of New York University who was serving his one term in Congress, moved an amendment which would prohibit the introduction of slaves into the new state and would free at the age of twenty-five all those born to slavery within its borders after its admission to the Union.

Considering the magnitude of the issue raised, the debate was remarkably brief, but it was clear and pointed. Clay championed the cause of the slaveholders, and John W. Taylor of New York spoke for those who favored restriction. Both knew that the extension or extinction of slavery was the real issue, and the North had the greater strength. The amendment was adopted after only three days of discussion, and on February 17 the amended bill was passed and sent to the Senate. There it went to a committee whose chairman was Charles Tait of Georgia, confidant of both Crawford and Calhoun, and on his recommendation the Tallmadge amendment was dropped. With the end of the session and of the Congress only two or three days distant, neither house would yield and the bill was lost.

The new Congress was scarcely organized in December, however, before Missouri's petition for statehood was again on the Speaker's desk, and once more it was referred to a committee. It was still in the committee's hands three weeks later when a bill admitting Maine to the Union as a state was taken up and passed; but when the latter reached the Senate, it was promptly amended to include Missouri in the same bill, without restriction as to slavery.

The debate was sectional from the start, with the Southern forces powerfully reinforced by the return of John Randolph to the House and the appointment of William Pinkney to the Senate from Maryland. In sheer ability, the Northern interests, with the single exception of Rufus King who still represented New York in the Senate, had no one in either house fit to cross swords with these two, or with a number of others such as James Barbour in the upper chamber and Henry Clay and William Lowndes in the lower. In the House the North had the advantage of numbers, but as King aptly phrased it, it was always militia against regulars.[3]

The reason for this disparity was inherent in the economies of the respective sections. The plantation system of the South resembled the society of England in the heyday of her landed aristocracy. Success as a planter depended on the possession of good land and ample labor, with adequate means of transportation for the crop. Given these, full-time personal supervision was no more necessary than it is today for a stockholder in a prosperous industry. Thus the more able and ambitious men of the South were free to enter politics. The North, on the other hand, was a commercial and industrial society, where success depended upon the personal guidance of the entrepreneur. There the more capable remained tied to business and let their lawyers handle their politics.

As the contest progressed, the number of visitors increased beyond the capacity of the galleries to hold them; and when Pinkney began speaking against the slavery restriction on January 21, 1820, Vice President Tompkins gallantly turned over to the ladies the seats usually reserved for foreign diplomats.[4] A Cabinet meeting scheduled for that day had to be postponed because Calhoun and Secretary of the Navy Smith Thompson had both gone to the Senate to hear the great Maryland orator; and on the twenty-fourth, when Pinkney concluded his speech, even John Quincy Adams was in the gallery.[5] Harrison Gray Otis, now Senator from Massachusetts, answered but seemed to miss the true significance of the contest. He was thinking back to the days of the Hartford Convention; and to him the whole question of admitting new slave territory was simply a question of increasing through the operation of the federal ratio the political power of the South.

Even Rufus King, who took up the argument on February 11, failed to exploit the full possibilities of the question. By this time the galleries were crowded with Negroes, who dimly realized that the servitude or freedom of their race was at stake.[6] To these the New York Senator addressed himself, and though he talked much of the political balance of power, he managed to convey to the blacks the impression that his people were champions of their freedom. The Calhouns entertained that evening, and no other topic was discussed. The speech was called by Southerners seditious and inflammatory; but Adams, already resolved that it would be better to destroy the Union than to permit the spread of slavery, thought King had been too timid.[7]

·4

The whole of New England and the Northern States were presently shaken by the reaction of the South, for the slaveholders saw with prophetic clarity that to permit restriction in Missouri would inevitably mean the ultimate extinction of their "peculiar institution." Northern men had generally assumed that the constitutional provision outlawing the slave trade after 1808 was the first step toward eventual emancipation, and idealists among them had taken it for granted that of course the South shared this purpose and meant to co-operate in achieving the final goal. Yet even while sincere and high-minded men and women in New England talked of freedom, New England ships were smuggling slaves by thousands to Southern ports,[8] and the profits of the outlawed trade were finding their way into the new manufacturing enterprises of the Eastern States. The already large proportion of Southern capital invested in slaves loomed larger still as land values fell with the onset of depression; and though the returns were small,[9] to wipe out the investment altogether would have meant disaster—the same disaster that did indeed befall the South in the tragic reconstruction period.

The South, in short, had given up all thought of an eventual emancipation, and was even looking to a demand for Negroes in the West to reduce both her dangerously large slave population and her exorbitantly high investment in human labor. Her reaction to the Northern proposal to restrict, and ultimately to abolish, slavery was precisely the same as New England's reaction to the embargo had been; and it was motivated by the same utterly human desire to avoid personal financial ruin even at the possible cost of national calamity. The pressure was relieved in the North by the rise of manufactures as an alternative and equally profitable source of investment, but no such outlet was open to the South. Indeed, the very protective policy on which Northern industrial prosperity was based served only to depress further the economy of the cotton states.

Just as New England only half a dozen years before had denied that Congress possessed the power to pass an embargo, so now the South denied that a restriction upon Missouri, or any other territory applying for admission to the Union, could be constitutionally imposed. To men like Randolph and John Taylor of Caroline, the Northern position was just another attempt at consolidation of the powers of government and meant, should it be accomplished, that the majority could plunder as they saw fit, under cover of law and without restraint. So Spencer Roane was willing that Virginia should secede if the extension of slavery were restricted, and John Tyler wrote that men talked in the halls of Congress "of a dissolution of the Union with perfect non-chalance and indifference."[10]

It was Senator Jesse B. Thomas, a Crawford man from the new state of Illinois, who proposed the basis on which the famous compromise was at last worked out, permitting slavery in Missouri but forbidding it in all the rest of the Louisiana Territory north of 36° 30'. The bill was finally passed on March 2, 1820, after protracted conference between House and Senate managers and a parliamentary maneuver more adroit than honest on the part of Henry Clay, which prevented a vote on Randolph's last-minute motion to reconsider.[11] At the same time, as part of the compromise, Maine was admitted as a free state, having received permission from Massachusetts to form a separate government provided she should be received into the Union by March 3, 1820.

5

The passage of the compromise was the "fire bell in the night" that filled Jefferson with alarm and led patriotic men both North and South to fear for the permanence of the Union. Calhoun watched the gathering storm with anxiety and foreboding. He did not believe that the question would bring dissolution, but if it should, he saw the South driven, however reluctantly, to an alliance with Great Britain.[12] It was a frankly sectional reaction, which revealed momentarily the widening gulf between the two great geographical regions of the country.

Monroe had long been under pressure from his Virginia friends to accept the State Rights position. In letter after letter Roane, John Taylor, Madison and even Jefferson urged upon the President the necessity for blocking the centralization toward which the Government seemed to be tending, subtly assuming that of course he agreed with their views. The method showed considerable insight into Monroe's character and seems to have had some effect. At least he made pointed overtures to Randolph as a result of the latter's uncompromising stand on the Missouri question—overtures as pointedly rejected. It is not, therefore, surprising that the final passage of the compromise found the President quite unprepared to act either way.

He resolved his personal doubts as he usually did, by putting the burden of decision on his Cabinet, this time taking the added precaution of asking opinions in writing—something he had never done before. His dilemma was whether the act was or was not unconstitutional, and accordingly whether he should or should not veto it; and he could hardly have been surprised when the Cabinet split, as Congress had, along sectional lines. The form in which Monroe posed the question to his advisers was whether the prohibition of slavery *forever* in the territory north of 36° 30' applied only so long as the territorial status continued, or remained applicable after statehood had been achieved. If only the former was meant, there was no constitutional question, for none of them denied the power of Congress to prohibit slavery in the territories. If the law intended that the prohibition should apply after the territories had become states, however, the three Southern members of the Cabinet were clear that it would not be constitutional, for Congress could not prohibit slavery in a state. With this view Smith Thompson, a former New York State Judge, agreed, much to the annoyance of J. Q. Adams, who thus found himself the lone advocate of the constitutionality of abolition.[13]

As the argument threatened to become warm, Calhoun suggested rephrasing the President's question to cover merely the constitutionality of the Missouri Compromise Act. That it was valid all could agree, though for different reasons. Adams could simply answer "yes," while the others could explain that they understood the prohibition of slavery to apply only to the territorial status. Both Adams and Monroe welcomed this bit of logic chopping, and the President signed the bill.[14]

After the discussion, Calhoun and Adams walked home together. The New Englander spoke of the equality of all men, of the dignity and worth of human life, and of the moral impossibility of justifying slavery. Calhoun conceded the justice and nobility of his colleague's views, but saw no other way to handle the labor problem of the South, given the presence of the Negro, and considering the existing prejudice and social structure of the South. Well though they knew each other, and familiar as each was with the other's mental processes, they arrived at no common ground.[15] Is it any wonder that the common people of North and South, who knew each other scarcely at all, whose means of livelihood, way of life and even speech were different, should fail to understand each other's point of view?

Seen from the vantage point of another century, the failure of North and South to understand each other can only be attributed to narrow and shortsighted self-interest on both sides. Southern planters imagined that cotton could not be grown without Negro labor; and the Negro was still too close to savage Africa from which he had been violently taken to be trusted to live at peace with those to whom he owed his misfortune, should he be set free. The conclusion appeared inescapable that any effort to abolish Negro slavery was a deliberate effort to destroy the whole economic structure of the South. The North, for its part, still resented the embargo and the commercial losses of the war, which together had very nearly destroyed the economic structure of New England. Both of these events were attributed to slavery, which gave to the agricultural states some twenty votes in Congress in excess of the number justified by their white population: twenty votes that had been enough to swing the balance against the commercial states.

Where the various selfish interests that make up a society can be consolidated into two major divisions, and where these divisions have no will or wish to understand each other, no power on earth can indefinitely prevent a conflict between them. In the 1820's interests were gradually coalescing. Prosperity for the free states appeared to lie in a policy of industrial and commercial expansion, subsidized by Government and buttressed by a judicial theory of contract which held legislative charters and private agreements to be alike inviolable. Such a policy required the intervention of a strong central government; and the supremacy of the Federal power became, therefore, the cornerstone of Northern hopes. The prosperity of the South, on the other hand, seemed to rest upon the maintenance of slavery and the continuance of a foreign market for an ever-growing output of cotton. The protective system favored by the North tended to destroy this market; and to break that system, as well as to ward off moves toward the abolition of slavery, it was necessary for the South so to weaken the Federal power that tariff laws could not be passed nor emancipation carried out. A theory of state sovereignty was the obvious rationalization of the Southern position.

CHAPTER XVI

THE GAGE IS THROWN DOWN

1

As WINTER settled over the Army outpost at Council Bluffs and the Engineer Cantonment just down the river, the Yellowstone seemed very far away, and even the Mandan Village was remote. The expedition had been slow and costly. The failure of the steamboats and the financial difficulties of the contractor had brought criticism. The ever-increasing economic distress, from which the West suffered even more keenly than the East, had led many to wonder if the cost of such pioneering was indeed justified. All these complaints and criticisms were enlarged and hammered home by the Missouri press under Benton's guidance, and slowly the original sentiment in favor of the expedition began to change.

Calhoun had lost no part of his faith in the venture, but he realized that its complete fulfilment would have to wait. The post on the Yellowstone was given up, and plans were made to occupy the Mandan Village only after another intermediate station could be garrisoned. For surely it was more important to have these far-flung outposts of a rising empire firmly and peacefully established, at the cost of speed, than to rush them and invite destructive opposition.[1]

On other fronts, however, the vast military program seemed to be moving smoothly. At the junction of the Minnesota and Mississippi Rivers, temporary barracks already stood on the site soon to be occupied by Fort Snelling. A splendid military road eighty feet wide had been completed between Detroit and Fort Meigs, a few miles southwest of the spot where Toledo now stands: such a road as might have averted the first disaster of the War of 1812, had it been in existence eight years earlier. Another road from Columbia, Tennessee, across Alabama and Mississippi to Madisonville, Louisiana, near the head of Lake Pontchartrain, was well advanced; and a third link in the system of military communications had been started between Plattsburg and Sackett's Harbor by way of French Mills (now Fort Covington) on the Salmon River and Morristown on the St. Lawrence.

The fortifications program too was well under way.[2] The appropriation for the first year had been made without question, and $650,000 had already been spent on various projects by the beginning of 1820. Fortress Monroe, a massive, seven-sided structure which was to mount 250 cannon, had not yet been started, but wharves, roads, machinery, workshops and barracks were complete, and material for the fort itself was ready. The stone foundations of Fort Calhoun, which was to round out the defenses of Norfolk and cut off the mouth of the James River, already showed above high water, though laid on a shoal from one and one-half to three fathoms below the bay. On them would rest a tower battery with three tiers of casemates, which like Fortress Monroe a mile away was to mount 250 cannon.

Far to the south Mobile Bay was to be defended by twin forts, pentagonal in shape and each carrying 118 guns, which could rake the five-mile-wide harbor mouth. One was to be on Mobile Point, the other on Dauphin Island. Neither had yet proceeded beyond the excavation stage, but much of the building material had been accumulated. Existing batteries about New Orleans were to be supplemented by smaller forts at Chef Menteur and Rigolets, commanding the entrance to Lake Pontchartrain and hence the northern approach to the city. The work at Rigolets had been started but had not progressed beyond the delivery of materials.

Forts Monroe and Calhoun were farthest advanced because of their strategic importance in the defense of Chesapeake Bay and of the Capital. These two were being built under a series of special contracts for materials and services. Each of the others was provided for in a single contract, under which the builder furnished both workmen and materials and was bonded for a sufficient sum to insure performance. Supervision of the work, however, remained in the hands of the Army Engineers.

For the first time in its history the United States had a thoroughgoing military policy, which appeared in a fair way to be carried out; but beneath the surface were personal animosities and jealousies and ambitions, sectional rivalries, and the kind of provincial

myopia from which Americans have always suffered with respect
to Europe and the world at large.

2

Save only for the rising discontent over the Missouri expedition,
the program was well received by the masses, whom it touched
more widely and more directly than most of the other activities of
government. Calhoun himself, with his youth and energy, his winning manners, and his truly national outlook, was also popular, and
it must have occurred to Adams and to Crawford at about the same
time that he might become by 1824 a dangerous rival. Each moved
in his own way to forestall that possibility.

Adams' way was to offer Calhoun the mission to France, which
Gallatin had expressed a desire to relinquish. He expected, he told
his young colleague, "more from him than from any other man
living, to the benefit of the public service of this nation," and he
thought that a tour of duty abroad would have a broadening influence.[3] The ultimate benefit to Calhoun would absolve Adams,
before his own conscience at least, of any intention merely to put
a rival out of the way. Naturally enough, however, the Carolinian
declined, saying simply that he could not afford it. Even had there
been no financial bar, an ambitious man could hardly have been
expected to give up a post which was bringing him widespread and
favorable notice for one in which he would, for all practical purposes, be buried.

Crawford's way was equally characteristic of the man. It was a
direct frontal attack, through his adherents in Congress, on the
whole defense program which appeared to be the source of Calhoun's popularity. Crawford too was doubtless sincere, for the depression was deepening day by day, and as revenues fell off, it was
increasingly necessary to find ways of reducing expenses. The military program was a large item in the budget. If trimming it should
react against the Secretary of War, was that any fault of the
Treasury?

The first move in this direction came on the day after Adams had
made his offer of the French mission and was in effect a resumption
of the Seminole inquiry. Again it was Lewis Williams who rose in

the House to call for information. He understood that a deserter
had been executed without trial by the commander at Pensacola,
and he wanted a report on all punishments inflicted in the Army
contrary to regulations since 1815. Lowndes pointed out that a
court-martial had already been ordered for the guilty officer in the
Florida case, but Williams was unsatisfied and his resolution was
adopted.[4]

For the next six weeks, or until the historic Missouri debate began late in January, scarcely a day went by that did not see a new
resolution pass the House, calling upon the Secretary of War for
information or explanation or authorizing an investigation of some
phase of the department's program. Members wanted a report on
the administration of the pension act of 1818, and the request was
so worded as to imply fraud on the part of the War Department.
They wanted a statement on the fortifications built or begun since
the beginning of 1816, with full particulars as to plans, expenditures and contractual arrangements. They wanted to know what
objects were intended by the Yellowstone expedition and how much
money had been and was to be spent in connection with it. They
wanted copies of the rules and regulations under which the department was paying for property destroyed by enemy action during
the war; and they wanted the Secretary to have prepared and laid
before the House at its next session "a system of martial law, and
a system of field service and police, for the government of the Army
of the United States."

It was not yet Christmas, but Calhoun was already obliged to
ask that four additional clerks be temporarily attached to his office,
to take care of the enormous amount of additional clerical work
thus being piled up.[5]

The request was laid on the table, and the House reassembled
after the holiday still bent on finding out some weak spot in the
military program. Before the first month of the new year was out,
the Crawford managers had engineered resolutions asking the cost
of the Military Academy to the Government, and how many cadets
from each state had matriculated there; what moneys appropriated
to the War Department remained unspent, and for what purpose
they were destined; and the aggregate strength of the military
establishment by years since the war, broken down by classes of

service. The campaign of harassment reached a peak on January 10, 1820, when the House resolved "to inquire into the expediency of reducing, or entirely stopping, the military fortifications," and at the same time requested a report on the precise nature and terms of the contract let by the Quartermaster General for supplying the expedition then ascending the Missouri River.

A week before the passage of the latter resolution, Colonel Richard M. Johnson had taken his seat in the Senate, but even though no longer in the House, he could not allow so open a thrust at his brother and himself to pass unchallenged. In a brief speech of January 12, to his own motion looking to the improvement of the system of Indian trade, he took occasion to voice the sentiment of the West in favor of the whole frontier policy. As to economy, he thought it necessary only to glance at the War Department's records to be "fully satisfied that the most rigid economy has been uniformly observed ever since the administration of it devolved upon the present incumbent."[6]

The Committee on Military Affairs had meanwhile submitted a statement from Quartermaster General Jesup showing that $200,-000 had already been spent on the Missouri and Mississippi expeditions, and that another $250,000 would be spent in the next three years. When the cost of maintaining the same forces at their normal stations was deducted, however, the statement showed a net gain to the Government, over the four years included, of some $40,000. The practice of having the troops at the Western posts raise most of their own food was expected to save in that time enough to cover the cost of transporting the soldiers to their new stations.[7]

John Cocke of Tennessee, who had been one of the prime movers in previous inquiries directed at the War Department, termed the report unsatisfactory and, taking due note of Colonel Johnson's remarks, pushed another resolution through the House on January 24, calling for a report on all moneys actually paid to James Johnson under his supply contract and on the circumstances under which the contract was awarded.

There for the time being the matter rested, while Congress devoted the next month to the most critical question that had arisen since the formation of the Union: the extension or restriction of slavery. The pause gave Calhoun an opportunity to catch up with the demands made upon his department and to prepare himself for the next onslaught, which was not long in coming.

3

No sooner was the Missouri question out of the way than Congress returned to the attack, bent on reducing military expenditures and cutting down the Army. Nor can they be altogether blamed. An election was coming in the fall, and hard-pressed constituents the country over were struggling to make ends meet while property values, wages and money itself continued to fall. So the Army, accepted only on sufferance in the best of times, was presented as the very symbol of central power—the despotic creature of a government that had already robbed the people through the unholy manipulations of its bank. Then, as all too often since, the welfare of the country and even its vital defenses were placed second to re-election.

Despite the heavy burden placed upon him by almost continuous calls from the House for information, Calhoun managed somehow to keep up with the demands; and however unpalatable they might be to some, his reports left no loophole for attack up to the time of the Missouri debate. There was one point, however, at which the department, if not its Secretary personally, appeared vulnerable; and that point was soon ferreted out. An anonymous letter reached the President calling attention to various alleged instances of maladministration, particularly on the part of the Engineers, and charging specifically that Major Christopher Van Deventer, the Chief Clerk, was financially interested in a contract awarded in the summer of 1818 to Elijah Mix for supplying stone at Old Point Comfort and the Rip Rap Shoal.[8] Calhoun recalled at once an incident that had taken place shortly after the contract in question had been let, and the Chief Clerk was promptly sent for. The facts appear to have been about as follows:

Mix and Van Deventer had married sisters, and the latter regarded his brother-in-law as an able and enterprising businessman. Van Deventer had no hand whatever in awarding the contract, that being a matter entirely in the hands of the Engineer Department which did not pass through the Secretary's office in advance; but he had no doubt of Mix's entire competence to perform it. In view of Mix's character as it was later revealed, however, it seems highly probable that the contractor meant from the start to capitalize on the relationship.

The fixed custom of the day, established in the War Department long before Calhoun's time, was not to advertise for bids but merely to notify a few competent individuals who were asked to make proposals. By accident or otherwise Mix happened to be passing Old Point Comfort on his way to Washington during July of 1818 and learned there that contracts were soon to be awarded for fortifications to be built in the neighborhood. He applied to the Engineer Department for details and entered a bid to supply between 100,000 and 150,000 perches of stone at three dollars a perch. The bid was the lowest received and was regarded by the Engineers as an unusually favorable one for the Government, as indeed it was, for the stone had to be of special quality for use under water. The contract was signed July 25, 1818, by Mix and General Swift, with Van Deventer as witness, subject of course to the necessary posting of bond.

Mix must have known perfectly well that his financial standing would never be approved by a bondsman, particularly in view of the fact that the contract appeared to be a losing one as prices of stone and labor then stood, but he kept his knowledge to himself until the contract was signed. Then he approached Van Deventer, explained his situation, and offered to sell his brother-in-law a one-fourth interest in the contract. Van Deventer went at once to Calhoun and, without going into details as to why he wished it, asked if he could legitimately accept Mix's offer. The Secretary's reply was that "it would not be illegal as there was no law to prohibit it," but he thought it would expose the Chief Clerk to "improper insinuations" and would be injurious. Van Deventer nevertheless did buy the proffered quarter-interest in the contract, though he was careful not to tell Calhoun he had done so. Another quarter-interest was disposed of in Norfolk, and with his cash reserves thus bolstered, Mix got his surety and proceeded with his work.

The contract continued to be a losing one, and in April 1819 Van Deventer was constrained to buy a further quarter-share to save his

original investment and perhaps also to avoid having his connection
with the affair revealed. He was becoming increasingly uneasy,
however, both because of the liability he had incurred and because
he was aware that he had acted without Calhoun's knowledge and
contrary to his advice in a matter that might well involve the department, should Mix default. The growing hard times saved him, for
by the fall of 1819 the cost of freight and labor had so declined
as to make the contract profitable, and he lost no time in unloading
his interest in it. Mix bought back one of Van Deventer's two
quarter-shares in October 1819, and the other was taken by the
father-in-law of the two men in January 1820.

Shortly thereafter Calhoun became aware for the first time that
his Chief Clerk had been dealing in departmental contracts, when
the anonymous letter already mentioned was turned over to him by
the President. He summoned Van Deventer, listened to his explanation, and then informed him, in the presence of a witness, that
should it ever become necessary for the department to make any
decision regarding the Mix contract, the Chief Clerk would have
to go.

Meanwhile, by way of a flanking movement in support of the
frontal attack represented by the letter to Monroe, a press and
whispering campaign began, tending to throw discredit on the work
for which the stone being supplied by Mix was intended. "Castle
Calhoun" was denounced as extravagant and unnecessary, and the
whole fortifications system of which it was a part was questioned.[9]

When the affair had been thoroughly aired in the public prints,
the House called upon the Secretary of War for copies of all construction contracts entered into by his Department since 1815, with
full details as to the manner of making the awards, the solvency of
the contractors and the quality of the performance.[10]

The excitement had already spread to New York, where General
Swift, speaking to a Republican mass meeting in Flatbush, denounced the whole assault on the War Department as a political
move by "Mr. Crawford's friends in Washington." The General
was appointed to a resolutions committee, which promptly affirmed
its high approval of the administration and its full confidence in the
President, the Vice President, "and in the persons composing the
cabinet of the Executive."[11]

4

Crawford's friends proved stronger in Congress than they were in Brooklyn, and they were aided by more than one member whose motives for doing so had nothing whatever to do with the political ambitions of the Secretary of the Treasury. The storm broke in full force on the eighth of March. The House was sitting as a Committee of the Whole when Cannon of Tennessee moved to reduce the total strength of the Army, including officers, noncommissioned officers and musicians, to five thousand men. For reasons of his own, Clay voiced his agreement, asking only that the question be postponed until the Foreign Relations Committee reported on Spain's failure to ratify the Florida treaty. His hold on his own state was threatened by Johnson, who had split with him over the Seminole affair, and Johnson was identified with the military program. So too was Andrew Jackson, who was the Speaker's most dangerous Western rival.

The postponement was in name only, for the House turned immediately to the military appropriations bill. The War Department budget had already been drastically cut by the Committee on Ways and Means, now under the chairmanship of the veteran Samuel Smith of Maryland. The allowance for clothing the Army was cut by a third, while Calhoun's estimate of a million and a half dollars for coastal fortifications, based on existing contracts, had been halved. The Dauphin Island fort which would command one of the two entrances to Mobile Bay, and without which the battery guarding the other entrance would be useless, was eliminated altogether.[12] Even this, however, did not satisfy the insurgents.

The first item in the bill was for support of the Military Academy, which Cannon proposed to abolish on the ground that it merely created a "privileged military order." He was followed by Williams of North Carolina, who saw no reason for including a sum to pay recruitment bounties to bring the Army to authorized strength. He thought it was already quite large enough. Then Slocumb, a Federalist member from the same state, charged the War Department with having "loaned to bankrupts" powder and lead valued at $240,000, though a report laid before the House in February had shown that three-quarters of this amount had gone to the entirely solvent firm of Du Pont and Company on terms highly favorable to the Government, and the rest was by no means yet lost. All the transactions, moreover, had taken place before Calhoun entered the department.[13]

Presently the discussion widened to include the size and disposition of the Army, which a New Hampshire member thought "too large and uselessly employed," with a disproportionately large staff. "It would take longer to collect this army, which was scattered about like the sheep of the shepherd among the hills—to bring them from the Yellow Stone, and the remote corners of the earth— than to raise up a new army." With that perhaps Calhoun would have agreed, but he certainly would have pointed out that this very necessity for keeping the Army stationed at distant and widely scattered places was precisely the reason why its numbers should not be reduced.

Since Calhoun was not there to answer for himself, however, his friend and successor in the House, Eldred Simkins, answered for him, not neglecting to suggest that recent wholly unwarranted increases in the pension fund had better be removed before the vital defenses of the nation were impaired. But the economy bloc was not to be silenced by mere reference to its own inconsistency. Cannon returned to the charge, followed by Williams; and the burden of both was that a republic was best defended by a citizen army, that fortifications need not be fully manned, if indeed they need be manned at all, in peacetime, and that there was no danger whatever of foreign war: all this despite the collapse of the Florida treaty, the rising power and admitted hostility of the Holy Alliance and British rivalry for the fur trade in the Northwest.

Next day, after an interruption only long enough to receive the promised report on Spanish relations, the subject was resumed and a determined effort was made to trim still further the allocation for coastal defenses. Arguments to prove that Congress had indeed sanctioned the program and was therefore bound by the contracts of the War Department produced only a denunciation of what members chose to call "legislating by executive departments" and "exceeding appropriations." Clay agreed with Williams that Congress had no liability for Executive agreements, or even for the commitments of previous Congresses, and the sum proposed by Ways and Means was accepted.

Before the bill was passed the Missouri expedition, too, came under fire, and after two days of wrangling, fifty thousand dollars was cut from the sum allotted to the Quartermaster's department, with the specific intention of stopping the expedition where it was.

Calhoun's efforts to get the more important items increased in the Senate [14] were unavailing, save only that Johnson managed to restore the appropriation for the Missouri expedition. The House, however, refused to accept the change and the Senate at last yielded despite all the not disinterested Kentuckian could do.

The expedition went no farther than Council Bluffs.

5

The nervous strain suffered by Calhoun during those middle weeks of March 1820 was not wholly due to the Congressional attack on his military program. In the interval between the passage of the Missouri Compromise and the beginning of the House debate, his little daughter Elizabeth, not yet five months old, fell ill. What appeared at first to be a cold soon took a serious turn, and within a week hope was virtually abandoned. The child died on March 22, after a painful and racking illness of sixteen days.

They were days of contrast that must have set the young father to speculating anew on the ways and wellsprings of political power; for while all his works were being castigated by the Representatives of the people in Congress, he and his pretty wife were receiving the high tribute of personal devotion. Fashionable ladies vied with each other for the privilege of nursing the ailing child, and busy Government officials hovered anxiously about the Calhoun home. President Monroe himself called daily, and his daughter, Mrs. Hay, insisted upon sitting with the stricken infant evening after evening although the bridal festivities for her younger sister were not yet over. Mrs. Adams also attended faithfully, and many more. The ebullient Margaret Bayard Smith hurried into the city as soon as she heard of Elizabeth's illness, but found the crowd of well-wishers and the offers of service already so great as to be actually injurious to the patient. Nor was it "mere tribute to rank," if Mrs.

Smith's judgment may be credited, but rather a spontaneous expression of good will toward a couple universally beloved.[15]

On the same day that little Elizabeth Calhoun died, the Capital was shocked by news of the duel between Stephen Decatur and Commodore John Barron, whose conduct as commander of the hapless *Chesapeake* Decatur had branded as cowardly. In the evening the popular, gallant and admired Decatur died and the whole city put on mourning.

Both Calhoun and Floride were exhausted by their long siege, but the press of work arising from the demands of Congress could not be avoided, even temporarily. Calhoun was at his office the next day as usual, perhaps glad to turn his thoughts and energies into other channels, while William Lowndes, with the unobtrusive indispensability of genuine friendship, made the necessary arrangements for the funeral.[16]

6

It was a bleak spring indeed that invaded the Capital in 1820, not alone because the angel of death rode with it. The fate of free government and of the Union itself hung in the balance as thoughtful men watched the Era of Good Feeling break down into partisan bickering and sectional strife. Even in foreign relations, where national unity is most of all essential, there was no common ground on which all Americans could stand. The Florida treaty remained unratified by Spain, and the slavery agitation had given it new significance.

The principle of sectional balance in the Senate was established by the simultaneous admission of Maine and Missouri, yet the vast bulk of lands still held in common by the nation lay north of the compromise line and so were closed to settlement by holders of slaves. Inevitably the South cast about for regions from which corresponding slave states could be carved. Aside from Arkansas, which already had territorial status, only Florida and Texas were available; yet the treaty which would extend American sovereignty over Florida seemed about to collapse, and should it be carried into effect it would by its own terms mean renunciation of any claim to Texas. The country between the Sabine and the Rio Grande had long been a magnet to adventurous spirits from the West and South alike. It had been in part explored late in 1818 by a small group of American officers and men acting under Calhoun's orders,[17] and he was loath to give it up, but he held Florida the more important to the defense of the nation and feared that both could not be acquired without war. Adams, too, thought the treaty he had made the best obtainable, and Monroe would not risk the hostility of the Northern states by seeking more potential slave territory at such a time.[18]

The terms of the treaty were hardly made known before Western interests, led by Clay in Congress and Benton in the Missouri press, began attacking the abandonment of Texas; and when Spain failed to ratify within the specified time, Clay proposed to reconsider the whole business. The move was not unrelated to the rival Presidential aspirations of the Speaker and the Secretary of State.[19] To add to the complexity of the problem, a revolution broke out in Spain in January. Such was the situation when Lowndes, speaking for the Committee on Foreign Relations, recommended that Florida be occupied forthwith as indemnity for spoliations.[20]

Congress was too busy curtailing the activities of the Army to consider taking any action that might require that Army to be used, and news of the success of the Spanish revolution offered a reasonable excuse to postpone a decision until another session. Again the Crawford and Clay forces joined, and on the Speaker's motion a resolution was passed directing the Secretary of War to report at the beginning of the next session "a plan for the reduction of the army to six thousand officers, non-commissioned officers, musicians, and privates." Only the Engineer Corps was excluded.[21]

CHAPTER XVII

THE CAMPAIGN BEGINS

1

OPPOSITION to the War Department program on the part of the Radicals, as the followers of Crawford were called, was directly connected with the Presidential succession. There was an appeal to the old Jeffersonians of the South in the argument against consolidation; economy might win support from the conservative business men of the East; and the prejudices of the debtor West might be turned to account by associating Calhoun with the Bank of the United States.

The attack on the Secretary of War, however, was only the negative side of Crawford's campaign. At a caucus early in April 1820 the Radicals tried unsuccessfully to substitute their candidate for Monroe as the party standard bearer; and before Congress adjourned they secured the passage of a law limiting the bulk of Presidential appointments to four years' duration. Though ostensibly an administrative measure to insure strict accountability, the law was made retroactive so that officeholders would begin seeking reappointments in the fall, and it was noteworthy that a majority of them would need the recommendation of the Secretary of the Treasury.[1]

John Quincy Adams, meanwhile, had been shown a letter from Judge Nathaniel Pope of Illinois, addressed to young Daniel Pope Cook, the judge's nephew and the state's lone Representative in Congress. It dealt with Illinois politics and showed, so the recipient noted in his diary, "how industriously Crawford is working there, as well as in every other part of the Union, by the means of his appointments, to promote his own future views, and says explicitly that if I have any future expectations I must interfere directly with the appointments. John Pope wrote much the same thing two years ago from Kentucky." Then he added, perhaps meditatively, that he had "hitherto scarcely interfered with any appointments, and in no instance with a view to provide for a political partisan."

Adams did not mean, of course, that he made no appointments, nor that he recommended no office seekers to the President. Monroe's practice was to consult his advisers when a vacancy occurred, and in general to name the candidate recommended by the particular Secretary most concerned. Thus diplomatic and consular offices were so far within Adams' control that he felt free, as we have seen, to offer the French Ministry to Calhoun without consulting the President. The State Department printing, including printing of the laws, was also his to award; and even outside his own department his influence was considered great enough to bring upon him almost daily visits from office-seeking Congressmen or their friends.

If Adams did not use his patronage for partisan ends, it was not because he had no patronage at his command, but because his own self-delusion was complete and all-embracing. What he chose to regard as a difference in principle was in fact only a difference in terminology. Where others sought plums for political partisans, Adams sought only to fill all public offices with the best and ablest men. But the "best men" were naturally those whose views were akin to his own; and he never for one moment doubted that when the time came they would support the Presidential aspirations of John Quincy Adams. To question that would have been to doubt his own merit and perhaps the justice of Divine Providence as well.

Cook was followed by Timothy Fuller of Massachusetts, whose daughter Margaret was to be his chief claim to fame, but the story was the same. Maine had been "sold" to Crawford, and Adams, for his own sake and that of his following, must reply in kind. "He asked me whether, as the slave-holder was buying up auxiliaries in our camp, some assistance against him could not be drawn from his side—how Calhoun and South Carolina were disposed? I told him that of Calhoun's disposition I knew nothing. . . ."[2] He was aware, however, that the young War Secretary perceived and resented the partisan motive behind the criticism of his department, and it was reasonable to suppose that resentment against Crawford could be turned into support for Adams.

2

Calhoun's strength in his native state was certainly increasing, in spite of the dominance Crawford's party still held over it, and would be no meager accession for any candidate. Both South Carolina Senators, John Gaillard and William Smith, had voted with the Radicals on the Army appropriation, and Smith was under Treasury orders on all questions; but the younger men, who were gradually taking over the places of power, were largely Calhoun's friends. His cousin and former law partner, Patrick Noble, was speaker of the state House of Representatives; his brother-in-law, John Ewing Calhoun, was a candidate for the next legislature; Robert Y. Hayne was Attorney General; and Joel R. Poinsett and George McDuffie were slated for seats in Congress.

McDuffie's relationship to Calhoun was intimate and personal. At the age of ten, an unknown and desperately poor Georgia country boy, he secured a job in James Calhoun's Augusta store, where he demonstrated marked ability and qualities of character no less striking. After two years in the store, James passed his young protégé along to William Calhoun's plantation, where he could attend Dr. Waddel's school and eventually South Carolina College. In due time he became law partner of Eldred Simkins in Edgefield; and now, after serving an apprenticeship in the state legislature, he was to succeed without opposition to Simkins' seat in Congress.

Calhoun's strength was growing in other quarters also. His cousin, Andrew Pickens, recently Governor of South Carolina, had emigrated to Alabama, where he and Charles Tait, now a Federal Judge, were rapidly acquiring influence. In the West his championship of internal improvements and a general desire for military protection overbalanced dissatisfaction in Missouri and the opposition of the fur interests. Even in the New England states, where antagonism to the rule of the South was strongest, he had a surprising number of friends. His defense of their commerce during the war led Northern merchants to regard him with favor, while the manufacturers of New England and Pennsylvania looked upon him as committed to their own tariff views.

Adams played in his mind with men, as on a chessboard, countering Clay in the West with Andrew Jackson and checking Crawford in the South with Calhoun. The one he would have for Vice President, the other for Secretary of State. But neither had yet been informed of his role in the Adams plans, and there were those who looked to each as having claims of his own upon the gratitude of his country. It was not long, of course, before the question was broached to Calhoun, who stated his mind in a long letter to Tait.

"The importance which you attach to the good and harmonious conduct of myself, and a few other individuals, I cannot but think is over estimated," he wrote. "The prosperity of our country never has, perhaps, depended much on the conduct of any single individual. Those rise whose principles and conduct are congenial to a majority of the people. . . . My politics, I think I may say with perfect truth, has been a system founded on certain fixed principles; and to carry them into effect has been my highest ambition. I would despise myself, if I were to change this noble object for the mean one of personal aggrandizement. Provided our country be free, powerful and moderate in her councils, I care not whether I have the principal sway, or not. With these principles, I hope and believe, there is not much danger of collision. . . ."[3]

But it would not be possible to avoid collision much longer. Crawford was already sure in his own mind that Calhoun meant to support Adams if he did not run himself, and in either case he was bound to interfere.

3

The Johnson contracts threatened to leave the War Secretary vulnerable. Through no fault of his own, but because of the President's interposition, the advances had been excessive. Johnson, moreover, had been given new contracts, though with great reluctance, by the Quartermaster General, in the hope that with renewed credit and returning prosperity he could recoup his and the department's losses. The hope was vain. By spring of 1820 the advances totaled well over three hundred thousand dollars, which was almost a hundred thousand more than the contracts would have called for had they been faithfully performed. Yet Johnson, on his way home after the adjournment of Congress, wrote from Cumberland that an additional twenty-five thousand would be essential to keep his brother going! Before Calhoun could reply he learned from Colonel Atkinson of another Johnson failure.[4]

When the Secretary refused, as tactfully as he could, to extend further credit, Johnson once more took his complaint to the President. His argument was frankly political. He needed the money to silence his foes, who were also the foes of the administration. For two years and more he had carried the Republican cause in Kentucky, almost alone, for which he thought some consideration was due. And by way of indicating the extent of his political power he revealed that his brother John would be sent to Congress in the fall without opposition. Monroe turned the letter over to Calhoun, who could only repeat that the advances already exceeded the amount of the contracts.[5]

The whole case had already been submitted to arbitration, the Johnsons claiming that since the actual cost of transportation up the Missouri was higher than could have been anticipated, they were entitled to more than the contract called for; and a very generous award had been made.[6] A dispute quickly arose, however, over interpretation of the arbiters' decision, which was still awaiting clarification when Johnson wrote again to Calhoun. He enclosed evidence to show that the transportation account would amount to forty tons more than estimated, on the basis of which he had drawn twenty thousand dollars on the War Department. He hinted delicately that if the contract would not cover, another contract for the next year would be in order, and closed with assurance that while Kentucky had been going "headlong to the devil" when he got home, he had since stumped the state, and all was now right again. Two weeks later came a statement from James Johnson showing forty thousand dollars to be due him still, though the books of the Quartermaster General and of the Treasury told a very different tale. When the Secretary refused to give ground, Johnson bluntly accused him of hostile intentions and threatened to seek Congressional intervention.[7]

In the midst of the controversy Calhoun left the city for a week, and it may be that he called upon the aged Sage of Monticello, Thomas Jefferson.[8] Aside from that brief interval, however, he had had no respite since his illness in December. By the time the humid midsummer arrived, he was physically and mentally exhausted. Yet still official duties kept him at his desk. Applications for pensions continued to pour in under a revision of the law which in effect required the Secretary of War to re-examine every case covered by the act of 1818, and Calhoun insisted upon a rigid construction despite the disappointments and complaints that were certain to follow. He had, moreover, only until winter to prepare a plan for the reduction of the Army.

The affairs of the Johnsons he wisely passed along to the President, noting that transportation contracts so far awarded the Senator's brother would "probably about square with the advances," but that he would "fall greatly indebted to the government on his provision contracts for 1815, '17, '18." Only contracts for the last year, of course, were of Calhoun's doing, and the excessive advances on them had been ordered by Monroe. This, however, he forbore to mention, adding only his own impression "that to avoid all censure" the contract now sought "ought to be made on publick proposals."[9]

In the same letter to the President he declined an invitation to vacation at some springs near Monroe's Loudoun County estate. He had determined, by way of holiday, "to take an excursion as far as West Point, or perhaps as far as Niagara," thus combining relaxation with an official survey of fortifications he had not as yet seen, providing, of course, he could find time to get away at all.

No doubt he had other reasons, too, for seeking a Northern trip. He wanted to get a firsthand impression of Northern sentiment on the sectional and partisan issues debated at the last two sessions of Congress. He wanted to find out for himself how the people of New York really felt about the fortifications program, and he wanted to consult General Brown on the impending Army reduction. Perhaps also in the back of his mind was another question of more personal import, in connection with the views of his Southern friends: he wanted to see how the populous Northern cities felt about John C. Calhoun.

4

It was the middle of August before he finally managed to get out of Washington, headed vaguely in the direction of "the Lakes," while Floride and her mother stayed behind to look after the children. With him went Peter Hagner, Third Auditor of the Treasury, and Major Roberdeau of the Topographical Engineers. After a brief stop in New York they embarked by steamboat for Albany, where they were joined by General Brown and his staff.[10] The next two weeks saw them at Ballston Springs, Utica and Buffalo, and on the morning of September 3 the guns of Fort Niagara boomed in salute to the Secretary of War.

On the way to the falls, Calhoun had found time for a visit with his friend and former colleague, General Peter B. Porter, a power in New York State politics, even though he had lost the Governorship in 1817.

Fort Niagara was little more than a ruin, according to newspaper accounts, though blockhouse and barracks were in good repair. The Canadian fort opposite, however, was strong and well built, with a garrison three or four times that of the American post. It was a state of things made almost inevitable by the penny-wise policy of Congress, but Calhoun must have been greatly heartened at the way the local citizens resented it.[11]

From Niagara Falls the party went down Lake Ontario to Sackett's Harbor, where new and imposing works were under construction, then on to Montreal and down Lake Champlain to Plattsburg.[12] Calhoun's original plan had been to proceed from Plattsburg directly to New York City, where preparations were already being made for his reception; but somewhere along the route he changed his mind and went instead to Boston.

It was the evening of September 15, a Friday, when he entered the city, as quietly as possible so that he might get a night's sleep before the round of official calls began. It was sorely needed, for the three days he spent in Boston were full indeed. After a morning call on the Governor at Medford, he inspected Fort Independence, where he received the salute, and Fort Warren, after which he dined with Jeremiah Mason, Federalist Senator from New Hampshire in the Fourteenth and Fifteenth Congresses. Before he left, he visited the Navy Yard at Charlestown, inspected numerous manufacturing establishments in the vicinity, and spent a day with Daniel Webster.

The day with Webster was devoted to something more than

official business, though it began with an inspection of Watertown Arsenal. George Ticknor, at least, recalled that on their return the two men spent hours together driving about the neighborhood in a phaeton; and later, at dinner, Calhoun was guest of honor with a large group of prominent Bostonians present. "Mr. Calhoun talked much and most agreeably at table," Ticknor reported, "and it was evident to all of us that Mr. Webster desired to draw him out and show him under the most favorable aspects to his friends. After dinner, a considerable number of young men, particularly of the young lawyers of the town, came in and were presented to Mr. Calhoun." The impression they got, though no overt word was said, was that Webster wanted Calhoun to be the next President of the United States.[13]

The Secretary left Boston abruptly the morning of the nineteenth and four days later was in New York, having visited Springfield and New Haven on the way. It so happened that genial William Wirt, the Attorney General, had reached New York the day before on business of his own, but he readily accepted an invitation to accompany Calhoun on a tour of the forts in the harbor. They set out in good faith with a committee of local dignitaries, but instead of to the forts they were carried without their knowledge and against their will to a silk factory on Staten Island. There they were detained the entire day, while the soldiers at the forts were kept under arms the whole of a warm September Saturday momentarily awaiting the arrival of the Secretary of War. It was dark before Calhoun and Wirt were returned to Manhattan, where they discovered that the afternoon papers had a full account of their adventure.[14] From the New York *American* one would gather that the two Cabinet members had made a special trip to New York for the sole purpose of visiting the silk-dyeing establishment of Messrs. Barrett, Tillotson and Company on Staten Island.

Through it all Calhoun appeared unruffled. Early Monday morning he was at the Battery to review an artillery brigade and a little later received the homage of parading troops in front of the City Hall. He also found time to visit the Navy Yard in Brooklyn before appearing as guest of honor at a dinner given by the Common Council of the city. The New York *Advocate* the next day commented "with great satisfaction" on "the civilities shown to

Mr. Calhoun, whose rapid advancement is the result of talent, industry, and correct moral and political conduct."

He was back in Washington the first of October, his health improved and his spirits revived by the trip. He was convinced that the people of the North as well as those of the South favored the defense program for which he stood, and he had faith that what the people approved the politicians could not indefinitely block.

5

The Northern trip served also to persuade Calhoun that the slavery issue raised in the Missouri debates did not forebode a struggle for power between North and South. He thought it, on the contrary, to be the work of a few ambitious men, mainly in New York and the Middle states, who calculated upon the Northern majority in Congress and in the electoral college to carry them to power.

"We to the South ought not to assent easily to the belief, that there is a conspiracy either against our property, or just weight in the Union," he wrote to Tait soon after his return. "A belief of the former might, and probably would, lead to the most disasterous consequence. Nothing would lead more directly to disunion with all of its horrors. That of the latter would cooperate, as it appears to me, directly with the scheme of the few designing men to the north, who think they see their interest in exciting a struggle between the two portions of our country. If we, from such a belief, systematically oppose the north, they must from necessity resort to a similar opposition to us. Our true system is to look to the country; and to support such measures and such men, without a regard to sections as are best calculated to advance the general interest. . . . Should emancipation be attempted it must, and will be resisted at all costs, but let us be certain first that it is the real object, not by a few, but by a large portion of the non slave holding states."[15]

That Calhoun had underestimated the extent of the cleavage on the Missouri question was evident as soon as Congress convened in November. The first business of the session was the choice of a Speaker to succeed Clay, who found himself prevented by "imperious circumstances" from attending until after Christmas; and it was immediately apparent that in making the choice the House would again be choosing sides on the slavery controversy.

The principal contenders in a struggle that lasted three days were John W. Taylor of New York, leader of the restrictionists, and the South's most able member, William Lowndes. Smith of Maryland and Sergeant of Pennsylvania had just enough strength to keep either Lowndes or Taylor from securing the needed majority. On the seventeenth ballot Lowndes fell short by one vote only, but on the twenty-second attempt Taylor was chosen. The next day Delegate John Scott presented a certified copy of the Constitution of the State of Missouri, which was referred by Taylor to a select committee consisting of his recent opponents for the chair: Lowndes, Smith and Sergeant.

The convention by which the Missouri Constitution was drafted had taken no pains to hide its work, and well in advance of the document itself the news reached Washington that free Negroes were to be excluded from the state. Calhoun and Adams had discussed the provision the day before Congress met, as they rode together to a Cabinet meeting, and the Carolinian had expressed deep concern over the reappearance of a question he had regarded as settled.[16] The article was plainly in violation of the Constitutional guarantee that gave to the citizens of each state the privileges and immunities that would be theirs in any other. Between the date of his discussion with Adams and the report of the House committee, Calhoun talked the whole thing through many times with Lowndes, who in the absence of his family was living with the Calhouns.[17] The conclusion they reached was that embodied in the report which Lowndes offered to the House November 23.

It was judicious and temperate, as was everything Lowndes did, but there was no flinching from the issue. Missouri had been given permission to form a constitution and become a state, and it would be difficult in the extreme to reduce her again to the condition of a territory. She was entitled to equal rights with the other members of the Union, including the right to have her laws evaluated not by Congress but by the courts. The unconditional admission of Missouri was therefore recommended, and the report was accompanied by a resolution to carry the recommendation into effect. Lowndes made it clear, however, that the committee was not unanimous, and the discussion soon revealed the sectional nature of the split. Sergeant was the dissident member. After a week of vigorous and sometimes heated debate early in December, the resolution was rejected by a strictly sectional vote of 93 to 79.

6

Among those who followed this new Missouri debate with the greatest interest were Thomas Hart Benton and David Barton, who had come to Washington to represent that state in the Senate. Born and bred in North Carolina, and allied by blood and by marriage with old Virginia families, Benton was yet as completely identified with the West as was Clay himself. For a time he lived in Tennessee, serving in the state Senate and fighting under Andrew Jackson in the War of 1812. Fearless and self-confident, he had genuine ability with which to back up his boastfulness, and it was not long before he was made the General's aide-de-camp, with the rank of Lieutenant Colonel. But he loved to fight almost as much as his chief, and was quite as unyielding and tenacious. The two were soon at odds with each other. A tavern brawl followed in which Jackson was seriously wounded, and Benton found it expedient to move to St. Louis. There he became publisher of the *Enquirer,* practiced law and in the swaggering manner of the frontier bully killed his man in a duel.

Benton will be remembered as the man who first attacked the Missouri expedition, and his appearance in the Capital boded no good for the War Department. His election had been by the narrowest of margins—a single vote; and there can be little doubt that he owed it to the American Fur Company. Astor's forces had become alarmed by Calhoun's attitude toward the Indian trade, including the tightening of the licensing system; and an act of March 4, 1820, continuing the Government trading houses, had galvanized them into action. Benton's election to the Senate was one result. Another was the arrival in the Capital of an able and experienced lobby, whose first victim seems to have been John Floyd of Virginia. Benton's disingenuous account of their initial operations is worth quoting:

"Two gentlemen (Mr. Ramsay Crooks, of New-York, and Mr.

Russell Farnham, of Massachusetts), who had been in the employment of Mr. John Jacob Astor in founding his colony of Astoria, and carrying on the fur trade on the northwest coast of America, were at Washington that winter, and had their quarters at the same hotel (Brown's), where Dr. Floyd and I had ours. Their acquaintance was naturally made by Western men like us—in fact, I knew them before; and their conversation, rich in information upon a new and interesting country, was eagerly devoured by the ardent spirit of Floyd. He resolved to bring forward the question of occupation [of the Columbia River country], and did so."[18]

Benton most certainly "knew them before," and he knew perfectly well what they were in Washington to accomplish. The occupation of the Oregon country, so that Astor's lucrative fur trade in that area might be fully protected, was only one purpose. The other was the destruction of the Government-operated Indian trading houses.[19]

Floyd's enthusiasm for the wishes of his new friends led him, before he had known them six weeks, to propose in the House the occupation of the Columbia River; and a month later he submitted to the President a detailed report, in the preparation of which Messrs. Crooks and Farnham had doubtless aided. Monroe passed it on to Adams, who pronounced it a "tissue of errors in fact and abortive reasoning, of invidious reflections and rude invectives."[20] It was laid before the House, nevertheless, and was accompanied by a bill that went a great deal farther than the report. For the bill was not confined in its scope to the Columbia River question, but dealt with the whole matter of Indian policy as well. It abolished the factory system, liberalized licensing provisions and set up a whole new method of handling the Indian trade—a method more congenial than the old to the American Fur Company. The bill did not get beyond a second reading, but it served as the opening gun in a determined and ultimately successful campaign.

Benton was in the Senate to help accomplish the same purposes that brought Crooks and Farnham to the Capital, and he was perfectly aware of it. Calhoun as yet was not, but he was conscious of increasing pressure from the West on the whole question of Indian policy. To the now familiar calls for information on every phase of military operations was added a persistent investigation of the affairs of the Indian department.

7

Reduction of expenditures meant to Congress, as it did to the Treasury, the curtailment of the whole military establishment. It had been obvious for some time that the best Calhoun could hope for would be a reduction so carried out as to leave the most vital services not too seriously impaired and to permit as rapid an expansion as possible in case of war—the third war with England, which he still believed to be inescapable. He had already given much thought to the problem when he was instructed by Congress to report a plan for reducing the Army, and over the summer of 1820 he worked out the details. The plan was presented December 12, 1820, in what must still be regarded as one of the ablest of American state papers.[21]

"However remote our situation from the great powers of the world, and however pacific our policy," wrote Calhoun, "we are, notwithstanding, liable to be involved in war; and, to resist, with success, its calamities and dangers, a standing army in peace, in the present improved state of the military science, is an indispensable preparation. The opposite opinion cannot be adopted, without putting to hazard the independence and safety of the country." He praised the militia and acknowledged their importance, but "to suppose our militia capable of meeting in the open field the regular troops of Europe, would be to resist the most obvious truth, and the whole of our experience as a nation. War is an art, to attain perfection in which, much time and experience, particularly for the officers, are necessary." No amount of military genius in a commander or courage in his men can take the place of organization, discipline, training in military tactics.

"The great and leading objects, then, of a military establishment in peace, ought to be to create and perpetuate military skill and experience . . . and the organization of the army ought to be such as to enable the Government, at the commencement of hostilities, to obtain a regular force, adequate to the emergencies of the country, properly organized and prepared for actual service." Only so can the first shock of battle be withstood, and time be gained to enlist and train new troops. Only so can initial disaster, with consequent loss of resources and prestige, be avoided.

Calhoun proposed to retain the staff at full strength and to make no change in the number of regiments, battalions or companies. The reduction from twelve thousand to six thousand men would be carried out simply by reducing the enlisted personnel of each company to half strength, so that in time of war there would be "nothing either to new model or to create." The strength of the Army could be doubled by adding privates to the existing companies, and could be still further augmented by splitting the expanded companies into two, doubling the number of officers and adding more recruits.

The plan was worked out only after suggestions had been asked and received from ranking officers, the most important contributors being Generals Jacob Brown and Winfield Scott, but the broad outline had been in Calhoun's mind since 1815.[22] It was intelligent and workable, and it conceded as much as anyone honestly desiring retrenchment from patriotic rather than partisan motives could reasonably ask. Even the leader of the Radicals in the House, Thomas W. Cobb of Georgia, agreed that it was "the ablest, the most ingenius, and, upon the whole, the best defence of a standing army in time of peace" which he had seen in print.[23]

Yet it was not acceptable to Congress because of the very principle that made it unique: it reduced only the line and left the staff where it was. Had not Jefferson warned against standing armies in time of peace? Had not all free governments from time immemorial been defended by citizen armies, whose love of liberty was equaled only by their courage? No one thought to point out that the United States was at that moment the only free government left on earth, nor to recall that the War of 1812 had been won by seasoned troops at the council table of Ghent rather than by militia on the field of battle.

From aged Timothy Pickering, with whom he had broken more than one lance in Congress, Calhoun received a letter commending his plan; but the members of his own party and his own generation abandoned him. It was not until 1903, more than eighty years later, that a similar organization was put into effect, long after it had become a commonplace in European armies; and the First World War was over before all of the plan was tried.[24]

CHAPTER XVIII

THE GLITTERING CROWN

1

THE rejection of Calhoun's plan for reducing the Army was but an incident in a long and unrelenting siege. The assault upon the War Department begun at the previous session had continued throughout the summer by rumor and innuendo in the press; and in the winter of 1820-1821 the Radicals were joined by Clintonians and Clayites as well. When the military program proved unassailable, they resorted to personal abuse of the Secretary of War. Request followed request for information; the Johnson contracts again came under scrutiny and were once more pronounced wasteful, extravagant and perhaps corrupt; the organization of the Army was ridiculed and its cost denounced. The whole theory of Calhoun's report was held up to scorn by such men as Floyd and Cocke because it presumed to insinuate that free men could not defend their own homes and that an army of officers could. The Military Academy was again condemned, and the Army appropriations offered new ground for the old objections to the whole military establishment and all it stood for. The Army was rendered unnecessary by the fortifications, and the fortifications cost too much.

The mental and physical strain on Calhoun was tremendous, and to his intimates was plainly apparent. In his preoccupation he forgot a dinner engagement with Adams, and his private correspondence and private affairs virtually went by the board until well after the adjournment of Congress.[1] Day after day he was on the defensive, watching his careful and intelligent plans crumbling under partisan attacks, helpless to do anything himself to save them, and knowing that the efforts of Lowndes, Simkins and the few who took his part on the floor of the House were futile. The observer unfamiliar with American customs might have thought Congress a grand inquest sitting in judgment upon usurping magistrates rather than a co-ordinate branch of a threefold sovereignty.

So far as the House was concerned, there was little other business worth its attention until the Army had been reduced and the military expenditures curbed. Even the much-agitated Texas question was subordinated to the crucifixion of Calhoun, and the finally ratified Spanish treaty was allowed to go into effect without more than passing comment. When the session ended with the expiration of the Sixteenth Congress, March 3, 1821, the Army had been reduced to four regiments of artillery and seven regiments of infantry, the number and rank of officers being explicitly stated. Only the Corps of Engineers remained substantially as it was, though its work was lightened by reduced appropriations. The reduction was to be effective June 1.

Military appropriations had been slashed all along the line, without regard to contractual obligations or essential functions. Items for pay, subsistence, clothing and medical services were cut disproportionately, although the reduction in numbers would presumably affect each to the same extent; and new restrictions were placed upon expenditures by the Quartermaster General. The most serious blow, however, was again in the sum allotted for fortifications. The inadequate $800,000 of the previous year was cut to $202,000, plus an unexpended balance of half that amount; and the works for which it could be used and the amounts to be spent on each were enumerated. Only Forts Delaware, Washington, Monroe and Calhoun, and the works at Rigolets and Mobile Point were named. The appropriation for the Indian department had also been halved, with no previous intimation that any cut was contemplated, though the cost of the department had been steadily rising as settlers encroached upon Indian lands in the West and new treaties and annuities were required.

On the final day of the session the members of the Cabinet were with the President at the Capitol, reviewing the bills hastily ground out as the hours and minutes ticked away. When the final gavel fell, the Secretaries of State and War walked home together, just as they had done on previous occasions. Adams noted that Calhoun was "dispirited by the results of the attacks systematically carried on through the whole Congress, but especially through the session

just expired, against his management of the War Department."
The Carolinian attributed his difficulties to the repeal of the internal
taxes and the too liberal pension act of Monroe's first year in office;
but he did not fail to note the apparent coalition of Crawford, Clinton and Clay in opposition.

Adams himself laid chief blame on Crawford and wrote in his
diary that "all the attacks against the War Department during this
Congress have been stimulated by him and promoted by his partisans. An essential impulse to this course on his part is the knowledge he has obtained that Calhoun is not prepared to support him
for the next Presidency." And almost as an afterthought he added:
"It has been the policy of all the parties to keep hostilities in reserve
against me this session, and to assail the War Department as an
outwork. . . ."[2]

2

With Monroe safely re-elected, by as near a unanimous vote as
any President save George Washington ever received, he passed
from the stage as an active political power. Nothing more was to
be expected of him in the way of patronage, and he was too weak
as a party leader to be worth cultivating for any influence he might
be supposed to have. The scramble for place was in full swing.
The opposition was factional, and even those who supported the
existing policies were divided among themselves. The old republicanism of the Revolutionary epoch was giving way before the
economic and social forces of the nineteenth century. The heredi-
tary planter and merchant ruling class was being replaced by a
newly arrived class of manufacturers, artisans and Western ad-
venturers, who called themselves "the people" and the form of
government that gave them power "democracy."

When Monroe took his oath for the second time and settled back
content to ride out his second term as gracefully as possible, Calhoun was not yet in the field. Both Adams and Crawford had
earlier feared his potential rivalry, but both seem to have decided
by 1821 that he would not run until a later time. So Adams
throughout the year made pointed overtures to win Calhoun's sup-

port, and Crawford, watching cynically, assumed they had succeeded.[3]

When Adams completed his scholarly and illuminating Report on Weights and Measures he offered it for criticism to Calhoun alone;[4] and a few days after the session ended Ninian Edwards, now Senator from Illinois, sounded out the Carolinian on Adams' behalf. He reported his disposition "excellent" and that he "had no views to himself for the next Presidency."[5] The New Englander took it as a commitment and made use of it accordingly.

After a Cabinet meeting later in the month, at which a decision to abandon the uncompleted fort at Dauphin Island was made, he came out of his shell to approach his colleague directly. "I spoke to Mr. Calhoun of the decision at the Cabinet meeting yesterday," he wrote next day in his diary, "and told him that on this or any other . . . subject of general consultation by the whole Administration, if he had any preference of views with regard to measures, I should always take pleasure in concurring with them and supporting them." Calhoun was grateful, but he wanted nothing except the French mission for Lowndes, should Gallatin still intend to retire. His friend's health had been seriously impaired by the strain of the past two sessions, and he thought the change of climate would be beneficial.[6]

Calhoun's reaction to what could only seem to him stupid, shortsighted and purely captious opposition to his defense program was precisely the reaction one might have anticipated. He attributed the attacks on his management of the War Department to Crawford, and he resolved in consequence that Crawford should never be President of the United States if he could prevent it. Neither would he lend support to Clay, who had joined in the opposition to his policy. If that meant coalition with Adams, he was prepared to accept it, though his recent New England visit had led him to doubt Adams' strength in his own country. If it meant he must run himself, he would do that too, but only as a last resort. His ambition was not blind. He must have known as well as anyone else that his chances of winning the highest office would be far better when more years had passed him by.

Equality was the genius of the age. The masses everywhere were surging upward to new political power, carried forward with the

forces released by Watt and Whitney and the others to new opportunities, and to a doubled and redoubled share in material things.
It meant the end of feudalism in Europe, and though Calhoun
would not carry his analysis that far, it spelled the end of slavery
in America. It meant also war and revolution and an ever-present
threat to the United States from the political and economic masters
of the Old World: men who knew that autocracy could not long
endure in any country while one nation remained free. With
British eyes fixed on Cuba and the Northwest, and the Holy Alliance half disposed to interfere between Spain and her revolting
colonies, it seemed sheer folly to weaken American power. Calhoun resolved that his own course in the next Presidential election
would be determined by the attitude of the candidates toward that
issue.[7]

3

The candidates, or two of them, were primarily concerned for the
present with other matters. The occupation of Florida meant new
Government jobs, and place seekers by hundreds pressed their
claims with Crawford and with Adams. Calhoun had no offices
to bestow. He was instead under the unpleasant necessity of dismissing numerous deserving public servants through reduction of
the Army, and there was no lack of pressure on behalf of those
likely to be dropped. To this he turned a deaf ear. If officers must
be dismissed, let them at least be the less able. If a staff sufficient
for an expanded Army could not be retained, so much the more
reason for making the remnant as efficient as was humanly possible.
A certain amount of leeway in shifting commands was authorized
under the regulations adopted by Congress, and Calhoun meant to
take full advantage of it.

The first problem occurred at the top, where the Army reduction
act had provided for only one major general. Since Jacob Brown
was his senior in the service, Andrew Jackson had to resign or be
demoted, with consequent demotions on down the line. Either
course was difficult, but Jackson himself preferred the former and
was promptly named by Monroe to be Governor of Florida. Calhoun then summoned Brown and Brigadier Generals Scott and

Gaines to Washington to advise him with respect to officers of lesser rank, and at the same time sent confidential letters to colonels, lieutenant colonels and majors of the line asking them to rate the officers under them in three groups according to ability.[8] The necessary demotions, dismissals and shifts of command were based on the recommendations of the officers themselves, and as far as the records go the political pressures were ignored.

One of those released was Dr. Benjamin Waterhouse of Cambridge, apostle of vaccination and distinguished scientist. Adams interceded vigorously and got Monroe to do likewise, but Calhoun refused to reconsider. However competent as a scientist, Waterhouse had proved less satisfactory as a physician than others in the area and was not trusted professionally by the officers.[9]

For the post of Inspector General the Carolinian was forced to choose among five men in line for the promotion. One he rejected out of hand because he had once threatened to use political influence to chastise a superior officer; and two others were eliminated as being less well qualified. The two who remained were Major Archer and Colonel Abraham Eustis, nephew of the Massachusetts Congressman and former Secretary of War. He chose to ignore the political good will that might have followed Eustis' appointment and named Archer for the post, "among the most important in our military establishment," because he was regarded as a little more able, though junior in rank.[10]

Full advantage was taken of the situation to reorganize the Army as far as it could be done under the law. At the same time the Northern and Southern Divisions were abolished and replaced by a more practicable split into Eastern and Western Departments, to be commanded by the two brigadier generals.[11]

4

The Army reduction prevented Calhoun from visiting his South Carolina home in 1821, although his personal affairs were sorely in need of attention. Despite the fact that his salary had been increased two years before to six thousand dollars, his official compensation continued to be less than enough to sustain his household on the scale required of Cabinet officers; and he had been pressed for funds ever since the Northern trip of the previous summer. Through the fall and winter of 1820 he was writing hopefully to his brother-in-law about selling his cotton crop promptly, collecting debts, and most important of all, making remittances. He hoped particularly that some money might be forthcoming by the end of January "should you be in funds for a few hundred dollars at that time."[12]

The reason was an expected addition to the growing Calhoun family. This time it was a boy, born February 9, 1821, and christened Patrick—the first of the children to be born away from South Carolina.

The "little Irishman," as his father called him, was growing fast when Floride's younger brother, James Edward Calhoun, put in an appearance to enlarge still more the family circle. James came from China and South America aboard the frigate *Congress,* which docked at Norfolk in May. An officer in the Navy, he had been almost continuously at sea for four years past, and his presence went far toward compensating for the loss of the trip to Carolina.

An unexpected rise in the price of cotton eased for the moment the financial pressure, and the Calhouns made plans for a holiday. Early in July, James Edward went to Philadelphia for a period of study and in August visited Montreal and the lakes, while his sister and brother-in-law vacationed at Bedford Springs in Pennsylvania, not far from the original Calhoun settlement of a century before. With them went the faithful Peter Hagner, who had also been on the Northern tour of the previous summer.[13]

The trip may indeed have served a political end, as Crawford and Adams later surmised,[14] but there is no hint of it in Calhoun's letters. To his brother-in-law he wrote of a day spent near Harrisburg with a farmer friend, probably his colleague of the Thirteenth Congress, Edward Crouch;[15] and he could speak of nothing but the excellence of the agriculture he saw there. Crops were better and more profitable than those in Carolina, though the soil was less rich; and Calhoun believed the difference lay in the method of cultivation, which he described minutely. On the basis of what he had seen in Pennsylvania, he urged John Ewing to secure an overseer "from about Hagerstown where the farming appears to be equally good," or from Loudoun in Virginia. He did not have any idea, apparently, that the difference might lie in the less efficient and more costly labor system of the deeper South.

What he may have seen in Pennsylvania besides superior agriculture we can only guess. A small, closely knit group of men, often called, from the relationships among them, the "family party," was then rising to political power in the state, and its leading spirits were Calhoun's old friends Samuel D. Ingham and George M. Dallas, son of the former Treasury Secretary. Others in the group were William Findlay, lately Governor and soon to be United States Senator; Richard Bache, Philadelphia journalist and postmaster whose wife was a sister of Dallas; and Thomas Sergeant, brother of Federalist Representative John Sergeant and brother-in-law of Bache.[16] If any of these happened to visit western Pennsylvania during Calhoun's stay there, no doubt politics were discussed; and any such visit would not have been accidental.

It should also be noted that the contract for construction of the fort at Mobile Point had lapsed with the death of the contractor, and that only a month before Calhoun's Bedford Springs trip Ingham had solicited the job for his friend and associate, Lewis F. Coryell. Efforts were even then in progress to iron out legal difficulties, although they ultimately proved unsuccessful.[17]

Whatever the truth of the matter may be, the "family party" was soon supporting the Secretary of War for the Presidency.

In late September the Calhouns returned to Washington only to find the city swept by fever. Old Mrs. Calhoun and James Edward went south to Pendleton, while Floride and her children visited with friends on higher ground a few miles from town; but Calhoun himself plunged at once into the affairs of the War Department. He took up his correspondence where he had dropped it early in the summer for the Army reorganization and wrote again to Southern friends to urge an end to the rising sectional hostility. He repeated and amplified his belief that the Missouri agitation did not mean an attack upon Southern prosperity by the North, but only a bid for power by a small, unprincipled group; and he pleaded earnestly for mutual good will.

"Were we to act," he wrote to Charles Tait, "on the supposition, that we cannot trust; that by giving power we arm a robber, we would no longer be one nation. We could not feel, or act other wise towards an avowed enemy. Thus virtually separated we ought to prepare for actual separation. Distrust must engender distrust. We will not trust them, they will not trust us. Conflict must follow, thence violence and then disunion. ...."[18] He saw it still as a political question, unaware that Lyman Beecher and other eloquent New England ministers had already made it a crusade.[19]

5

His speculations were rudely interrupted by news from Florida. The province and its archives were to be surrendered, under the treaty with Spain, within six months of the final ratification. When the time was up, those terms were yet to be carried out; and the archives, in particular, had not only not been surrendered but were being removed to Cuba. So Jackson, in his capacity as Governor of the Territory, took possession by force; and when Colonel Callava, a Spanish official, refused to give up papers Jackson believed him to possess, he was unceremoniously put in jail. At that point Eligius Fromentin, whom Monroe had named to be Federal Judge in Florida, stepped in and issued a writ of habeas corpus in Callava's behalf and was himself ordered before Jackson to answer for his action.

So far the imbroglio belonged to John Quincy Adams, and we may be sure Calhoun was glad enough to have the strong-willed Tennessee general out of the Army. He was not through with Jackson yet, however. A letter to General Brown from the ranking officer at Pensacola was presently laid before him, explaining that Jackson had been issuing military orders as though he were still commander of an army, and asking if they should be obeyed. Brown's answer, routed through the War Department before being delivered, replied emphatically "no."[20] The truth of the matter was that Jackson, as usual, had taken to himself and was exercising the utmost limit of power to which he might conceivably be entitled under the broadest possible interpretation of his orders. Until a territorial government could be set up, he had been told to assume the powers formerly held by the Spanish Governors, and they had been in theory absolute. Jackson merely translated the Spanish theory into such action as suited his purposes.

Led by Ritchie's Richmond *Enquirer,* which had become the acknowledged voice of the Virginia State Rights school, the press of the country far and wide denounced Jackson's newest venture into autocracy. Monroe was still vacationing at Oak Hill, his Loudoun County estate thirty miles or so from the Capital; but Calhoun and Adams, talking over the affair, agreed that he ought to return without delay. Calhoun's fear was that the case would be tried and settled in the newspapers before the administration could act upon it, thus biasing the public mind before the facts could be made clear. Adams recorded the conversation in his diary and added a judgment of his younger colleague, after four years of close association. "Calhoun," he wrote, "is a man of fair and candid mind, of honorable principles, of clear and quick understanding, of cool self-possession, of enlarged philosophical views, and of ardent patriotism. He is above all sectional and factious prejudices more than any other statesman of this Union with whom I have ever acted."[21] It was perhaps the last favorable estimate of Calhoun Adams was to make, but for its time and place it was eminently just. Though he is known today primarily for his sectionalism, Calhoun was the last of the great political leaders of his time to take a sectional position—later than Webster, later than Clay, later than Adams himself.

Monroe came hurriedly back to Washington and the Cabinet met daily for a week. His initial reaction was that Jackson had again exceeded his powers, both in holding a Federal Judge accountable to himself and in issuing military orders. It was perfectly clear to the President, to the Attorney General, and to the Secretary of War that the civil Governor of a Territory had no military command and could exercise no jurisdiction over the United States Courts. The fact that Judge Fromentin had no authority to issue a writ for Callava's person did not alter the fact that Jackson had no right to question it.

Calhoun summed up the general feeling of the Cabinet majority when he said "he had no doubt that Jackson's intentions were perfectly pure and upright; but his disposition was to exercise to its utmost extent every particle of power given to him. He had not sufficient regard to the genius of our institutions and to the popular opinion."[22] But it was not "popular" opinion Jackson was prone to disregard—it was the opinion of scholars and politicians and theorists of all sorts: the opinion, if you will, of all those who had better heads and sounder judgments than his own. The opinion of the people he always understood and followed. It was Calhoun rather than Jackson who lacked regard for the masses.

As usual where Jackson was concerned, Adams disagreed with his colleagues. He thought Jackson combined in his person military and civil power and was ready to justify everything he had done. Day after day he hammered at the President, frankly using the political argument of Jackson's great popularity when others failed, and urging that the newspaper attacks on the General were in fact aimed at the administration. At last Monroe gave in and discreet letters were drafted, telling Jackson and Fromentin very gently that each had exceeded his powers. Calhoun was not satisfied; but since Jackson was to be told he had no military command, he offered no further objection.

6

Florida was only one of many issues upon which the new Congress would pass judgment. The military and Indian policies were sure to be debated again, and Calhoun hoped this time to sustain his course with votes. In addition to McDuffie and Poinsett, he could count on active support from Micah Sterling, a classmate at Yale and Litchfield, who now represented a western New York district, and on his brother Ansel Sterling, from Connecticut. Another friendly member from the latter state was Henry W. Edwards, an associate of Calhoun's student days in New Haven; and the Pennsylvania delegation, dominated by the "family party," was well disposed. The opposition would at the same time be weakened by the loss of Clay, who was remaining at home to mend his private fortune and his political fences.

A few days before the session began Calhoun sought a conference with Adams, who had shown every evidence of good will and had even offered to aid the War Department program whenever he could. Monroe's hands-off policy with regard to Congress had proved thoroughly disastrous for the administration, and Calhoun now proposed to try the other tack. With good reason he attributed the increased violence of the opposition at the last session to the hostility of the Speaker, and he now sought Adams' assistance in preventing Taylor's re-election.[23] He had no candidate of his own to offer, since Lowndes was unwilling to run for the office; but he was clear that Taylor, who had been consistently allied with Crawford and Clay in opposition to the military program, should be replaced.

Adams demurred on the ground that any interference by the administration would be construed as intervention in a New York state quarrel; but the truth was that Taylor had anticipated Calhoun's intention to replace him and had made his peace with the Secretary of State. The conference had taken place two days before Calhoun made his request, and Adams had agreed to use his influence to prevent administration pressure being used. He did in fact secure from Monroe a promise of neutrality, which he relayed to the New Yorker.[24] He still believed himself, of course, to be above any kind of political bargaining; but it may not be without significance that Taylor from that time forth was an active Adams partisan and took a leading part in the campaign.

Calhoun met a more favorable response from Secretary of the Navy Smith Thompson, who carried the problem to his old associate and party chief, Martin Van Buren, newly elected Senator from New York. Witty, cheerful, conciliatory, with a genius for making friends, Van Buren's reputation as a political manipulator had preceded him to the Capital, where his good will was eagerly sought by the rival factions. Taylor professed to have broken with Clinton, but the Clintonians had supported his election, and that was enough for Van Buren. The New York delegation was quickly whipped into line, and when the House met on December 3 seven ballots were taken without making a choice among Taylor, McLane and Rodney of Delaware, and Smith of Maryland. The next day Philip Barbour of Virginia appeared as a candidate, and on the twelfth ballot secured the necessary majority.

As soon as the various committees were appointed, Calhoun knew he had erred. For the chairman of Military Affairs was William Eustis of Massachusetts—the same Eustis whose administration of the War Department he had vigorously criticized in 1812 and whose nephew a few months before had failed to receive an important military appointment. Adams caustically reminded Calhoun that he had only himself to blame, but that was but partially true. Eustis was an Adams partisan, and the Congressional supporters of the various candidates were expected to reflect the views of their principals.

The choice of Barbour as Speaker of the House was a Crawford victory, as well as a sectional victory for the South. It meant also the triumph of the Bucktails over the Clinton faction in New York's heated political struggle and helped to give smiling little Martin Van Buren, before he had been a month in the Senate, fair claim to being "perhaps the greatest manager" in Washington.[25] For Calhoun, however, it meant the almost certain defeat of his military and Indian policy. Crawford did not attempt to conceal his hostility toward the Secretary of War and sided openly with the disgruntled victims of the Army reduction.[26] He entered, too, with increasing vigor into the local politics of South Carolina, and Calhoun replied in kind. In November John Clark, a personal foe of Crawford, was re-elected Governor of Georgia by two votes and was generally believed to have won out through Calhoun's influence.[27]

At this critical moment the South Carolina Legislature took a hand. On the evening of December 18 some two-thirds of the combined membership of the two houses met in caucus, and by the narrow margin of 58 to 54 it was declared expedient to nominate a candidate for the Presidency. The dissenters were primarily Calhoun's supporters, who felt that any such move would be premature; but once the decision was made, they joined the majority to place in nomination, by a unanimous vote, the name of William Lowndes.

The resolutions adopted at the meeting spoke of "sectional divisions of alarming magnitude" and of the necessity of uniting upon some candidate who would command the respect and esteem of West, East and South alike: "who, remote from any connection with a cabinet succession, shall be brought forth truly, strongly, and indubitably, as the *national candidate.* . . ." It was made clear in the nominating speech that Lowndes's name was proposed because the "principles of State sovereignty" and the "unrelenting economy" associated with Crawford were regarded as dangerous to the country.[28]

Lowndes meanwhile was on his way to Washington, quite unaware that he was being made the favorite son of South Carolina by a group of enthusiastic supporters. He had deliberately stayed away from Congress until the contested Speakership was settled and did not take his seat until December 21. It must have been very shortly after his arrival that Calhoun called on him to discuss one of the most crucial decisions of his career.

Adams had long counted on Calhoun's support in the Presidential race, and as the breach between War and Treasury Departments became more obvious and outspoken, he counted on it the more. Calhoun had assured him, through Edwards, as lately as the past summer, that he had "no views to himself" for the coveted office; and it was plain enough that he could not support Crawford. Clay, who had joined in the moves to reduce the Army and was the chief exponent of the tariff, was equally out of the question, so that Adams was perhaps justified in his assumption. Calhoun, however, was playing a negative rather than a positive role. He was not seeking the election of any particular individual, but rather the defeat of Crawford; and he could support Adams, therefore, only so long as he appeared likely to win out over the Georgian. The opening days of the Seventeenth Congress, together with what he had learned on his Pennsylvania junket, convinced him Adams could not win New York or Pennsylvania, and he had no chance anywhere in the South since the Missouri Compromise.

Such was the situation when Calhoun learned that his own name was being linked with that of Adams by the New Englander's partisans. Whoever was responsible, it was a shrewd political move, for if Calhoun publicly denied it, he would seem to be taking sides against the administration. If he did not deny it, however, he would be irrevocably associated with the political fortunes of a man he believed unable to win and would be compelled to watch in sheer impotence the collapse of his cherished defense program. The alternatives were to come out for some other candidate or to run himself, and the former was out of the question because no man he could honestly support was then in the field. Moreover, the very viciousness of the Radical assault on the War Department and all it stood for had made Calhoun, through no volition of his own, the natural and obvious leader of the anti-Crawford forces.

The idea of running himself had, of course, been in his mind for a year and a half, and an increasing number of friends were insistent that he should do so. His own natural self-confidence, the very genuine cordiality with which he had been received in the Northern and Middle states, his susceptibility to flattery, and above all his political naïveté combined to force a decision upon him. It was this decision he took to Lowndes, who "answered him without hesitation that equally from public and private motives I should greatly prefer his election to that of any of his competitors for the office."[29]

On the evening of Friday, December 28, 1821, Calhoun gave to a group of Congressmen who called on him permission to regard him as a candidate for the Presidency.[30]

It was in all probability the following morning that Lowndes received a hasty note from James Hamilton, Jr., a supporter in the South Carolina Legislature, telling him briefly of the action of the caucus in Columbia. He went immediately to Calhoun, and the two friends canvassed the entire situation. Later in the day Lowndes wrote to Hamilton. He had not sought and did not then seek the highest of public offices, but "the Presidency of the United States is not, in my opinion, an office to be either solicited or declined." He then hastened to make clear his position relative to Calhoun:

"I understand from Mr. Calhoun that he has already written to several friends that he has found himself obliged by a state of things which left him no alternative, that he should consent to be held up for the Presidency." A note by Lowndes attached to this passage adds that Calhoun "had not done so until he found that his name was being improperly associated with Mr. Adams's. This communication he had made to me with his characteristic frankness some days before I received your letter. . . ." Then follows the expression of his own preference already quoted, and the note concludes: "The friends whom he has consulted think it impossible that he should now retract what he has done. Immediately upon receiving your letter I communicated its contents to Calhoun. Our conversation you will readily suppose to have been without reserve. He has seen the letter which I now write you. . . ."

The remainder of the letter was an expression of his hope that South Carolina would not permit any expressed partiality for himself to stand in Calhoun's way, should the state's influence be needed by the latter. "I am not surprised," he wrote in conclusion, "at the conduct of Mr. Calhoun's friends. I know him and estimate him too well to be mortified by any preference which they may express for him."[31]

CHAPTER XIX

CANDIDATE

1

THE forces which led Calhoun to declare himself in December of 1821 as a candidate for the Presidency were both numerous and complex. First of all, of course, he wanted to be President; but he was far from the impatient, overeager opportunist that he appeared in the eyes of some of his contemporaries. Let us examine for a moment the political scene as it must have been shaping up in Calhoun's eyes since he had entered Monroe's Cabinet.

As a member of Congress, he had been through the full bitterness of New England's revolt against Southern domination, but he had understood what lay behind that revolt and had sought to the best of his ability to remove the causes. He was, moreover, himself New England trained, and he knew as well as any man in America how deep-seated was the feeling of the North and East against the long line of Southern Presidents. It must therefore have been perfectly obvious to him from the start that his own chances of occupying the White House would be best in succession to a Northern and preferably a New England man.

When he supported Monroe in the caucus of 1816, he probably gave little or no thought to the sectional question. He was a bare thirty-four years old, and six full Presidential terms would have to pass before he would reach the average age at which the office had up to that time been filled. He had no thought of himself as Monroe's successor or even necessarily as the successor once removed. When he became Secretary of War, however, it was immediately apparent that Adams and Crawford were already candidates for the election of 1824, and it seemed entirely probable that the choice would lie between them, or perhaps among them and Henry Clay. Among these Calhoun would almost of necessity have favored Adams, and so he appears to have done. The election of another Southerner, like Crawford, would postpone indefinitely his own chances; and Clay, like Calhoun himself, was young enough to wait. Probably before his first year as a member of Monroe's Cabinet was up, he had accepted Adams in his own mind as the next President, and was content to let time determine what part he himself should play in 1824 and later. Having thus made up his mind, he devoted himself with all his characteristic energy and enthusiasm to the task of reorganizing the War Department.

Then two circumstances led him to reconsider his position. One of these was the slavery question opened up by the Missouri Compromise, and the other was the determined and it seemed to him inexcusable opposition on the part of Crawford's Radicals to the most elementary measures of national defense. Perhaps the military policy to which he was committed loomed more important in Calhoun's eyes than it really was, but that is no more than a human failing. If he erred, it was at least on the side of safety. Crawford's opposition was carried far beyond the bounds of mere retrenchment; and as it took more and more the character of political reprisal, Calhoun made up his stubborn Scotch mind the more firmly that as long as he could prevent it, William H. Crawford should not be President of the United States.

The Missouri agitation he thought to be the work of a small group of Northern politicians who hoped to profit by it. His conviction that the North as a whole was not bent on abolition and that the South, by acting as though it were, would only inflame sectional hostility and in the end make the Union itself untenable, was the reaction of a true nationalist; but it left both Adams and Crawford censurable. Adams had not attempted to conceal his own abolitionist sentiments, and Crawford had been among the first to take the very extreme Southern view that Calhoun deplored. It was obvious after 1820 that the election of either Adams or Crawford would tend to deepen sectional animosities. Nevertheless, until 1821 he remained willing to support Adams, as the most available Northern man.

It has generally been assumed by historians, and even by some of Calhoun's biographers, that he saw a chance to win the Presidency without waiting eight or sixteen years, and with all the tricks of the politicians at his command went after it. It is necessary to assume no such thing. We have only to keep clearly in mind his conviction that public policy and personal ambition alike demanded the defeat of Crawford and to remember that in 1821 Adams' chances looked very slim indeed, even to Adams.[1] Calhoun knew as a result of his Northern excursion in 1820 that Adams was unpopular in his own section; and after the Missouri Compromise, it seemed hardly probable he could poll any strength in the South. Giving him New England, however, and conceding the West to Clay (remember Jackson not only was not yet an avowed candidate but still insisted he would not consider running), all political observers agreed that the Middle states would decide the contest. In other words, if Crawford was to be beaten, he would have to lose either part of the South or both New York and Pennsylvania.

In 1821 Van Buren secured political control of New York. He was not yet publicly committed to any candidate, but his methods, the nature of his organization and his alignments within the state, made it hardly probable he could support anyone but Crawford. If Van Buren could deliver New York, it would mean that the Georgian was as good as elected; for his strength in Congress and in the hinterland would grow as the prospect of his victory, with its accession of patronage, grew more sure. It would mean to Calhoun complete defeat of his cherished military program, and probably also the frustration of his own political ambition. He had already been urged more than once to run himself. He knew he could give Crawford a stiff fight in the South and that he might even challenge Clay in the West, where his advocacy of internal improvements was popular and his military policy still had friends. He had willing adherents in New England and in New York; and above all, he had been assured by Ingham, George M. Dallas, Thomas J. Rogers and others close to the scene that he could carry Pennsylvania against either Crawford or Adams.

It seems highly doubtful that he had any idea in 1821 that he could himself be elected, but he felt sure he could get enough electoral votes to keep Crawford from winning. That was his main object, and declaring his own candidacy was the only way he saw of accomplishing it.

It was very similar reasoning that brought the South Carolina caucus to nominate Lowndes, and led such able political leaders as Robert Y. Hayne to feel that the concurrent candidacies of Lowndes and Calhoun would be beneficial rather than otherwise. The two men would appeal to different types, and should either of them develop genuine strength, the following of the other could be thrown to him.[2] The chances of seriously cutting into Crawford's Southern vote would be greater and the Georgian's prospect of ultimate victory less sure, if both of South Carolina's favorite sons opposed him, than if only one were in the field. Calhoun himself did not share this view. He thought the caucus nomination of Lowndes a "very rash and foolish" move, but less because it put another rival in the field than because he thought the caucus system had a bad odor and because it seemed to imply a lack of confidence in himself.[3]

2

The opposition between Calhoun and Crawford, personal though it was, was only one manifestation of a fundamental clash of principles. Ever since its weakness had been exposed by the War of 1812, Calhoun had consciously striven to guide the Government of the United States into the path of power; for Napoleon and George III alike had shown that only strength gives safety. To this end he had supported a moderate tariff, a national bank, a large Navy, a well-equipped and well-officered Army, and a unified system of transportation by road and canal; and he had consistently argued that the Constitution granted all powers necessary to bring these things to fruition. If they did not differ materially from the powers claimed by the old Federal Party, Calhoun had his answer ready; for, as he once told a small gathering of Army officers, when the Republicans "stormed and carried the citadel of Government, in 1801, they were not such fools as to spike the guns."[4]

Yet to grant these powers at all was to grant them to a majority in Congress, and Congress had shown itself again and again to be moved by sectional demands and partisan considerations rather than by any grandiose conception of the national good. The very *raison d'être* of the State Rights school was the realistic belief that the strongest interest would always control the central government, and that to confer upon that government the broad powers that were attributes of sovereignty would simply be to give to this stronger interest a legal right to exploit the weaker.

In the mismanagement of the bank the South and West saw ample proof of the danger of central power, just as the North and East had seen it in the embargo and the restrictive system of the war. The answer in both cases was the same—opposition in the name of the states, and moves to curb the expanding central government. Crawford championed the State Rights party; and Calhoun, because of all he stood for and all he wished to achieve, was sure that broad powers were "indispensible to our happiness and permanent prosperity."[5]

Chief Justice Marshall, born controversialist that he was, watched closely the progress of the State Rights movement. The exoneration of the bank by the Supreme Court had been widely resented, and Ohio had gone the length of forbidding the bank to do business in that state. In Cohens vs. Virginia, a case trumped up for the purpose, he made himself an opportunity to reply, and laid down the rule that the states were subordinate to the authority of the National Government. The decision provoked a most able and searching journalistic debate in which Judge Roane and John Taylor of Caroline (not to be confused with John W. Taylor, the New York Representative) spoke for the State Rights party. R. M. Johnson spent days in the Senate attacking the whole principle of judicial review, and it looked as though the explosive question of sectional versus national interests was to be exhumed again, after its hasty burial with acceptance of the Missouri Compromise.

It was at the height of this controversy that Calhoun entered the Presidential race, to oppose at one and the same time sectionalism, state sovereignty, machine politics and William H. Crawford.

3

One of Calhoun's contemporaries was not far wrong in calling him "a giant of intellect, who was a child in party tactics."[6] His reasons for entering the campaign seemed to him entirely sufficient, and the equally gifted but unworldly Lowndes agreed; but Adams and Crawford took a very different view of things. Shortly after it was noised about the Capital that Calhoun was a candidate,

Adams' friend and supporter, William Plumer, Jr., discovered pressing business at the War Department where he "took advantage of some enquiries of Mr. Calhoun, to introduce the subject of his being a Candidate, & had a very long, & apparently free conversation. . . ."[7]

This conversation Plumer immediately carried to Adams and later summarized in a long letter to his father. Calhoun, he wrote, "began with stating that he had been for years in favour of giving to the North the next President, leaving us to select him; that his own wishes had always been in favour of Mr. Adams, on whom he pronounced a very warm eulogium as a man of talents, of integrity, & correct political opinions—that his opponent, Crawford, was the reverse of all this, a man whose course he could not approve, & with whom he could not act—that there were many at the south who thought with him on all these points, & were ready to support Mr. Adams, if he could be supported with the United force of the north—but that without this support from us, his case was hopeless—that it began to be believed in the south that Mr. Adams was rather unpopular in New England, & would be deserted by New York & Pennsylvania—that in consequence of this Crawford was gaining strength in the middle states, & would certainly secure a majority throughout the Union, if some more popular man could not be nominated, to prevent these deserters from the north falling into the scale of the Treasury candidate. . . ."

The impression Plumer got and conveyed to Adams was that Calhoun was running "rather against Crawford than Adams, & with a view to prevent the election of the former, if the latter was not likely to succeed." But he discounted the explanation, and Adams rejected it entirely.

From that day forward Adams regarded Calhoun with a boundless and unreasoning jealousy, strikingly reminiscent of the attitude taken by his father in 1796 toward the Presidential aspirations of the younger and abler Jefferson. But the earlier rivalry was frank and open, and the quarrel was in the end made up. John Quincy Adams did not avow his sentiments and his relations with Calhoun remained on the surface cordial. Not once did he drop a hint that he doubted the explanation Calhoun had given Plumer, but in his diary he grew daily more rancorous and bitter. His pages are filled with suspicion and distrust; and he saw hidden and hostile meanings in all the Carolinian said or did not say, did or did not do. He seemed to feel, as his father had felt before him, that he had some sort of divine right to succeed to the Presidency without opposition. He insisted, too, that the office must come to him without his seeking it; and so, while the other aspirants engaged in public exchanges of journalistic invective, Adams poured out his venom and his suspicions, his surmises and his conjectures, in his diary. Consciously or not, he preserved for posterity all the misunderstanding and misrepresentation, all the wounded pride and personal rancor, of one side of a peculiarly vicious Presidential campaign, while the other sides (for there were as many sides as there were candidates) have been mercifully buried in the files of the partisan press.

The point is of the utmost importance, because the interpretation of Calhoun's career through the 1820's as that of a vacillating and unprincipled politician, ready to sacrifice friends and country alike to his own ambition, dates directly from the publication of Adams' diary in the 1870's. It is a view flatly contradicted by the overwhelming mass of contemporary evidence from other sources: letters and journals, many of which are cited in these pages, of protagonists and onlookers in the same struggle in which Calhoun and Adams were engrossed. Following the Civil War, when all those not of the winning side were discredited, the famous diary was accepted as giving a faithful picture of men as well as of events; and the contrary estimates of scores of other equally high-minded and patriotic observers of the political scene were ignored or heavily discounted. Von Holst and most of those who followed him accepted Adams' judgment of Calhoun as uncritically as they accepted the New England estimate of the whole period preceding the war.

4

Calhoun continued to take Adams in his carriage to various engagements and to call upon him for friendly talks—talks that, so far as Adams reports them at least, seem just as frank as ever. If Calhoun had suspected for a moment the things his colleague was writing about him, he would surely never have discussed political questions with such unreserve. He would more probably have ceased all intercourse with Adams as he had with Crawford, aside from that made necessary by his official post.

But fortunately perhaps for his peace of mind, he did not know what Adams was thinking; and the response to his candidacy from other quarters was more favorable. True, Albert Gallatin, a shrewd and usually competent judge of men, put him down as merely "a smart fellow, one of the first amongst second-rate men, but of lax political principles and a disordinate ambition not over-delicate in the means of satisfying itself"; but Gallatin had been a member of Jefferson's administration, belonged to the State Rights party, and got his political gossip at second hand from Crawford.[8] True, Senator James Brown of Louisiana called him "the most presuming man in the Nation,"[9] but Brown was a brother-in-law and partisan of Henry Clay. New England-born Joseph Story thought him "superior to most, if not all of the candidates," with only his youth against him;[10] and Webster thought Calhoun alone could challenge Crawford's strength.[11] It may indeed be that President Monroe himself preferred Calhoun as his successor, though he studiously avoided any appearance of taking sides. Van Buren thought him "the undoubted favorite of the President"[12]—or wished it to appear that he thought so; and one of Calhoun's more ardent supporters was the President's son-in-law and secretary, Samuel L. Gouverneur. Even his technical rival, William Lowndes, was generally believed to be a Calhoun supporter.[13]

Nor was his appeal confined to those in high places. His Pennsylvania ancestry and New England education tended to obliterate any thought of sectionalism in connection with him. He was popular alike with officers and rank and file of the Army; his personality was winning; his character spotless; and his record in public life admirable. His boldness and energy and his profound belief in the future greatness of his country, as well as his own comparative youth, made him a universal favorite among the younger men; while his demonstrated competence as an administrator and the moderation of his views on the controversial questions of the day appealed to men of more experience and years. Even those who most opposed his course admitted his genius.[14]

His very efficiency in his official position gave him an advantage, for by 1822 he had the work of the War Department so well organized that it practically ran itself. Business was referred almost automatically to the appropriate clerk or bureau, and matters requiring the personal attention of the Secretary steadily decreased, giving him time to devote to politics.

Whatever Calhoun did he did enthusiastically, with his whole energy and will. Whatever he undertook, he invariably had superb confidence in himself and in his ability to carry it through. Once he had entered the lists, the Presidential campaign was no exception, and he put into it all the resources of his powerful and aggressive nature. Yet he remained almost wholly innocent of the practical political knowledge of such men as Crawford and Van Buren. He did not see, or preferred to ignore, the obstacles in his way; and as the optimistic reports of his followers began to come in from Pennsylvania and New York, from North Carolina and Ohio, from New England and the West, he began to believe that he could win.[15]

His friend and Washington neighbor, William Winston Seaton of the *Intelligencer,* was one of many who thought his candidacy premature; and one evening as the two men walked together along the river bank, Seaton urged Calhoun to give it up. "At the end of your second term," the editor argued, "you will be still in the prime of manhood. What would you do?" And Calhoun replied, "I would retire and write my memoirs."[16]

He was not to be moved by argument, for his mind was made up; and in this he was no different from lesser men. As he was himself to learn in time, the mass of mankind is indifferent to mere reasoning, however brilliant it may be. So it was that to Marshall's decisions and the Virginia answers the common people paid little or no attention. In the West they had lost their property, their land, their means of livelihood, by foreclosure to the banks; and they were therefore against banks. In the South the price of cotton fell lower and lower as import duties rose, and so the South opposed the tariff. It is by interest rather than by argument that men are moved, and even interest must be clear and definite and independent of verbal proofs.

CHAPTER XX

CALHOUN FIGHTS BACK

1

THE simultaneous entrance of Calhoun and Lowndes into the Presidential race eliminated any lingering hope of constructive legislation for the remainder of the session. Congress became at once a battleground where first one aspirant and then another gained the upper hand, while pandemonium reigned and the high calling of statesmanship went by the board. Calhoun's candidacy, which was explicitly directed at Crawford, naturally aroused the Radicals to do their utmost; and an opening soon presented itself. The appropriations for support of the military establishment had been so severely cut by the preceding Congress that money was not available to meet legitimate expenses, and the Secretary was forced to ask for a deficiency appropriation. The deficits included $450,-000 for payment of the inflated Revolutionary pensions and $70,-000 for the Indian service.[1]

In connection with the latter item, it will be recalled that the Indian appropriation had been reduced without warning from $200,000 to half that sum on the last day of the previous session, although the system of expenditure authorized by various acts of Congress required the larger amount. Calhoun had already brought considerable improvement into the fiscal procedure of the Indian department by exacting quarterly budget estimates from the field before making disbursements; but the distances involved and the often primitive communications made it inevitable that a considerable time must elapse before any sweeping change could go into effect. With many posts the department could communicate not more than twice a year, and with several only once, because of their remoteness. It had, therefore, been quite impossible to reduce expenditures in keeping with the reduced appropriations in time to avoid an initial deficit.

The House took up the question on January 3, 1822, and for

days the Secretary of War was held up as extravagant, inefficient and a contemner of law, bent upon usurping powers that belonged rightfully to Congress. An air of mystery and intrigue was thrown over the Indian expenditures, of the nature and purpose of which the Radicals professed to know nothing. At last, after a week of wrangling, the House voted to call upon the department for information. Another of Calhoun's lucid reports was presented,[2] but it was all to no purpose. The debate served only to reopen the controversial question of Indian trade, which became the next object of attack.

The Senate Committee on Indian Affairs, of which the pompous and complacent Benton was a member, took the lead, calling upon the Superintendent of Indian Trade for a report on the operations of the Government factories. Along with the routine statistics, McKenney restated the policy to which Calhoun had committed the department. The Indians were no longer free but were utterly dependent on the white man. To cut off their trade would be to doom them to extinction; but unless those who had commerce with them were held to full responsibility, the Indians would be unmercifully cheated, as those of lesser knowledge or intelligence or shrewdness have been cheated in trade since time began. The Government factors were responsible, as no private traders could ever be, for the welfare of the savages. To abolish them would only make it harder to keep whisky out of the Indian country, would expose the frontier to perpetual warfare, and would place in private hands a monopoly of the rich fur trade with consequent monopoly prices for the consumer.

The traders, led by the American Fur Company, wanted precisely that, and they turned to their own uses the widespread sentiment of the West and South against the factory system: a sentiment which had nothing to do with free or restricted enterprise, but sprang from a deep-rooted dislike and distrust of the Indian. To accept the policy Calhoun had done so much to foster meant to concede to the Indians a right to the lands on which they dwelt and hunted, and this neither Western settlers nor Southern planters could ever be brought to do. So those who coveted the Indian lands united with those who were greedy for the profits to be wrung from a monopoly of the fur trade.

McKenney's report was tabled, but its mere existence was enough for Benton, who immediately set to work on a detailed exposure of the system. He secured statements from four persons familiar with the operations of the trading houses who happened to be in Washington—all of them personally known to the Senator, "and known to be gentlemen of truth and honor."[3] Three were Indian agents, who had little of importance to say, but the fourth and most prolific of testimony was Astor's lobbyist and associate, Ramsay Crooks. McKenney was permitted to interrogate the witnesses in the presence of the Senate Committee on Indian Affairs, and to file counterstatements, documents and statistics. Nothing that he could say, however, in any way altered Benton's predetermined conclusion that the goods supplied to the trading houses had been of types not adapted to the Indian trade, were of bad quality, and had been purchased "at improper places."

While this voluminous sheaf of documents was being compiled, a bill to abolish the Government trading houses was introduced in the Senate. Benton's report followed, and the Missouri Senator spoke to it late in March—a speech so filled with abuse of McKenney that Chairman Johnston of the Indian Affairs Committee felt called upon to interpose. The bill, he hastened to explain, had been reported through no suspicion of malfeasance on the part of any official, and he had found nothing in Benton's report to prove that the superintendent had not fulfilled the duties of his office with ability and integrity. McKenney, for his part, replied in the *Intelligencer* and asked for a Senate investigation to clear his name, but was denied a hearing.[4]

The bill abolishing the trading houses passed the Senate without a record vote on April 1, and a month later was approved by the House, virtually without discussion, and again without a roll call. We may be sure, however, that a new member from New York, Churchill C. Cambreleng by name, had a hand in it. Intimate and confidant of Martin Van Buren, Cambreleng was a former partner of Astor in the American Fur Company, for which he had traveled widely. Benton, for his part in securing abolition of the trading houses, received the special commendation of Astor's board of strategy and the more substantial appointment as attorney for the company.[5]

Even as the votes were being cast, new swarms of settlers moved in upon the Indian lands, while agents of the American Fur Company and other traders distributed largess of whisky among the savages.[6] Calhoun's humanitarian policy was followed by a long period of exploitation and a half century of Indian warfare.

2

While the fate of the trading houses still pended, the House Committee on Military Affairs made known its opinion that various appointments under the Army reorganization act were illegal. The particular cases objected to involved shifts of command between line and staff, carried out in accordance with the Army regulations. Eustis denied that the changes were sanctioned, and when the disputed appointments went to the Senate for confirmation they were rejected. It later developed that, as a result of carelessness on the part of the House Committee, the text of the regulations printed by Congress differed from the official copy being used by the War Department.[7] The circumstance did not change any votes in the Senate, however, and the offices, including that of Adjutant General, remained vacant for the rest of Monroe's term.

The Radicals followed up immediately with a move to reduce the Army still further, which presently became another investigation of the whole military establishment. Special committees were hand-picked to serve Crawford's turn, and for a time the War Department looked routed. It was not until the military appropriation bill reached the Committee of the Whole late in February that Calhoun's strength showed. From that time, however, he gained steadily. On the floor of the House McDuffie and Poinsett, the Sterling brothers and the Pennsylvanians proved more than a match for their opponents. McDuffie, spare of frame and nervous of manner, with brilliant deep-set blue eyes, black hair and expression permanently grim, was a veritable host within himself, and he led the fight for the War Department appropriation in a manner that drew biting words from Randolph. The young South Carolinian replied in kind with a fervor that made even the caustic Virginian wince, while a wag in the gallery called out, "Lay on, McDuff, and damn'd be him who first cries, 'Hold, enough.' "[8] The incident made McDuffie a marked man, but it did nothing to injure Calhoun's cause.

It was soon clear that a potential President had more influence in Congress than a mere department head. Calhoun's strength grew with his prospects and one after another his budget requests were passed. Even the Indian office deficiency appropriation was made, and only the much-debated fort on Dauphin Island was finally lost. A new investigation of the Mix contract produced only a censure of Van Deventer and criticism of methods already superseded.[9] At no point could further attacks on the military program be sustained, and a report from Calhoun on Army expenditures lent added emphasis to the solid nature of his achievement. During his regime as Secretary of War the yearly cost of maintaining a soldier had been reduced from $451 to $299.[10]

As Congress dissolved into factions and cabals, the battle between Calhoun and Crawford, though it remained dominant, became only one of many political sorties. Clay and Adams were also attacked, and though the Kentuckian himself was absent, his partisans were much in evidence. Jackson was again denounced by Crawford and Clay, and again defended by Adams and Calhoun; and even Clinton, though not on the scene and not openly in the field, did not lack for attention from his rivals. Only Lowndes, of all the major aspirants for the Presidency, escaped, and his candidacy was not taken very seriously, even by himself. His health was visibly failing, and it was plainly apparent that he had small hope of living out a Presidential term. He was granted a leave of absence on April 25 and resigned his seat May 8, the final day of the session. Toward the end of October he sailed with his family for Europe in a last vain effort to regain his health, and six days out from Philadelphia he died. His campaign had been passive from the first; and if he had few opponents, he had also, as Calhoun wrote to his brother-in-law in March, "still fewer ardent friends."[11]

Where Lowndes had been content to let honors seek him out or pass him by, Calhoun was aggressive, and his fighting qualities won him both followers and foes. Having determined to stand for the Presidency, he took active steps to secure his election, while Crawford openly and Adams behind the scenes as actively tried to block his path. In March the *Franklin Gazette* of Philadelphia, organ of the "family party," began publishing a life of Calhoun which ran through nine installments over a four-month span. Probably the work of George M. Dallas, it was well enough done to call forth increasingly violent blasts in Jonathan Elliot's pro-Crawford Washington *Gazette* and in Adams' diary.[12] Adams was particularly incensed, for only a short while before he had withdrawn the Government printing from the hostile *Democratic Press* of Philadelphia and had given it to the *Franklin Gazette*. Here was base ingratitude.[13]

Calhoun had intended to take his family south as soon as the session was over; but the accumulated business of his department and the tense political situation led him to alter his plans. "The sacrifice is great," he wrote to his brother-in-law, "but it must be made, particularly as my friends the radicals have selected me as the object of their peculiar favour, as you no doubt have seen by the papers. I must be prepared for them. They have gained nothing yet but defeat, and I am determined that they shall gather no other harvest."[14]

3

In the deeper South the quarrel between Calhoun and Crawford was taking a more serious form. In July of 1821 a series of articles had appeared in the Milledgeville *Gazette* championing the extreme State Rights position and Crawford, the State Rights candidate. The articles were signed "Trio." They were answered with the biting sarcasm of which he was a master by George McDuffie, who wrote in the *Georgia Advertiser* under the signature, "One of the People." His identity, however, was revealed by the editor at the request of Colonel William Cumming, one of the "Trio," who immediately challenged when he learned with whom he had to deal. Cumming had been named Quartermaster General of the Army under the reorganization of 1818, but did not keep the position long.[15] He was reputedly a skilled marksman and an experienced duelist, while McDuffie was quite unfamiliar with the business. He nevertheless accepted the challenge, as the code of the Southern gentleman still required. The meeting was arranged to take place early in June 1822.

To Calhoun it seemed little short of a deliberate attempt by the Crawford forces to assassinate a rival who could not be silenced, and it revealed dark reaches of politics of which he had not previously been aware. He had supposed that political rivalries, like those in law or business, were conducted under rules; that he who sought high office stood upon his own character and convictions, which his fellow citizens approved or disapproved with their suffrages. But the Greek ideal of the wise man, the statesman, as lawgiver and judge had ceased to have meaning for a society in which not only the direct rewards of office but enormous indirect power to enrich or impoverish half the population lay with government. In such a society the right to wield this power must inevitably create parties and factions whose struggles would become more violent and more unprincipled as the prize grew in magnitude with the growth of national wealth. Political judgments were no longer made in terms of men, but in terms of benefits, the anticipation of which brought together in a single organization men of all classes and conditions. The organization thus created was the political machine, like other machines direct and efficient if kept in repair, but impersonal, irresponsible and amoral.

As the time approached for the duel, Calhoun confessed to "a strange foreboding," a sense of impending tragedy for which he felt responsible, and his relief when he learned that McDuffie had come through the ordeal alive was profound. It was the eighteenth before he received the news, and he passed it on immediately to the others of his own inner circle. "The mail of this morning has spread joy over our city," he wrote to Micah Sterling. "McDuffie is not only alive, but is believed to be safe. . . . Never have my feelings undergone so great a change in so short a time."[16]

The ball had entered McDuffie's side and lodged against the spine, where the doctors feared to probe for it. It seemed to cause no ill effect, however, and the young Carolinian was soon around again, engaging in another newspaper battle with his Georgia adversary which led to another challenge and another duel later in the year. On the second occasion McDuffie's arm was broken. The back injury began to give him trouble too, and between them they kept him away from all but the last few days of the short session of Congress, thus achieving at least one of the ends his adversaries sought.

The personal quarrel between McDuffie and Cumming was but an incident in the battle for control of South Carolina, and it stung Calhoun into taking a more active part in state politics than he had hitherto done. When John Ewing Calhoun, disgusted after a single term in the legislature, determined to withdraw, his brother-in-law urged him to reconsider. "It is the duty of those, who have the means and capacity, to serve the country," he wrote, "and we ought to resist that tendency to disgust which is so apt to be excited by the many proofs, which we daily see of the want of Candor and integrity." He had spoken in an earlier letter of the importance of replacing the pro-Crawford Senator William Smith, whose term was about to expire, but this time he went farther. "Hayne is the man that ought to be elected. He has talents and eloquence and will honour the state." And to represent Pendleton District in the House he endorsed Warren R. Davis, whose sister had recently married John Ewing Calhoun.[17]

At about the same time a new element entered into the campaign, when a slave revolt led by a free Negro broke out in South Carolina. The Army reduction had left a mere two companies as garrison at Charleston, and the frantic appeal of the Governor for troops put Calhoun under the necessity of dangerously weakening some other point to reinforce the threatened city. A company was promptly sent from St. Augustine, though the action left Florida exposed to Indian attack.[18] The uprising was quickly suppressed, but the trial of the conspirators revealed that behind it lay a pamphlet version of Rufus King's speech on the Missouri Compromise, from which the half-literate Negroes had concluded that their servitude was in defiance of the law.[19]

The incident fanned to a flame the smoldering fires of sectional intolerance—a flame that was not stilled by the formal entrance of another slaveholder into the Presidential race. Late in July the Tennessee Legislature nominated Andrew Jackson, and it must have appeared to many as it did to Calhoun that the presence of five candidates from the slave states to only one from free soil ought to give Adams a distinct advantage.[20]

Though he did not care to have his share in the state election publicized, Crawford's friends were quick to see in Hayne's victory the hand of the Secretary of War. Calhoun was denounced in the

JOHN QUINCY ADAMS
by Thomas Sully

CALHOUN AS SECRETARY OF WAR
by Rembrandt Peale

Radical press for trying to control the state, as though Crawford were not also trying to control it; and it was freely predicted that when the proper time came Calhoun would withdraw and throw his support to Adams or Clay. Both of these gentlemen were highly unpopular in South Carolina, the one for his abolitionist views and the other for his advocacy of the tariff. Calhoun stood between Crawford and the electoral vote of Pennsylvania, New York and New Jersey, where the Presidential contest would be decided, and no journalistic effort was spared to put him out of the race.

He prepared to reply in kind.

4

Late in July, Thomas L. McKenney, whose job as Superintendent of Indian Trade had been legislated out of existence, issued a prospectus for a semiweekly paper, to be called the Washington *Republican and Congressional Examiner*. A few days later Calhoun and Adams were dinner guests at the country estate of a mutual friend, and on the long drive home in the early evening the younger man did a great deal of talking. He spoke of the consistent opposition of Clay and Crawford to the administration, each for his own ends, and of the bitter partisanship of the press, leading up at last to McKenney's proposed journalistic venture. Adams was noncommittal, but he confided to his diary that night his suspicion that "it originated in the War Office, and will be Mr. Calhoun's official gazette, as long as it lasts."[21]

Both men were aware of the sources of Crawford's strength, and both knew that his organization was good enough to carry him to the White House unless it could in some way be broken. But Adams was content merely to deplore the facts in his diary, while he thanked God he was above such methods. Calhoun, with his bolder, more direct nature, was inclined to believe that God helped those who helped themselves. The physical attack on McDuffie and the unparalleled viciousness of the newspaper denunciations of himself had opened his eyes. He realized that he must fight fire with fire, and he was offering Adams an opportunity to join him in a counteroffensive against a common foe, quite unaware that his colleague now regarded him as no better than Crawford.

The first number of the Washington *Republican* appeared on Wednesday, August 7, 1822. It was a four-page sheet, carrying its own prospectus on page one. On page three was a long, controversial letter from Adams, but the feature was an article on the second page addressed to the people of the United States. The first of a series, it dealt with foreign relations, particularly with Spain; but succeeding numbers turned to domestic affairs, exposing the tactics of Congress and the motives behind them, tracing the growth of the existing party divisions, and at every turn castigating the Radicals. The "Trio" articles from Georgia were held up as typical of the purely partisan attacks being made on the administration, excepting only one member of it, and more than passing notice was given to false economy and to the Senate's failure to confirm appointments under the Army reorganization. The articles ran until August 28 and were remarkably well written by the newspaper standards of the day. Indeed, the style bore various resemblances to that of the Secretary of War.

The effect was instantaneous. Before the last number appeared, Jonathan Elliot's Washington *Gazette* had come out unequivocally for Crawford, whom it had hitherto supported only by indirection; and Adams noted in his diary that the new paper had "already manifestly disordered the composure of Mr. Crawford's editorial phalanx."[22] Unable to answer the arguments of the *Republican,* Elliot resorted to the familiar *argumentum ad hominem,* and soon the columns of the *Gazette* were filled with personal abuse, first of McKenney, then of Calhoun and finally sparing not even the women of the Calhoun household. Nothing the Carolinian had done was overlooked, and malfeasance of office and corruption were terms commonly used. Even his age was misrepresented by a good ten years, thus distorting almost to absurdity the only real argument against his candidacy. McKenney was accused of having been "turned out of office, by special act of Congress," and before long the *Gazette* appeared to be arguing that the whole Indian trading system had been abolished for no other reason than the dishonesty and mismanagement of the superintendent.

But the *Republican* stuck to its policy and made it good. Before September was over, Adams had forgotten his doubts and wrote gleefully in his diary that the two papers were still "in deadly conflict, but with such unequal force, all reason, argument, and demonstration on one side, and all scurrility and billingsgate on the other, that the National Intelligencer has been compelled to step in to the relief of the Treasury."[23]

Then McKenney read one morning a newspaper insinuation that, when his Indian trade accounts should be settled, he would be found in default by $120,000. A check-up with the Auditor's office revealed that the vouchers which had accompanied his accounts when turned in were now missing, and "the whole package bore marks of mutilation." McKenney, with uncanny foresight, perhaps induced by the repeated efforts to upset the Indian system, had retained in a private safe a duplicate set of vouchers and with these hastened to Calhoun. The accounts were settled and that matter, at least, cleared up, but McKenney's official integrity continued under fire until he could almost literally "see confidence in [him] giving way."[24] He had been imprudent enough to pledge his own credit and that of his brother to the Treasury for the debts of the Johnson brothers, and in other particulars also his financial transactions were obscure—matters of which his enemies made the most. In the end, his usefulness as an editor was destroyed and the paper changed hands, but not before it had amply served its purpose.

5

After the appearance of the Washington *Republican,* Calhoun's relations with Crawford were openly hostile, but with Adams his intercourse remained, on his side at least, friendly. After a Cabinet discussion Adams paid his younger colleague the compliment, rare at this date, of a grudgingly favorable notice in his diary; and the two men discussed at length the quarrel between Colonel Cumming and McDuffie, whose second meeting was impending.[25] It was not in Calhoun's nature to talk of so personal a matter to anyone whom he held in suspicion or distrust. When the President's message to Congress was being drafted, he revealed his mind again, asking Adams not to press an objection the latter had raised to a paragraph dealing with the Military Academy—a request he would hardly have made of a man he knew to be his political enemy. He agreed readily to omit the parts Adams particularly opposed, but hoped the rest of the paragraph might stand. To this Adams consented, then ruminated in his diary on "the state of Mr. Calhoun's mind." He thought the latter had no motive but to prevent loss of patronage by curtailment of the academy.[26]

Adams still refused to accept the instruments of party as tools fit for his hand to touch, and would not countenance partisanship in his behalf lest he be committed to reward the faithful. Calhoun was less fastidious, though he remained far behind Crawford or Clay, and behind Jackson too, as it proved, in the matter of party organization. The patronage at his disposal, since the reduction of the Army, was negligible, and what he had was strictly circumscribed: a limited number of cadets at West Point, Indian commissioners and agents, and occasional legal counsel to defend suits involving the department. Supply and construction contracts did not pass through his hands, even had there been appropriations for such work. He doubtless hoped, however, to turn to account the unwillingness of Ohio and Kentucky communities to see stores and supply depots withdrawn, as they must be in view of the reduced funds; and the names of Congressmen occasionally appeared as War Department attorneys.[27]

Some partisans were provided for in other departments, but of these there were probably not many. We know that Calhoun had as early as 1820 solicited an office for William P. Duval,[28] and he may therefore be given credit for Duval's appointment as Territorial Governor of Florida; and it was on his recommendation that John McLean of Ohio, a colleague of the war days in Congress, became Commissioner of the General Land Office; but if there were others during the first year of his candidacy, they do not appear in the records. These two alone, however, were enough to arouse the ire of Adams and of Crawford, for the Territorial Governors were under the State Department, and the Land Office belonged in the Treasury.[29]

In the Congressional elections he confined himself to expressing his preferences privately, and even that much he did in only three cases. His friends in the state legislature secured the election of Robert Y. Hayne to the Senate; and Elias Earle, whose course he condemned in a letter to John Ewing Calhoun,[30] was not returned to the House; but the voters of Pendleton District did not see fit to follow his advice. Whatever he did was done from his desk in Washington, without any noticeable neglect of his official duties. Crawford, on the other hand, spent nearly four months of the recess of Congress in Georgia, campaigning for his candidates for state and national offices, while the Treasury got along as best it might under its Chief Clerk.[31]

6

On the score of patronage, a question of military precedence must also be mentioned, more because of the emphasis later given it by Adams than because of its intrinsic worth. At the time of the Army reorganization an old quarrel between Generals Scott and Gaines as to which of them was the senior came to a head, and both appealed to Calhoun to settle it. This he prudently declined to do, saying only that the succession to the chief command would be determined by the President when that post should become vacant. In the fall of 1821, however, General Brown suffered a paralytic stroke which prevented his attending to his duties, and Scott pressed his claims once more. Again Calhoun refused to decide the question, but as Brown's illness lingered through 1822, Scott continued to demand that he be called to Washington to take over the interim command. Brown eventually recovered, and the dispute between the two generals remained unsettled when Calhoun's term as Secretary of War came to an end.

It was still unsettled in 1826 when Scott pressed his claim on Adams. The latter then charged that Calhoun had written to the importunate general in 1822, telling him that Monroe had decided to give him the coveted rank should Brown's illness persist. He elaborated the charge after Brown's death in 1828 and his own retirement from the Presidency, insisting that Calhoun's purpose was solely to gain Scott's political support and that his letter was written after Brown's recovery was so far assured that he was already at Philadelphia on his way to Washington.[32] No such letter appears in the letter books of the War Department, and there is no reference to it in Scott's subsequent correspondence on the subject. Save for Adams' assertion there is no evidence that it ever existed. Even he does not say he had seen it, but we may presume that he learned of it through Scott, who was eager to add the weight of Monroe's authority to his claims. Adams' two stories, moreover, do not agree, for it was not until the spring of 1823 that Brown recovered sufficiently to leave his New York home.

Even had such a letter been written, it could not have been for the purpose alleged, because Scott was already a Calhoun partisan and in the spring of 1822 had considered resigning from the Army to run for Congress in the Secretary's interest.[33] Yet September of that year saw him still asking for the interim command in terms leaving no room for doubt that his claim had been pointedly refused. He continued to press for a decision after Brown's return to Washington—something he would hardly have felt it necessary to do had he considered the case settled in his favor. Scott doubtless did believe that he would receive the chief command in due season, should Calhoun be elected to the Presidency, but he would have expected as much from any candidate he backed. It does not appear from the correspondence, however, that he had received any promise or even any real encouragement from the War Department.[34]

7

The short session of Congress in the winter of 1822-1823 was marked by a counteroffensive in which Calhoun's partisans in both chambers carried the fight to Crawford. This time it was the Secretary of the Treasury who was under constant pressure, and his record was scrutinized as minutely and as eagerly as ever Calhoun's had been by the Radicals. When the weak spot was found, the technique made familiar by the Georgian's own followers was turned against him. On January 20 a letter addressed to Messrs. Gales and Seaton in their capacity as printers to Congress appeared in the Washington *Republican* over the signature "A. B." It recalled a Treasury report of the preceding winter dealing with the deposit of public funds in certain Western banks, and charged that portions of the supporting documents had been suppressed.[35]

The printers demanded an investigation by the House, the published documents were compared with the originals, and various passages were indeed found to have been omitted, some of them being enclosed in penciled brackets and others covered by blank sheets of paper. They revealed, if nothing else, an extralegal generosity on the part of the Treasury; but though Crawford's chief clerk admitted having marked some of the omissions, the Secretary himself had no recollection of them or of having ordered them. The committee professed itself satisfied, but A. B. was not, and was soon accusing Crawford of willfully mismanaging the public funds. A second committee investigated more thoroughly, and the practices alleged against the Treasury were eventually justified on the ground that the financial distress of the West required some relaxation of the rules to prevent great hardship.

The identity of A. B. was not revealed until the following year, but it was in fact Senator Ninian Edwards of Illinois, who continued throughout the hearings to publish letters under his alias in the *Republican*. When the Congress came to an end March 3 he was still publishing, having broadened the scope of his attack to include in detail the relations between the Treasury and the banking institutions of the West.

The whole affair was very like the repeated investigations of the Mix and Johnson contracts, but with the shoe now snugly fitted to the other foot. The only differences were that Calhoun had replied promptly and frankly, while there was at least an appearance of evasion on Crawford's part. The A. B. letters were not in any sense scurrilous or abusive, which could not be said of Jonathan Elliot's anti-Calhoun literature; and last but not least, no evidence was presented by Crawford that disproved, or even threw serious doubt upon, the charge that he had received as legal tender bank notes that were not such in fact or that, whether at his instigation or not, documents had been withheld from the House.

The publicity was widespread and effective. Calhoun thought in April 1823 that "the Radicals are much broken; and . . . their Chief is also much depressed,"[36] while Ingham wrote jubilantly to Edwards in August that Crawford's popularity as a candidate was definitely on the wane. He dated this decline in public favor from the appearance of the A. B. papers.[37]

CHAPTER XXI

MOSTLY PERSONAL

1

THE very success of his drive against the Crawford forces left Calhoun with an added burden of work which precluded any thought of a vacation in the South. The military appropriations for 1823 had found much easier going in the House, with most of the items, including fortifications, increased over the previous year; but a last-minute stand by the Radicals left his desk piled high with resolutions and requests for information. It was six weeks before he was satisfied that his work was caught up, and by that time it was too late to go South, since Floride was expecting a confinement in May.[1]

For all his political ambition, his preoccupation with the affairs of his department and his intellectual pursuits, it was his family that came first in his thoughts and in his plans. During the soul-trying days of his first campaign for the Presidency, when he saw his every word and act distorted and misconstrued, his motives questioned and his character vilified, it was from Floride and the children that he derived renewed strength to go back day after day into the turmoil of the political world—a world that fascinated him and lured him on, and which he came to understand as few men have ever done, yet one that eternally remained in its methods as in its ultimate reward beyond his grasp.

Self-contained and with a reserve approaching austerity where intimate details of his life were concerned, it is only from letters to members of his family that any consistent picture of him as husband and father may be drawn. One such letter he addressed to John Ewing Calhoun early in 1823. "To be placed in the situation of father," he wrote by way of congratulating his brother-in-law on the birth of a son, "is among the greatest changes which we experience through life, and tho' it has its anxieties, it is not without its prepondrance of happiness. I find my children the great solace of life, and midest all of the anxiety which must occasionally be felt, there is still that which makes you feel how much more happy you are with them and how disconsolate you would be without them. . . ."[2]

He had occasion to recur to the same theme late in May, to announce "the addition of a fine boy" to his own family. He and Floride were amply compensated by the event which had kept them from visiting the South that season, but they felt more and more keenly the comparative isolation of Washington. The new arrival was not yet named, for they did not know the name of John Ewing's first-born, and they wished to avoid any duplication. There was a disposition, however, to call him John; and John Caldwell, after his father, he was ultimately christened. With fond gossip of the other children the letter closed.

The children were always in evidence in his letters to close relatives. Andrew was in school and doing well, a "stout, hearty boy" and growing fast. Anna Maria, already her father's favorite, was tall, slender and sprightly, with features resembling her mother's and something of her father's mental grasp and quick perception. Patrick was, in his parents' eyes at least, "the picture of beauty," blue-eyed with hair of lightest tow. Watching his growing, active family, the busy father regretted only that he could not bring them up in Carolina, among the numerous members of the Calhoun clan. He shared the deep-rooted highland respect for kinship, and thought those who lived under its influence "more disposed to a virtuous life."[3]

2

Calhoun's mind was quick and essentially speculative, and he turned naturally to books and to similarly congenial outlets for his superabundant energy. He was thoroughly versed in the literature of politics and economics, he was fond of history, and he followed the best in contemporary thought through the pages of the *Edinburgh* and *Quarterly Reviews* and their transatlantic counterpart, the *North American*.[4] Yet he read little if at all for the sheer pleasure of reading, but always for the improvement and extension of his own knowledge.

He kept in touch with science and the arts, and retained all his old contacts with the educational world. Moses Waddel, now president of the University of Georgia, remained a lifelong friend, and he kept up a desultory correspondence with Benjamin Silliman and Jedidiah Morse at New Haven. In the spring of 1822 he took a prominent part in collecting funds for the relief of old Judge Reeve, long since retired and destitute;[5] and later in the same year he received an honorary degree from Yale.[6]

Whatever the task before him might be, Calhoun always applied himself to it wholeheartedly and with an intensity of concentration that soon made him master of his subject. He was always busy, and to those who saw him only at his work he appeared to have no recreations at all. He did not play cards. He never indulged in jest, nor in the conviviality of the table. He drank only wine, and that in moderation. He did not even smoke. Yet he was far from the cold, unemotional thinking machine that his habitual gravity and dignity of manner seemed to imply. If he indulged in none of the dissipations of his time, even the mildest and most innocent of them, it was through no assumption of moral superiority but because he did not need them. His own inner resources, his family and his friends provided him with all the relaxation he found necessary.

He loved to be surrounded by friends, to be in the midst of people, though he dwelt for the most part among the towering pinnacles of abstract thought to which few of his listeners (for to converse with him was generally to be a listener) could ever climb. He would talk inexhaustibly upon almost any subject that might slip into a discussion. His knowledge was enormous, and the way he molded and refined it was sheer genius. Unless it might have been soft-spoken William Lowndes, not one among the contemporaries of all his forty years of public life ever matched Calhoun in the brilliance of his intellect, and none surpassed him in the purity of his character.

Floride too was at her best in society, and entertainments at the Calhouns' were among the most popular in Washington. For balls the rooms were crowded, and political feuds, for the evening, were set aside. Even the formal dinners of the Secretary of War were events of note, for guests were tactfully chosen and, in defiance of time-honored custom, the ladies were present. In small, informal groups, Floride sometimes played the piano or took a turn at chess with the guests, while Calhoun talked on and on, of history or philosophy, agriculture or science or literature as the fancy struck him, his strong face changing in an instant from the thoughtful repose of chiseled marble to complete mobility and animation. From the warm hazel color they bore in calm, his large, luminous eyes seemed to alter as he talked, appearing now gray, now deepest blue or black, but always brilliant with some hidden inner fire. They were piercing, too, and seemed to see the inmost thoughts of those who met them squarely.[7] There was about him a magnetic compulsion that made him stand out in any gathering, even when he was not speaking, and as he talked, he seemed to grow until his presence filled the room.

His conversational powers were remarked upon by all who came in contact with him, yet it was more by the force of his personality and the matter of his discourse than by any arts of the speaker that his influence was exerted. He was not, like Webster, a master of poetic imagery, nor gifted like Clay in the art of anecdote. His conversation, like his speeches, was unadorned by rhetorical flourishes, making up in vigor and clarity and solid worth what it lacked in stylistic charm. Partly, perhaps, it was the novelty and boldness of his ideas and the abundant variety of his information; but most of all it was the quality of his voice, the earnestness of his manner, and the indescribable way in which something of himself seemed to accompany his words that accounted for his fascination. To friend and foe alike, Calhoun was "a most captivating man."[8]

3

It was Floride's mother, the wealthy landowner who had used to spend her summers at fashionable Newport, who really understood and knew how to appeal to the mass mind. In the late summer of 1822 the dreaded cholera threatened to sweep down upon the Capital, and all who could leave the city did so. The stout Huguenot soul of old Mrs. Calhoun saw no terror in the epidemic, but a God-given instrument of salvation; and she gave all her energy to a religious revival which made its appearance, not altogether without her assistance, in the fall. Despite the remonstrances of her daughter and son-in-law, she would visit the public houses and even private homes, whence she almost literally dragged the unregenerate off to be saved.[9]

Her movements were uncertain and unpredictable; and she spent money recklessly, mostly on others, without concerning herself seriously as to where it was coming from, leaving it to John Ewing and to her nephew, J. E. Bonneau, in whose hands much of her property was placed, to find ways of paying the bills. Possessions she seemed to regard as inconvenient rather than otherwise, and the partition of her wealth, begun at the time of Floride's marriage to Calhoun, continued as a sporadic process for many years. Thus her investments were often made in the names of her sons. Clergy Hall, the summer residence at Pendleton, stood in the name of John Ewing; and in the fall of 1822 she bought a beautiful home on the heights above Georgetown which was deeded to James Edward.

James was not even in Washington when the purchase was made, and Calhoun did not think it wise, but had long since learned to offer no interference. "Your Mother has bought a splendid establishment in Georgetown at $10,000," he wrote to John Ewing. "The finance is low, but as she has no need of it, I fear she will in the long run find it dear."[10] And so indeed she did, for the property sold six or seven years later at a considerable loss.

It was once said of old Mrs. Calhoun that she and Andrew Jackson were the "only independent characters" in Washington. The statement does less than justice to her son-in-law, but the implied comparison with the Hero of New Orleans was not without its point. Both were tough-minded and strong-willed, and both were Calvinists. Later in the campaign, after Calhoun's withdrawal, his mother-in-law gave her own preference to Jackson and remarked that, should he be elected, she would spend the next winter in the Capital in order to see a President who went to church.[11]

Calhoun, too, had been reared a Calvinist, but during his student days in New England he had been attracted to the more philosophical Unitarian faith, and he was one of the founders of the first church of that denomination in Washington. He contributed liberally toward the cost of the spacious, well-lighted building erected to house the congregation by Charles Bulfinch, architect of the Capitol, and was doubtless among those present at the dedicatory service on June 9, 1822. The building stood at the corner of Sixth and D Streets, only a few blocks from the Calhoun home. Convinced by the logic of Unitarianism, he assumed that others must likewise be convinced, and that this faith must ultimately prevail throughout the world.[12] It was a characteristic utterance, revealing at once his profound belief that truth is absolute and all men rational. Despite his conviction, however, he could not, or at least he did not, convert the members of his own household. Floride preferred the more ceremonious Episcopal ritual, and her husband often accompanied her to that church, while old Mrs. Calhoun remained a devout and active Presbyterian.

4

In the summer of 1823 the Calhouns moved to the beautiful tree-girt house on Georgetown heights, which old Mrs. Calhoun had purchased in the name of her younger son. The estate included twenty acres of rolling turf, woodland and rocky hillside in a section known as the Rock of Dumbarton. The magnificent red brick house had been built in 1800 and was a veritable mansion for that day. Surrounded by a walled garden and spacious lawns, it stood high above its grounds, which sloped away in unobstructed grandeur toward the Capital. It had been called by its previous owner "Acrolophos," or Grove on the Hill, but the Calhouns gave it the simpler and equally fitting name of "Oakly." It is the house that is known today as Dumbarton Oaks. John McLean, Postmaster General since July, lived across the street, and Thomas L. McKenney was also a neighbor.

The clearer, drier air of the high ground wrought marked improvement in the health of the children, and a new buoyancy and optimism pervaded the household. There was something of the farm about it, and Calhoun was always at home with plants and trees. Just now he was interested in the manufacture of wine, a topic which entered freely into an otherwise purely political correspondence with General Swift, who brought and planted in Calhoun's garden the first Isabella grapes in Washington.[13]

Calhoun's own qualities alone would have brought him many visitors. His office brought him more, and his candidacy still further increased the demands upon his hospitality. Like his mother-in-law, he gave generously, and though Spartan in his personal habits he spent freely on his family. He was often in want of funds, and time and again was forced to sell portions of his South Carolina property and to seek advances from his brother-in-law, who remained in charge of their joint affairs.

Financial transactions among the Calhouns were free and frequent, with John Ewing doing most of the bookkeeping. William apparently continued to manage his brother's Willington plantation, and we find him depositing funds to Calhoun's credit with his Augusta factors, or paying money over directly to John Ewing, who in turn paid various bills on his brother-in-law's behalf. John Ewing was always the agent when land was to be sold or rented, while Calhoun advised when to hold and when to sell the stocks they owned in the old United States Bank. Sometimes one and sometimes another of the clan would be in funds, but they were always freely at the disposal of the others. In part these complex financial dealings were a consequence of fluctuating money values and an exchange which was generally against the South, but they bespeak a rare degree of intimacy and mutual good will within the family.[14]

Oakly proved impracticable as a winter home, because of its distance from the War Department offices and the generally poor condition of the roads, but the Calhouns were back the following spring. It was there that another child, Martha Cornelia, was born in April 1824, while an important Cabinet meeting was delayed by the absence of the Secretary of War.[15] In the big, rambling house with its adjacent woods and tree-dotted lawns one could look down upon the city and yet feel apart from it and from its mad scramble for place. It was easier there to forget the bitterness of the Presidential contest, and to magnify the fair report of over-sanguine friends.

Though he tried to play the political game according to the rules, Calhoun remained much what he had been at the start: a theorist, a metaphysician, a man of thought rather than of action. He descended early to the political arena and spent his whole life there, but he never became a skilled politician. He regarded himself as a democrat but he never really accepted the principles of democracy and never learned to cope successfully with the vast unpredictable force represented by the common man. He regarded his cause as that of "truth and the people, against corrupt and unprincipled combinations," and he professed complete faith in the virtue and intelligence of the common man; but the "people" meant, in McDuffie's phrase, the "substantial yeomanry of the country," who were placed in specific opposition to the "grog shop politicians of villages and the rabble" of the cities, with whom he conceived Jackson's strength to lie.[16] His appeal was to the middle class, as Jackson's was to a conscious proletariat, but the machine politics of Crawford and Van Buren knew no class distinctions.

CHAPTER XXII

CANDIDATE NO LONGER

1

CALHOUN's major claim to the Presidency lay in his consistent nationalism, and upon that point his campaign was chiefly waged. Adams and Clinton were frankly Northern candidates, Clay and Jackson as frankly favorite sons of the West, while Crawford's appeal was primarily to the South. Calhoun had strength in every part of the country, and he seemed to many to be the logical successor of Monroe. Through a dozen years of public life his course had been uniform and consistent, and his views on all the major questions of the day were fully known.

He stood for a nation unified and free, strong to defend itself but yielding special privilege to no class or group. He was identified with the second war for independence, and to a greater degree than any other individual with the policy that grew out of it: a moderate tariff, a national bank, internal improvements, a strong Navy and an Army adequate to the defense of long and distant frontiers. He stood solidly against all sectional movements, and was willing to make whatever compromises should be necessary to bring harmony from conflicting points of view. He called himself Republican, tracing his creed to the principles of '76 and '98, but he opposed explicitly both the extreme State Rights position of the Radicals and the ultraconsolidationism of the older Federalists.[1]

Just as he appealed to those who held national views the country over, Calhoun's supporters represented all shades of economic and political belief. Many were men who had sat with him in Congress in the old war days, such as John McLean, Samuel Southard of New Jersey, and Ingham; some were old college friends, like Micah Sterling and Henry W. Edwards, now Representative and soon to be Senator from Connecticut; some were in or of the Army, like Joseph G. Swift and General Winfield Scott; and still others were the friends or relatives or neighbors of other days, like McDuffie,

Governor Pickens of Alabama, and Virgil Maxcy, a Maryland lawyer whose father had once been president of South Carolina College. But there were many who supported the young Carolinian for the things he represented or the character he bore, and these were confined to no special place or party. Among them were old-line Federalists, like Daniel Webster and William Gaston of North Carolina; legalists, like Henry Wheaton and Judge Ambrose Spencer of New York and Roger B. Taney of Maryland; and politicians of the stamp of Ninian Edwards, George M. Dallas, and Duff Green of Missouri, who had succeeded Benton as publisher of the St. Louis *Enquirer.*

At one and the same time Calhoun won the endorsement of Supreme Court Justice Joseph Story, whose thinking followed Marshall's pattern, and of old John Tayler of Caroline, since the death of Roane the active leader of the Virginia State Rights party.[2] He did it, moreover, without misrepresenting or concealing any part of his political creed. He made no concessions of doctrine to gain followers, and it was to his credit that many—perhaps most—of his partisans disagreed with him in one or more particulars.

With scores of his lieutenants he kept up a voluminous political correspondence, and his letters were passed on from one to another, while the partisans wrote back and forth among themselves. In every state he had supporters actively at work, and in many he had well-developed local organizations. There were conferences at Oakly and gatherings of the faithful in other cities, while trusted henchmen like McDuffie and Hayne and Van Deventer traveled widely in Calhoun's interest.

2

New York and Pennsylvania were the prizes most eagerly sought by rival managers, and in both states Calhoun's claims were vigorously pressed. In Pennsylvania his partisans controlled the powerful *Franklin Gazette,* they dominated local politics in Philadelphia, and the state offices were largely in their hands. When the time seemed ripe for a formal endorsement of their candidate, a caucus was called to meet in Harrisburg following adjournment of the legislature in March 1823. But the Jackson managers had anticipated the move, and the delegates from Westmoreland County, Scotch-Irish stronghold west of the Alleghenies, had been instructed for the Hero. As a dangerous party split threatened to develop, the majority discreetly voted to make no nomination at all. It was a setback which foreshadowed coming events, but Calhoun remained optimistic. He distrusted the caucus system and professed to be satisfied with the assurance of Dallas that he could have had two-thirds of the delegates had the matter been pressed.[3]

In New York also he seemed to be strong, and the end of May saw the appearance in his cause of the New York *Patriot*. The editor was Colonel Charles K. Gardener, former aide to General Brown, but the moving spirit was Henry Wheaton, a man of rare ability and character. Both these contributed to the paper's financial support, as did Swift, Scott and Samuel Gouverneur, and all of them wrote for it on occasion. Most articulate of them all, however, was young Lieutenant John A. Dix, who succeeded Gardener as aide to General Brown and devoted himself to the defense of Calhoun's military policy.[4]

The *Patriot* made immediate inroads upon Crawford's strength with the people, but it could not shake Van Buren's control of the legislature, which would in the end choose the Presidential electors. When the suggestion was made, however, that the election be given to the people, the *Patriot* seized upon the idea; and soon such a tide of popular sentiment was generated for it that no candidate for the legislature dared avow opposition. The Clintonians eagerly took it up as their own, and a People's Party formed around it. Thus DeWitt Clinton, whose partisans in Congress had joined the Radicals in attacking the War Department, and Calhoun, who had denounced Clinton as early as 1808 in the South Carolina Legislature, came to be fighting side by side against a common foe—the little magician from Kinderhook. There is some evidence that Calhoun's partisans, who were in fact mere babes in the murky wilderness of New York politics, built hopes upon this temporary union of winning for their man the ultimate support of the powerful Clinton faction, but the adroit Clinton managed to channel in the other direction any benefits that may have been derivable from the association.

Later in the year Wheaton himself was sent to the assembly on the People's ticket, and was even prepared to run for speaker should Calhoun think it desirable, in event of failure to elect the pro-Adams Tallmadge.[5] He introduced and drove through the assembly a bill providing for popular choice of Presidential electors before he took leave to resume his duties as Supreme Court reporter; but Van Buren still held the upper hand, securing the defeat of the bill by indefinite postponement in the senate.

Another Calhoun paper, the *Virginia Times,* had meanwhile been started in Richmond, and the War Secretary built high hopes upon the approval of the venerable John Taylor of Caroline, whom he had visited in the spring.[6] But he had only arguments to offer, and these were wasted against the armor of self-interest. Spurred on by Van Buren, Thomas Ritchie brought the influential Richmond *Enquirer* out for Crawford. Calhoun was held up as a high-tariff man and a consolidationist, and he pleaded in vain that he had never expressed a sentiment hostile to the true Virginia doctrine. Had not Jefferson himself approved, and Madison signed, the tariff of 1816—the only tariff ever supported by Calhoun? Had not Roane endorsed the bank, and was not the Cumberland Road Jefferson's doing? Had not Monroe conceived the chain of coastal forts, and Gallatin the inland waterways? But this was no longer enough for such as Ritchie, Floyd, the Barbours and Tyler, who were contesting the leadership of the state with the Dynasty. The *Virginia Times* changed editor and name toward the end of July and passed out of existence altogether in another month.

Calhoun's claims to the Presidency were ably publicized, but they were not backed up by appeals to sectional or class prejudices or by tangible promises of gain. In Virginia General Scott, under the pseudonyms of "Pendleton" and "Wythe," challenged the Radicals in their own stronghold with a series of articles in the *Enquirer;* an *Address to the People of North Carolina,* written either by Calhoun himself or by McDuffie, came out in November; and a similar pamphlet entitled *Measures, not Men* was published at about the same time in New York.[7] They provoked only counterblasts in kind. The versatile president of South Carolina College, Thomas Cooper, charged that the whole defense program was designed merely to increase the patronage of the War Department, while the

Raleigh *Register* and the Columbia *Telescope* re-examined the Johnson and Mix contracts in terms not flattering to the Secretary.

3

There were those among the young Secretary's followers who read the signs aright, but they failed to influence their candidate. In the unwillingness of the Pennsylvania Legislature to make a nomination, such skilled politicians as John McLean saw the ultimate collapse of Calhoun's chances, and the Postmaster General, at least, urged his friend at that time to look no higher than the second office.[8] But Calhoun was too confident and too unskilled in practical politics to perceive his danger. Though he despaired at times of his own chances, he never once doubted the success of his cause.

Paradoxical as this may seem, he was in fact still following the policy he had originally laid down for himself. His whole campaign was directed first of all to the defeat of Crawford, and only secondarily to his own election. "I hold it certain that our side must prevail," he wrote to Ninian Edwards in July, "but whether it will be under myself, may be more doubtful." He thought Adams the stronger and believed New York would decide between them, but it was clear that he regarded the election of Adams, no less than that of himself, as a defeat for Crawford and consequently as a victory for "our side."[9]

Jackson, too, he regarded as on his side, and the two men kept up a correspondence in which political questions were freely discussed. He took it for granted that the General's primary object, like his own, was the defeat of Crawford, and so he counted Jackson's strength as his own.[10] "Keep separate, but attack none, save only the Radicals" was his advice to his partisans.[11] He was prepared to inherit the strength of Adams, of Jackson, and of Clinton, should any or all of them fade in popularity. To each of these in his own territory Calhoun was second choice; and he counted on this secondary strength to make him the most available compromise choice, should the election go, as it now seemed certain to do, to the House of Representatives.[12]

4

The first real setback encountered by the Radicals came in September, through no effort on the part of their opponents. Crawford was taken ill while visiting Senator Barbour in Orange County, Virginia, and the local doctor, noting only an initial chill and subsequent sharp rise in temperature, dosed his distinguished patient for bilious fever. The disease was probably erysipelas, which was no doubt aggravated by the Secretary's fondness for the table; but whatever it was, the treatment was wrong. Crawford's enormous bulk settled back in bed, and there he remained for six weeks or more, partially paralyzed and almost blind. It was November before he was really well. For other endless weeks he remained in darkness and helplessly crippled. It seemed impossible that he should ever live to be President, and that he did live was surely no tribute to the physicians who bled him twenty-three times within three weeks.[13]

Adams meanwhile had gone to his Massachusetts home for a brief vacation, and almost simultaneously with his arrival in Boston his confidential clerk, John Bailey, who had not actually lived in the state for six years, was elected to Congress. It looked to the *New England Galaxy* quite indistinguishable from the sort of thing Crawford was doing in Georgia, and the editor said so. In a subsequent issue there were some references to "rotten boroughs," and later still some remarks, duly restrained, in praise of the Secretary of War.[14] The same Massachusetts election saw William Eustis chosen Governor of the state, without interference from Adams if not with his avowed support. He had also overcome his scruples in another direction. In August a fulsome newspaper prospectus came out of Washington, and on November 12 the first issue of the *National Journal* appeared, edited by Peter Force and devoted to the interests of the Secretary of State.

The defection of the *Galaxy* and objections by War Department adherents to the election of Eustis came at a time when Adams' suspicions were already thoroughly aroused. McLean's appointment as Postmaster General had been followed in September by that of Senator Samuel L. Southard of New Jersey, another Calhoun supporter, to be Secretary of the Navy, following the elevation of Smith Thompson to the Supreme Court; and the mistrustful New Englander fitted the sequence into a pattern of his own imagining. Through the important Cabinet discussions during November, out of which the Monroe Doctrine was born, the entries in his diary were increasingly bitter toward his younger colleague. In Calhoun's willingness to risk war to keep the Holy Alliance out of Latin America, Adams could see nothing but a deliberate wish to make trouble for the next President; and even after he had himself swung around to a similar position, he retained his belief that the War Secretary was merely trying to embarrass him.

On the eve of the meeting of Congress he had a long political discussion with Plumer, in the course of which he declared that Calhoun had been "laboring incessantly" to advance himself at Adams' expense, while professing friendship and good will, and charged that his rival, having given up any hope of success, was already scheming to lead an opposition.[15] After two years of pretense, Adams prepared to bring his animosity out into the open, and within the week the *National Journal* began an attack on the Secretary of War.

5

Crawford was still ill when Congress met, and the efforts of his party were principally directed toward getting him nominated by a caucus as quickly as possible. From the first day of the session, the business of President-making was in the forefront, and even the changes in membership bore directly on that question. Clay was back after a two-year absence and showed that he had lost none of his old magic when he won the Speakership again by an overwhelming majority. The seat so long and so capably filled by William Lowndes was now occupied by James Hamilton, Jr., already at thirty-seven a power in South Carolina politics, and soon to be among the foremost of Calhoun's adherents. Daniel Webster, whose recent visits to Washington had been confined to Supreme Court sessions, took his seat as a Representative from Massachusetts. So did John Bailey of the State Department, though his right to sit was immediately challenged.[16] Edward Livingston, brother of the late New York Chancellor and steamboat magnate, arrived from Louisiana; and from Tennessee came towering, black-browed Sam Houston, who had an old grudge against the War Department.[17] In the Senate new faces included Henry W. Edwards of Connecticut, "promoted" from the lower branch; handsome and eloquent Robert Y. Hayne; and most important of all, General Andrew Jackson, who alone in his adopted state had had the political strength to defeat the veteran John Williams.

The President's message, with its historic warning against further European intervention in the New World, created scarcely a ripple as Congress and Cabinet played at politics. The Washington *Republican* took up the cudgels against the *Journal,* and was soon reinforced by news that Calhoun had been nominated by an almost unanimous vote of the South Carolina Legislature. The action was spontaneous and even against the advice of his Washington managers, but the candidate himself thought it just as well.[18] When Maxcy proposed to seek a similar endorsement in Maryland, however, Calhoun stayed his hand, fearing to risk another failure. McDuffie continued to represent him as the "most national candidate & most likely to unite the votes of the different sections,"[19] but his chances were waning, and Duff Green wrote significantly of supporting Jackson should the Carolinian be out of the running.[20]

Crawford was still strongest of the candidates in Congress, where it was evident that efforts to block a caucus would be futile. Slowly but surely now his health was improving, and his confidence had never failed. In mid-January the burly Georgian started the political auction going with a bid for Adams, the price being the Vice Presidency.[21] He was believed to have made the same offer to Clay. Colonel R. M. Johnson presently turned up in the State Department offices with a proposal that, in return for support, Jackson should be Vice President, Clay Secretary of State, and Calhoun Secretary of the Treasury, and indicated that the arrangement had been suggested by Calhoun, "not as a bargain or coalition, but by the common understanding of . . . mutual friends."[22] Adams, always ready to believe the worst of any man he disliked,

did not question the authenticity of the story. He merely took it as
evidence that the War Department was weakening. Calhoun, on
the other hand, still thought his own chances good and denied all
rumors of coalition with Adams as "one of the devices of the
enemy."[23]

It was not Johnson but Ingham who spoke for Calhoun, as
Adams knew very well, and the Pennsylvanian followed hard upon
Johnson's heels to the State Department. He had no fantastic
offers to make. He wanted only two things: to know why Adams
had so suddenly and violently turned against Calhoun; and to solicit
for George M. Dallas the appointment as Minister to Mexico. As a
matter of fact, Adams' animosity toward Calhoun had been growing steadily for two years, but he had dissembled it so well that no
one could have suspected it who had not read his diary. His sudden
avowal of it when Congress met took Calhoun as well as the Capital
generally by surprise. The question of an envoy to Mexico had
been simmering almost as long. Calhoun had originally proposed
Ninian Edwards, but Adams had prevailed upon Monroe to offer
the place to Jackson, who promptly declined it. Under prodding
from Cook, who was now Edwards' son-in-law, Adams agreed to
accept the Illinois Senator; but Ingham had meanwhile got the
President's promise to appoint a Pennsylvanian. Baldwin had been
suggested, but his high-tariff views made him unacceptable to the
Calhoun faction in the state, who wanted Dallas.

The conversation was interrupted at this point, and it was several
days before it could be resumed. When Ingham called again, he
found Adams ready to unburden his heart in a "full and explicit
conversation." The complaints he detailed were too petty or too
farfetched for serious consideration. What he resented most was
that after he had given the public printing to the *Franklin Gazette*,
the paper had come out for Calhoun instead of for himself. Calhoun had received support from the Boston Federalists, and Adams
had been abused by the *New England Galaxy* which professed to
favor his rival. He argued finally that the election of Calhoun
would be against the traditions and spirit of American institutions—immoral, if not absolutely illegal. Why? Because no man
older or more experienced than Calhoun could honorably serve
under him, and his elevation to the Presidency would therefore

exclude "*all* the other men who were distinguished before the nation"![24]

The *National Journal* had already said as much in only a slightly different way. Adams, asserted the editor, was the only candidate who was "an avowed advocate and strenuous supporter" of what he was pleased to call "the present system of policy." Calhoun had repeatedly said that policy should be carried forward. Therefore, Calhoun should be supporting Adams. That he was not, proved that his ambition was merely to advance himself against the interests of his country. To Adams the "present system of policy" apparently did not include the military program, though it did extend to the unqualified justification of Jackson's Florida exploits.

Ingham pointed out, apropos of the *Franklin Gazette,* that since Adams was being supported in Philadelphia by the Federalist *National Republican,* the Democratic papers were almost forced to oppose him; but the argument was wasted. So was the visit, for Adams made it clear he would not accept Dallas as Minister to Mexico.

6

The Presidential caucus—the last ever held—met on February 14, 1824, in spite of the combined opposition of Adams, Calhoun and Jackson. In this opposition Calhoun took the lead, as he had from the beginning led in all moves aimed against Crawford. Late in January Ingham had called an anticaucus meeting, which consisted primarily of Calhoun's friends,[25] but no effective action was taken. The opponents of the system could not make up their minds whether to attend and vote down a nomination or to stay away and let Crawford's friends enjoy a hollow triumph. In the end they chose the latter course.

The caucus was attended by only sixty-six members—hardly a quarter of the combined total of the two Houses. The carefully laid plans of Van Buren and Ritchie to build upon it a coalition of Virginia, New York and Pennsylvania came to naught, as the Pennsylvanians stayed away and half of the New York and Virginia members did the same. For this failure Calhoun was held primarily responsible.[26]

Needless to say, Crawford received the nomination, the only curious part being that it was not unanimous. Adams got two votes, and Jackson and Nathaniel Macon one each. Counting two proxies, Crawford had sixty-four. Albert Gallatin, returned home at last, was named the Vice Presidential candidate, partly in the hope of yet influencing the choice in Pennsylvania, partly to reassure the Virginia Dynasty whose collaborator and friend he had so long been. The meeting was open, and the nomination was hissed from the galleries;[27] but public disapproval in no way lessened the real importance of the move for the other candidates. Carried through though it was by a faction, it yet had the full weight of tradition behind it and aligned Crawford with the procession of Presidents. The opposition vote was weakened in proportion as it was split among many candidates.

The caucus was indeed the natural outgrowth of the political system envisioned by the founders. The nominating convention on any widespread scale was an impossibility before the railroad age. The idea had already been suggested, however, by Calhoun's partisans in Pennsylvania, and though they could not carry it through, they did succeed in calling a state convention to meet in Harrisburg on March 4, despite the opposition of both Crawford and Jackson parties.[28]

The convention was expected to nominate Calhoun; but Jackson's candidacy had been slowly gaining momentum, like a football team being pointed for a particular game. In the Senate the crotchety and dictatorial Hero had charmed friend and foe alike by his mild and courteous manner, his dignity, and his transparent freedom from guile; yet though he mingled graciously with the rich and powerful, he remained the favorite and champion of the common man—the "rabble of the cities" who were contemptuously neglected by Calhoun's partisans.

Calhoun's fortunes in Pennsylvania had been skillfully linked to those of the anti-Radical Schulze, selected by the "family party" as their candidate for Governor, but after his election in the fall of 1823 Schulze had repudiated his obligations,[29] and the resulting breach opened the way for the Jackson managers. Dallas recognized the inevitable. On February 18 he addressed a Philadelphia town meeting, called to select delegates for the coming state convention. He moved resolutions condemning the recent caucus nomination of Crawford and called for party unity even though it meant the sacrifice of personal preferences. His own preference, he reminded his hearers, was well known, but the party itself was at stake; and he called upon Pennsylvania to support Andrew Jackson for President.[30]

For this blow Calhoun was utterly unprepared. "Mr. Dallas had informed me about a week before," he wrote to Maxcy on the twenty-seventh, "that he thought the cause was lost in Penna and that we should have to yield there, at the Harrisburg convention. Tho' prepared for a defeat [at] Harrisburg, no movement in advance was anticipated. What took place was unpremeditated and under a sudden impulse received from the caucus nomination here, and the loss of Berks which decided the contest in favor of Genl. Jackson in Penna. I have no doubt the motives were pure; and tho' ill timed as it regards Dallas and our cause, yet not unfavorable to the great point of defeating the Radicals."[31]

Thus he adhered still to his first intention, that Crawford must be kept from the Presidency, whoever might win. Nor did his optimism fail him, even now. He still thought he could hold South Carolina and New Jersey. Jackson's managers had agreed not to enter in North Carolina, with the understanding that the ticket already formed should be his if Calhoun appeared hopeless, while Calhoun was to receive the Jackson votes in Louisiana, Alabama, Mississippi, Missouri and Tennessee if he should appear the stronger. The "understanding" with Jackson, however, went no farther than this, and certainly did not include any arrangement whereby Calhoun was to withdraw and receive the Vice Presidential nomination.[32] "Jackson's friends indicate a disposition to add my name to his ticket in Penna as V. P.," the letter to Maxcy continues. "We are determined in relation to it to leave events to take their own course, that is to leave the determination to his friends. Standing as I do before the American people, I can look to no other position than that which I now occupy."

When the Harrisburg convention met, Jackson received 124 out of 125 votes, and his friends indicated their choice by giving Calhoun 87 votes for Vice President. Though his name was not formally withdrawn as a candidate for the first office immediately, the campaign, so far as Calhoun was concerned, was over.[33] He had been from the first unaware of the forces combined against him and had remained sanguine to the end. Now, disappointed, bewildered and unwell, he withdrew to his Georgetown home to reflect and get his bearings.

He had thought to carry the manufacturing states on his record on the tariff of 1816; but the meager duties Calhoun was willing to support had long since been rejected by the manufacturers as a pittance, and his reasons for supporting any duties at all were not calculated to appeal to men whose hands had just found the way to the public pocket. His championship of internal improvements was not enough to overcome the popularity of either Jackson or Clay in the West, where he had antagonized the powerful fur interests; and although he was perhaps personally more popular than Adams in New England, his Southern birth alone disbarred him there. His appeals to the "people" against the machine politics of Crawford had only prepared the ground for the proletarian movement launched by Jackson. Even the Army, on which he had depended, went over to the military chieftain; and Calhoun had to choose between withdrawal and the risk of splitting the anti-Crawford forces and giving the election to the Radicals. He did not hesitate over the choice, but withdrew from the contest.

CHAPTER XXIII

NATIONALISM CRUMBLES

1

THE decade between the second war with England and the retirement of President Monroe saw the emergence of the forces which molded modern America. It was during this era of depression, expansion and heated controversy that the young nation, stimulated by far-reaching technological developments and given impetus by the individualistic philosophy of the Revolution, turned from commerce to industry, with all that choice implied. It was within this brief ten-year span that America turned from the policy of free trade, in defense of which the war had been fought, to the economic nationalism which played so large a part in bringing on the civil struggle of the '60's: the same economic nationalism that led through the corruption and the extravagance, the wealth and the poverty, of the age of big business into an era of economic chaos and world-wide conflict.

The peace of Ghent was in reality a declaration of economic war, which only intensified long-standing rivalries between the two nations. The points at issue were the navigation of the Mississippi and the Great Lakes, the vast fur trade of the Central and Pacific Northwest, the North Atlantic fisheries, and most important of all, the carrying trade of the world, to which was soon added a struggle for markets between America's war-inflated manufactures and the hitherto unchallenged industry of Britain. These economic conflicts formed the central problem of the decade, the two general solutions offered being free trade and national self-sufficiency.

Calhoun never doubted the desirability of the free-trade policy, but he knew that it would mean continuing rivalry with Great Britain, accompanied by repeated and destructive wars. He sought in consequence a Navy powerful enough to keep the sea lanes open for American ships wherever they might seek to go; an Army large enough, and well enough equipped and based, to fight off immediately any challenge to American supremacy on the continent; and a system of internal transportation adequate for free and rapid movement of troops and supplies from one extremity of the land to the other. He would mitigate the financial strain of war by linking the Treasury to a National Bank; and he favored a tariff sufficient to insure necessary industrial production, should the paths of commerce be closed by war. He believed that goal had now been in large measure assured. Clothing and supplies of the Army were of domestic origin; the Navy was growing; internal transportation was greatly improved; the nation was independent and free. Further extension of the duties would only jeopardize the final achievement of the program, for it must result in declining revenues and in the end in declining agriculture.[1]

The alternative solution abandoned altogether the policy of free trade in favor of the continuous and increasing protection of American industry through prohibitive duties on competing foreign products. From 1816 to 1824 the issue between these two solutions was fought out, but the argument came to be more and more one-sided. The profits of industry, even under the mild protection of the 1816 tariff, mounted as high as twenty-five percent, while agriculture yielded no more than four and the slave-tilled Southern soil often returned as low as two percent.[2] It was inevitable that capital should flow to industry, and inevitable that political power should follow. Nor is it surprising that the cleavage should come along sectional lines, for representation in Congress was sectional and each member generally if not invariably spoke for the dominant interest of his constituents. Ever since Alexander Hamilton's assumption law, wealth had been flowing to the North and East, and such measures as military pensions and the United States Bank only hastened the process. With the abandonment of free trade, shipping declined; and the wealth of the North and East was invested in manufacturing, at home or in the West. Tariff sentiment rose with rising profits, and the Ohio Valley lost its early leadership of the protectionist movement, which came to be as completely sectional as slavery itself.

Moves to increase the tariff had been made in every Congress since 1816, but so far sweeping changes had been defeated, albeit by narrowing margins. The Eighteenth Congress, however, was a different proposition. The apportionment following the census of 1820 was for the first time in effect. Those sections which had been overwhelmingly in favor of the tariff of 1816—New York, Pennsylvania and the West—had gained twenty-eight seats. The sections that had split more or less evenly on the earlier tariff had lost three seats; and the South, which alone had vigorously opposed from the start, had gained only six members. At the same time, eight of the twelve seats added in the Senate since 1816 went to tariff regions.[3] This time success seemed assured; and a long and detailed bill revising the duties upward was introduced into the House on January 9, 1824, by Representative John Tod of Bedford, Pennsylvania, chairman of the Committee on Manufactures.

Before the bill was called up in February, the sectional nature of the issue was pointed by a measure providing Federal funds to survey routes for roads and canals. The question as to whether these public works were ultimately to be constructed by the nation or by the states was left in abeyance; but the discussion soon turned into a disagreement over the meaning of the Constitution. Since the proposed surveys would be made by the War Department, Calhoun was called upon for an opinion, and he skillfully steered a middle course. He still believed that the power to build roads and canals belonged to Congress, but except in some grave emergency he would not exercise it without the consent of the affected states.[4] The answer was too equivocal for the Virginians, who were bent upon preventing any enlargement by construction of the powers of the Federal Government. John Randolph, always a gadfly and often a prophet, minced no words in explaining why. "If Congress possess the power to do what is proposed in this bill," the shrill, piping voice rang out above the murmur in the chamber, "they may emancipate every slave in the United States. . . ."[5]

The surveys for roads and canals were authorized notwithstanding, but more than one Southern member turned to the tariff debate with Randolph's warning still ringing in his ears.

2

The various duties embraced by the tariff bill were taken up, one at a time, and each separate item had its partisans. Although members might be only lukewarm on some points, the particular product of their own section was, of course, a special case in which further protection would be desirable. It was lead in Missouri and Illinois, hemp in Kentucky, iron in Pennsylvania, wool in Ohio and New York, and so on down the line. It was only when the general principle of the bill, protection itself, was debated that the argument rose above the level of petty trading. The weight of eloquence was all against, with Hamilton, Poinsett and McDuffie taking leading roles; but the most important debate was that between Henry Clay and Daniel Webster.

Clay spoke on the thirtieth and thirty-first of March, spoke as well as he had ever spoken in his life, to proclaim an "American System," a nationalistic economy self-contained and self-sufficient. He was answered by Webster on April second. Though the Massachusetts hinterland was turning steadily to manufactures, Boston still wavered. Her old allegiance to the sea was strong; and when Webster circularized fifty businessmen of his acquaintance for opinions on the tariff, they were dominantly for free trade which had once passed the wealth of the continent through their hands.[6] So Webster opposed the protectionism of Clay, after a single evening's preparation, in a speech which he thought "clumsy, wanting in method, and tedious."[7] It was in fact one of the best arguments of his brilliant career, and one of the most embarrassing; for the tariff of 1824 dealt the final blow to Boston's commerce, her capital shifted to industry, and Webster turned in consequence to the protective policy, but never was he able to refute effectively this anti-tariff speech of 1824.

On the sixteenth McDuffie closed the case for free trade but his opponents, sure of their strength, did not bother to reply. They called instead for the question, sustained the call, and the bill was carried 107 to 102. The vote was strictly sectional, with only one Southern member favoring. That one was Johnson of Virginia, who represented Monongalia County, then as now in the Pittsburgh area. The lines drawn by the Presidential campaign were not in evidence, as each man voted according to the whim of the economically dominant group in his district, regardless of the stand taken by the particular candidate whose partisan he was.

In the Senate the process was repeated, with, if possible, an even greater preponderance of ability on the side of free trade, for the Senate had no Henry Clay. Young Robert Y. Hayne led the fight against the tariff, but was ably seconded by such battle-scarred veterans as Rufus King, Samuel Smith of Maryland, back once more in the upper chamber, and old John Taylor of Virginia. The protectionists said little, but when the votes were counted the bill had passed, 25 to 21. Here, too, the vote was sectional, with the South solidly against, the West solidly for, the tariff. Pennsylvania favored the bill, Massachusetts and Delaware opposed, Maryland and New York were split. A conference report on amendments was accepted by both Houses on May 19, and the President signed the bill on the twenty-second.

The average rate of duty was thirty-seven percent, or almost twice the rate under the act of 1816.

3

The passage of the tariff of 1824 marked a turning point in Calhoun's intellectual growth, though he was himself only dimly aware of it at the time. For the tariff showed that self-interest rather than reason determined the votes of the people's representatives, and that the self-interest of a Representative or Senator was dictated by the beliefs of the dominant—or most articulate—economic group among his constituents. It showed that no real barrier existed to prevent the majority from voting into their own hands the wealth and property of the nation.

The Constitution has always been the refuge of the minority, and so it was in this case; but there were those who saw, as early as 1824, that the appeal must be futile. Since the tariff would be in effect a subsidy to the manufacturers at the expense of agriculture, and particularly of the cotton planters, it was the latter who first raised the question of constitutionality. A vigorous memorial from the citizens of Charleston in February affirmed that the power to regulate commerce with foreign nations had not been given to Congress for any such purpose and that, if the contemplated act were not actually unconstitutional, it was yet "inconsistent with the character and spirit of our confederated Government."[8] James

Hamilton, Jr., repeated the charge in the House,[9] but it was the Virginians who most clearly saw the implications of the policy.

It was a policy intended less to encourage manufactures than to enrich a pecuniary aristocracy: in the words of John Taylor of Caroline, a "bill of bargains" by which many local interests were to be brought to serve a capitalist master, and which must in the end destroy the essence if not the forms of representative government.[10] Brilliant, erratic Randolph impatiently brushed the constitutional argument aside. "If, under a power to regulate trade, you prevent exportation; if, with the most approved spring lancets, you draw the last drop of blood from our veins; if, *secundum artem,* you draw the last shilling from our pockets, what are the checks of the Constitution to us? A fig for the Constitution! When the scorpion's sting is probing us to the quick, shall we stop to chop logic? Shall we get some learned and cunning clerk to say whether the power to do this is to be found in the Constitution, and then, if he, from whatever motive, shall maintain the affirmative, like the animal whose fleece forms so material a portion of this bill, lie quietly down to be shorn?"[11] In vain did Poinsett warn that Great Britain would seek cotton for her mills in Mexico and Brazil if American ports were closed to her manufactures. In vain did McDuffie argue that the tariff was not even in the real interest of those sections by which it was supported. It would bring wealth to a class, and that class had influence in Congress out of all proportion to its numbers.

It was a foregone conclusion that the opposition to the tariff would eventually be absorbed into the State Rights school, for where but in the states could power possibly be found to arrest the advance of the subsidy system? And where but in the states, in the role of economic minorities, lay the will? Since they could not outvote the tariff advocates in Congress, the only avenue left open was to deny the right of Congress to legislate on the question at all; and such an approach had been the very substance of the State Rights tradition since the Alien and Sedition Acts and the famous resolutions of '98 and '99. Already the spirit of nullification was implicit in the particularist attacks upon the Supreme Court, which had in five leading cases upheld the Federal Government against the states and in a sixth, the Dartmouth College case, had pro-

claimed the inviolability of the corporate charter. Two other cases
in which the same principles were at stake were before the court
while the tariff fight was on and were decided before the subsidy to
industry was voted. In Osborn vs. Bank of the United States,
decided March 19, the doctrine of Federal supremacy was reaffirmed, after the court had, on March 2, elaborated on the theory
of corporations in Gibbons vs. Ogden.

In the latter case the Livingstons' monopoly of New York
waters for purposes of steam navigation was broken. The commerce moving over the Hudson and New York Bay was interstate,
and only Congress had the power to regulate it. There is little
doubt that the monopoly in question was vicious, but in destroying
it the court opened the way for vast interstate monopolies beyond
the power of the states to regulate or control. Control by taxation
had already been denied in M'Culloch vs. Maryland, and now regulation by charter was also forbidden; yet for generations the obvious corollary, that if the states could not regulate business the
nation must, was rejected. The decision in Gibbons vs. Ogden was
in effect a recognition of the fact that economic interests might
transcend state lines; but it provided no means by which the power
of these interests, the greater for their territorial extent, might be
controlled if Congress chose to leave them unhampered.

At the time these decisions were made, the court was already
under fire in a number of states where local laws had been overruled, and the tariff issue then pending in Congress had already
been linked in Taylor's *Tyranny Unmasked* with the criticism of
judicial supremacy. Allusions to the Federal nature of the Union
were common in the tariff debate as they had been in the debates on
the Missouri Compromise, and the State Rights school gained an
impetus it could never have had on the merits of its political
arguments alone.

4

Calhoun himself took no active part in the tariff discussion, although it was well understood that Hayne, Poinsett, Hamilton and
particularly McDuffie expressed his views. He was too deeply involved in the Presidential campaign to seek any controversy that

could be avoided, and he was already having all he could do to keep clear of the latest onslaught by the Radicals.

In the interval between the Presidential caucus and the Pennsylvania State Convention, Monroe had nominated Ninian Edwards to the long vacant Mexican mission. The Crawford followers in the Senate immediately attacked the appointment on suspicion that the A. B. papers of the previous year had been the work of the Illinois Senator, but the storm subsided and he was confirmed by a large majority. He was on the very point of leaving for his post when a report from the Treasury, in which his testimony in the A. B. investigation was flatly impeached, was laid before the House. Apparently timed to coincide with Edwards' departure, it would presumably be months before he heard of it, and long before any counteraction could be taken the election would be over. Almost at the moment of his boarding the stage, however, a copy of the report was placed in his hands by his son-in-law, Illinois Representative Daniel P. Cook. He prepared his answer on the way to Wheeling, mailing it back from that city on April 6.[12]

The answer was addressed to the Speaker of the House, but was actually mailed to Calhoun, who was expected to supply any documents needed in support of it, and probably also to intercede with the President should that become necessary. In it, Edwards acknowledged himself the author of the A. B. papers and repeated in summary form all the charges he had there made against Crawford. A committee whose leading members were John Floyd, Daniel Webster and Edward Livingston was appointed, and a messenger was immediately dispatched to find Edwards and bring him back to Washington. The Radicals spread the story that the Mexican mission was his reward for destroying Crawford, and Monroe was with difficulty restrained by his Cabinet from removing Edwards without waiting for the hearing.

The committee sat until well into June, although Congress had long since adjourned, but in the end it was political expediency that won the day. Edwards was discredited, not because his charges were demonstrated to be false, but because strong testimony was presented to show that he had denied his authorship of the A. B. papers in order to secure Senate confirmation of his appointment to Mexico. The evidence did in fact weigh heavily against the Treasury, but the report which Webster handed to the President on June 21 concluded that nothing had been proved "to impeach the integrity of the Secretary, or to bring into doubt the general correctness and ability of his administration of the public finances."

The Cabinet, save for Crawford, had been on hand since early morning and remained with the President the rest of the day, the question being whether Edwards should be removed, and what if any action should be taken. The group met again at eight the next morning—an unheard-of hour for Cabinet discussion—and did not break up until after nine at night. In the course of the day Edwards' resignation was received and was finally accepted, although Calhoun, Southard, Wirt and even Adams agreed that the committee's conclusion was not justified by the evidence.[13] It was simply the easiest course and the one that would bring least criticism upon the President.

The last chapter in the case was written on the Fourth of July, 1824, when the former Illinois Senator was excluded from the Independence Day dinner in the Capital. In consequence, Adams, Calhoun and Postmaster General McLean publicly withdrew their own subscriptions to the dinner; and Wirt, who was to be out of the city, publicly endorsed the stand of his colleagues.[14]

5

Even more serious for Calhoun's future than the "A. B. plot" was a quarrel with Georgia over the removal of the Cherokees which reached its climax at about the same time and was undoubtedly inspired in part by the hostility of the Crawford faction which controlled the state. The origin of the difficulty went back to 1802 when the territory comprising the future states of Alabama and Mississippi had been ceded by Georgia to the United States. As its part of the bargain the Federal Government agreed to secure extinguishment of the Indian title to all lands still held by the tribes in the mother state as soon as it could be done peaceably and on reasonable terms. Although much had been accomplished, some ten million acres still remained in Indian hands after twenty years, and Radical politicians blamed the delay on the Secretary of War.[15]

Egged on by the Georgia delegation, Congress at last appropriated money for the purpose, and late in 1823 negotiations with the Cherokees were started, only to meet with a polite but definite refusal to sell. Word of the failure was followed almost immediately by the arrival in Washington of four Cherokee chiefs, who informed the President, not at all submissively, of their determination to cede no more lands.

Calhoun answered near the end of January 1824, pointing out how impossible it would be for the tribe to maintain itself for long as an independent nation within the limits of Georgia or any other state. He offered them tribal lands beyond the Mississippi or cash with which to purchase land as individuals, in Georgia or elsewhere. They must move outside the states altogether or merge with the white population and become themselves citizens.[16] The Indians did not see why they had to do either. They were satisfied with their situation and were unfavorably impressed by the experience of those of their tribe who had emigrated. Since they did not intend to move or sell out, the time would never come when their title could be extinguished peaceably and on reasonable conditions, so it was manifestly impossible for the United States to carry out its part of the compact with Georgia.

Calhoun had long advocated the civilization of the Indians, and the astonishing articulateness of these Cherokee chiefs must have pleased him even while it forced upon him a most unpleasant dilemma. He could do nothing, however, except to refer the correspondence to the Georgia authorities. For three weeks the question simmered while Congress debated the tariff and the Indians moved freely in the society of the Capital, acting, in Adams' phrase, like "well-bred country gentlemen."[17] On March 10, however, the Georgia Senators and Representatives stated their case in unmistakable language. If the Indians were now unwilling to emigrate, they contended, it was the fault of the policy pursued by the administration since 1819: Calhoun's policy of civilizing the red men. It was up to the United States Government to fulfil its compact and remove the unwanted occupants. Georgia would under no consideration accept the Indians as citizens. They must go. If not peaceably, then they must be evicted by force.

Though the Indians were clearly in the right, the moral issue

was bound to be disregarded. Land speculation still raged in the
state, fostered and encouraged by rival lottery schemes of the Clark
and Crawford factions. If the Cherokee lands had not been sold
already, they soon would be; and the dominant majority was hardly
likely to give in on merely ethical grounds, particularly where the
minority was despised because of race and customs. It was the
prejudice against the Indian as such that lent point to the present
argument; for even had they not coveted their lands, the Geor-
gians—and generally speaking, the whites everywhere—would still
have resented Calhoun's efforts to civilize the "savages." The fact
that the Cherokees had their own courts, Lancaster schools and
other civilized institutions was in itself enough to arouse the indignation of their white neighbors; and Calhoun's inadvertence in
addressing the visiting chiefs as "Gentlemen" was the ultimate
insult.[18]

Monroe laid the matter before Congress early in April, reaffirming his wish to civilize the Indians and his hope that they could yet
be induced to remove beyond the Mississippi, but explicitly denying any obligation or right on the part of the United States to
force them to do so. The message and an accompanying report
from Calhoun were referred to a special committee. Its chairman,
however, was John Forsyth, who had drafted the letter from the
Georgia delegation, and its report was merely a reiteration with
footnotes and documents of the position taken by the Georgia members.

The four Cherokee chiefs chose the same day to address to the
Senate a commentary on the President's message with its supporting papers. They denied that they had been inspired in their attitude by any white man and called the Georgia charges a subterfuge.
They had accepted the civilization of the whites and now made
their living by agriculture, manufactures and mechanic arts. They
were "peacefully endeavoring to enjoy the blessings of civilization
and Christianity on the soil of their rightful inheritance," and they
did not intend to be pushed back again into barbarism by being
transported to a wilderness where they must resume the chase and
defend themselves in arms against more primitive tribes.[19] Calhoun
could have asked no better proof of the practicability of his Indian
policy, if only the greed and the prejudice of the whites would per-

mit it to operate; for these same candid and cultivated Cherokees had been marauding savages harrying the Long Canes settlement within the memory of men still living.

6

A separate Office of Indian Affairs was created in the War Department in March 1824, under the superintendency of Thomas L. McKenney. Crawford had first proposed such an office in 1815, and Calhoun had sought Monroe's consent to the move in 1818 and again in 1822. It was not until the controversy with Georgia, however, that the President at last approved.[20] The immediate result was to relieve the Secretary of an immense amount of administrative detail, leaving him free to give his best energies to the major problems of his office.

All summer long and on into the fall, Indian chiefs in buckskin and feathers or in the soberer dress of the white man moved in and out of the building that housed the War Department, as Calhoun tried to effect a permanent solution of the Indian problem. The only answer that would be acceptable to the whites was to transport the Indians beyond the confines of the United States, but to gain the consent of the Indians Calhoun knew that they must be guaranteed security in their new homes. Patience and forbearance, he was sure, would overcome friction between neighboring tribes, if only Congress would provide that, once relocated, their lands would not again be encroached upon and themselves required once more to move. By the end of 1824 plans were complete to resettle eighty thousand Indians in the country west of the existing territories: in the present states of Oklahoma, Kansas, Nebraska, Iowa, Wisconsin and if need be Minnesota and the Dakotas. He insisted on only one point. The Indians must be guaranteed permanent, undisturbed possession of the lands allotted to them. [21]

The plan came to nothing through the sheer inertia of Congress, and Calhoun was charged later with having cleverly designed the scheme to thwart the Missouri Compromise. For had it become law, there would have been no land north of 36° 30' to which settlers from the free states might emigrate.[22] Such a Machiavellian design would have been far beyond him, even had he wished at that date to upset the compromise. He had, moreover, advanced the same general plan in 1818, well before the Missouri question arose. He simply failed to realize, as did those who were to criticize him later, the terrifying speed with which the continent would be occupied. He thought the civilization of the Indians could be accomplished long before the Western lands would be needed for settlement by the whites.

During the summer, too, he worked long and enthusiastically on surveys for roads and canals. When his old teacher, Benjamin Silliman, visited Washington late in May, he found Calhoun full of plans for internal improvements; and Nathan Sargent—Oliver Oldschool of the *United States Gazette*—calling at the War Department in June, reported that the Secretary "soon had his table and floor covered with maps" to illustrate his program.[23] Later in the summer he visited the "summit of the Allegaheny" to satisfy himself that there was "an ample supply of water" for one of his projects, presumably Gallatin's old plan for a canal to link the Susquehanna and Allegheny Rivers.[24]

To such questions he could turn with real relief, once he had withdrawn from the Presidential race. At the same time his military program began to appear to Congress in a new light, and he experienced no difficulty in getting appropriations for the disputed coastal forts, Dauphin Island alone excepted. Those who most objected to him as a President were quick to note, as soon as there was no possibility of his becoming one in the near future, that he had, after all, made a very good Secretary of War. "Judging by the various reports that all of us have seen from the war department," wrote Niles, "the order and harmony, regularity and promptitude, punctuality and responsibility, introduced by Mr. Calhoun in every branch of the service, has never been rivalled, and perhaps, cannot be excelled—and, it must be recollected, that he brought this system out of chaos."[25]

It was indeed an enviable record Calhoun had made in his first administrative post. The organization of the War Department was given a form so nearly definitive that no essential changes were needed, even to cope with the shock of Civil War forty years later, and it long served as the model after which other departments were patterned.[26] Annual reports covering both finances and activities were inaugurated. Forty-five million dollars of unsettled accounts were reduced to three million, and a system instituted which had already cut defalcations from three percent of the amount disbursed to two-tenths of one percent, and in another year would eliminate them entirely. Despite checks and setbacks the military frontier had been pushed westward by three hundred miles. The coast defenses had been immeasurably strengthened. The Military Academy had been modernized and given something like academic standing. An artillery school had been established at Fortress Monroe. The per capita cost of the Army had been materially lowered while rations and equipment were greatly improved, and its effectiveness increased in spite of reduced numbers and wider territorial distribution. Its organization was more efficient than it had ever previously been, even in wartime.

If Calhoun's Indian policies were less successful than his efforts in behalf of the Army, it was not because they were less sound but rather that they were too advanced for the time. A man of enormous energy and dominant ambition, for his country as well as for himself, Calhoun conceived his schemes in terms of his own capacity and vision. He credited others with an intelligence, a will and a patriotism equal to his own; and when they failed him, as men invariably will when asked to keep pace with genius, his plans fell through; yet even in his failures he surpassed the triumphs of ordinary men.

CHAPTER XXIV

CLAY MAKES A PRESIDENT

1

As THE first hesitant buds began to show in the hills behind Oakly, Calhoun watched the Presidential contest from which he was now withdrawn, and pondered his own position. Adams, for all his ability, was temperamentally unfit for party leadership, and Jackson was too precipitate and headstrong to be entrusted with executive power; yet it was now clear that if Crawford was to be defeated it must be at the hands of one of these two. He saw little to choose between them and was reluctant to ally himself with either. His own chances of succeeding to the Presidency would not be improved by supporting a losing candidate nor by serving an unsuccessful administration. The Vice Presidency seemed the only neutral station he might occupy, and the Pennsylvania state convention showed him the way out of his dilemma. Adams and Jackson were runing as candidates of the same party. There could be no incongruity, therefore, in his appearing on both tickets for the second office, and immediately after the Harrisburg nominations he sought the blessing of the Adams faction.

From the initial overtures early in March until the very eve of the election itself, negotiations continued through various intermediaries, the most frequent of these being John W. Taylor and General Jacob Brown. Since he still suffered from a partially paralyzed hand, Brown was usually accompanied by his aide, Lieutenant John A. Dix, in the capacity of amanuensis, and it is from a memorandum prepared by Dix immediately after the election that most of our knowledge of the circumstances comes.[1]

When first approached, Adams would not consider the proposition. Forgetting his animosity of the winter, he had reverted to his original plan, which was to have Jackson for Vice President and Calhoun in the State Department or, if he preferred, in the Treasury. It was an arrangement that would combine in one party the three men who professed to stand for the policies of Monroe's administration and to oppose the rising influence of machine politics, drawing strength at the same time from all sections of the country. In the abstract, it was a logical grouping, but in practice, as Calhoun tried again and again to make Adams see, it was impossible; for Jackson was after the Presidency, and the more support Adams' friends gave him for the second office, the more they strengthened his chances of the first. Calhoun, moreover, did not wish any place in an Adams Cabinet. He knew all too well his colleague's "peculiarities of temper" and had no intention of identifying himself with an administration he believed doomed to certain failure.

Adams refused to accept the possibility of neutrality. In return for endorsing Calhoun's Vice-Presidential aspirations, he wanted a public declaration in his own favor, and regarded the Carolinian's unwillingness to give it as proof that he was secretly supporting Jackson. He branded the whole scheme as selfish and unprincipled, but he continued the discussions in hopes of winning Calhoun over to his own plan.

In the midst of these negotiations Crawford, whose health had been slowly improving for the last four or five months, suffered a sudden relapse and was again the bedridden, helpless, almost sightless wreck he had been early in the winter. This time even his best friends doubted that he could pull through, and his managers began to look frantically for a substitute.[2] Late in May Colonel John Taylor of Caroline, aged and ill but with no jot of his mental powers impaired, suggested to Adams that he might now carry Virginia.[3] In such a contingency an alliance with Calhoun would be a burden, and the discussions abruptly ceased.

But Crawford, far from being withdrawn, miraculously began to mend; and Adams, on a visit to his native Massachusetts, finally conceded that Jackson would not be content with the secondary role.[4] The New Englander's friends made new overtures to Calhoun and negotiations were resumed. General Brown again took the lead in almost daily conferences and even committed his impressions to paper in the form of letters to John W. Taylor, written by Dix at the General's dictation. From these it was possible to infer a pledge of support for Adams from Calhoun, if one wished to infer it; but Dix, though he transcribed the letters, insisted that no such promise had at any time been made. Brown himself believed that Calhoun preferred Adams to Jackson, as indeed he did at that time; but it was Brown and not Calhoun who construed this preference into an avowal of partisanship.

The Secretary of War was not in the city when the final conferences were held. He had gone to Yorktown in company with the nation's distinguished guest, the beloved Lafayette, who was beginning an extended visit in America. He returned near the middle of November to learn that Adams had at last agreed to accept him as his own candidate for Vice President. It was a concession largely meaningless, for Calhoun's election to that office was already a certainty.[5]

2

The election went far to confirm Calhoun's claim to being the most national of the candidates, for he had polled 182 electoral votes for the second office, from every corner of the Union. In only four states—Connecticut, Georgia, Ohio and Virginia—did he fail entirely; and his total was but one short of the combined strength of the two leaders for the Presidency. True to the stand he had taken from the beginning, he rejoiced in the defeat of Crawford and regarded Adams' success in New York no less than Jackson's in the Carolinas as an overwhelming victory.[6]

For the Presidency no candidate had a majority and so the final choice, as had long been anticipated, would have to be made by the House. Adams had carried all of New England and most of New York, to get 84 electoral votes. Crawford had polled only 41, mainly from Virginia and Georgia where the State Rights movement was strongest; and Clay received 37, the bulk of them from industrial Kentucky and Ohio. It was Andrew Jackson who led the procession with 99 electoral votes, and in his case alone sectional issues did not appear to be decisive. In reality Jackson's too was a sectional following, but of a type less easy to distinguish. It was not regional but stratified, coming from a section not bounded by state lines but by property and debt; and since the dispossessed always outnumber those with means, he rolled up a decisive margin in the popular vote.

When the delayed returns from Louisiana were received in Washington in the middle of December, showing that Crawford rather than Clay would go to the House with the two leaders, it was apparent that the Kentuckian's partisans might well determine the choice.[7] The rivalry between Calhoun and Clay for the succession made it inevitable that they should now be on opposite sides, and that the ambitions of these future aspirants to the crownless throne should influence the present contest.

This outcome was implicit in the circumstances and was unquestionably fully perceived by the protagonists themselves. It had been foreseen by Plumer before the end of 1822, and so we may be sure it had not escaped Adams.[8] The Pennsylvania nomination of Calhoun on the Jackson ticket implied a similar understanding of it on the part of the Jackson managers. Adams' appreciation of this conflict between Calhoun and Clay for the succession was one of the factors that led him to resist so long accepting the former as his own running mate; for he feared that should he thus tacitly endorse Calhoun's pretensions as Jackson had already done, Clay would be driven into the arms of Crawford whom he might thereby elect.

Just what Adams, as a result of General Brown's oversanguine reports, may have expected from Calhoun is not clear; but the election was no sooner over than he began to voice his disapproval of the Carolinian's conduct to various of his intimates, including Plumer and Brown.[9] Brown indeed took credit to himself for "having obtained the Vice Presidency" for Calhoun, and was, if anything, more dissatisfied with the result than Adams. He remained displeased, even after seeking and receiving an explanation, which was most probably a denial from Calhoun that he had ever pledged support to the New Englander and a reiteration of his intention to remain neutral.

It was at this point that the election returns arrived from Louisiana, and Clay's friends let it be known that their principal "was much disposed to support" Adams, "if he could at the same time be useful to himself." A day or two later Robert P. Letcher went so far as to hint that the Kentucky members might even be willing to disregard instructions from their state legislature if they could be sure that Clay would be offered a suitable place in the administration.[10] At the same time, Clay's partisans were sounding out the Crawford and Jackson factions, but the terms were too harsh. They wanted nothing less than the succession at the end of a single term.[11]

Adams, too, was looking around. Shortly before Christmas he interrupted his discussions with Letcher long enough to have a "confidential conversation of more than two hours" with Senator James Barbour of the Radicals. He explained that he had meant no disrespect to Crawford when he had refused to attend the Fourth of July dinner from which Ninian Edwards had been excluded, and that he would favor reducing the tariff if it "should be found to bear hard upon the agricultural and commercial interests." Barbour's contribution to amity was an assurance that Adams would be Virginia's second choice.[12] Adams also considered Webster's desire for the London mission, expressed to Plumer;[13] gave favorable attention to a consular appointment desired by Van Buren for a constituent;[14] and hearkened attentively to General Brown's wish for "a good understanding" with Clinton, whom he hoped to see in the next administration.[15]

There was no doubt, however, that the proposition from Clay struck Adams most favorably. Letcher made it clear before the end of December that the Kentuckian's friends could elect Adams in the House on the first ballot and were disposed to do so, with the definite expectation of throwing the South into opposition and making Clay the next President.[16] Adams maintained his reserve, but as the new year dawned he agreed to a tête-à-tête. On January 8, the anniversary of Jackson's triumph at New Orleans, Clay wrote to Francis P. Blair that while the choice was a choice of evils he meant to support Adams. He did not wish to give further impulse to the military spirit. And the next day he called on the Secretary of State. "He wished me," the latter wrote in his diary, "to satisfy him with regard to some principles of great public importance, but without any personal considerations for himself."[17] Presumably the principles referred to were those which made up Clay's American System; and Adams seems to have been able to satisfy the foremost champion of the tariff as easily as he had satisfied the strongly antitariff Barbour. At any rate, Clay publicly declared for Adams on January 24.

3

As Adams became more deeply entangled with the Clay faction, he became increasingly hostile toward Calhoun, who still strove to preserve an uneasy neutrality. Appearances pointed to the conclusion that he favored Jackson, as his own interests would seem to have required. John McLean, who was close to him at the time, believed that he had cast in his lot with the General, and there was a common impression that such was the case.[18] The fact remains, however, that the Vice President-elect, whatever his personal predilections may have been, studiously avoided any move that might influence the election one way or the other. He might better have supported Jackson actively; for Adams had decided to accept Clay's aid, which meant to all minds but his own committing the Presidential succession and thereby renouncing any claim he may have had on Calhoun.

Once his decision was taken, nothing the Carolinian did or failed to do found any favor in Adams' eyes. Brown still sought interviews with his chief, and continued to come away dissatisfied. He reported to Adams on January nineteenth Calhoun's conviction that the Western states would be solidly for Jackson, which would insure the General's election; and Adams answered that the War Secretary "must either be grossly misinformed or too well informed." As it happened, it was misinformation, for Calhoun did not yet know that Adams had come to an understanding with Clay. The next day Cook brought the same information and went on to explain that he too would have to vote for Jackson if all the other Western states did so. Adams was quite prepared for Cook's follow-up that Ingham, R. M. Johnson and McDuffie had been trying to swing his vote, by threats and promises, and had hinted at an organized opposition should Adams win. He blamed it, of course, on Calhoun, as he blamed every move of the latter's former partisans that was not directly in his own interest.[19] He could not, or would not, see that with Calhoun's withdrawal from the Presidential contest, his party had passed into other hands, and his partisans, being beyond his power to reward, were also beyond his power to control.

For the record Adams asked Cook to reduce to writing the substance of his conversations with Ingham and McDuffie, which he promised to do; but as Adams repeats Cook's story there are certain essential departures from the original version.[20] This time there are no threats but only a prediction, eminently sound. Cook was seeking appointment as Governor of Arkansas Territory, and Ingham, he alleges, told him he would get it by voting for Jackson. Cook's answer was admittedly offensive, and the subject was dropped. McDuffie's threat of "a formal, determined, and organized opposition" in event of an Adams victory was now reduced to a prophecy that the coalition with Clay would arouse such popular indignation that Adams would be ruined.

Surely there was nothing here beyond accepted political usage, and nothing whatever to connect Calhoun with it, save only that Ingham and McDuffie had been his partisans. Yet as early as 1821 Adams had been told by Jackson's personal representative that McDuffie was the particular friend of the General in the House;[21] and with Pennsylvania committed as she was to the Hero, it would have been political suicide for Ingham to remain passive. Other former Calhoun men, like T. J. Rogers, Webster, Edwards, McLean, Southard and the whole Calhoun faction in New York were actively supporting Adams; but he chose to regard as a breach of faith anything less than the full and complete endorsement of himself by each and every one of Calhoun's onetime partisans.

Even after the public announcement that the Kentucky and Ohio delegations would vote for Adams, Calhoun repeated to General Brown his assurances of neutrality between the two leading contenders and expressed a personal preference for the New Englander.[22] It was obvious he saw no harm in what had taken place. The Jackson managers, however, saw both harm and an opportunity. On the twenty-eighth an unsigned letter appeared in the *Columbian Observer* of Philadelphia, a Jackson organ, charging that Clay had thrown his strength to Adams in return for the first office in the Cabinet and the succession; and the "corrupt bargain" became thenceforth the Jackson rallying cry.

Clay's answer was the impetuous publication of a "card" in the *National Intelligencer* calling the writer of the letter "a base and infamous calumniator, a dastard and a liar," and demanding satisfaction; whereupon Representative George Kremer of Pennsylvania, plump and simple and incapable of guile, declared himself the man; and the laugh was on Clay. He knew, of course, that behind Kremer lay the Jackson machine, he had reason to believe in the person of Major John H. Eaton, but no proof could be had and so there occurred no duel. Instead Clay demanded an investigation of the charges by the House and a committee was chosen, but nothing came of it.[23]

The charges against Clay were of course charges against Adams also; and though he reacted in his own peculiar way, he was quite as extravagant as the Kentuckian. The entries in his diary for this period seem designed to show that political pressure of the strongest kind—promise of office and threat of ruin—was being brought to bear on members of Congress in Jackson's interest, and that at the bottom of it all was Calhoun who, since he could not be President himself, was bent upon making and controlling a President.

4

Feeling was running dangerously high when the long-awaited day arrived. Promptly at noon on February 9, 1825, the members of the Senate, preceded by the Sergeant at Arms and their President pro tempore, John Gaillard, filed into the chamber of the House. Outside there was snow on the ground and an ominous chill in the air not altogether attributable to the weather. Elsewhere in the city an effigy of John Quincy Adams was ready for the burning, and men with hard hands and leathery faces recalled approvingly the well-known Jackson way of righting wrongs.

In the almost offensively new Hall of Representatives the electoral votes were ceremoniously counted, though everyone had known the result for two months already. Calhoun was duly declared elected Vice President of the United States; the names of Jackson, Adams and Crawford were laid before the House as the men from whom a President must be chosen, and the Senators withdrew.

In the Speaker's room, meanwhile, a venerable, silver-haired old man whose work was all but done and two who were to inherit the future had been enacting a dramatic scene. The old man was

Stephen Van Rensselaer, known to all New York as "the Patroon"; and his companions were tall, persuasive Henry Clay and "Black Dan" Webster of the massive head and golden tongue. The votes of twelve states, thanks to Clay, were assured for Adams, but thirteen were needed to elect a President. The New York delegation stood seventeen for the New Englander and seventeen against, which meant no choice on the first ballot, and perhaps the failure of Clay's plan. For Van Buren had a plan also. He would foil Clay for a ballot or two by keeping the New York vote tied. Then he would break the deadlock in Adams' favor and he, not Clay, would be the President-maker. So Webster and Clay had cornered the Patroon, originally a Crawford man, and proposed to change his vote.

They told him the election rested with him alone, for should he not switch to Adams there would be no majority, and the most dire consequences must ensue. No doubt anarchy was the theme most often dwelt upon, for Van Rensselaer was a man of property and wealth. When they left him he was confused and indecisive. Louis McLane met him and tried to refix his mind on Crawford, but the confusion only grew worse. As the roll of the states was being taken, the old man bowed his head in prayer, and when he opened his eyes, lo, at his feet lay a sign: an Adams ballot. He picked it up and hastily stuffed it into the ballot box. New York cast her vote for Adams, and Clay had made a President.[24]

That evening Monroe gave his last Presidential levee. The rooms of the White House were crowded to overflowing with heroes of the past, the present and the future. Lafayette, the President-elect, Calhoun, Jackson and a host of other distinguished political figures were in the company. Among the guests were Samuel F. B. Morse and a young English visitor, Edward Stanley, member of Parliament and one day as Earl of Derby to be Prime Minister of Great Britain. To Morse, who studied men to paint them, Adams "seemed in some degree to shake off his habitual reserve, and, although he endeavored to suppress his feeling of gratification at his success, it was not difficult to perceive that he felt in high spirits on the occasion."[25] The Englishman's opinion was a very different one. "I never saw a more sinister expression of countenance," he wrote, "than that of Mr. Adams—his figure is short & thick, and his air is that of low cunning & dissimulation, which I believe has not been much belied by the course of his political career."[26]

Jackson, dignified and unaffected, congratulated his successful rival with seeming sincerity; and President Monroe, determined as always to avoid unpleasantness, treated both men with studied impartiality. He did not even congratulate Adams lest it be construed as indicating a preference, and the next evening at a military ball he deftly steered the conversation away from the election. On the eleventh, however, the President-elect sought out his predecessor at the Executive Mansion; and with no prying eyes to see, Monroe offered the customary felicitations and said he would stand ready at any time to help in any way he could. Adams told him he had asked Crawford to retain the Treasury (in spite of his expressed belief that the A. B. charges were substantiated by the documents) but the Georgian had courteously declined. Monroe got the impression James Barbour was second choice. Southard would retain the Navy, and Clay was to be Secretary of State. Monroe feared the consequences but gathered that the offer had already been made, so he said nothing.

Adams went from the White House direct to an interview with Clay, where the first office in the Cabinet was in fact tendered to the Kentuckian, while Monroe retired to his study and wrote an account of his interview with Adams. The prospect of Clay in the Cabinet after all the "bargain" charges so troubled the President that he wondered if there were yet time to interfere, and after sleeping on it he sent General Brown to make sure that he had not misunderstood. Brown apparently did not say he came from Monroe, but did expostulate vigorously against Clay's appointment, arguing that the place should go to Clinton. Adams assured him the offer to Clay had already been made, and Monroe wrote another memorandum.[27]

Calhoun himself did not take seriously the bargain charges leveled at Adams until the rumor became current that Clay would indeed become Secretary of State. In such an eventuality, his own political future was at stake and the prosperity of the South in jeopardy. With this the South Carolina delegation in Congress agreed, and one of its members, probably Poinsett, conveyed to Adams an offer of support on condition that Clay be excluded from the Cabinet. The overture was rejected.[28] It could hardly have been otherwise, for the very foundation of the coalition was a sectional alliance between New England and the West.[29]

A new age had dawned in America: an age of science and technology which promised new and limitless sources of wealth for the few, while holding out to the many the glittering promise of more and better things to gratify ancient instincts of acquisition. It was an age of power, of organization, and of pressure politics: an age in which representative government would stand not for popular will but for the concentrated might of special interests sharing a common source of wealth or a common aim. No public man could much longer remain aloof, allied to no interest or cult; for these were fast becoming the organs through which the collective will was to be made manifest. In the absence of adequate transportation and communication, interests were necessarily local and sectional; and the choice each man had to make was thereby immensely simplified. He could go with his section, or leave it and seek a new career. Adams chose to go with New England, and Calhoun chose to go with the South.

5

The Senate of the Nineteenth Congress met on the morning of March 4, 1825, having been called together in special session by the retiring Chief Executive. The members were called to order at about ten-thirty, whereupon Senator Mills of Massachusetts moved that the oath of office should be administered to the new Vice President by Andrew Jackson, the oldest member of the Senate present.[30] So Calhoun stood, tall and erect, before the straight military figure of the popular Hero. For a long moment his brilliant, magnetic eyes were fixed on those of the General. He pronounced the oath in his clear, matter-of-fact voice, and it was done. Then taking the gavel from the perennial President pro tempore, John Gaillard of South Carolina, he spoke briefly to the assembled Senators.

His theme was the varied powers of the Senate, which shared the legislative duties of the lower house, partook of executive functions in its control over treaties and appointments, and served as a court in impeachment cases, at the same time acting as representative of the states and "the guardian of their rights and sovereignty." The functions were wisely assigned, the organization excellent, but he added "what must be known to all, that a successful discharge of the duties assigned by the constitution to the senate, must depend, notwithstanding the skill of its organization, almost wholly on the patriotism and wisdom of the members."[31]

So Calhoun made his bow in the Senate of the United States, where almost all of his remaining years were to be spent. More than once he was to see the patriotism and the wisdom of its members fail; but he never swerved from his conception of its functions, though he came more and more, as the industrial revolution advanced and political power followed the curve of profits, to emphasize and elaborate "its peculiar character, as the representative of the states."

New members, and old members reappointed to new terms, were sworn in; and the Senate adjourned as the playing of the Marine Band outside announced the arrival of the President-elect. Adams was escorted to the Senate chamber, and thence by the members of the Senate to the Hall of Representatives, already filled with visitors and officials of the Government. Clad in a plain black suit of domestic manufacture, he stepped to the Speaker's table and read his inaugural address.

He reviewed briefly the first generation of American independence and summarized the policies of his predecessor who sat behind him on the platform. He called for an end to party feeling, urged his countrymen to yield their confidence to virtue and talents alone, and closed with words of praise for internal improvements which, Monroe's opinion to the contrary notwithstanding, he avowed to be within the constitutional competence of the national Government. Then "in a loud and clear voice" he took the oath from Chief Justice Marshall. Among the first to congratulate the new President, as an artillery salute boomed outside, was General Andrew Jackson.[32]

In the inaugural address Adams had made his own one of Clay's articles of faith; and no one doubted that he had embraced the tariff also when his nominations to Cabinet posts were sent to the Senate. Richard Rush was to be Secretary of the Treasury, James

Barbour to be Secretary of War; and Southard, Wirt and McLean were to remain in the offices they then held. But the appointment of Clay as Secretary of State was to most minds the barefaced sealing of an unholy bargain, which could mean only one thing: a union of Northern and Western interests for a higher tariff, with the inevitable consequence of ruin for the agricultural South. When the division came on the seventh, more than a third of the Senators present voted against confirmation, among them Jackson and Eaton of Tennessee, Hayne of South Carolina, Tazewell of Virginia and both the Senators from Georgia and from North Carolina. The cotton states feared this new industrial party, as well they might; and the Jacksonians had already decided to go into opposition.

6

Was there indeed a bargain between Adams and Clay? It has been usual for historians to accept the assurances of both men that there was not, and to justify Adams' choice as well as Clay's vote on the ground that each was acting according to his lights in the best interests of the country. It is doubtless true that Clay could not in any circumstances have supported Jackson, and there is no reason to doubt the sincerity of his belief that Crawford was physically unfit for the office. That left only Adams for whom he could vote, and surely no recrimination would have followed had that been all he did. Not content with merely casting his own ballot as one member of the Kentucky delegation, however, he persuaded his political friends to do as he did.

Benton's argument that Clay had indicated his intention to vote for Adams before there were any contacts between them is quite irrelevant, though it has gained wide currency through frequent repetition. The important point is not when Clay decided to give Adams his own vote, but when he decided to convey that of his partisans also, and why. His own justification in his "Address to His Constituents" boils down to this: that those many individuals who had voted for him had in effect placed their interests, so far as the next Presidency was concerned, in his hands. It was therefore his duty to support actively the candidate he considered most likely to carry on the policies for which he himself had stood. By the same token, if the new administration saw fit to use his services, he could not reconcile it with his conscience to refuse. But the truth was that he could not swing the West for Adams without consenting to go into the Cabinet himself, however impolitic the move might seem.[33]

As to Adams, his contention that Clay alone was qualified to hold the office of Secretary of State is unconvincing in view of the opinion he had held of the Kentuckian since they had clashed at Ghent, and had repeatedly entered in his diary. He had called his erstwhile rival ill-informed, and in foreign affairs incompetent; half-educated and of loose morals. Only a year ago he had written his future first Secretary down as "so ardent, dogmatical, and over-bearing that it is extremely difficult to preserve the temper of friendly society with him."[34] These judgments were now reversed, though no new evidence, unless it was the evidence of Clay's strength in the House, was introduced.

Prate about honor and high-mindedness and duty all you like. Make every possible allowance and reservation. The fact remains that Adams was elected only through Clay's active aid, and that President Adams promptly named Clay his Secretary of State. Whether or not there was an explicit understanding between the two men in advance of the election is immaterial. From the dawn of time political favors have commanded political rewards; and though done from the purest motives on earth, no man who had ever had any hand in politics could have doubted the direct relation between the two. Had Adams lost the election, and Clay or any-one else been appointed in like circumstances by the successful candidate, he would have been the first to cry "bargain" and "cor-ruption." Such are the rules of the great game of politics. We may close our eyes and say that bargains are never made by our side, or we may condemn all coalitions as immoral and corrupt; but we cannot change the rules till we change the nature of the players, and the players, in the last analysis, include us all.

Bargain or not, the deed was done; and neither the two pro-tagonists nor the nation could now escape the consequences. For Adams had, in truth, accepted the protective system, in spite of the solid Massachusetts vote against the tariff of 1824; and whether he liked it or not, the forces that had made and would control him represented that very concentration of financial power that old John Taylor of Caroline, now six months dead, had foreseen and feared. He had solidly behind him the well-organized manufacturing interests, with their demands for Government aid; he had the advocates of inland commerce; and he had the bank, through its attorneys, Daniel Webster and Henry Clay.[35] If Adams had ever been a nationalist, he was so no longer. He was merely New England's President, the President of the industrial Ohio Valley and of the Eastern financial centers, the President, if you will, of the abolitionists. He had received less than a third of the popular vote, but had none the less accepted the Chief Magistracy from the hands of those who had it to bestow—the special interests of a portion of the country.[36]

7

Three days after Clay's appointment had been approved by the Senate, Calhoun unburdened himself in a letter to General Swift.

"We have passed through many and strange events during the last winter," he wrote, "which are but little known to the country. The result of which is, that we have triumphed in part and been defeated in part. The policy of Mr. Monroe's administration I consider fixed. He is too popular to be attacked. This is a great point; but there ends our victory. The mass of political and moral power, which carried the late administration through in triumph, has been wholly neglected in the new organization; and in the final stages of the election, the voices and the power of the people has been set at naught; and the result has been a President elected not by them, but by a few ambitious men with a view to their own interest, I fear. This result has caused the deepest discontent, and in my opinion deservedly. There is a solemn feeling of duty, that it must be corrected at another election, or the liberty of the country will be in danger. It is my opinion, that the country will never be quiet till the example is corrected, and the Constitution so amended as to prevent the recurrence of the danger. The country will appear to subside, but the appearance will be deceitful. Principles cannot be violated in this country with impunity. In four years all that has happened will be reversed, and the country will settle down on sound principles, and wise policy.

"As to myself, I do not think of moving under existing circumstances. I know the force of my position, and my friends need not fear, I trust, either ambition, or imprudence on my part. I however, cannot but see what must come; and I shall never separate from principles, let the consequences be what it may. I see in the fact that Mr. Clay has made the Pres't. against the voice of his constituents, and that he has been rewarded by the man elevated by him by the first office in his gift, the most dangerous stab, which the liberty of this country has ever received. I will not be on that side. I am with the people, and shall remain so."[37]

To be "with the people," he was presently to learn, meant to join forces, for better or for worse, with Andrew Jackson.

CHAPTER XXV

A VICE PRESIDENT IN OPPOSITION

1

AFTER the election Calhoun remained in Washington only long enough to dispose of his E Street home. Having recently suffered the loss of his ginhouse and a season's cotton crop by fire,[1] he was badly in need of ready cash, and the thousand-dollar reduction in income which his new position entailed only emphasized his financial difficulties. He soon found a purchaser, however, in the person of his successor at the War Department, James Barbour, and was fortunate enough to realize on the property the same sum he had invested in it: nine thousand dollars.[2]

Again the Calhouns established themselves for the summer at Clergy Hall, the Pendleton estate of Floride's mother, but the Vice President found little time to devote to his family. As South Carolina's most distinguished citizen, he went triumphantly from one public dinner to another; and even in Augusta, where business took him later in the year, he was toasted and feted. He spoke often, but always briefly, and his remarks were always apt. Now and again the toasts offered by enthusiastic friends looked forward to a day when he should be not the second but the first officer of the Republic, and in 1825 they did not seem farfetched nor premature. For at forty-three Calhoun could boast a record of political achievement equaled by no other man of his years in American history, unless perhaps it were Alexander Hamilton. He had been elected Vice President of the United States by an overwhelming vote after proving his fitness by six years in the national legislature and more than seven as Secretary of War. In both places he had been outstandingly successful despite partisan attack. Who could doubt that in his new position, too, he would succeed? For the next four years he would be in the very center of the political whirlpool, but in a capacity virtually nonpolitical, where he might cultivate the friendship of all parties and avoid antagonizing any. Even the

315

bitter Smith faction seemed willing for the moment to let bygones be bygones, and everywhere he was received with the honors due to his position and his genius.

Like his friends, Calhoun regarded the Vice Presidency as a steppingstone to the highest office; but it was not his intention to wait passively while new honors sought him out. As he toured the state attending dinners and talking to all manner of people, he was appraising the popular reaction to Adams' election and gauging the sentiment of his fellow citizens on the issues before the country. At the same time Van Deventer in Washington, Maxcy in Baltimore, Swift and Gouverneur in New York and other adherents scattered throughout the country kept him informed as to the prevailing sentiments elsewhere. He chose the occasion of a public dinner at Abbeville, where he was among his oldest friends, to review his own career and to reaffirm his faith that the measures he had advocated were justified and wise.[3]

Neither publicly nor privately did he express any criticism of President Adams; but he retained the opinion he had already formed, that the result of the election had in fact gone against the popular wish and that the appointment of Clay to the Cabinet, in the circumstances, had opened the way to the virtual "sale" of the office by the House. "I do firmly believe," he wrote to Gouverneur early in June, "that an amendment to the Constitution, as to the mode of choosing the President, is indispensible. The present mode will end in deep corruption." And to Swift later in the month he expressed his fear that "the election hereafter will go habitually to the House, where under the cover of the recent example, if not reversed, the country will be as regularly sold, as the Roman Crown was by the Pretorian Band."[4] Yet he not only had no thought at this time of organizing an opposition to the Adams administration; he did not think there would be any organized opposition, unless the policy pursued by those in power should prove "systematically wrong." He noted a general disposition to support the President so long as he should maintain the policies of his predecessor, and he was willing to wait for a further expression of policy before charting his own course.

If the path he meant to follow seemed perfectly clear to him, however, it appeared less so to those who controlled affairs in Washington. Adams' partisans, not unreasonably, wanted to know just where the Vice President stood. Major Van Deventer, who retained his clerkship in the War Department, relayed the query to his former chief, but Calhoun did not choose to be explicit. "I had supposed," he countered, "that my course had been so uniform, and the principles on which I acted so distinctly stated, and openly avowed, that no man of intelligence could doubt how I would act in my present situation. . . ."[5] Adams and Clay were not deficient in intelligence, and their doubts were soon resolved. Before the summer was over, the supporters and particular friends of Calhoun and Jackson alike were being treated by the administration as foes. The decision was only natural, and no action of Calhoun's could have changed it; for Adams could hardly regard as a supporter the man from whom he had snatched the coveted prize, nor was Clay likely to treat as a friend his own most dangerous rival for the succession.

2

Even before he took the Presidential oath, Adams had determined upon the elements from which he intended to forge a party. The backbone of the administration was, of course, to be the fusion of his own comparatively small following with that of Clay, and to this end the distribution of Federal offices and largess in the West went to the Kentuckian.[6] His tariff stand was calculated to give him strength in Pennsylvania, buttressed by the appointment of Richard Rush to the Treasury, and in his inaugural address he made a bid for Federalist support. Both in New York and in the South, however, he had to choose between two rival factions, almost necessarily throwing the other into opposition. The choice fell upon the Crawford Radicals and the Clintonians; and its first fruits were the investment of James Barbour with the War portfolio and the offer of the British mission to Clinton.

The adroitness of Adams' manipulations may well be questioned. His own victory in New York was due to neither of the two major parties in that state, but rather to a third group, drilled and managed by Thurlow Weed, a young Rochester editor and member of the Assembly. Weed thought to build a machine on the basis of the Federal patronage he expected from Adams, but was by no means displeased when the British mission was tendered to Clinton. It would mean the latter's resignation as Governor and the elevation of Lieutenant Governor James Tallmadge of the Adams party. When Clinton declined, however, and the appointment went instead to Federalist Rufus King, Weed became alarmed and hastened to Washington to explain to the President who were his friends in New York. The President was not interested; and in August he further clarified his position by the appointment of Alfred Conkling, a Clinton henchman, to be United States Judge for the Northern District of New York despite the united opposition of the Federalists and of his own followers.[7]

Equally beset with political difficulties was the determination to cultivate the Radicals in the South. For one thing, Van Buren represented that party in New York, and he had been cut out by the administration's overtures to Clinton, which left Adams in the awkward position of wooing the Radicals in one section while opposing them in another. The powerful Virginia wing of the party soon split into two factions, with James Barbour going into the Cabinet and Governor Pleasants and his successor, John Tyler, friendly, while the veteran Jeffersonian, William Branch Giles, came out in opposition. Crawford's own Georgia was effectively alienated when Adams refused to recognize a one-sided treaty negotiated by the state with a minority faction of the Creek Nation.[8] In Tennessee the President cultivated the anti-Jackson forces of former Senator John Williams, who was himself given a diplomatic post.

In the lesser offices Adams left untouched a majority of the employees of the consular and customs services, pointing to this fact as proof that his administration was but a continuation of Monroe's. It was notable, however, that the bulk of those retained were associated with the parties he wished to conciliate. The military appointments which had been vacant since 1822 now went to officers whom Calhoun had passed over, and of the former War Secretary's friends only Southard, McLean and Poinsett remained in high offices. Monroe's offer of the long-delayed Mexican mission to Poinsett was confirmed more through sheer necessity, however, than from any wish to gratify the Vice President; while Southard and McLean had worked actively for Adams' election. Even so the President soon grew suspicious of the Postmaster General because of a clerkship given to Henry Lee, a Virginia journalist and erstwhile Calhoun partisan.[9]

Those excluded from the calculations of the administration were quick to realize their position and to act accordingly. As the alliance of New England and the West gained Southern followers, Van Buren made his peace with Clinton, and the Tennessee Legislature nominated Andrew Jackson for the Presidency in 1828. Old Hickory forthwith resigned his seat in the Senate, and in his letter of acceptance denounced the appointment of Congressmen to executive posts and called for limitation of the Presidential office to a single term.

3

Late in September Calhoun and his family left Pendleton for Abbeville and Willington, staying two or three weeks at Bath before setting out at a leisurely pace for Washington. Again he was dined and toasted wherever he stopped, and even his personal habits were imitated by his admirers. He often wore a short fringe of beard over his throat, primarily for protection against cold, and he was wearing it when he and his party stopped for lunch at Cheraw. For the next six months, so the story goes, all the men in the vicinity wore similar fringes of beard.[10] Interrupted again and again for some formality or function, it was near the end of November before the Calhouns were settled once more in their Georgetown home.

Soon after his arrival in the Capital the Vice President called on Adams, with whom he discussed "the prosperous state of the country." He received the customary courtesy calls from returning members of Congress and the Cabinet, but the President was distinctly cool, and the Secretary of State was hostile.[11]

By the narrow margin of five votes, John W. Taylor was elected Speaker of the House, where the administration forces were led by Daniel Webster and Edward Everett, late professor of rhetoric at Harvard and editor of the *North American Review*. In the Senate, however, there was no clear majority either way. Count-

ing the Jacksonians and the friends of Calhoun as potentially of
the opposition, the President's strength would depend largely on
how many of the Radicals he could win over, and perhaps ultimately
upon the seats vacated by Barbour and Rufus King. Small wonder that after sending his first annual message to Congress, Adams
confided to his diary his "intense anxiety" as to the outcome.[12]

Calhoun listened as intently as any Senator in the hall while the
President's declaration of policy was read. The message began
with a discussion of foreign affairs and referred to a Congress of
Latin American nations, soon to be held at Panama. The United
States had also been invited, the invitation had been accepted and
ministers would shortly be named to attend. A bankruptcy law, a
unified militia and a better-disciplined Army were recommended.
There were programs for dealing with the public lands and with the
Indians, and a call for less rigorous interpretation of the laws be-
stowing pensions on Revolutionary veterans. There was a rhap-
sody on the flourishing condition of the finances and a long and
loving dissertation upon the needs of the Navy, for which the elder
Adams had first stood sponsor.

The President was fully warmed to his subject by the time the
constructive heart of the message was reached. Hoping to capitalize
on the wave of enthusiasm following completion of the Erie Canal,
he proposed a program of internal improvements so vast that even
Clay had been staggered by it when it was discussed in Cabinet
meeting.[13] He called for a national university, for scientific exploration, for standardization of weights and measures, and in poetic
terms he begged his countrymen to build astronomical observa-
tories for the public good. He traced the growth of the nation
since the Government was first set in motion, and concluded that
a new Department of the Interior was needed; he wanted better
patent laws; and he demanded the long-promised monument to
Washington.

But what of the authority of Congress to do all these things?
Adams reviewed the powers enumerated in the Constitution and
declared his opinion that "to refrain from exercising them for the
benefit of the people themselves . . . would be treachery to the most
sacred of trusts." He saw the spirit of improvement abroad upon
the earth, sharpening the faculties of man and challenging the

betterment of his condition, and in the language of the Harvard professor he had once been rather than that of the minority President he was, he accepted the challenge. "While foreign nations, less blessed with that freedom which is power, than ourselves, are advancing with gigantic strides in the career of public improvement; were we to slumber in indolence, or fold up our arms and proclaim to the world that we are palsied by the will of our constituents, would it not be to cast away the bounties of Providence, and doom ourselves to perpetual inferiority?"

The reaction was as swift as it was inevitable. Here in a new guise were the old heresies of Federalism. The men who had repudiated consolidation and central power in 1800 were little likely to accept them now, least of all from the son of the man who had last represented those doctrines in the Presidency. The very purpose of the Revolution had been to restrain the power of rulers to the popular will, and the conflict remained green in the memory of the Nation. Innocent and moderate as Adams' proposals were in the light of governmental functions today, they seemed like tyranny to many of his contemporaries. Crawford at his Georgia home pronounced the message "replete with doctrines which I hold to be unconstitutional," and the aged author of the Declaration of Independence agreed with him. Thomas Ritchie threw the Richmond *Enquirer* into the opposition scale, while in the West, Francis P. Blair, Kentucky editor who had supported Clay, went over to the Jackson forces.[14]

Calhoun offered no comment, but he noted a general belief that the message was unsatisfactory. "The friends of state rights object to it as utterly ultra, and those, who in the main, advocate a liberal system of measures, think that the message has recommended so many debatable subjects at once, as to endanger a reaction even to those measures heretofore adopted and apparently acquiesced in."[15]

As the clouds of opposition gathered in the hinterland, the news reached Washington that John Randolph of Roanoke had been chosen by the Virginia Legislature to succeed Barbour in the Senate—John Randolph of the acid tongue, whose distaste for the Adams clan was almost as old as he was himself. Too late, the President surveyed the scene and moved to modify his stand. Representative John Bailey of Massachusetts, his protégé and former clerk, hastily introduced an amendment to the Constitution which would grant to the general Government all the powers so recently claimed as already belonging to it.[16]

In South Carolina Judge William Smith, late of the United States Senate and now in the state legislature, seized the occasion to drive through that body a set of resolutions condemning as unconstitutional both internal improvements and the protective tariff.[17] They were aimed less at Adams than at Calhoun, and Eldred Simkins recorded his protest in vain. The middle ground he had so carefully maintained had already cost Calhoun much of the strength he had once had in the North, and he now saw his hold on his own state slipping away to the Crawford faction.

4

Calhoun took his responsibilities as Vice President with an untraditional seriousness. To an office that had come to be a sinecure he brought new dignity by attending to his duties with meticulous care. Day after day, from the beginning of the session until just before its close, when custom bade him withdraw to permit election of a President pro tempore, he was in his seat as presiding officer of the Senate. It was he who began the practice of addressing the members as "Senators" in preference to the more common "Gentlemen," and he found ways to make his office one of far greater influence than had any of his more recent predecessors.

His position was greatly strengthened by an act of the preceding Congress which gave to the Vice President the appointment of committees, a function theretofore exercised by the Senate itself.[18] In using this new power, Calhoun strove for rigid impartiality. His appointments gave control of eight of the fifteen major standing committees to the administration, and seven to members hostile or potentially hostile to Adams' program. The division came as near as was mathematically possible to reflecting the actual division of strength, and in the light of the President's annual message it was not unfair. While the important Committees on Foreign Relations and Finance fell to unfriendly hands, the administration had clear control of those on Commerce, Manufactures and Public Lands. Internal improvements, moreover, which Adams had chosen to make one of the basic policies of his party, were assigned to a select Committee on Roads and Canals which the administration dominated by four members to one.

Neutral or unfriendly Senators were in the majority on the Committees on Agriculture, Military Affairs, Indian Affairs, Naval Affairs and Judiciary; but the program outlined by the President made only the last two of these of more than routine importance. The Committees on Militia, Claims, Post Offices and Post Roads, Pensions and the District of Columbia went to the administration. In most cases the committee chairmen were the men who had filled the same posts in the preceding Congress, or the senior members who remained in the Senate, regardless of political affiliation; and even the exceptions were fitting and impartial. General Harrison, a presumptive Adams man, succeeded Jackson as head of the Military Affairs Committee; and Lloyd of Massachusetts, one of the administration leaders, headed the Committee on Commerce, separated from Manufactures for the first time. Since no Senator was permitted to head two committees, Lloyd gave way to Hayne as chairman of Naval Affairs; and Findlay of Pennsylvania took over the newly created Committee on Agriculture. There were no other exceptions to the seniority rule.

Adams wanted no neutrality, but full acceptance of his leadership; not half the Senate committees, but all of them. The appointments were almost immediately assailed, with the Committee on Foreign Relations being singled out for special criticism. Consisting of Nathaniel Macon, Littleton W. Tazewell of Virginia, John Gaillard, Elijah Mills and Hugh Lawson White, Jackson's successor from Tennessee, it presented a majority personally unfriendly to Henry Clay, and Calhoun was accused of demonstrating a calculated hostility to the President and his Secretary of State.[19] These attacks on the Vice President were not accidental or irresponsible. Adams, or more probably Clay, had correctly sized up the situation, and the administration was bent upon carrying the offensive while its foes were still disorganized. For disorganized they were. The Jackson following was in more or less open opposition on general principles, but the Crawford partisans were divided and the Calhoun faction aloof. Clay saw that, should these dissident elements combine, the administration would be in the minority, and he set out to destroy them one at a time. Calhoun was in the weakest position and so was first marked for the sacrifice.

The possibilities of the situation were not lost upon Martin Van Buren. Suave and smiling, the little magician sought out the Vice President in the solitude of his Georgetown home. Was Calhoun in favor of sending delegates to Panama to meet with representatives of Latin republics some of which, like Haiti, were actually in control of Negroes? He was not. In Clay's crusade to extend the institutions of democracy throughout the hemisphere he saw only the development of a potential rival for the cotton markets of the world. He had first heard of the proposal while on his way to the Capital and considered it so unwise that immediately upon his arrival he had stated his objections to a friendly member of the Cabinet in the hope of forestalling it, but had been told it was too late. The invitation had already been accepted.[20]

Van Buren, too, was against the proposition, and so were the Jacksonians. Why should they not combine to oppose it and at the same time protect themselves against Clay's strategy of "divide and conquer"? If such a combination should lead to the ultimate overthrow of the administration, what then? Had it not come to power by intrigue and corruption and against the popular will? Calhoun was not yet ready to enter into an opposition coalition, but he could not fail to see the political wisdom of the plan, and he agreed to lend his aid in defeating the Panama mission.

The names of the commissioners were sent to the Senate on the day before Christmas, together with a message which took notice of the criticism already expressed and emphasized the limited nature of American participation. "Although this measure was deemed to be within the constitutional competency of the Executive," Adams declared, "I have not thought proper to take any step in it before ascertaining that my opinion of its expediency will concur with that of both branches of the Legislature: first, by the decision of the Senate upon the nominations to be laid before them; and secondly, by the sanction of both Houses to the appropriations, without which it cannot be carried into effect."

It had too much the appearance of conferring as an Executive favor what the Senate claimed as a right, and it was cordially resented. John Branch of North Carolina promptly countered with a resolution. "That the President of the United States does not,

constitutionally, possess either the right or the power to appoint
Ambassadors or other public Ministers, but with the advice and
consent of the Senate, except when vacancies may happen in the
recess."

The Senate referred the matter to its reprobated Committee on
Foreign Relations, and a long and skillfully drafted report was
presented on January 11. Written by Tazewell, the report explicitly condemned the acceptance of the invitation without consulting Congress. It noted from the documents most recently sent that
objects were contemplated by the Panama Congress not mentioned
in the President's message and disapproved those objects, and it
discussed at length the probable results of participation by the
United States. The committee felt "most sensibly" the embarrassing situation in which they were placed, but they recommended
that it was "not expedient, at this time, for the United States to
send any Ministers to the Congress of American nations, assembled at Panama."[21]

5

Both sides accepted the Panama mission as the first test of
strength, and both knew that mere argument was not to be the
major weapon. There were perhaps sixteen Senators, or a third
of the total, who were unconditionally opposed to the administration, and another eight or ten personally hostile but under varying
degrees of local compulsion. By adroit use of the advantage that
always belongs to the party in power, Adams believed that a majority could be secured. He had at most to win over only three or
four.[22] The moves he had already made to appease the Crawford
and Clinton followings strengthened his hand, while the opposition
was seriously weakened by past feuds between Calhoun and Crawford, Crawford and Jackson, and Van Buren and Clinton.

When the nominations were taken up in executive session February 15, Van Buren proposed that the Panama question be
debated with open doors, "unless . . . the publication of documents,
necessary to be referred to in debate, will be prejudicial to existing
negotiations." The Senate agreed by a close 23 to 20 vote and
called upon the President to state whether such was the case.

Adams replied stiffly a few days later that his communications on the subject had been made in confidence according to usage, and he deemed it his "indispensable duty to leave to the Senate itself the decision of a question, involving a departure . . . from that usage, and upon the motives for which, not being informed of them," he did not feel competent to pass judgment.

Not a few of the Senators resented this insinuation that their motives were questionable, but they sustained the President and voted down resolutions of censure. For the next three weeks the rival factions battled for the handful of votes that would carry the day. Both Clay, who was the real manager for the administration, and Webster, who was its leader in the House, thought Calhoun was the moving force behind the opposition and that his hope was to weaken or destroy Clay by defeating a measure with which the Kentuckian was intimately connected.[23] There is little doubt that they were correct. Calhoun was entirely sincere in his disapproval of the Panama mission, but he knew as well as Clay that while the immediate struggle for power might lie between Adams and Jackson, the long-range contest lay between the two heirs apparent. So did the partisans on both sides; and when the question reached the House later in the session, the rivalry of the Vice President and the Secretary of State overshadowed all other aspects of the discussion.

It was a contest destined to last for many a year, but the first round went to Clay. On March 14, 1826, a resolution pronouncing the mission inexpedient was defeated, 24 to 19, and the nominations sent by the President were confirmed. An analysis of the various votes over a six-weeks period as they concerned this question shows that toward the end of February the administration secured a majority, which thereafter varied in strength but was never lost. In the process a sharp and clear-cut line was drawn between the sheep and the goats.

By the time the Senate was ready to act on the Tazewell report the Vice President had been forced, however reluctantly, to go all the way with Van Buren and the Jacksonians. He had from the beginning been willing to support such administration measures as he could honestly approve, but that was not enough for the coalition. "We must be identified with them, and give an unqualified support or be denounced, as in opposition," he wrote to Swift a few days after the Panama debate opened. "We must go farther, we must pledge a support to Mr. A's reelection, and [renounce] all those principles, for which we have ever contended, in favor of the Democratick basis of our government. There must be opposition in the opinion of those zealous advocates; and I make it, if we do not oppose them, they must oppose us. Be it so. One can make war, tho it takes two to make peace. If we are to be assaulted at all events, *it is only left to defend*. Acting defensively, we will at least have choice of position; and occupying as we do, the great Democratick principles, on which our whole political institution rests, I do not fear, that our position can be forced or turned."[24]

The new majority included recently seated Senators from Maryland and New York, E. F. Chambers and Nathan Sanford; and it counted four members who had previously voted now one way and now the other: Harrison and Ruggles of Ohio, Hendricks of Indiana and Holmes of Maine. Holmes came back to the opposition on the final vote, but on that crucial test R. M. Johnson of Kentucky went over to the administration. The opposition, on the other hand, lost Gaillard through death and Tazewell through prolonged illness.[25]

The channels through which political pressures operate are obscure enough at best, and they have in this instance been further beclouded by the widely accepted notion that John Quincy Adams of all men was above the use of patronage.[26] Adams had a convenient way of not knowing exactly what his lieutenants were doing and of failing to mention in his diary all that he did know. For him, it sometimes appears that the end not only justified but sanctified the means. The means in this case, at least in the universal opinion of his opponents, men no less honest or honorable than himself, were the familiar ones by which an executive wins over recalcitrant legislators. Van Buren said the administration victory was achieved after "unmistakable indications of effects produced by Governmental influence." Benton wrote that a few members of the opposition party voted to confirm the mission and that to these "there was afterwards, either to themselves or relatives, some large dispensations of executive patronage." And Calhoun charged the administration with seeking to "mould the publick voice at pleasure by an artful management of the patronage of office."[27]

CHAPTER XXVI

ONSLOW AND PATRICK HENRY

1

THE tactics of the coalition in securing confirmation of its delegates to the Panama Congress served only to fuse the divergent elements of the opposition into a party, with all the tools of partisanship at its command. First of those tools in importance was the *United States Telegraph,* which made its appearance on February 6, 1826. In its prospectus Adams thought he recognized "a sample of bad English peculiar to Calhoun,"[1] and its owner was rumored to be Senator John H. Eaton of Tennessee.

The rumor was not quite correct but near enough, for the followers of Jackson and those of Calhoun had combined to underwrite the venture. Eaton had endorsed the editor's note for three thousand dollars, but two-thirds of that sum was guaranteed by a group of Representatives and Senators which included James Hamilton, Jr., and Samuel D. Ingham.[2] The publisher was John S. Meehan, a true Jacksonian, but the active management soon passed into the capable hands of Duff Green, friend and partisan of the Vice President.

On March 27, two weeks after the Panama mission had been approved, the *Telegraph* charted the course of the opposition with a blistering editorial on "Bargain, Management and Intrigue," and three days later a direct assault upon the Executive began in the Senate. Branch of North Carolina, one of the sponsors of the paper, brought up his earlier resolution declaring the President to be without power to name envoys save with the advice and consent of the Senate. He had examined the documents in the case and thought he saw a deliberate intention to encroach upon the powers of the legislature. But John Randolph, who followed him on the floor, saw a great deal more than that.

Eccentric to the point of chronic insanity, and nourishing an aversion to the House of Adams that went back to the days of the

328

Sedition Act, Randolph had set out on his arrival in the Senate to make himself obnoxious to the President, and he pursued that single aim with all the skill and wit, all the venom and viciousness of which he possessed full measure. He had no fondness for Calhoun, either, and is said to have begun one of his speeches with the words: "Mr. Speaker! I mean Mr. President of the Senate and would-be President of the United States, which God in His infinite mercy avert . . .".[3] He was willing, however, to act with anyone who was seeking the same goal; and Calhoun and Van Buren both made strenuous efforts to harness the Virginian's outbursts to the needs of party discipline. It was an impossible task. Day after day Randolph entered the Senate chamber booted and spurred, secured the floor as soon as he could, and talked—for two, four, sometimes six hours at a stretch, drinking porter, pacing up and down the room, hurling his thunderbolts with deadly effect into the enemy's camp.

This had been going on already for three months when the Branch resolution reached the floor, and Randolph rose to speak on it. He was in rare good form. In his rambling, seemingly aimless fashion, he yet moved steadily around his subject in contracting circles. When he got to the coalition of East and West, Hayne tried to stop him, but in vain. The rules required that a point of order could only be decided after the objectionable words had been reduced to writing, and the Virginia scourge was wont to convey his meaning by tone and gesture. He continued, back and forth, through ancient and modern history, through the Presidential election, to the Panama mission and the message in which Adams had questioned the motives of the Senate. Calhoun sat imperturbable in the chair as Randolph paid his respects to the "evil genius of the American House of Stuart," castigated the President as only his glib and subtle tongue could, and likened the coalition to that "of Blifil and Black George . . . the puritan with the black-leg."[4] He was still not through, but he had said enough.

Clay conceived himself to be insulted and delivered a challenge. The preliminaries were arranged; and on April 8, 1826, the Secretary of State and the Senator from Virginia exchanged shots at a spot on the southern shore of the Potomac. Clay's seconds were General Jesup, the Quartermaster General, and Senator Josiah S.

Johnston of Louisiana; Randolph's were Edward F. Tattnall of Georgia and James Hamilton, Jr., both members of the House. Benton attended as friend of both parties. No one was hurt; and Randolph presently resumed his tirades against Adams and Clay, individually and collectively. Rumor soon had it that another duel was impending, between Clay and McDuffie; and a story made the rounds in Kentucky that the Secretary of State and the Vice President had fought and that the latter had been killed.[5]

The incident revealed an unexpected sensitiveness on the subject of the coalition, but it served a useful purpose for the administration also. It permitted Adams' partisans once more to single out Calhoun for individual attack. Had he not sat immovable in his seat while a flagrant abuse was committed on the floor of the Senate? It was less, perhaps, the single instance that had produced the spark than it was the cumulative effect of Randolph's withering blasts over a period of many weeks.[6] When news of the affair reached Boston, Federalist Christopher Gore sent it on to Rufus King with the comment that the "Vice President neither accords to the Dignity of his Station, nor the Expectations of the People"; and Webster thought that Calhoun's course in the matter had produced a "very strong sensation throughout the Country."[7]

2

Opposition leaders in the House, meanwhile, had chosen another means of harassing the President and his unhappy Secretary of State. Too far outnumbered to succeed with tactics similar to those adopted in the Senate, they concentrated on a single issue which the administration could not brush aside: the amendment of the Constitution as to the manner of Presidential elections. From mid-February until April, when the Panama question came down from the upper House, the Hall of Representatives had rung with furious debate on the old bargain and corruption charges. McDuffie led the fight for amendment and made of it a vigorous assault on the administration. It was in fact so vigorous that his language, on March 31, rivaled and even surpassed that used by Randolph in the Senate the day before, and it, too, produced an abortive duel. Representative Thomas Metcalfe of Kentucky entered into a correspondence with the South Carolina hotspur with the intention of drawing a challenge and succeeded, but the meeting was not held. The Kentuckian insisted upon rifles, which James Hamilton, Jr., McDuffie's second as he had been Randolph's, refused to recognize as a dueling weapon.[8] It is noteworthy that no effort was made in the House to call McDuffie to order for his remarks, and that neither Adams nor his partisans saw fit to criticize the conduct of the presiding officer, McLane of Delaware.

The Senate found another issue hidden in a bill from the House to add three judges to the Supreme Court and three new circuits to take in the Western states. It was true that some change in the judicial system was badly needed, but those who sought the overthrow of the administration were not willing to increase the patronage of the President to that extent, especially since it was widely believed that one of the places would go to John McLean. The Postmaster General was in command of the largest block of job holders in the Federal service and he was unwilling to clean house among them for the benefit of the coalition. Clay had long urged his removal, but his personal following in the West was large, he was strong with the militant sect of Methodists, and he had done too good a job of administering the postal service to offer Adams an excuse for dropping him. Promoting him to the Court, however, would serve the purpose equally well.[9]

The judiciary bill lay dormant in the Senate through the long Panama debate, but on April 7 Van Buren reported it out of committee with two amendments. In setting up the new circuits, Ohio was to be combined with Kentucky instead of with Indiana and Illinois, and the judges were required to be residents of their respective circuits. The amendments would automatically exclude McLean, because there was already a Kentucky judge on the Supreme Court. The Senate accepted the amendments, refused to recede when the House balked, and the bill was lost.

The next step in the campaign was a report from Benton calling for a reduction in Executive patronage. It was accompanied by six bills which were designed to cut the President's influence to almost nothing while proportionately increasing that of Congress. One bill would regulate the publication of the laws and public advertisements; another would virtually repeal Crawford's four-year law, save where defaulters were concerned; and the others were intended to regulate the appointment of postmasters, cadets and midshipmen, and to prevent the dismissal of Army and Navy officers by the Executive.[10] Perhaps these "reforms" were not seriously meant by their authors, who expected to come into power themselves in less than three years now and would have use for such patronage as there was; but the mere existence of the report served two useful purposes. It called the attention of the electorate to the power in the hands of the President, at the same time insinuating that it had been or was going to be misused; and it was a warning to the coalition that it must be circumspect indeed in its distribution of Executive favors. No action was taken, but the bills were laid on the table, whence they might be resurrected whenever the need arose.

If the report was largely propaganda, the warning was not without foundation. The evidence of Adams' purposes was slowly piling up and with it a suspicion as to past transactions. Despite the opposition of the Postmaster General, of ten of the eleven members of Congress from Tennessee, and of a substantial body of citizens, John P. Erwin, a brother of Clay's son-in-law, had been appointed postmaster at Nashville.[11] A stepson of Crawfordite Senator Thomas of Illinois, lately a clerk in the Treasury department, was named agent to the Osage Indians over the almost unanimous protest of Missouri; and Thomas' record showed consistent support of the administration after an initial vote against the confirmation of Clay. The strong Radical party in North Carolina was wooed in the person of Bartlett Yancey, who was tendered a diplomatic post but refused it; the veteran Gallatin, after repeated offers of foreign missions, finally agreed to go to England, where Rufus King's health had failed; and an unsuccessful candidate for the Senate from Connecticut was solaced with a seat on the Federal Bench in that state.[12] There was evidence, too, if such were needed, that internal improvements were to be so allocated as to win over doubtful states.[13]

To foes of the coalition all this appeared transparent. Adams and Clay were painstakingly building a party and were hopeful of incorporating into it at least a portion of the well-oiled Crawford machine.

3

The gains of the opposition were countered by renewed attacks upon Calhoun for the license permitted to Randolph on the Senate floor. So vigorous and pointed was the criticism following the bloodless duel between the Virginia Senator and the Secretary of State that formal notice was taken of it by the participants. On April 15 Randolph moved to rescind the rule of the preceding Congress under which committees were appointed by the Vice President. The debate was not reported, save only that no reflection on the presiding officer was involved. The action seems rather to have marked a turning point in the history of the Senate, for it was designed to recapture for that body functions earlier surrendered and was thus both an assertion of independence and a display of power. In introducing the subject, Randolph talked of the powers of the Vice President in general and alluded unmistakably to the charges being leveled at Calhoun.

After the vote, which was almost unanimous to repeal the rule in question, Calhoun explained briefly what he understood to be the extent of his own authority under the rules of the Senate. He conceived that "the right *to call to order,* on questions touching the *latitude* or *freedom* of debate, belongs exclusively to the members of this body, and not to the Chair. The power of the presiding officer, on these great points, is an appellate power only; and consequently, the duties of the Chair commence when a Senator is called to order by a Senator." It was a limitation he considered fair and just, for he was not himself a member of the Senate and hence not responsible to it but to the people who had elected him. It was proper that only members should exercise the privilege of challenging the language of their fellows.[14]

In the May 1 issue of the *National Journal* appeared an answer, signed with the pseudonym "Patrick Henry," but bearing strong resemblances to the style and intellectual processes of John Quincy Adams. "Patrick Henry" argued in biting phrases that the power to call to order was inherent in the office, and he referred to Calhoun as the "residuary legatee of General Jackson's pretensions to the Presidency." It was the kind of challenge that the confident and pugnacious Carolinian would not refuse, and the presumption that the President himself was the challenger made it politically necessary that he reply. He did so under the signature of "Onslow," most famous of the Speakers of the British House of Commons, but the letter was rejected by the *National Journal*. It appeared May 20 in the *Intelligencer*, and the public beheld the rare spectacle of the President and Vice President of the United States tilting at each other in a newspaper battle in which neither side gave or asked quarter.

"Patrick Henry" renewed the attack on June 7 in a long, learned and able argument, still couched in the cutting language of sarcasm; and "Onslow" stated his case in full, with equal ability and learning, in two papers in the *Intelligencer* for June 27 and 29. In three more numbers, appearing in the *National Journal* for August 4, 5 and 8 (after Calhoun was safely out of the city), Adams addressed himself "to the Honorable John C. Calhoun, Vice President of the United States"; but Calhoun's last word, in the *Intelligencer* for October 7, 10 and 12, maintained the detachment of anonymity.[15]

In his last numbers Adams took up the committee appointments, arguing that the administration should have been given a majority on all standing committees, and that such had been the invariable usage in the past. Calhoun did not fail to remind his opponent of the many hostile committees Clay had named during Monroe's term of office, nor of the many times that Clay in the Speaker's chair had allowed Randolph and others to say what they pleased. It was in fact a speech of Clay's own—his attack on Josiah Quincy in 1813—that was remembered by many as the most vituperative ever heard in Congress, yet no question of order had been raised.[16] As for the Senate committees, the only quarrel with them was that their members were foes of the President, but was that not merely following his own example, who boasted of appointing his enemies to office to the exclusion of his friends?

4

It is scarcely possible today to reconstruct the scenes that produced this undignified controversy, nor to evaluate the arguments.

Both Adams and Calhoun were positive and inclined to be self-righteous. Both were masters of dialectic, with Calhoun colder and more detached, Adams more censorious and vindictive. Given two such men, each convinced the other is trying to destroy him, any point of contact between them is sure to produce sparks sooner or later. Calhoun had already been rebuffed by the administration in his effort to stop the Panama mission before the session started, and he was therefore not exactly well disposed toward the President when the committees were named. The appointments, particularly Foreign Affairs, Naval Affairs and Judiciary, which put favorite administration measures in unfriendly hands, confirmed Adams in his preconceived belief that Calhoun was hostile; and the course of events during the session only drove it deeper.

Then came the Randolph affair, which took the Vice President at a disadvantage. While the eccentric Virginian was speaking, it probably never occurred to Calhoun that a point of order was involved. He had heard Randolph deliver many a tirade in the House fully as damaging and fully as provocative—tirades directed, moreover, at persons for whom he had more respect than he then had for Clay or Adams; and on not a few of these earlier occasions Henry Clay had been in the chair and had not interfered. It could hardly have occurred to him that a duel might result, since he had already seen more than one challenge pass without producing any fighting as a result of Randolph's invectives. It was not until the thin-skinned Adams accused him publicly of dereliction of duty that Calhoun realized the nature of the situation in which he was placed.

Adams might well have asked why no member of his own following in the Senate, technically a majority since February, had raised the point of order, but he did not. The opportunity to demolish the man whom he regarded as his major adversary was too tempting to weaken it by criticizing his own friends for the same fault. He might also have denounced McLane, who was presiding in the House when McDuffie's opinion of the coalition was aired; but he was not seeking a quarrel with McLane. Or he might have glanced back through his diary to the afternoon half a dozen years before that he had spent in the House gallery listening to Randolph speaking on the Missouri question. His entry would have shown him that the Virginian was twice called to order, that he had disputed the call, receded, tacked and gone on as before. And Adams' comment was: "It was useless to call him to order: he can no more keep order than he can keep silence...."[17]

Calhoun seized the first opportunity after the criticism was launched to explain his position, which he did, as we have seen, on the occasion of the rescinding of the rule giving him power to appoint committees. Naturally enough, Adams was not satisfied, and the change in rules was in itself a further annoyance, for Calhoun's appointments had at least given the administration control of half the committees. Under a system of selection by majority vote, the party in power would have to have a majority in the Senate to control any committees at all. Had Adams been born a Virginian, he might have challenged his Vice President to exchange shots with him. Being a puritan, he challenged instead to a duel of rhetoric.

The issue was not finally resolved until 1828, when the rules were amended after full debate to give to the presiding officer the right to call a Senator to order for words spoken in debate, subject to appeal to the Senate. Calhoun took the vote to be a justification of his course, since it was in effect an affirmation of his contention that he had not possessed the power in 1826. To Adams it was merely a way out of an embarrassing position: a whitewashing of the Vice President, preparatory to running him again.[18]

5

Two days before the end of the session, Calhoun withdrew according to custom to permit the election of a president pro tempore. With Gaillard dead, the two outstanding veterans of the Senate were Nathaniel Macon of North Carolina and Samuel Smith of Maryland. In point of experience there was little to choose between them. Each had served in both Houses and the career of each went back for more than thirty years. Both were experienced in the duties of a presiding officer, Smith having been President pro tempore of the Senate during Jefferson's second term, and Macon Speaker of the House under the same President.

The election took place the evening of the twentieth of May; and in the Senate gallery were John Quincy Adams and Henry

Clay, bent upon securing the choice of the pro-administration Smith. Tazewell protested this intrusion of the Executive, but without effect other than to bring upon himself charges of drunkenness, and there were dark hints of undue influence and of a vote changed in Smith's favor. It was not until the seventeenth ballot, two hours after the first roll call, that either candidate secured a majority; but the issue was in favor of Macon, and so the session closed with honors even.[19]

A few days later the *National Journal,* reviewing the events of the last five months, concluded that the Senate had changed for the worse and hinted that responsibility lay with the Vice President. The Alexandria *Gazette* took up the cry, lamenting that it was no longer an honor "to be in a Senate where a monster of depravity presides, and where the most [remorseless] and adroit vilifier that ever disgraced deliberative body, is permitted to consume more than half of the time of the Senate in the indiscriminate butchery of private character. . . ."[20] Like the "Patrick Henry" letters, the newspaper criticisms were meant to discredit Calhoun in the eyes of the electorate and thereby to render him a politically undesirable ally to the other elements in the opposition camp.

Most of the Crawfordites, the Clintonians and some of the Jackson following were actually or potentially hostile to the Vice President, and the strategy of the coalition throughout the session was shrewdly designed to take advantage of this lack of unity.[21] Calhoun saw his danger and took the only road open to him: he went over unreservedly to Jackson. If he had had any doubts before, Adams had resolved them for him. The re-election of the President must mean the succession of Clay and the annihilation of his own political prospects. Jackson, on the other hand, had proclaimed himself in favor of one term only for the Chief Magistrate, which left the way open after four years; and Jackson professed to stand for a program which Calhoun found acceptable.

When Major Eaton left Washington for his Tennessee home early in June, Calhoun entrusted him with a letter to Jackson, in which he virtually placed himself at the Hero's disposal. "An issue has been fairly made," he wrote, "between *power* and *liberty;* and it must be determined in the next three years, whether the real governing principle in our political system be the power and patron-

age of the Executive, or the voice of the people. . . . It will be no
small addition to your future renown, that in this great struggle
your name is found, as it always has been on the side of liberty,
and your country. Occupying the grounds that you do, there can
be no triumph over you, which will not also be a triumph over
liberty. That you may live to witness a successful termination of
the struggle, and that you may be the instrument, under Providence, of confounding political machinations and of turning the
attempts against the liberty of the country, into the means of per-
petuating our freedom, is my sincere wish."

He concluded with a few words about himself and his own position, after expressing his willingness to accept any consequence of
victory. "I know that much of the Storm will fall on me; but so
far from complaining, I deem it my glory to be selected as the
object of attack in such a cause. If I had no higher object than
personal advancement, my course would be easy. I would have
nothing to do, but to float with the current of events. I feel,
however, that such a course would be unworthy of the confidence,
which the American people have reposed in me, and of the duty
which every citizen owes his country."[22]

If Eaton gave his chief as accurate an account of the session as
Calhoun indicated the General was to expect, Jackson may well
have smiled over these last few lines; for the Tennessee Senator
knew as well as did the Vice President himself that neutrality
would be fatal. Calhoun's political strength, however, was not underestimated by the Jackson managers, and his tender of alliance
was gracefully accepted. "I trust," Jackson answered, "that my
name will always be found on the side of the people, and as their
confidence in your talents and virtue has placed you in the second
office of the government, that we shall march hand in hand in their
cause. With an eye single to the preservation of our happy form of
government, the missiles of slander will fall harmless at your
feet."[23]

For different but equally cogent reasons, Van Buren also placed
himself (although not yet overtly) under Jackson's banner. To
him it was a case of victory or defeat, and in Jackson he saw the
only leader who could win against the coalition. Because Clinton
was already in the Jackson fold, Van Buren had made his peace

with his old New York State foe; and through Ritchie, Randolph, Tazewell and a few others, he carried the bulk of the Crawford Radicals with him. Few were entirely satisfied with Jackson, but from sheer necessity he became the leader about whom all the dissident factions in the opposition rallied.[24] Thereafter there were only two parties: the administration, soon to call itself National Republican, and the Jacksonians, or Democrats.

CHAPTER XXVII

PLANTERS AND PLAIN REPUBLICANS

1

THOUGH he lived in a world of controversy and recrimination and presided daily over the stormy sessions of a Senate whose members were locked in a struggle for power, it was the big house hidden among the trees on Georgetown heights that was for the time being the center of Calhoun's world. It was there that Floride, in mid-April 1826, gave birth to an eighth child, while her husband defended himself as best he could against an onslaught he had not foreseen. The new arrival was a boy, the fourth, and was named James Edward in honor of his uncle who was visiting with the family at the time.[1]

Floride had scarcely recovered from the effects of her confinement when an epidemic of colds seized upon the children; and just two days before Calhoun yielded his gavel to Macon, five-year-old Patrick fell from a rocking chair and seriously injured his elbow. The next day little John Caldwell was taken with a cough and fever, but in the alarm over Patrick's condition the younger child did not receive proper attention. The disease quickly took a dangerous turn, and ten days went by before hope for his recovery was entertained.[2]

The damp, sticky heat of the Washington summer found the child still too weak to permit his being moved, and all thought of returning to the South before fall was abandoned. The Calhouns determined, however, to avoid any possible repetition of the siege by making their permanent home thereafter at Pendleton where the children could grow up in the bracing air of the Carolina highlands. Andrew and Anna Maria would benefit by uninterrupted attendance at school, and the move would also do much to relieve the financial pressure that life in the Capital entailed.

The decision was made with characteristic promptness, and Calhoun wrote at once to John Ewing to have necessary alterations made at Clergy Hall. "We wish the piazza to be repaired and such an enlargement of the space, through which the Stair case passes, as will give a pantry of good size, and a comfortable bed chamber instead of the little room, that Andrew used to occupy, with a door to open between it and your mother's chamber." For a permanent home he hoped to build on the hill a little way up the road, provided the land could be acquired by exchange; and he charged his brother-in-law to enter into negotiations with the owner, Colonel Lewis. For sound business reasons, however, he wanted the purpose of the transaction to remain undisclosed. "If he knew of my intention he would doubtless avail himself of it to rise in his demands, and on that account as well as others I do not wish my intention to be known at present, and I wish the exchange to be effected before my return." By the same mail he wrote to his mother-in-law to learn whether she would prefer that Oakly be sold or rented.[3]

Almost immediately John suffered a relapse. For weeks the child hovered between life and death, while the harassed father wrote the "Onslow" letters in his own political defense. There appeared to be no change in his condition by July 4 when Calhoun attended, along with the President, the official ceremonies marking the fiftieth anniversary of the Declaration of Independence. So deep was his affliction, as John sank slowly lower, that he scarcely noted the almost superstitious awe which greeted the news that Jefferson and old John Adams had died together on that same fiftieth anniversary of their own greatest work. At last one hope alone remained, and that was more a counsel of despair than a hope. If they could only get the child to a more healthful climate! They grasped the straw and set off for Pendleton shortly before the end of July.[4]

As Calhoun later described it, John "was so low, that it seemed almost desperate to think of moving him. He continued to sink on the journey till we reached Salisbery; where he became so feeble, that he could no longer stand the motion of the carriage. We then resorted to medicine again, and by the blessing of a kind Providence, with success. His desease so far yield[ed], that we were enabled to reach home by slow travelling and on the very day of our arrival his cough ceased, and has not since returned."[5] The child continued to improve steadily, and by winter was fully recovered.

2

Back once more among his own people, Calhoun fell quickly into the mood of the serene blue mountains that stretched away before him. The petty political squabbles of the past months were largely forgotten as he devoted himself to the affairs of his community and of his family. He did not succeed in acquiring the Lewis tract, and so his first care was to begin extensive alterations on Clergy Hall. The remodeling continued at intervals over three or four years until the entire character of the house was changed. At this time, and for another decade, the hall and the six hundred acres of land along the Seneca River that comprised the estate were rented from Floride's mother for $250 a year. It was not until 1836 that Calhoun purchased the property from his brother-in-law, to whom the deed had originally been assigned. The name of the estate was changed in 1830 to Fort Hill.[6]

When the summer was over a teacher was secured for the younger children, Patrick, John and Cornelia. Andrew went to school in Pendleton village, and Anna Maria was sent to a "female academy" at Edgefield, where she lived in the family of her father's old friend and neighbor, Eldred Simkins.[7]

The last and most unworthy numbers from "Patrick Henry's" pen reached South Carolina about the time the Vice President himself arrived, but he waited a month or more before dispatching a reply. Only once, so far as the records go, did he allude to the matter in public, and that was when compelled to by the wording of a toast at a dinner in his honor. On that occasion he referred briefly and without rancor to the attacks upon him, and declared once more his own political creed—the principles of the Declaration of Independence, of the Constitution, of Madison's Report of '99, and of "the great civil revolution that brought Mr. Jefferson into power in 1801."[8]

A few days later Calhoun and his family attended an anniversary meeting of the Pendleton Farmers' Society, at which he was admitted to membership. There was an address by the president of the society, his cousin and brother-in-law John Ewing Calhoun, followed by a dinner; and no one seemed to mind the trifling circumstance that the low floor of Farmers' Hall gave way beneath the strain.[9]

John Ewing Calhoun, whose own plantation, "Keowee," lay some two miles northwest of Clergy Hall, took charge of his brother-in-law's affairs when official business called the Vice President back to Washington; and one gathers from the correspondence of the two that Floride, though a charming and accomplished hostess, was not equal to administering an estate or supervising slaves. Whatever the difficulties, however, the new life was more satisfactory than the old. At the first opportunity Oakly was sold and the last property tie with Washington was broken.[10]

3

The fall elections showed a definite trend against the administration despite the best that Clay, Webster and Adams himself could do, and the path of the National Republicans was not made easier by Duff Green's renewal of the "corrupt bargain" hue and cry in June and again in November. Calhoun's friend Virgil Maxcy withdrew his own candidacy for Congress in favor of the incumbent, a Jacksonian; and Warren R. Davis was at last elected, though by a bare twenty-five votes, to represent Pendleton District. In the choice of a successor to Gaillard in the Senate, however, the influence of the Vice President proved insufficient. By a close vote of 83 to 81 in the legislature, William Smith won out over Daniel E. Huger. It was no gain for the administration, but it was another defeat for Calhoun in his contest with the Radicals for control of South Carolina.

Smith's dislike for Calhoun amounted to an obsession, but the latter treated his erstwhile opponent with unruffled cordiality. Smith could not fail to notice it, and once declared to Huger, "Do you know, sir, that Calhoun, on my return to the Senate of the United States, treated me with so much kindness and consideration that I could not hate him as I wished to do." The story got around, and one acquainted with both men commented that "he had no doubt Smith hated Calhoun the more for not being able to hate him!"[11]

The Vice President was again in the chair when the Senate

convened for the second session of the Nineteenth Congress, December 4, 1826. Under the amended rules of the Senate, standing committees were chosen by ballot. With forty-two members present, the coalition commanded twenty-three votes, and the outcome in every case was determined by that margin. A very well-informed correspondent of the Richmond *Enquirer,* possibly Tazewell, charged that the "tickets of the ministerialists were all made out, and kept in their drawers, and taken out as occasion required." The result, as might have been anticipated, gave the administration control of all the standing committees. Randolph got no assignment at all and the others on the proscribed list, instead of the usual two, got only one each: Berrien of Georgia, Dickerson of New Jersey, Hayne, Macon, Smith of South Carolina (a signal distinction for a newcomer), Tazewell, Van Buren, White and Woodbury of New Hampshire.[12] McDuffie and Floyd were similarly left off all committees in the House, and Ingham got no better than the comparatively unimportant Post Offices and Post Roads.

The attention of party managers centered on two still undecided Senatorial contests, involving Van Buren and Randolph, and for the time being Calhoun was let alone. As he left Washington to spend the Christmas holidays with Van Buren and Stephen Van Rensselaer at the Fairfax County home of his Virginia friends, the William H. Fitzhughs, he wrote with genuine relief that he had ceased to be "the object of the malignant attack of those in power."[13]

It was premature. On December 28 the Alexandria *Gazette* published, with editorial comment, a letter from Elijah Mix of notorious memory. The letter was dated November 1, 1825, and was addressed "To the author of Hancock," the signature over which an attack on the Vice President had recently been made in a New York paper. It charged that Calhoun as well as Van Deventer had been financially interested in the Rip Rap contract and offered to produce proof if desired. The editorial comment in the *Gazette,* while it acquitted Calhoun of profiting from the contract himself, specifically charged the former Secretary of War with complicity in the gains of his Chief Clerk. It was indicated that the incriminating document had come to the editor from the War Department.

The next morning a letter from Calhoun was placed in the

hands of the Speaker of the House, requesting an immediate and full investigation of the charges. At the same time the Secretary of the Senate received a brief note from the Vice President explaining his action and stating that "a sense of propriety" would keep him from presiding over that body until the matter had been disposed of.

Secretary Barbour, meanwhile, had sent Colonel R. M. Johnson, in the role of mutual friend, to explain to his predecessor how the Mix letter had come into his hands and how it had reached the public. "Hancock" was in reality Major Satterlee Clark, one-time Army paymaster who had been dismissed by Calhoun for failure to settle his accounts. At the time of the Hancock letters he was being sued by the Treasury for the amount of his default, some thirteen thousand dollars.[14] He had pocketed Mix's communication and at the appropriate time had given a copy to a competitor of that gentleman, Howes Goldsborough. The latter had used it to prove to the War Department that Mix was unfit to receive a contract and had then permitted a copy to be taken by the editor of the *Gazette*.

The administration apparently had not anticipated Calhoun's prompt request for an official investigation, for Clay hurriedly appeared in the House when the Vice President's letter was read,[15] and the Adams press argued that it was not a matter for Congressional action. It was no administration supporter but John Floyd of Virginia who rose to move that the investigation be made. Floyd will be recalled as the man who more than any other except perhaps John Cocke had made Calhoun's life as Secretary of War miserable. The Virginian now branded as a calumny the charge he had once pressed. He was followed in the same vein by Cocke, who declared that the previous investigations of the contract had not revealed "the most trivial circumstance going to show that the then Secretary of War was in the remotest degree improperly concerned in it."[16] A seven-man committee was appointed by Speaker Taylor, who under Clay's eye followed meticulously the rule laid down by the President: four of the seven members were strong administration men, and one of the others was personally hostile to Calhoun. Besides Floyd, the chairman, only one other member, James W. Campbell of Ohio, could be considered friendly.[17]

To the National Republicans Calhoun's demand for an investigation was made solely in the hope "of enlisting public sympathy, and regaining the ground he has of late lost in the public favor." To the Democrats it was another milestone on the road to political power. The Vice President was invited guest at the Jackson Day dinner, already a purely party affair, where he was toasted by name; and as his "inquisition" dragged on through January, he thought the overthrow of the coalition would be sure and complete.[18]

The investigation did indeed speak ill for the motives if not the prospects of those who conducted it. McDuffie attended the sessions as personal representative of Calhoun, but was able to accomplish little. The committee heard masses of testimony on virtually everything concerned with the War Department except the charge against the former Secretary. Major Satterlee Clark and Mix swelled the record, and so did various officers of the Army, but little of the evidence was to the point. General Swift, who had made the disputed contract, was not called at all until McDuffie insisted. The hearings were closed on January 27 without witnesses on behalf of the Vice President being summoned, and in a long letter dated two days later McDuffie denounced the whole proceeding. The report, which was delayed until February 13, concluded that Calhoun had not shared in the Mix contract, but aside from that was so confusing and equivocal that the reader might infer what he would. Floyd submitted a statement for himself and Campbell which cleared the Vice President of any suspicion of wrongdoing, in connection with the Mix contract or any other, but as a parting shot the House voted 81 to 78 not to receive McDuffie's protest, which was thus omitted from the printed record.[19]

The only tangible result of the investigation was that Van Deventer was relieved of his duties as Chief Clerk in the War Department. Administration supporters exulted that the report left Calhoun "much worse than he was before moving the business"; while the friends of the Vice President rejoiced "at the triumphant issue of the investigation."[20] On the fourteenth Calhoun resumed his duties as presiding officer of the Senate.

4

The Mix investigation was of a piece with the "Patrick Henry" letters in that its underlying purpose was to render Calhoun a political liability to his coadjutors. The allegiance which bound the Democratic leaders together was tenuous, and jealousies lay close to the surface. Calhoun had assumed as a matter of course the intellectual and social leadership of the party, giving by his presence respectability to a group that contained a high proportion of the unlettered and uncouth. Among all the Jacksonians he occupied the pre-eminent position, and his followers stood out for ability above the Crawfordites and the original Jackson men alike. There were those among the latter who resented the too-confident Carolinian, and among the Radicals of other days were many who remembered old scores. To these the Mix investigation offered an excuse for dropping the Vice President from the Jackson ticket, and even before the committee hearings were completed a move toward that end was on foot.[21]

Van Buren privately sympathized with those who sought the elimination of Calhoun, for in that direction lay his own chance at the Presidential succession. With the Erie Canal completed, New Yorkers did not look with favor upon the idea of building competing transportation routes with public funds, and Van Buren proposed to turn this feeling against his rival by associating Calhoun with Clay and the administration program. "You must advise me as soon as the Legislature are in session," he wrote to one of his lieutenants, "whether I can safely make my constitutional speech & therein reprobate strongly but respectfully the heresies of Messrs Calhoun and Clay on the subject of the powers of the Federal Government before my election. It would be most gratifying to do so. . . ."[22]

It would have been, in effect, to read the Vice President out of the party, with unforeseeable consequences, but the speech was not made. Before the appointed time word came that the South Carolina Legislature had followed the lead of Georgia in giving Jackson an almost unanimous caucus nomination, and perhaps the New York Senator was influenced by it. At any rate he postponed a public break, and the two men worked together to bring Northern and Southern interests into political harmony.

Out of their discussions came a detailed plan of campaign which was to bring Jackson into the White House in 1828, but which looked far beyond that eventful year. The first step was to be a national nominating convention, which would go far to restore the old two-party system by cutting out local candidates like Clinton and Adams; but the basis of the plan was no less than a renewal of the political alliance between New York, Pennsylvania and the South that had elected Jefferson and Burr in 1800. Until destroyed by Monroe's antipartisan policy, that alliance had operated to allay sectional hostility by substituting for geographical loyalties an allegiance to a party which cut across sectional lines. Ingham, Tazewell and doubtless a number of others participated in the discussions, so that it is not possible to assess the contributions of each, save that the national convention was Calhoun's idea and the North-South alliance probably Van Buren's.

To the South the proffered union would be a bulwark against the rising antislavery agitation, and it was not to be lightly refused, even if it meant giving the Presidency for a time to a "military chieftain." In January the scheme was submitted to Thomas Ritchie, who spoke for the Virginia Radicals. "We must always have party distinctions," Van Buren wrote to the Richmond editor, "and the old ones are the best of which the nature of the case admits. Political combinations between the inhabitants of the different states are unavoidable and the most natural and beneficial to the country is that between the planters of the South and the plain Republicans of the north. The country has once flourished under a party thus constituted and may again. . . ."[23]

Ritchie had already been a tower of strength to the opposition, but he had been reluctant hitherto to accept Jackson. Circumstances now combined, however, to bring him into the camp of the Hero. On the very day that Van Buren's letter was written, the Virginia Legislature met to choose a United States Senator. P. P. Barbour and John Floyd had both refused to run, and Ritchie had taken it for granted that Randolph would be unopposed. At the last minute, however, Governor John Tyler permitted his own name to be used, and he was elected by the narrow margin of five out of more than two hundred votes. Personally extremely popular and known as a strong State Rights man, Tyler was supported by all those who had once been Federalists, by all those on the Republican side who thought Randolph mentally unbalanced, and most strenuously by the administration members; and though the change would not alter the policy pursued, it was decidedly a triumph for

Adams and Clay. Randolph, the most outspoken member of the opposition, had been beaten, and that by a man who only two years before had written an unsolicited letter approving the appointment of Clay.

As the administration crowed in triumph, Ritchie pondered Van Buren's letter, swallowed his pride and at last came out for Jackson.[24]

Thus was the union of the Jackson, Calhoun and Crawford forces made complete, but it was still a union of political necessity. Even before Ritchie's decision had been made, he received a letter from Tazewell inviting him to come to Washington and edit an opposition paper. Van Buren concurred in the invitation, and significantly, the support of Jackson would be only incidental. The primary aim was "to inculcate and to keep alive by frequent repetition and argument, the great principles of the Republican party, as they were manifested and expressed prior to 1801. To support those who support them, and to oppose those who oppose them."[25]

Once before, in July of 1826, Van Buren had sought unsuccessfully to establish another Democratic paper in the Capital,[26] when it appeared that the *Telegraph* was being edited rather in the interests of the Vice President than in behalf of Andrew Jackson; and now again the old Crawford Radicals were seeking to curb Calhoun's influence in the new party by dividing Duff Green's power.

Even this, however, was not the full extent of the revelations in Tazewell's letter; for if the Virginian and the New Yorker could agree that the South Carolinian would bear watching, they were also suspicious of each other. "For my part," Tazewell went on, "I look forward beyond the 4th of March, 1829. Should we be defeated then, it would be necessary to take a new departure. Should we then succeed (of which I have no doubt) it is possible, nay probable, that our party will soon be in danger of separating from the very fact of its overwhelming and unmanageable numbers. Then will arise a new crisis, for the occurrence of which timely preparation should be made; & I feel solicitous that a Southern Editor should have acquired and established the reputation of the proposed Journal before that day arrives. What may be Mr. Van Buren's views upon this point of the subject I know not, nor does he know mine. In your reply, therefore, to this letter (which I shall be compelled to show him) you will not of course notice this."

Ritchie declined to leave Virginia and Duff Green was left in command of the Jackson press. More by the failure of others than by any skill of his own, Calhoun remained one of the chiefs of the rising Democracy. Van Buren, meanwhile, was re-elected Senator despite the strenuous efforts of the administration to defeat him, and in his letter of acceptance he publicly ratified the North-South alliance. It would, he wrote, be his "constant and zealous endeavor to protect the remaining rights reserved to the states by the federal constitution; to restore those of which they have been divested by construction; and to promote the interests and honor of our common country."[27]

5

As Adams and Clay carried the National Republicans down the old Federalist road toward centralized power, it became increasingly clear that the Democratic opposition, whatever form it took otherwise, would have to stand for the State Rights position. To Van Buren and to many of the Jacksonians such a choice was mere political expediency; to the Virginians and to the Radicals of the deeper South it was a victory for the principles they had championed undeviatingly since Jefferson's day; and to Calhoun it was a means to an end: the reform of a government he believed, not without provocation, to have become corrupt. Even as the union of Northern and Southern opponents of the coalition was being forged, Webster drove through the House "the most unprincipled tariff & more sectional than any ever before passed"[28]—a bill to increase the duties on wool and woolens for the benefit of New England. The policy he had roundly condemned a few years before was now desired by his constituents and, like the able lawyer he was, Webster had changed his convictions to suit the views of his clients.[29]

The woolens bill reached the Senate on February 13, but action on it was delayed until the last day of the month. It was an issue on which the Jacksonians preferred to remain uncommitted, for the General was being represented in Pennsylvania as in favor of protection and in the South as opposed. Van Buren had skillfully avoided taking a positive stand, while Calhoun was still believed by many to have propagated if he had not originated the policy. The tariff was a rock on which the North-South alliance might well founder, and Hayne moved accordingly that the bill lie on the table. It could be as effectively killed in that way as by voting it down, since the Congress had only three more days to run. At the same time the Vice President was urged to withdraw lest a tie be manipulated, forcing him to cast a vote that would necessarily be unpopular with one or the other wing of the party.

But Calhoun refused to yield his seat. The tariff appeared to his mind more dangerous in its consequences than a possible rift within the Democratic ranks. As the roll was called, more than one member failed to answer to his name, and among them was Martin Van Buren. The anticipated tie resulted, and the Vice President ended the hopes of the protectionists for the session.[30]

A few days later Van Buren and Churchill C. Cambreleng left for the South, accompanied as far as Charleston by William Drayton and James Hamilton, Jr. The purpose of the visit was to bring Crawford unreservedly into the new Democratic Party. The Radical leaders were well disposed toward the North-South alliance but remained unalterably hostile to Calhoun. The price of their support was the elimination of the Vice President, and there is little doubt that Van Buren's assurances were satisfactory.[31]

CHAPTER XXVIII

DEMOCRACY ADVANCES

1

CALHOUN'S vote to table the woolens bill reflected the growing unrest in his native state. An unhealthy economy will boil over sooner or later into political channels, and the economy of cotton was very unhealthy indeed. The great Southern staple had averaged nearly 21 cents a pound for the year 1825 and had reached a peak of 29.5 cents in June of that year. By that time most of the crop had been sold, but the rise stimulated heavy planting and increased the next year's crop by nearly forty percent. At the same time the tariff of 1824 operated to restrict the market and to bring advances in the cost of manufactured articles to the planters. The price of cotton fell to an average of 12 cents for 1826, and dropped to a low point of 8.8 cents in 1827. The average price for the year at Charleston was 9.3 cents and at Liverpool less than sixpence. The state of South Carolina saw a corresponding decline in the value of exports from $11,000,000 in 1825 to $8,000,000 in the year ending September 30, 1827.[1]

These economic conditions were reflected in hard times all over the state, and it was a state whose property-owning class was peculiarly articulate. By and large they blamed their plight on the protective policy and looked for relief to Jackson, whom they regarded as one of themselves because he, too, owned slaves and planted cotton. The defeat of the woolens bill was a step in the right direction, but the tariff interests, spurred on by Mathew Carey and the voluble Hezekiah Niles, soon made it clear that the fight would be renewed. They cared for neither one party nor the other but concentrated their efforts, like the efficient lobbyists they were, on winning individual Congressmen and Senators.

The Pennsylvania Society for the Promotion of Manufactures and the Mechanic Arts called a convention to meet at Harrisburg late in July, "to take into consideration the present state of the wool growing and wool manufacturing interests, and such other manufactures as may require encouragement," and urged "farmers, manufacturers, and the friends of both branches of industry" to hold preliminary state conventions in June in order to select delegates.[2] Indefatigably publicized by Niles and his fellow editors, and surreptitiously stimulated by Clay and Adams, meetings were duly held in state capitals throughout the North and East, while meetings of protest matched them in the South.

One such gathering, held at Columbia, South Carolina, on July 2, was addressed by pugnacious Dr. Thomas Cooper, friend of Jefferson and Priestley, noted scientist and among the first economists of his time. Governor Taylor was in the chair and a distinguished audience approved as Cooper traced the flow of wealth from South to North under the operation of the tariff. He foresaw that in the not distant future submission to such a system would be stark ruin and the South, ere long, must "calculate the value" of the Union. On the Fourth, McDuffie told his constituents the nation could not last twenty years under a policy that took the property of a part for the benefit of the rest; and the *Charleston Mercury,* edited by Henry L. Pinckney, a brother-in-law of Hayne, and hitherto strongly nationalist in its tone, approved both speeches.[3]

The same papers that were clamoring for a higher tariff to benefit one section alone cried "treason," and Cooper and those who thought as he did were roundly denounced by the administration. Cooper stuck to his guns and amplified his argument in letters to Van Buren. He foresaw that South Carolina, so desperate was her economic plight, would be ready to leave the Union should the tariff be increased, and urged Van Buren to oppose any such move.[4] Calhoun watched closely from his Pendleton retreat and knew that a crisis was approaching. "Our system," he wrote three weeks after Cooper's speech, "has reached a most important point in its progress, and one that will go far to determine the question of its durability. Few men in my opinion realize the magnitude of the present juncture; but it cannot pass away without testing severely the character of those, who are prominently before the nation."[5]

2

On July 30 an even hundred delegates from thirteen states assembled at Harrisburg. Niles was among them, but though he emphasized in his report of the proceedings the large number of "farmers" present, the list of participants does not bear out his claims for their disinterestedness. There were undoubtedly farmers there, including Jesse Buel of Albany and massive Joseph Ritner from western Pennsylvania; but those who held the offices and formulated the program of the convention were not moved by altruism. Even Buel had until recently been an editor; and Ritner, who presided over the meetings, had just completed two terms as speaker of the state assembly. Most, if not all, of the farmers present were sheep raisers, whose interest was as personal as that of Abbot Lawrence, one of the members from Massachusetts.

Besides those already mentioned, the list included Mathew Carey; Charles J. Ingersoll, president of the Pennsylvania Society for the Promotion of Manufactures; administration Senators Samuel Bell of New Hampshire and Ashur Robbins of Rhode Island; R. C. Mallary of Vermont, chairman of the House Committee on Manufactures; Ezikiel Webster, who came at the behest of his brother Daniel; Gideon Welles, the young editor of the Hartford *Times;* David Wilkinson of Pawtucket, father of the American machine tool industry; Clay's intimate, Jeremiah Morrow, lately Governor of Ohio and onetime Representative and Senator from that state; James Tallmadge of the administration party in New York; George Tibbits of New York, onetime merchant and former Congressman who had propagandized for the tariff as early as 1804; and assorted Congressmen, ex-Congressmen, merchants, manufacturers and publicists.[6]

The convention ended after five days with a memorial to Congress proposing prohibitive duties on wool and woolens and recommending additional protection for iron, flax and hemp, distilled spirits and cotton goods. The drafting of an "Address to the people of the United States" expressing the general sense of the meeting was left in the capable hands of Hezekiah Niles, who did not finish the task until October.[7] The address is a complete and documented statement of the tariff argument, the propagation of which was, to sincere protectionists like Niles and Carey who had no personal axes to grind, the real purpose of the Harrisburg Convention. But to the politicians present, and they were many and adroit, a more compelling purpose was to identify Adams with the tariff and thus to make it a campaign issue. They thought Jackson would then be forced either to accept the convention's report and lose the South or to oppose the system and lose Pennsylvania, New York and Ohio.[8]

Since the tariff of 1824 it had been obvious that no opponent of the protective system could be elected, but it was equally clear that no protariff man could carry the South. For Jackson to take either stand explicitly would be to give the election to Adams or to risk another decision in the House, so protectionist and free-trade Democrats agreed on a noncommittal policy. Jackson ignored the whole affair, and the manufacturing states continued to regard him as a tariff man while the South remained confident he was not. The famous Coleman letter, in which the Hero had expressed himself in 1824 in favor of a "judicious examination and revision" of the tariff, was exhibited in Pennsylvania to prove that he stood for the whole protective system, and in the cotton states it was cited as "authentic evidence that Gen. Jackson's opinions, on the subject of the Tariff, are materially variant from those of the present administration."[9]

The economic theory of the Harrisburg Convention, however, precipitated a new wave of protest from the South and from the importers of New England and New York. Best of the arguments produced were those of Henry Lee of Boston, representing the the views of a committee of merchants, and of Robert J. Turnbull, a retired South Carolina lawyer and planter.[10] Turnbull's work first appeared as a series of essays in the Charleston *Mercury* during August and September, over the signature of "Brutus," but was reprinted in a stout pamphlet called *The Crisis* late in October. The reasoning is in the vein of Thomas Cooper, whose friend Turnbull was, and its influence in South Carolina was immense. The central theme of the work was stated in a preliminary quotation from John Randolph: "There is nothing but power that can restrain power." The Revolution was fought not for union but for liberty, and liberty can only be preserved by force. That force lies with the states, which have a right to interpose to arrest unconstitutional and oppressive acts of the general government. For authority Turnbull relied on the *Federalist* and on Madison's Report of 1799 on the Alien and Sedition Acts.

Among those who read *The Crisis* eagerly and with approval was the Vice President of the United States, but Calhoun did not need the help of others in making up his own mind. Before more than one or two of Brutus' numbers could have reached him, he explained his reactions and his fears at length in a letter to James Edward Calhoun.[11] He thought that, in the face of a wave of popular hostility growing out of a general conviction that Adams had achieved the Presidency against the public voice, the administration was resorting to dangerous and corrupt means to sustain itself. Among these, he wrote, "there is one, in particular, that, in my opinion even threatens danger to the Union, I mean that of arraying the great geographical interests of the union against one another. The wisest men of the country, have divided in opinion, how far Congress has the power, and admitting they possess it, how far, on principle, encouragement may be given to domestick manufactures, as connected with the great consideration of the defence and independence of the country. But whatever may be the diversity of opinion among the wise and patriotick, as to the discreet exercise of this great power of changing the capital and industry of the country, there cannot among such, be any doubt, that the power itself is highly dangerous, and may be perverted to purposes most unjust and oppressive. Through such an exercise of it, one section of the country may really be made tributary to another; and by this partial action, artful and corrupt politicians may use nearly half of the wealth of the country to buy up partisans, in order to acquire, or retain power. This very use of it, many, and they highly intelligent, below the heads of the Administration are attempting to employ."

Then follows a reference to the woolens bill and his own agency in defeating it and to the Harrisburg Convention which resulted. Thus, he declares, "the dangerous example is set of seperate representation, and association of great Geographical interests to promote their prosperity at the expense of other interests, unrepresented, and fixed in another section, which, of all measures that can be conceived, is calculated to give the greatest opportunity to art, and corruption, and to make two of one nation. How far the administration is involved in this profligate scheme, time will determine; but if they be, the curse of posterity will be on their head. In the mean time, the South has commenced with remonstrating against this unjust and oppressive attempt to sacrifice their interest; and, I do trust, that they will not be provoked to step beyond strict constitutional remedies."

He was thinking of Cooper and Turnbull, perhaps also of the younger and more impetuous of his political friends, McDuffie and Hamilton. He foresaw that from the tariff great events would spring. "It must lead to defeat or oppression or resistence, or the correction of what perhaps is a great defect in our system; that the seperate geographical interests are not sufficiently guarded." He had not yet fixed upon the remedy, for the effort to increase the duties might still be defeated and make other measures unnecessary; but he was already seeking for a conservative solution to a problem which threatened an explosion.

3

Beyond watching with genuine concern the growing spirit of resistance among his followers and friends, Calhoun held himself aloof from politics. Throughout the summer he was the chief target of the administration press, but he steadfastly refused to visit the North for electioneering purposes, despite the urging of his partisans. "I cannot doubt," he wrote to Van Deventer late in July, "but my enemies have succeeded in making an impression against me to the North by grossly misrepresenting my opinions; but I trust time, and circumstances will finally remove all error on that point. I am willing to trust to their slow, but certain operation, aided by the fidelity of friends. . . ."[12] He was thoroughly occupied with his plantation, his large and scattered family, and the inevitable guests who find their way to the homes of public men. He was raising corn and small grains as well as the ever-present cotton, was experimenting with fertilizers, and was trying his luck with wine grapes. A month-long spell of bitter weather in October cut the cotton crop by a third and gave the Carolina planters, Calhoun among them, something besides politics to worry about.[13]

Then too there were numerous domestic concerns of greater or less importance, and in all of them Calhoun took an interest. His niece Lucretia, daughter of his brother William, was married during the summer; and a little later his cousin Francis Pickens and Eliza Simkins, daughter of Eldred Simkins, were the principals in another wedding. On both occasions the Vice President was among the guests, and we may be sure he was as gay as any there, with his pleasant wife and his graduated brood of youngsters. Andrew was already grown to man's size, though he was not yet sixteen, and his father was debating whether to send him to West Point. John had thrown off all trace of his illness of the previous summer and was stout and healthy; and James, the youngest, blue-eyed and flaxen-haired, already walked and talked, though little over a year old.[14]

Outside of South Carolina, meanwhile, the campaign was being waged with increasing fury. In the matter of Executive patronage Adams cast discretion to the winds, while Clay and Webster raised funds to subsidize the administration press.[15] The public printing contracts of three Jackson papers, the *Argus of Western America,* the *Maine Argus,* and the *New Hampshire Patriot,* were summarily canceled, and Clay also demanded cancelation of mail contracts held by Isaac Hill, editor of the last-named sheet. When McLean refused to indulge in political reprisals at Hill's expense, Clay sought the removal of the Postmaster General.[16] At the same time Webster made strenuous efforts to bring the Federalists into the National Republican Party.

New York elected a legislature in the fall, and when the returns were in they showed a sweeping victory for the Democracy. Clay and Barbour both charged the Postmaster General with using his influence against the administration, and Adams himself thought that "the influence of almost every officer, both of the custom-house and of the post-offices, has been violently hostile." As a result, another flood of criticism was directed at McLean, whose only fault appears to have been that he consistently blocked all efforts to influence the votes of post-office employees, one way or the other.[17] It should be noted, however, that though Adams blamed McLean bitterly, he said never a word against Rush; but the officers of the custom houses, also mentioned in the indictment, were under the Secretary of the Treasury.

The New York elections brought many of the old Federalists into the Jacksonian ranks, more because Adams had failed to conciliate them than through any real sympathy with the Democratic cause; and the incident served to show once more the superior political acumen of the opposition. In bringing over the Federalists, Van Buren exploited to the full Jackson's letters to Monroe of 1816, held out hope of 'an end to the proscription of their party, and gave them an excuse to come over to what already appeared the winning side.[18]

In almost every phase of political activity the story was the same. The administration press was less effective than that of the opposition; and such men as Peter Force and Charles King of the New York *Advertiser* were not able to cope with Duff Green and Thomas Ritchie. Both sides were completely organized, with national committees in Washington, state central committees, and local committees of correspondence which held frequent meetings and prepared "addresses" to the public; but the Jackson committees were more active and more enthusiastic.[19] For the opposition, the "corrupt bargain" charge had been so effectively hammered home that Clay was out again denying it; but the countercharges made by the coalition were generally ineffective.

4

Calhoun reached Washington only the evening before Congress met, having again left Floride at home with the children. Somewhere in the vicinity of Norfolk on the journey north he passed out of unseasonably mild and springlike weather, which had followed the cold of October, into damp, clinging fog persisting long after he reached his destination. The change was too abrupt for a constitution always inclined to be delicate, and he came down with influenza; but he did not let it keep him from presiding over the Senate.[20]

He was perhaps the more eager to be in his place because he expected to share in the first fruits of victory. For the Twentieth

Congress showed majorities against the administration in both Houses—the first time since the adoption of the Constitution that a party had been repudiated at the first election after it took office. The hated John Randolph, to be sure, was out of the Senate, but he was back in the House, as uncompromising and sharp-tongued as ever. Only one change could be counted a gain for Adams— the transfer of Daniel Webster from House to Senate, replacing the ailing Mills—and even that was questionable.

The President's message was almost querulous at times, with its repetition of recommendations earlier made and unfulfilled; but it was only another step in the crumbling fortunes of Mr. Adams. John W. Taylor had been beaten for Speaker of the House by Andrew Stevenson of Virginia, 104 to 94, with seven votes scattered, and these seven were also against the administration. Immediately after the reading of the message, Duff Green was chosen printer to the Senate; and a few days later the two Houses proceeded to the selection of committees.

In the Senate, where the choice was by ballot, the procedure introduced by the administration members at the previous session was now turned against them. All committees showed an opposition majority, and Macon went back to the chairmanship of Foreign Relations. In the House too the choice of committees became a party affair, with Ingham, McDuffie, and Hamilton prominently concerned. When the last named of these asked the Secretary of the Navy whom he would like to have representing the administration on the Naval Affairs Committee, Adams wrote testily in his diary: "It seems Hamilton disposes of the places on committees as if he were himself the Speaker."[21] The remark was not quite true, but near enough. It was not Hamilton alone, but a party steering committee, on which Calhoun's friends were predominant.

The House committees were as hostile as those of the Senate; and "the most unkindest cut of all" was the appointment of John Randolph of Roanoke to the chairmanship of the key Committee of Ways and Means—the place he had occupied twenty years before. It was merely nominal and meant only as a rebuff to the President, for Randolph was ill and quickly asked to be excused; but the blow was not materially softened when McDuffie took his place.

5

As the campaign swung into its final year, the press on both sides showed a heightened temper and a lowered regard for honesty. The slander that Jackson had knowingly lived with his beloved Rachel before she was divorced from her first husband was exploited in a sort of serialized political handbook called *Truth's Advocate and Monthly Anti-Jackson Expositor.* By way of reprisal Duff Green launched the weekly *Telegraph Extra* to serve the same purpose, and the administration countered with *We the People,* edited by Jonathan Elliot. These various special editions were confined to campaign material, which could in this way be sent out to editors all over the country at nominal cost.

In addition to its press attack upon the character of Mrs. Jackson, the administration went in for pamphlets and handbills, most popular of which was the notorious "coffin handbill" depicting six coffins and detailing the story of Jackson's cold-blooded murder of six militiamen who wanted to go home when their terms of enlistment were up. As a matter of fact, their terms were not up, and they had been shot as deserters after court-martial in due order; but the administration clung to its own version. These documents were conceived and issued by John Binns, editor of the *Democratic Press* of Philadelphia. They were distributed in enormous quantities, and in many variants. Isaac Hill replied for the opposition with an accusation that Adams, while Minister to Russia, had attempted to prostitute a beautiful American girl to the Czar; and soon there were stories of the President's extravagance and his waste of public money, not failing to mention the billiard table and chessmen bought for the White House.

The sudden death of De Witt Clinton early in February 1828 removed the last possibility of a third hat in the ring and intensified the struggle for New York. The devices of politics, including the appointing power, continued to be used by the administration in the same way they have always been used by all administrations, the only difference being that Adams professed to know nothing about the activities of his friends, and to protest vigorously in his diary of his great disinterestedness.[22] He nevertheless persuaded Webster, whose services in the Senate were invaluable, not to insist just then on going as Minister to England. He had been promised that post "at a proper time" as the price of his support, but was again put off, this time in favor of James Barbour.[23] Thus a Cabinet vacancy was created for Peter B. Porter, whom Clay had long sought to bring into the administration. In the hope of winning New York, Smith Thompson was put on the Adams ticket for Governor of that State, and the President himself decided that it would not be necessary for Thompson to resign his Supreme Court seat.[24]

In Virginia both Monroe and Madison were put on the administration ticket as Presidential electors, without either their knowledge or their consent. The whole affair was engineered by Clay's friend Francis Brooke, who neglected to forward the official notification to the two ex-Presidents until some time after it had been printed and distributed where it would do the most good. Both immediately declined, but the impression that they would serve had already been created in widely scattered places.[25]

On the other side, the Jacksonians harassed the members of the Cabinet with calls for information in the same way that Calhoun had been plagued a few years earlier by these same men, who were now, by the turn of the political wheel, his friends. Led by John Randolph, the opposition continued to harp incessantly upon the "corrupt bargain" theme, and Randolph, at least, used language as strong as that which had led to the duel with Clay. The foreign appointments, and particularly the London mission, were repeatedly assailed in the press and on the floor of Congress, until Clay's health broke under the strain, and he seemed too feeble by late April to continue in the flesh, much less in office. He managed, however, to do some vigorous campaigning in Maryland on his way home from a visit to the celebrated Dr. Physick of Philadelphia.

6

The united front which the Jacksonians presented to the administration concealed a well-developed schism within their own ranks. Many of the Democratic leaders continued to resent Calhoun's dominant position in their organization and the confident way in which the Carolinian was talked of as Jackson's political heir. For the time being his experience, intelligence and social position made him necessary to their cause; but they were fully prepared to get rid of him when the time came.

Late in February of 1827, while the North-South alliance was still in the formative stage, the Vice President had learned that an old letter from Monroe to himself dealing with the Seminole campaign was circulating among the Jacksonians. A hasty check revealed that such a document, dated September 9, 1818, had been removed from his files. An exchange of letters with Monroe served to state the case, and Calhoun contented himself with assuring his former chief that nothing in the letter could be interpreted to detract from his fame.[26] He heard no more of it for some months. Toward the end of the year, however, certain Georgia newspapers accused the former War Secretary of ingratitude toward Crawford, to whom they alleged he owed his place in Monroe's Cabinet. Calhoun wrote again to the former President, enclosing clippings and asking that the allegations be contradicted. A few days later he heard of the stolen letter again under circumstances which left no doubt as to its whereabouts, and he suddenly realized that the shaft was aimed at him as much as at Monroe— perhaps in the end at him exclusively.[27]

The letter had found its way into Jackson's hands, partially mutilated and attended by anonymous commentaries, all of which led the highly sensitive General to recall that Monroe and a part of his Cabinet had been willing to repudiate him over the Seminole episode. Correspondence between Monroe, Calhoun and Jackson over the affair dragged on for months until the whole question was put aside lest it jeopardize the election. Calhoun did not fail to see that his own destruction was intended, and he was keenly aware of the awkwardness of his position; for he had indeed, and with perfect sincerity, regarded Jackson's actions in Florida as a breach of discipline and had only yielded that judgment to the majority opinion in the Cabinet. He probably believed it still, but he could not now avow it unless he wanted to commit political suicide. So he adroitly sidestepped. "I never did suppose," he wrote Jackson, "that the justification of yourself or the government depended on a critical construction of [your orders]. It is sufficient for both, that they were honestly issued and honestly executed, without involving the question, whether they were executed strictly in accordance with the intention that they were issued. Honest and patriotick motives are all, that can be required, and I never doubted but that they existed on both sides."[28]

As this controversy was developing, Crawford was strenuously pressing the efforts he had begun on Van Buren's visit to the South to take Calhoun's name off the Jackson ticket. In a letter to the New Yorker late in December 1827, he proposed that another candidate for Vice President, preferably Macon, should be launched during the session of Congress, and expressed his confidence that Calhoun could not carry Virginia, Georgia, North Carolina or New York.[29] A week earlier, Crawford had written to another correspondent in a similar vein, with a blanket permission to use the letter as he saw fit. He asserted that Calhoun had favored Adams until Clay declared for him, and passed along the report that the Carolinian's friends had been as ardent as Clay's in bandying about the term "Military Chieftain."[30]

The attempt to displace Calhoun was unavailing, more because of his own personal popularity than through any effort in his behalf by those associated with him. When the caucuses were held, he was unanimously nominated by the legislatures of Pennsylvania, New Jersey, Ohio and Kentucky, and got 164 out of 188 votes in Virginia. Only in New York did he fail, the caucus making no nomination at all for the second office, after giving Jackson a unanimous vote for the first.[31] Winning the election seemed too important to Jackson, and the newly welded North-South alliance to Van Buren, to risk an open break with Calhoun's still formidable following; but neither forgot that the Seminole campaign might contain the seed of his destruction or that Crawford held the key.

CHAPTER XXIX

THE TARIFF OF ABOMINATIONS

1

THE America of the 1820's epitomized within herself the major conflicts of the modern world. In these states whose union was a bare half century old might be found the same diversity of interest and culture, the same disparity of wealth and position, and the same political and economic forces that were creating modern Europe. Here, too, was intellectual ferment, with theory piled upon theory, and a restless, questing energy pervading all the life of the continent. Americans were no different in character from their cousins abroad, but only a little freer to seek fulfilment of their own desires; and by and large what they desired most was wealth. Practical and self-reliant, they keyed their pursuit of fortune to the facilities and resources offered in the places where they dwelt, and developed in the process local interests and institutions compatible with their needs.

In the manufacturing and commercial states the depression that began the decade gave way to redoubled business activity, stimulated by, and nourishing in its turn, new avenues of transportation. Through the Erie Canal flowed grain, timber, minerals and even manufactured products from the West. Almost at once the cost of moving a ton of goods from Buffalo to New York dropped from one hundred dollars to less than a tenth of that sum.[1] Boston, Philadelphia and Baltimore saw their own commercial doom in DeWitt Clinton's ditch and set themselves to follow suit as rapidly as possible. For the benefit of her great port, Pennsylvania built an elaborate system of canals with inclined planes to carry freight across the mountains. The National Road that had once funneled the Western trade to Baltimore could not compete with these cheaper water routes, and so 1826 saw the Chesapeake and Ohio Canal Company chartered by the states of Maryland and Virginia. It was obvious, however, that Washington, where the canal reached tidewater, would be the chief beneficiary, and Baltimore merchants soon began to look in a new direction.

Already at Quincy, Massachusetts, and at Mauch Chunk, Pennsylvania, wagons with flanged wheels were being drawn on wooden rails by horses or mules; and in 1825 old John Stevens, who had failed to convince the Erie Canal commissioners ten years before, had set up in his yard a circular track over which a steam locomotive ran.[2] A wave of railroad enthusiasm set in. Boston demanded a connection with Albany where she, too, might share the traffic of the Erie Canal; and Baltimore translated demands into prompt action. On the last day of February 1827 the Maryland State Legislature chartered the Baltimore and Ohio Railroad. The stock was snapped up as soon as it came on the market, and the cornerstone of the line was laid on July 4, 1828, with Charles Carroll of Carrollton, last surviving signer of the Declaration of Independence, officiating.[3] In Washington on the same day President Adams took the first spadeful of earth from the C & O Canal.

Inland commerce throve, manufacturing establishments of all kinds sprang up under the fostering influence of the protective system, and prosperity settled over the North and East. It was accompanied, to be sure, by various unhealthy manifestations. Workmen occasionally struck for higher wages, and many were displaced by laborsaving machinery. Factories were largely operated by children whose standard day was fourteen hours. Pauperism rose alarmingly. But there was always the West, with its exhaustless heritage of land. A veritable mania for speculation seized upon otherwise sober citizens who saw enormous profits being made by a fortunate few. One had only to start a business, complain to Congress that foreign competition was ruinous, and a subsidy would be forthcoming in due time. Forgotten were the days of black depression through which the country had so recently passed. Forgotten was everything but the possibility of bigger and ever bigger profits.

2

Shortly after the Twentieth Congress met in December 1827, a considerable group of substantial citizens who knew what they wanted quietly entered Washington and put up at the various hotels and rooming houses with which the city was liberally supplied. They were manufacturers from a dozen states and journalists interested in the cause of domestic industry, and their purpose was to influence the passage of a new tariff act. Late in January a group of some thirty "wool growers, and other friends of the protecting principle," with Hezekiah Niles at their head, called on Clay to pay their respects; and we may be sure that no Congressman capable of being impressed was neglected. A rumor was already current, however, that tariff increases were to be denied by a combination of New York, Pennsylvania and Virginia to appease the South.[4]

In anticipation of the drive of the protectionists, and with full knowledge that the administration would make an issue of it, the House Committee on Manufactures had been carefully chosen. Its chairman, Mallary of Vermont, was an Adams man and a protectionist, but the majority of the committee members were Jacksonians, and the dominant personality among them was Van Buren's henchman Silas Wright of New York. To this committee went reams of petitions and memorials for and against increasing the duties. These were supplemented by lengthy hearings quite in the modern manner and by reports from the Treasury and from the Committee on Ways and Means. Petitions for the tariff were generally arguments for an increased duty on a single product; memorials on the other side were theoretical disquisitions against the whole protective system. The Treasury, under Rush, was in favor of increased duties, and the Ways and Means Committee, under McDuffie, was for free trade.

The Committee on Manufactures heard twenty-eight witnesses, and it is a fair guess that many of them were of the party chaperoned by Niles. They came from eight states and the District of Columbia; eight of them were members of Congress; and six of them had been delegates to the Harrisburg Convention. One was interested in hemp growing, one in the manufacture of sail duck, and one was a cotton manufacturer. Two were glassmakers, three iron manufacturers, and five distillers; but fifteen were concerned in the manufacture of wool. About half of these also raised sheep, keeping flocks of from one hundred to four thousand, and so could

be put down by Niles as "farmers," but they were in no legitimate
sense. One of their number, E. I. Dupont of Wilmington, Delaware, spoke for most when he testified that he had bought a farm
for the purpose of raising sheep to supply his woolen mill, but
thought it a losing business.

First and foremost these men were industrialists, one of them
even at that early date an absentee owner who knew nothing of the
business and had brought a manager along to answer questions.
They were concerned solely with profits, and they assumed that
the members of Congress were similarly moved. There was not
entire agreement as to what should be further protected. The
Eastern distillers wanted cheap molasses, the sailmaker cheap
hemp, a Pittsburgh glassmaker cheap woolens for his workmen.
But the wool manufacturers spoke with one voice, and the weight
of numbers was on their side.[5]

Their recommendations followed closely those of the Harrisburg Convention, with which Mallary was in full agreement, but
he was overruled. The tariff schedule offered to the House on
January 31 was the work of Silas Wright, and it represented one
of the fruits of the political alliance of North and South. In the
matter of woolens the Harrisburg demands were reduced to a level
no longer prohibitory, but in all other respects the fondest hopes of
the protectionists had been exceeded. The duty on raw wool was
high enough to raise the price to domestic manufacturers. There
were heavy duties on iron, hemp and molasses, all anathema to New
England and to shipbuilders, merchants, distillers and fabricators
of machinery elsewhere. Any tariff bill would be objectionable to
the South. This one was carefully and deliberately framed to be
objectionable to New England also. Thus Jackson's Pennsylvania,
New York and Ohio followers could vote for it, and Southern
Jacksonians could oppose. The bill would be defeated by New
England to the great damage of the administration; the South
would be satisfied; and Jackson would remain on both sides of
the question.

We do not know who conceived this cunning scheme, but we
may guess. Stevenson, who appointed the Committee on Manufactures, was Van Buren's friend, and so were Wright who wrote the
bill and a majority of his colleagues. It was entirely in keeping

with the "little magician's" methods and at least appeared to be in
his interest. Calhoun, too, was intimately concerned and undoubtedly knew about the plan in advance. Whether he had any
hand in formulating it or not, he accepted it as offering the best
prospect of breaking the protective system. As McDuffie expressed
it later, "We saw this system of protection was about to assume
gigantic proportions, and to devour the Substance of the Country,
and we determined to put such ingredients in the chalice as would
poison the monster and commend it to his own lips. This is what
is sometimes called 'fighting the devil with fire', a policy which,
though I did not altogether approve, I adopted in deference to the
opinions of those with whom I acted."[6]

3

The success of the scheme depended on voting down all amendments that might make the duties acceptable to New England. This
the Southern members agreed to do after receiving satisfactory
assurances from the Jackson tariff men that they would not unite
with the administration forces in the end to pass the bill. Calhoun
was not a party to this agreement, but was aware of it and advised
its acceptance. The intermediary between the two groups was
Representative Warren R. Davis of Pendleton District.

Debate began in the House early in March, with Mallary opposing the bill of his own committee and seeking amendments to bring
it into line with the Harrisburg proposals. It was clear to everyone what had been done, and why; but for the moment the administration appeared to be trapped. "We have just begun on the tariff,"
wrote John Bailey, who did most of Adams' official denying. "The
bill you are aware was framed precisely to defeat itself, as it will
if not amended as Mallary has proposed. . . . Without [the amend-
ment] the bill is not worth having." A little later he was more
specific still, charging that it "was engendered between the avowed
anti-tariff men of the South, and the *professed* tariff Jackson men
of the middle states, and framed most pointedly so as to bear
heavily and injuriously on New England, in the hope that it would
thus be defeated."[7] Genial Judge Story, who thought himself
above all merely sectional prejudice, wrote wrathfully to Ticknor

that the question "must finally come to the sheer point, whether the South shall govern the East, now and forever"; but Clay saw the situation more clearly when he wrote in February to Crittenden, "The Jackson party . . . do not really desire the passage of their own measure, and it may happen in the sequel that what is desired by *neither party* commands the support of both."[8]

No one seriously defended the bill, but the Northern and Southern wings of the Democracy voted down every attempt at amendment. Only one modification, a slight lowering of the duty on raw wool, was passed, and that by one vote only. As the end of the debate neared, the administration forces were faced with defeat and loss of prestige on the issue they had tried to make peculiarly their own. At that point Clay gave the word to pass it anyway, bad as it was, and on April 23 the bill was carried in the House 105 to 94.[9] Only three Southerners, all from western Virginia, voted for it; the Jacksonians from the tariff states of Pennsylvania and Ohio went on record as favoring protection; and New York cast a heavy party vote in the affirmative. But it was eleven votes from New England that carried the day.

Before the tariff went over to the Senate, Wilde of Georgia and Drayton of South Carolina sought to amend the title to avow the protectionist character of the measure so that a ruling on its constitutionality might be secured from the courts. Wilde called it an act "for the encouragement of domestic manufactures." Drayton said it was "for the purpose of increasing the profits of certain manufacturers." But John Randolph, caustic as always, termed it "a bill to rob and plunder nearly one half of the Union, for the benefit of the residue."

Less than two weeks before the tariff was disposed of in the House, Thomas Cooper, whose ears must still have rung with the cries of "treason" leveled at him for his antitariff activities of the preceding summer, wrote a long letter to Van Buren. He urged upon the New Yorker that he could, if he chose, be President of the United States in succession to Jackson. Calhoun alone stood in his way, and he was "too pretending, too fond of the brilliant, the magnificent, the imposing, too calculating how all his sayings and doings will work with respect to his own honor and glory."[10] All he need do, Cooper urged, was to follow the straight course on the tariff—come out squarely against it and compass its defeat. But Van Buren thought his road lay in a different direction.

The tariff bill went in the Senate to the Committee on Manufactures, from which it was reported on May 5 with fourteen amendments designed to re-establish the Harrisburg schedule. Much maneuvering had been going on behind the scenes; and Webster, who was identified at once with the administration, with New England, and with the point of view of conservative business, was often closeted with other members. It was known that the division would be close; and Calhoun was urged by some of the Jacksonians to withdraw, lest the administration deliberately manipulate a tie and force the Vice President to cast the decisive vote against the tariff, but he refused. The defeat of the protective system was more important in his eyes than was the alliance with the North, and he did not mean to let it go by default in his absence. If need be, he told his advisers, he would withdraw from the ticket, but he would not absent himself from the Senate.[11]

What he saw by remaining in his place was not heartening, nor calculated to create sectional good will. The plan so carefully arranged between the two wings of the Democratic Party for defeating the protective system was scrapped before his eyes, as the solemn assurances he had received from the Jackson managers were repudiated by the votes of those who had given them. The amendments that would make the policy acceptable to the wool manufacturing states were taken up, seriatim, as soon as the question reached the floor; and seven of the fourteen—enough to give the New England members an excuse for approving the measure— were passed. On five the vote was 24 to 22, with Van Buren favoring the amendment; on one the count was 25 to 21, with Eaton also on the majority side; and on one the roll was not called.[12]

Even as amended, Webster still doubted that his constituents would like it, and the administration regarded its fate as doubtful as long as their leader could not make up his mind. Adams was accordingly asked to speak to the Massachusetts Senator to "fix his indecision," and the next day Webster called on the President. The tariff was discussed, but we are not told what was said on either side. Shortly after the conversation, however, the confidence of the administration Senators returned.[13] On May 13 the bill was passed by 26 to 21. Voting for it were Benton of Missouri and Rowan of Kentucky, who dared not oppose the declared will of their respective states; Van Buren, who had engineered the passage by the New York State Legislature of a resolution instructing him to do so; and Eaton, who was closer to Jackson than any man in Washington.[14]

4

To the political managers of the Jackson party the result was satisfactory. They, too, had voted for the tariff, and in so doing had destroyed its usefulness as a campaign issue for Clay. To Calhoun it was a breach of faith; and to South Carolina, where economic depression was becoming daily more acute and the rising spirit of rebellion more difficult to stem, this newest and most vicious of tariffs—"this bill of abominations"—spelled disaster. The tone of the South Carolina newspapers while the measure was under discussion, the tenor of letters from observers on the ground, and perhaps most of all the memory of the excitement produced by the Harrisburg Convention, left no doubt in the minds of members of the state's Congressional delegation as to what the reaction would be at home; and with sound reason they feared its effect upon the forthcoming election.

Immediately on the passage of the bill members of the delegation were invited to meet at Hayne's home, and all except Senator Smith accepted. At that and at a succeeding meeting, various propositions were discussed. A proposal was made that a formal protest against the tariff be presented to Congress and to the various state Governors by the Representatives of the antitariff states; but only Georgia would agree, so the matter was dropped. James Hamilton, Jr., most hot-tempered of the group, announced his intention of withdrawing from Congress and refusing to return unless specifically instructed to do so by his constituents. He felt that he could no longer do anything for them. He was dissuaded by Drayton, Hayne and McDuffie.

It was finally agreed that they should not leave their seats until Congress adjourned, that they should then go to their districts and inform each other by letter of the state of public feeling, and that they should meet at Columbia in the fall when the legislature was to convene, to be on hand for consultation or action as the circumstances might warrant. Above all, in the words of Colonel Drayton, "they should endeavor to prevent public meetings, and every expression of public opinion connected with the tariff, until after the result of the presidential election should be ascertained." It was the unanimous conviction that the choice between Adams and Jackson was of small importance in comparison with the issue raised by the restrictive system, and they would not risk confusing that question with the election.[15]

Discussion at the meetings was free and informal, and the whole situation, including possible results of the continuation of the protective policy, was fully canvassed. McDuffie said, as he had said in public more than once, that the system if persisted in must ultimately lead to a dissolution of the Union. Such a result was deprecated by all; but the remark led on to a discussion of the military and economic resources of the state, against the possibility that coercion should be applied to her at some future time. Such a discussion, under the circumstances, was by no means far-fetched. These men, one and all, believed that the Constitution had been violated, not once but persistently, and the state militia at that date were universally regarded as a defense against the possible usurpation of the general government.[16] The leaders of the group, Hayne, McDuffie, Hamilton and Drayton, all were militia officers, and it would have been surprising had they not brought up the point of military power.

Owing to the deliberately indiscreet revelations of one of the South Carolina Congressmen, Thomas R. Mitchell, who belonged to the Smith faction, the activities of the group received wide and unfavorable publicity. They were played up by the administration press as treasonable in character, and were added to the sayings and doings of Dr. Thomas Cooper and other outspoken antitariff men as further proof that the Jackson party meant to break up the Union to provide an imperial throne for the Hero. Yet in their inception and in all that transpired at them, these meetings at Hayne's home were conservative. Calhoun, of course, was not present, but the majority of those who were belonged to what Mitchell termed "the Calhoun party." They were political and personal friends of the Vice President, and they reflected his attitude toward the problem.

Above all things, Calhoun wanted to avoid a radical solution, and he looked with grave misgivings upon the protest meetings and intemperately worded memorials that were becoming commonplaces in South Carolina. He was now convinced that the tariff was the major issue before the country, and he agreed with McDuffie that it would ultimately mean the destruction of the Union if it were not modified; but he wanted to change the system by the orderly processes of law—not by force or violence. The first step was to repudiate an administration definitely committed to the protective policy, and to be sure of that result it was necessary to avoid any revolutionary outburst in South Carolina. What the next step would be must depend on Andrew Jackson.

CHAPTER XXX

SOUTH CAROLINA OBJECTS

1

IN THE South, with her semifeudal economic structure, the depression of 1818-1821 had never really receded. There had been brief intervals of prosperity and of optimism, but over the decade the spiral had moved inexorably down. "Never was there such universal, and severe pressure on the whole South," Calhoun wrote to his absent brother-in-law while the tariff of 1828 was before the Senate, "excepting the portion, which plants sugar. Our staples hardly return the expense of cultivation, and land and negroes have fallen to the lowest price, and can scarcely be sold at the present depressed rates."[1] All over the South the mass of people were in distress. Never before, not even during the embargo in 1808, had the times been as hard. The new tariff act seemed to end once and for all any prospect of relief, and many were ready for outright rebellion, even as New England had been in 1814.

That the tariff was responsible for rising prices on manufactured articles seems hardly open to question. Also undeniable is the still more serious charge that, like the old embargo and nonintercourse acts, it created inequality and bred suspicion, distrust and in the end disunion. But the tariff was not the sole cause of Southern distress. The root of the trouble lay in the economic system inherited from colonial days and perpetuated by a profoundly conservative system of government. The impact of the industrial revolution served only to fix it the more firmly, by enormously enlarging the demand for cotton and increasing in proportion the burden of slavery.

It was in essence a colonial economy, colonial to the North as well as to England, and its guiding genius was the cotton factor. After the War of 1812 the rising manufacturer replaced the merchant as entrepreneur of the North, but the factor maintained and extended his economic mastery of the South. The planter contracted to de-

liver a specified number of bales of cotton each season, and often
paid the factor a forfeit if the total fell short. He was generally
in debt to his agent, and planted more and more cotton in a vain
effort to clear himself of it. Everything the plantation bought or
sold passed through the hands of the factor; and the bulk of it was
cotton which was stored in great warehouses in Charleston, Savannah, Augusta, Mobile, New Orleans and numerous other points.
Against this cotton the factor drew notes of hand which circulated
as specie all over America and Europe.[2]

By this means the single crop system was maintained and extended until the whole life of the South was centered around cotton. Southern capital came to be concentrated in the factorage
cities, with their miles of wharves and acres of warehouses, and
the small rural community did not develop as it had in other parts
of the country. Interest in improved transportation lagged, for
cotton could be hauled in the slack season and there was no need to
pay turnpike tolls or taxes for Government-sponsored improvements. Even the Charleston and Hamburg Railway, chartered in
1828, though seemingly an exception, was a product of the system,
for it grew from the competition of Charleston and Augusta
factors.[3] The industry that had early taken root in the upcountry
of South Carolina became less profitable than cotton and fell into
disuse; and the wealth of the section, like colonial wealth in all ages,
was slowly drained off to centers of industry, banking and trade.
Commerce with Europe shifted to Northern ports, particularly to
the growing metropolis of New York, as Southern purchasing
power declined; and every bale of cotton indirectly reaching the
markets of the world increased the dependence while it diminished
the revenue of the South.[4]

But most important of all was the institution of slavery, for it
was slavery that kept Southern economy static and precluded
change. By the mid-1820's Southern capital to the total of some
$300,000,000 was tied up in slaves, and other millions in land.[5]
These sums could not be reclaimed for investment in manufacturing or other enterprises, the way New England's merchant capital
had been put into industry; and they could be made to pay interest
only in cotton culture. The Southerner could not seek a new career
in the remoter West, as his Northern compatriot did, without

leaving his slaves behind, and so those that emigrated only served to concentrate still further the slave population. Unable to sell them and not daring to grant them freedom, the South was herself in fearful bondage to her slaves.

Is it any wonder that intelligent Southerners looked upon the tariff with deep anxiety? Calhoun spoke for the overwhelming majority of his fellows when he expressed his own conviction that the tariff was "one of the great instruments of our impoverishment; and if persisted in must reduce us to poverty, or compel us to an entire change of industry."[6] The enormous capital immobilized in slaves and land precluded the possibility of a change of industry except with foreign resources, and to accept impoverishment with resignation was not in the American character. Every visit to the North, every Northern paper that came into Southern hands, served only to emphasize the more the growing disparity in wealth between the sections and to strike deeper the feeling of injustice and oppression.

2

Immediately after the adjournment of Congress May 22, Calhoun hurried back to South Carolina and to his family. The state seethed with suppressed excitement, but her leaders stuck to the decision reached in Hayne's rooms after the passage of the tariff. There was to be no violence and no irresponsible talk that might jeopardize the election. But no plan of action was offered; and at such times of political and economic stress only action will serve. Before any decision was made in authoritative quarters, a new and younger leadership invoked the sword. At Walterboro in Colleton District far to the south, Robert Barnwell Rhett, twenty-seven-year-old member of the state legislature, translated the arguments of *The Crisis* into terms of action in a fiery speech early in June. In the name of union he called for resistance to a form of taxation peculiarly oppressive and unjust, and appealed to the Governor to convene a special session of the legislature where appropriate steps might be taken.[7]

The Governor declined, but the whole incendiary issue was open again. The papers took up the challenge, with all the old arguments pro and con, and rallies and mass meetings far and wide echoed the call to resistance or proposed new remedies. The state was torn between those who courted rebellion and those who believed there must still be some peaceable way out of an intolerable situation. While a cheering crowd at Columbia burned effigies of Clay, Webster and Mathew Carey, the state's political leaders found excuses to visit Pendleton where long and earnest conferences took place.

Despite the fulminations of the administration press against the *"Mercury* junto"* and its alleged disunion purposes, Calhoun was no clearer than the others as to what action should ultimately be taken. He thought the tariff "the most dangerous question that has ever sprung up under our system,"[8] but he counseled patience and moderation until the election should be decided. Though he was convinced that no appeal to Congress, with its fixed tariff majorities in both Houses, would be fruitful, he still hoped that Jackson would use the influence and power of his office to bring about a reduction. Beyond that many lines were open, but most of them meant forcible resistance, which he was unwilling to accept. The remedy must be constitutional as well as effective; and to find it, Calhoun turned his great powers of analysis and his abundant energy to a re-examination of the Constitution.

His attitude at this time is well expressed in two letters, both dated July 10, 1828. To Monroe he wrote of the discontent he saw around him, but expressed his confidence that "attachment to the Union remains unshaken with the great body of our citizens." It could not be doubted, however, "that the system pushed to the present extreme acts most unequally in its pressure on the several parts, which has of necessity a most pernicious tendency on the feelings of the oppressed portions. I greatly fear, that the weak part of our system will be found to consist in the fact that in a country of such vast extent and diversity of interest, many of the laws will be found to act very unequally, and that some portions of the country may be enriched by legislation at the expense of others. It seems to me that we have no other check against abuses, but such as grow out of responsibility, or elections, and while this is an effectual check, where the law acts equally on all, it is none in the case of the unequal action to which I refer. One thing seems to me certain, that the system is getting wrong and if a speedy and effective remedy be not applied a shock at no long interval may be expected."[9]

To Jackson he issued a blunt warning that, strong as Southern attachment to the Union was, "an impression of long continued wrongs would not fail to shake it." After the votes of Eaton and Van Buren for the tariff, Calhoun himself had grave doubts as to how much relief was likely to be forthcoming from Jackson; but he made it abundantly clear that the support the General would receive in the South would be support for tariff reform. The belief "that those now in power will be displaced shortly," he wrote; "and that under an administration formed under your auspices, a better order of things will commence, in which, an equal distribution of the burden and benefit of government, economy, the payment of the publick debt, and finally the removal of oppressive duties, will be primary objects of policy is what mainly consoles this quarter of the Union under existing embarrassment. That your administration may be the means of restoring harmony to this distracted country and of averting the alarming crisis before us is my sincere prayer."[10]

3

In December of 1827 the South Carolina Legislature had condemned the tariff as unconstitutional and had asserted its right as representative of one of the parties to the constitutional compact to remonstrate.[11] A committee had been named to prepare an exposition of grievances and a protest against the tariff for consideration at the next session, and a spokesman for this committee, William C. Preston, called at Clergy Hall during the summer. At Preston's request, Calhoun undertook to draft the Exposition and Protest, and it was in the process that his own views as to the nature of the American Union were formed.

Many other thoughtful men were engaged in similar tasks, and the air was full of arguments, plans, proposals and contention. It was the prologue to the great debate over the Constitution and the nature of government which was to continue for a generation until the issue was resolved by arms in favor of power. Calhoun followed the discussion closely, though he took no active part in it, and it forms the essential background of his *Exposition*.

One proposal well received in many quarters was made by Governor William Branch Giles of Virginia in a letter to that state's two Senators immediately upon the passage of the tariff. He argued for two excises to be levied by the respective states: one upon domestic manufactures equivalent to the tariff on the foreign article, and the other upon all animals driven on foot into the state. The plan had previously been discussed with McDuffie, who offered a modification of it later in the summer, proposing to tax all goods manufactured in the tariff states after they had entered into and become a part of the mass of property in South Carolina.[12]

A great popular meeting at Edgefield on July 26, said to be the largest ever held in the state, took up the cry and pledged its participants to use neither Northern manufactures nor Western livestock. The tariff of 1828 was freely compared to the Stamp Act of 1765, and to drive the resemblance home a committee of correspondence was appointed to keep in touch with similar groups in other parts of the South. At the dinner which followed, the toasts, scheduled and volunteer alike, breathed a spirit of rebellion reminiscent of Revolutionary days. Similar meetings with similar sentiments were the order of the day up and down the state and over the line in Georgia. At Pendleton Calhoun toasted "The Congress of '76— They taught the world how oppression could be successfully resisted, may the lesson teach rulers that their only safety is in justice and moderation." James Calhoun and Patrick Noble were among those who arranged the Abbeville meeting, where Hayne and Hamilton were guests and McDuffie speaker. Over and over again, in district, parish and town, the scene was re-enacted; and the upshot of it all was that almost to a man South Carolinians thought themselves the victims of oppressive taxation.[13]

That it was also illegal taxation many doubted; and still others who held the protective policy unconstitutional saw no remedy but the ballot box. In the latter group belonged Senator Smith, Poinsett, John B. O'Neall, Hugh S. Legaré and James L. Petigru, and many who had once been Federalists, like Drayton, the Gaillards and the De Saussures. General David R. Williams held opposition to be futile as well as wrong, for the majority had spoken. The only remedy was to stop buying Western stock and Eastern manufactures and begin producing both in South Carolina. To Williams this did not mean a change of industry, for he was already a manufacturer, successfully using slave labor, mostly that of small children, in his textile mills.[14]

To all these arguments Calhoun gave due consideration, but he found none of the remedies satisfactory. He knew that the South could not change her industry as Williams, Niles and even Madison argued she ought to do, because her capital was not convertible. Isolated factories might indeed be successfully established—his own brother-in-law was interested in one such venture at Pendleton[15]—but to go in for industry on a large scale would require borrowing from Northern banks and relying on Northern skill, to do either of which would merely be to supplant one form of subservience by another. Even if it were tenable, such a sweeping change in the whole economic structure of the region must take years to carry out and would bring with it hardships as great as those attributed to the tariff. But equally unpalatable to Calhoun's conservative mind was the remedy advanced by Robert Barnwell Rhett. A revolutionary movement that would inevitably bring on a clash with the general government could lead only to added suffering and, unless one or the other party backed down, to bloodshed.

To escape these two alternatives, and at the same time rescue the state from the position into which she had drifted was Calhoun's task, as he searched the Constitution and the already voluminous literature of constitutional interpretation.

4

He had carried home with him from Washington a number of volumes pertinent to his study, and others were already in his hands. From the Library of Congress he drew a collection of the political pamphlets of 1799, fruit of a controversy in which Jefferson himself had directed nullification of the Alien and Sedition Laws and Thomas Cooper had gone to jail for doing so. He drew also Henry Wheaton's Supreme Court Reports, which contained in half a dozen cases the complete exposition of John Marshall's doctrine of centralized power; and to these he added the works of

Thomas Hobbes, who taught that "covenants, without the sword, are but words."[16] With the immediately contemporary literature on economics and government he was undoubtedly familiar: with Thomas Cooper's *Lectures on Political Economy,* and with the *Notes on Political Economy* of another South Carolinian, Jacob N. Cardozo, editor of the *Southern Patriot.* Of course, he knew Turnbull's *Crisis,* which parts of the *Exposition* closely follow; and he knew the *Journal of the Constitutional Convention,* published in 1818, and Yates' Minutes, given to the world three years later, both of which had been reprinted in 1827 as the first volume of Elliot's *Debates.*

But of equal and perhaps greater importance for an understanding of the situation out of which the *Exposition* came is the *Southern Review,* the first number of which appeared in February 1828. The *Review* had been conceived in the fall of 1827 at an informal gathering to which Senator Hayne was host. It was meant to be to the South what the *North American* was to the New England States, but the times it served dictated an emphasis more political than literary. It was edited by Hugh Swinton Legaré, a future Attorney General of the United States, and Stephen Elliott, president of the Bank of the State of South Carolina, professor of botany and natural history at South Carolina College, statesman and man of letters; and in the course of a brief sixteen issues it numbered among its contributors many of the most distinguished of South Carolina names.[17]

The first number included an article on the Colonization Society by Chancellor William Harper. The second, distributed in May, began with a fifty-four-page study of the Constitution of the United States, the *Federalist* and *The Crisis,* by Stephen Elliott. In the August number Legaré reviewed Kent's *Commentaries;* and the issue for November 1828 contained a review of the *Journal of the Constitutional Convention* by D. J. McCord, state court reporter and editor of the outspoken State Rights Columbia *Telescope.* More pointed still were articles on internal improvements by Elliott, the Georgia controversy by William Drayton, and the tariff by McDuffie, the latter essay being a review of Niles' Harrisburg Convention Address and of Lee's Boston report against the increase of duties.

That Calhoun was familiar with the *Southern Review* is certain, and he may even have helped, through Hayne or others, to plan its policy. We find him, at least, forwarding to the editor a list of subscribers apparently sent to him by Bartlett Yancey in North Carolina; and his paragraph in the *Exposition* on the Roman tribunate, with its parenthetical reference to Niebuhr, was almost certainly taken from a review of Niebuhr's newly translated *History of Rome* by Professor Robert Henry in the May number.

"I am pleased," he wrote Yancey in July, "that you think so well of the first No. which seems to be very able. The second, I think equally so; and I feel much confidence that it will be able to sustain its character."[18] In the same letter he commented on the political and economic crisis, reaffirming his faith in South Carolina's loyalty and his hope that Jackson would exert his power as President to remedy the situation; but he was ready, as a last resort, to appeal to the states. "That they have adequate power, when all other fails to apply Constitutionally an efficient remedy I do not doubt. The Virginia Report and resolutions in '98 are conclusive on that point."

There was nothing surprising in his thus falling back upon the sovereignty of the states. Judge Reeve must have taught the doctrine at the Litchfield Law School, for it formed the basis of the creed on which he acted. It had been repeated over and over again in resolutions of state legislatures, in New England, the West, or the South according to the direction of the political wind. The *Federalist,* the Virginia report, the proceedings of the Convention, even the Constitution itself, gave countenance to it. Studying this body of constitutional literature, Calhoun could not fail to find the remedy he sought for the abuse of power. It lay in the right of each state, as one of the parties to the constitutional compact, to declare null and void laws made in violation of that instrument.

After a visit to Clergy Hall, James Hamilton, Jr., proclaimed the remedy in a speech to his constituents on October 21. As though to contrast it the more sharply with the appeal to force, Hamilton's speech was delivered where Rhett's had been, at Walterboro.[19] He repeated the fear of Calhoun, Hayne and the other South Carolina leaders that the election of Jackson would not arrest the evil. "He cannot repeal a law. The government of this country is not in the executive. It resides in a despotic sectional majority of both houses." He traced the course by which an economic minority had in the past and would again fix its will upon the community, and the picture was black indeed. Then with all the skill of the brilliant orator he was, Hamilton pierced the gloom and revealed the way by which the South might rid herself of the tariff: by nullification within the respective sovereign states of laws manifestly unconstitutional. Such was the remedy invoked by Jefferson and Madison against the Alien and Sedition Acts, and in the very words of these venerable patriots he repeated the unequivocal phrases. "That the several states who formed the constitution being sovereign and independent, have the unquestionable right to judge its infractions: and that a nullification by those sovereignties of all unauthorized acts done under color of that instrument, is the rightful remedy."[20]

5

The reaction in other quarters to the agitation in South Carolina and Georgia forms an instructive commentary on the democratic process. The rest of the South was apathetic, with only Virginia showing any signs of interest; and her efforts were more in the direction of quieting the protest than of ameliorating the cause of irritation. To Virginia, which did not plant cotton herself but did a brisk business in slaves with states that did, the North-South alliance that was to bring Jackson to power was more important than the tariff. And in the North and West, the whole thing was set aside as politics. Niles spoke for the manufacturing interest in this as he so often did in other cases, when he simply denied flatly that any economic distress existed in the South. To the editor of the widely circulated *Weekly Register* the whole agitation was the work of a few "ambitious men" whose purpose was "to preserve or obtain political power";[21] and the protectionists among the Jacksonians were equally anxious to gloss over the economic question.

The National Republicans seized upon the tumult as campaign material, once more singling out Calhoun for individual abuse. Adroitly chosen excerpts from his tariff speech of 1816 were quoted, and his present course was attributed to disappointed ambition. It was even insinuated that as he held the seat Burr once occupied, his course might yet be similar, since others of his party were already advocating disunion.[22] Through the summer and on into the fall the administration press hammered away at the Vice President, but he took no notice of it. He was absorbed in writing the draft of an Exposition and Protest, which under his hand was growing into the statement of a complete theory of government.

It was a theory that received embellishment from an unexpected quarter. In October the *National Intelligencer* published a letter from Jefferson to Giles, dated nearly three years earlier. Obviously responding to a query, Jefferson stated that at the time of the embargo J. Q. Adams, then Senator from Massachusetts, had informed him of a plot which would have taken New England out of the Union. An answer authorized by Adams appeared in the same paper October 21, the day of Hamilton's nullification speech in South Carolina. The President corrected Jefferson's account of their interview and specified his charges against the responsible leaders of New England Federalism. No names were mentioned by the *Intelligencer,* but the *Jackson Republican* of Boston, edited by Calhoun's friend Theodore Lyman, was less circumspect. Lyman printed the story in his issue of October 29 with names, among the others that of Daniel Webster, and pointedly asked why Adams remained on personal good terms with men he had once called traitors. Webster promptly brought a criminal action for libel. The outcome of the trial was a split jury and two postponements, after which, the political purpose having been served, the charges were dropped.

Through the agency of the Lyman trial and the controversy into which Adams found himself plunged, the whole philosophy of the separatist movement in New England and of the Hartford Convention was reviewed in the press at the very time that Calhoun had fallen back upon a similar doctrine in defense of South Carolina. At one point in the trial Lyman's counsel stated unequivocally that, "A confederation of the New England States to confer with each other on the subject of dissolving the Union was no treason. The several States are independent and not dependent. Every State has a right to secede from the Union without committing treason." No protest or objection from Webster is recorded; and in fact his own pamphlet of 1808, "Considerations on the Embargo Laws," and the Rockingham Memorial of 1812 were offered as evidence in support of the statement.[23]

Thus, beginning in the fall of 1828, as Calhoun was completing the *South Carolina Exposition and Protest,* and running on into the succeeding year, the literature of controversy was enriched by a complete restatement of the American precedents for nullification, which fitted well the mood of the South and helped to provide the materials for the ideological debate of the 1830's.

CHAPTER XXXI

CALHOUN TAKES HIS STAND

1

THE controversy over sovereignty, which is what it came to in the end, was of importance only to the philosophically inclined. To the masses the election overshadowed everything else. The propaganda efforts of the campaign, far surpassing in intensity and sheer viciousness any previous display of the kind, had stirred the body politic to its foundations, and the largest popular vote in the nation's history was recorded. In the four years since the last election the common man had become articulate and had made his power felt. In 1824 six of the twenty-four states in the Union, including New York, chose Presidential electors through their legislatures; but by 1828 only Delaware and South Carolina still resisted the tide of change. In the other twenty-two states more than a million qualified voters—three times the total of 1824—went to the polls.

Jackson's victory was so overwhelming that some of his own followers feared the party had become too strong for its own good. Clay confessed his mortification and distress, while Adams consoled himself with the assurance that his rival was unfit to be President and that his administration would therefore collapse. The New Englander had actually carried, in addition to his own section, only New Jersey, Delaware and half of Maryland, for a total of 83 electoral votes. He had even lost one electoral vote in rock-ribbed Maine, and his showing was much less impressive than his father's had been in 1800. Calhoun was triumphantly re-elected to the Vice Presidency, but his strength in the electoral college fell seven votes short of Jackson's 178: seven votes that were significantly cast by Georgia in favor of Senator William Smith.

Like his father before him, Adams salved his wounds by trying to perpetuate the principles of his defeated party in the courts. Associate Supreme Court Justice Robert Trimble of Kentucky having died during the summer, Adams nominated Clay's partisan,

387

John J. Crittenden, to be his successor. So eager had Clay been
to have the appointment made that he had even tried to persuade
Chief Justice Marshall to intercede with the President.[1] It was all
to no avail. The nomination was sent to the Senate as the Kentuckian wished, but the Senate refused to act on it, and so the
vacancy remained for Jackson to fill.

The election was no sooner over than the internal strains in both
parties revealed themselves on the surface. Clay's friends, who
filled most of the Federal offices in the West, rallied to their own
leader and did not spare the retiring President.[2] Adams had failed.
Next time would be Clay's turn, and they meant to see that he got it.
Clay himself asked Everett point-blank if he might count on the
support of the Eastern states in 1832, and Everett carried the query
to Adams, as it was intended he should. The answer was vague
and unsatisfactory. Adams was ready to say that the party stood
dissolved, and apparently assumed that he was thereby relieved of
any obligations he might have had toward the man who had made
him President.[3]

The victors, too, were divided among themselves. Van Buren
had been elected Governor of New York, but it was not anticipated
he would be long out of national politics; and his partisans and
those of Calhoun were quickly at odds. The question on everyone's tongue was whether Van Buren or Calhoun or Jackson's own
intimates would control the Cabinet, and which among them would
gain the upper hand and be the Democratic candidate in succession
to the Hero.

In addition to the personal clash of rival ambitions within the
two party organizations was a more fundamental division along
class or economic lines. Jackson had polled a heavy vote among
the landless, the debt-ridden and those who worked with their
hands; and his obligation to these "lower classes," as the Adams
men were inclined contemptuously to call them, was great. But he
had also been supported by the landed aristocracy of the South and
by a substantial group of second-generation Federalists in New
England. If there were rival ambitions within the Jackson party,
there were also rival interests, and the two lines of cleavage were
bound to run together sooner or later. In the Richmond *Enquirer*
for December 11, 1828, Ritchie expressed the concern of the South

for the future when he republished as a warning to Jackson, Edmund Pendleton's pamphlet of an earlier day, *The Danger Not Over*. In South Carolina Calhoun's *Exposition* went farther still. It was at once an admonition and a challenge, transcending personal and sectional rivalries to strike at the heart of the economic conflict.

2

The South Carolina Legislature did not meet until late November, when the outcome of the election was no longer in doubt. Its primary business was to consider means of dealing with the situation created by the tariff. All agreed that the protective system was unequal and unjust. The majority thought it also unconstitutional, and resolutions to that effect were quickly adopted. On the course of action beyond that, however, there was less unanimity. One group led by Legaré thought protest sufficient, while the party of the other extreme was led by Chancellor William Harper and Rhett. Calhoun's influence was cast into the conservative scale and for the time being no drastic move was made.

The Special Committee on the Tariff reported the *Exposition* to the House on December 19 and it was ordered printed without other formal action being taken.[4] It was not Calhoun's intention to nullify the tariff, but merely to state the grievance and assert the right to nullify should it not be removed. He still hoped that the threat alone would be enough; and to make doubly sure that no radical action was taken, he deliberately held back Hamilton and acquiesced in the election as Governor of conservative Stephen D. Miller.[5]

So anxious was he over the action to be taken by the legislature that for the first time in his term as Vice President Calhoun was not in Washington when Congress met. He remained in South Carolina until he was sure of the outcome and did not take his seat on the Senate rostrum until December 22, three weeks after the session had begun.

Five thousand copies of the *Exposition* were printed and distributed through the state and nation. Although the document had no official standing save the endorsement of the committee that reported it, Thomas Cooper included it in the laws of the state for that session.[6] Calhoun's authorship was not avowed, but neither was it denied. The stamp of his mind was upon it, and it had not been long in circulation before it was generally understood to be his work. He had given the committee permission to use his name if it was thought desirable, but his position as Vice President made it seem better that he remain in the background.[7] He had Jefferson's precedent to follow, for the great Virginian had been Vice President at the time the Kentucky Resolutions came from his hand, but had not until much later avowed the authorship.

There was absolutely no question of concealment for political purposes. Calhoun's views were widely known and freely acknowledged—so much so that the fire of the administration press was directed almost exclusively at him during the final weeks of the campaign. If his prospects were thereby destroyed, as some of his friends thought, he was willing to accept the situation. He had deliberately and after mature reflection chosen the course he meant to pursue, and he was ready to abide the consequences.

3

The *South Carolina Exposition and Protest* made Calhoun the acknowledged head of the Southern State Rights party—an honor he would have indignantly rejected only half a dozen years before. But it is far more than a mere State Rights document, and it is distinctly not the public avowal of a change of view. It is as clear and penetrating an analysis of the problem of government as had been produced by any American pen up to that date, not excepting the *Federalist* or the treatises of John Taylor of Caroline. It is a sincere, patriotic and fearless attempt to solve a problem that the constituted rulers of the nation still refused to face, though it threatened the very existence of that nation.

Calhoun's point of departure was the tariff of 1828; but to a mind that habitually dealt in universals the tariff was only a special case, just as the embargo which had brought New England to the verge of secession had been a special case. He had opposed the restrictive system in 1812 because it was class legislation, unequal in its operation and condemned by public opinion in a substantial area. He now opposed the tariff for the same reason; and to make his position clear, he outlined the whole theory of government on which it rested.

It was obvious that as long as the national legislature possessed the power to make or mar private fortunes by subsidy or tax, it would be subject to pressure from selfish interests. The tariff represented an instance of successful pressure and nothing more. It is no solution to fall back upon the ballot box, for the omnipotence of the legislature only precipitates a scramble to control it, and the franchise is extended until those without property are in the majority. When that happens, property changes hands. It was to prevent this kind of class legislation that the Constitution was drawn up, but some means had to be found to keep the instrument from being violated. The search for such a means led Calhoun to the State Rights theory, which he embellished and refined.

The *Exposition* begins with a statement of the case against the constitutionality of the tariff. The general Government is one of specific powers, and the promotion of industry is not among them. A proposal to include it was even rejected in the Convention. Congress may impose duties on imports for revenue purposes, and a revenue bill may legitimately be arranged so as to afford incidental protection to industry; but the system set up by the tariff of 1828 was avowedly for protection and nothing else, though by its title a revenue act and so not subject to review by the courts. Unlike other advocates of State Rights, Calhoun always conceded the power of judicial review.[8]

The economic argument which follows is largely a restatement of the free trade position as it had been upheld for the past decade; but even in restating familiar theses, he projects his analysis farther into the future than others were able or willing to do. The essence of the argument is that while the domestic manufacturers were seeking a monopoly of the home market by eliminating foreign competition, the staple states were competing in the world market, and others stood ready to take their place whenever the cost of production rose above the competitive level. The tariff added forty-five percent to the cost of tools and supplies and proportionately increased the cost of production, with corresponding losses in the world market. The contention of the protectionists that prices would not be raised was mere duplicity, for the avowed purpose of the tariff was to equalize a high with a low cost of production, which could be done only by raising prices. Continuance of the system must throw the South exclusively upon the home market, which could not consume a quarter of her products.

Instead of supplying the world, the *Exposition* continues, "we would be compelled to abandon the cultivation of three fourths of what we now raise, and receive for the residue, whatever the manufacturers, who would then have their policy consummated by the entire possession of our market, might choose to give. Forced to abandon our ancient and favorite pursuit, to which our soil, climate, habits, and peculiar labor are adapted, at an immense sacrifice of property, we would be compelled, without capital, experience, or skill, and with a population untried in such pursuits, to attempt to become the rivals instead of the customers of the manufacturing States. The result is not doubtful. If they, by superior capital and skill, should keep down successful competition on our part, we would be doomed to toil at our unprofitable agriculture,—selling at the prices which a single and very limited market might give. But, on the contrary, if our necessity should triumph over their capital and skill,—if, instead of raw cotton, we should ship to the manufacturing States cotton yarn and cotton goods, the thoughtful must see that it would inevitably bring about a state of things which could not long continue. Those who now make war on our gains, would then make it on our labor. . . ."

To the argument that overproduction was the real cause of Southern distress, Calhoun retorts that in that case the manufacturers who seek higher prices for their products should limit their own supply instead of seeking a bounty from the public treasury. Then, in more serious vein, "We have no monopoly in the supply of our products; one half of the globe may produce them. Should we reduce our production, others stand ready, by increasing theirs, to take our place; and, instead of raising prices, we would only diminish our share of the supply." He goes on to argue that the West also loses by the system, in so far as it is agricultural, and that lavish expenditures for internal improvements cannot compensate for loss of markets. Indeed, in the end the manufacturing states themselves must also lose by the policy they now so strenuously champion.

"The system has not been sufficiently long in operation with us, to display its real character in reference to the point now under discussion. To understand its ultimate tendency, in distributing the wealth of society among the several classes, we must turn our eyes to Europe, where it has been in action for centuries,—and operated as one among the efficient causes of that great inequality of property which prevails in most European countries. No system can be more efficient to rear up a moneyed aristocracy. Its tendency is, to make the poor poorer, and the rich richer. Heretofore, in our country, this tendency has displayed itself principally in its effects, as regards the different sections,—but the time will come when it will produce the same results between the several classes in the manufacturing States. After we are exhausted, the contest will be between the capitalists and operatives; for into these two classes it must, ultimately, divide society. The issue of the struggle here must be the same as it has been in Europe. Under the operation of the system, wages must sink more rapidly than the prices of the necessaries of life, till the operatives will be reduced to the lowest point,—when the portion of the products of their labor left to them, will be barely sufficient to preserve existence. . . ."

Karl Marx was ten years old when that paragraph was written, and the theory of the class struggle was far in the future. So, too, were the consequences of the subsidized industrial system in America as Calhoun envisaged them; but the student of the decades following the Civil War will appreciate the accuracy of the analysis, even though the members of the committee for which the report was prepared did not. The paragraph does not appear in the version printed by the legislature.

4

From the economic argument Calhoun turned to the political, to give us the first complete sketch of the theory later enlarged in his posthumous *Disquisition on Government*. He starts with the simple proposition "that irresponsible power is inconsistent with liberty, and must corrupt those who exercise it." For this reason

Representatives are held responsible to their constituents through periodical elections; but this alone cannot prevent the abuse of power. If the interests of different groups of people differ, as they must in any substantial community, the laws are bound to affect them in different ways. One group may gain by exploiting another and for that purpose sanction an abuse of power by its Representatives. Opposing interests would thus become hostile parties, "the stronger of which, if the Government provided no efficient check, would exercise unlimited and unrestrained power over the weaker. The relation of equality between the parts of the community, established by the Constitution, would be destroyed, and in its place there would be substituted the relation of sovereign and subject, between the stronger and weaker interests, in its most odious and oppressive form."

That this situation had actually come about in the United States by 1828 he did not doubt. The tariff represented a gross abuse of power by the majority with the consent of their constituents; and if the sovereignty rested with the majority, it was legitimate. What was to be done? Calhoun remained in 1828 what he had been in 1812—at heart a metaphysician rather than a practitioner of politics; and it was perhaps inevitable that he should seek a metaphysical solution. It was equally inevitable that the solution must be ineffective in practice because it rested upon principles which the common man could not grasp.

The rallying cry of the American Revolution had been the Rights of Man. They were natural, universal rights, inherent in the world order, serving as the basis and model for all law. They could be discovered by reason, and were everywhere at work in the world. The fight against the tariff had much in common with the Revolutionary struggle, and there were those who took part in it who repeated the old appeal to natural rights; but the appeal was no longer valid, and Calhoun rejected it. In many parts of the world a new concept had grown up, which most lawyers, consciously or otherwise, accepted—the notion of law as posited or made. Law, in the nineteenth-century jargon, was simply the will of the sovereign. If the sovereignty rested with the majority, the tariff was law and to be obeyed as such. To reject the tariff and still be logically correct, only two courses were open. One could admit the sovereign character of the act but forcibly oppose it on ethical grounds, which would simply be rebellion; or one could deny that the sovereignty, defined as the power to make binding law, belonged to the majority. It was the latter course that Calhoun, after careful study of the Constitution, chose as best; but to people of more prosaic minds the two were not distinguishable. To most of those who opposed the tariff, nullification (or state interposition as Calhoun preferred to call it) was just another name for resistance or rebellion; and to those who favored the protective system, it was very close to treason.

But to return to the *Exposition*. What Calhoun did was to locate the seat of sovereignty in the states rather than in the national government. The Constitution was a compact between the several states in their corporate character, each of which was at the time of the formation of the Union sovereign in its own right. That is to say, it owed no allegiance to any superior power. The exercise of certain sovereign powers is delegated to the general Government under the Constitution, but not the sovereignty itself. The government of the Union and those of the states exist side by side; but the former may exercise only delegated powers, while the original power remains with the latter, modified only to the extent that the relationship can be altered by three-fourths of the states through the amending process. Out of this relationship comes the remedy for the tariff, for the making of law is a sovereign function which, though delegated, remains under the control of the sovereign. The states, clearly, may interpose to arrest the operation of a law deemed unconstitutional. There was precedent in the Virginia and Kentucky Resolutions, and clear justification of the theory in Madison's Report to the Virginia Legislature on the Alien and Sedition Acts. The *Federalist* itself indicated the path, and the debates in the Constitutional Convention bore out the intended roles of state and general Governments.

All this was pretty technical, but it had a core of solid sense. In the forty years which had passed since the Constitution was written, changes of incalculable magnitude had taken place, not alone in America but in the world. The population of the United States had increased threefold and its area had doubled. Wealth had multiplied and under the combined stimulus of science and Yankee ingenuity much of it had been invested in manufacturing enterprises. These manufacturing interests developed a theory of government in keeping with their special needs, just as the commercial world of Federalism had done. Under a high tariff they prospered, and naturally they wanted a national government strong enough to impose it. As they became prosperous they achieved political power, which may generally be found on the side of property; and they used it to establish the tariff policy and to modify the law of corporations so as to permit industrial combinations of unlimited size and means. Their theory of government was derived from Alexander Hamilton's Federalism and became the Whig doctrine of Webster.

Since the South with its inexhaustible raw materials and its imperial trade suffered under the tariffs which meant prosperity to industry, Southern statesmen opposed the tariff; and their method was almost necessarily to oppose the theory of government on which the tariff rested—the Federalist-Whig theory of a strong central power able to foster money-making and in the control of those who made the money. The states with their own traditions and separate governments were simply the instruments most readily available for the building of an opposition theory which was the more plausible because the historical analysis which supported it was undoubtedly correct. Despite the denials of the constitutional lawyers of today, the record is clear that the men who wrote the Constitution and those who adopted it believed it to be in fact a compact among the states, which delegated to the general government the exercise but not the substance of their sovereignty. The federal structure of the Government formed a convenient basis on which to erect an opposing dogma; but if the federal structure had not existed, the Whig theory would still have been opposed, perhaps along class rather than sectional lines.

In developing and advocating the State Rights doctrine in 1828, Calhoun was not turning from nationalism to a narrow sectional point of view, and he was not from motives of personal ambition seeking to destroy the Union. He was, in a very genuine sense, trying to save the Union in the only way in which it could be saved— by preserving the loyalty of its citizens. It is not in human nature for the victims of legalized plunder to be loyal to the government that has brought about their ruin, and in the unguarded talk of his fellow citizens Calhoun saw that loyalty slipping away. A dozen years earlier he had proclaimed himself "under the most imperious obligation to counteract every tendency to disunion";[9] but the wisdom, justice and moderation of Congress on which he had then relied had failed. A single selfish interest had gained control of the machinery of government and was indirectly but none the less thoroughly looting a third of the nation.

5

The democratic process had run its full cycle before his eyes, and he saw the problem at last as Randolph and John Taylor had seen it long ago. He realized now that men were moved primarily by love of gain, and that it was asking more than human nature could give to ask for personal disinterestedness in the majority of any body of men on earth. Men did not come to Congress to weigh in intellectual detachment the best interests of the human race. They came as advocates for the special desires of those who elected them, and so it must be eternally as long as man's consciousness centered in himself, which is to say as long as he retained his will to live.

The art of governing as he had observed it over twenty years was the art of keeping in precarious balance powerful and antagonistic interests, by means of bribes and threats, rewards and punishments. The bribes were pensions, roads, canals, cheap lands, tariffs and other forms of class legislation. The rewards were offices and contracts. And the result, whenever the balance should be lost, was tyranny; for as long as a minority remained with property or labor to exploit, a majority could be bought on the promise of sharing in the spoils. With the coming of the industrial revolution the balance was destroyed. The geographical basis of representation gave preponderant strength to the manufacturing states, and they used their power as power is always used—for their own gain.

So Calhoun fell back upon the sovereignty of the states, as the only hope of preserving the Union. His illusions were gone, and in the full maturity of his powers he set forth in the *Exposition* the creed he was to follow for the rest of his days. His stand was taken, his mind made up, his purpose clear. He rejected the major premise of democracy because he saw that a majority may be the worst of tyrants. He turned his back upon an economic nationalism that was in fact national isolation for the personal profit of a few industrialists, because he foresaw the human misery that such a course must bring. Thenceforward he stood out as the great defender of federal as opposed to centralized government, of cooperation as against coercion; and in the process he made himself the supreme champion of minority rights and interests everywhere.

APPENDIX

APPENDIX A

The *Life of John C. Calhoun, presenting a condensed history of political events from 1811 to 1843* was published anonymously as a campaign biography in 1843 and was generally attributed to Robert M. T. Hunter. In 1908, however, Gaillard Hunt published in the *American Historical Review*, XIII, 311-312 a letter from Robert Barnwell Rhett to Calhoun's editor, Richard Crallé, dated October 25, 1854, in which the following statement is made: "There is one thing written by Mr. Calhoun that you ought not to publish as his—and that is—*'his life'*. He wished me to Father it—but I told him, that it was impossible for me directly or indirectly to allow anyone to understand that I was the author of a publication which I had not written. Hunter and I read it over together in my house in Georgetown. He inserted about a page and a half, and became the putative author; and it has done more to lift him to his present position than any thing else in his public life." From this statement Hunt concluded, reasonably enough, that the *Life* was in fact an autobiography, and it has since been so regarded.

Although the volume was certainly prepared with Calhoun's active assistance and has the value of an autobiography as a source book, I am unwilling to accept it as having come from his hand. His own first reference to it is in a letter to Hunter, September 30, 1842. "I have had several letters," he writes, "from [Joseph A. Scoville], in which he presses me, as he has you, on the subject of my life . . . but it appears to me to be much more important, that it should be well done, than speedily done. . . . I shall, however, with the materials I have get a friend next week to commence preparing such a biographical sketch as Mr. Scoville desires. . . ." C. H. Ambler, ed., *Correspondence of Robert M. T. Hunter,* 49. On October 25 Scoville, who was a New York journalist active in Calhoun's behalf, referred to it in a letter to Calhoun. "As soon as possible I would advise your sending me the proposed life etc. I have seen the publishers, and they will wait very willingly. I will select some one here to edit it." *Correspondence,* 856. In a letter to his daughter, February 6, 1843, Calhoun says that "Mr Hunter has rewritten most of [the biographical sketch]; so much so as fairly to be entitled to the authorship." *Correspondence,* 524. And in a letter to Hunter, February 1, 1844, he refers to "my life, prepared by yourself, and published by the Harpers." *Correspondence,* 562.

These statements do not of course altogether disprove the assertion of Rhett, but they do throw some doubt upon it. More important, however, and more conclusive is the resemblance between the *Life* and various other sketches of Calhoun which preceded it. The first of these appeared in the *Franklin Gazette* of Philadelphia during the spring and summer of 1822, and was believed by contemporaries to be the work of George M. Dallas. The pamphlet, *Measures not Men,* which appeared in 1823 and was fathered by General Joseph G. Swift, was little more than a reprint of the *Franklin Gazette* articles; and the sketch

401

in the *National Portrait Gallery of Distinguished Americans,* edited by J. B. Longacre and J. Herring in 1834, carries the story down to that date. The *Life* follows closely a pattern common to these earlier versions and is in fact only an expansion of them, with additions to cover the later years. We may therefore suppose that these various sketches, together with copies of the speeches liberally quoted in the *Life,* were the materials referred to in Calhoun's first letter to Hunter quoted above. They were whipped into shape, either by Calhoun himself or by the friend to whom he expected to assign the job, and the resulting manuscript was revised by Hunter after Rhett refused that responsibility, if indeed it was actually offered him.

Rhett's statement a dozen years after the event that Hunter did no more than add a page and a half must be weighed against Calhoun's contemporary remark that Hunter had rewritten most of the sketch; and even if we accept Rhett's view, it still does not follow that it was Calhoun rather than someone else who prepared the first draft. Rhett could have had no personal knowledge to that effect, since he was in Washington at the time while Calhoun remained in retirement at his South Carolina home. It must also be borne in mind that Rhett was given to exaggeration, that he had quarreled with Calhoun between the date of the *Life* and the date of his letter to Crallé, and that he was probably jealous of Hunter.

Taking all of the circumstances into consideration, the most that can be said is that the *Life* is an "official" biography, prepared under Calhoun's eye and perhaps in part by his hand; but it is not in any legitimate sense of the word an autobiography.

APPENDIX B

State and Sectional Analysis of Votes in the House of Representatives
on the Tariff of 1816 and on Internal Improvements in 1817

Section and State	Tariff of 1816			Internal Improvements		
	For	Against	Not voting*	For	Against	Not voting*
New England						
Connecticut	2	2	3	----	6	1
Massachusetts	7	4	9	4	16	----
New Hampshire	1	3	2	1	5	----
Rhode Island	2	----	----	----	2	----
Vermont	5	1	----	----	5	1
Total	17	10	14	5	34	2
South						
Georgia	3	3	----	5	1	----
Louisiana	----	1	----	----	1	----
North Carolina	----	11	2	6	6	1
South Caroina	4	3	2	6	3	----
Virginia	7	13	3	6	14	3
Total	14	31	7	23	25	4
West						
Indiana	—†	---†	---†	1	----	
Kentucky	6	1	3‡	4	5	1‡
Ohio	4	----	2	5	----	1
Tennessee	3	2	1	1	3	2
Total	13	3	6	11	8	4
Middle States (I)						
Delaware	----	----	2	----	2	----
Maryland	2	5	2	2	6	1
New Jersey	5	----	1	3	3	----
Total	7	5	5	5	11	1
Middle States (II)						
New York	20	2	5	25	2	----
Pennsylvania	17	3	3	17	4	2
Total	37	5	8	42	6	2
Grand Total	88	54	40	86	84	13

* Includes absences and vacancies.
† State not admitted to the Union until December 1816.
‡ Includes the Speaker, who favored both measures.

403

APPENDIX C

Tariff Votes and Representation 1816-1824

Section and State	Total Representation (1816)	Tariff Vote (1816) For	Tariff Vote (1816) Agai'st	Tariff Vote (1816) Not voting	Total Representation (1824)	Tariff Vote (1824) For	Tariff Vote (1824) Agai'st	Tariff Vote (1824) Not voting
New England	41	17	10	14	39	15	23	1
Connecticut	7	2	2	3	6	5	1	----
Maine	----	----	----	----	7	1	6	----
Massachusetts	20	7	4	9	13	1	11	1
New Hampshire	6	1	3	2	6	1	5	----
Rhode Island	2	2	----	----	2	2	----	----
Vermont	6	5	1	----	5	5	----	----
South	52	14	31	7	58	1	57	
Alabama	----	----	----	----	3	----	3	----
Georgia	6	3	3	----	7	----	7	----
Louisiana	1	----	1	----	3	----	3	----
Mississippi	----	----	----	----	1	----	1	----
North Carolina	13	----	11	2	13	----	13	----
South Carolina	9	4	3	2	9	----	9	----
Virginia	23	7	13	3	22	1	21	
West	22	13	3	6	40	31	7	2
Illinois	----	----	----	----	1	1	----	----
Indiana	----	----	----	----	3	2	----	1
Kentucky	10	6	1	3	12	11	----	1
Missouri	----	----	----	----	1	1	----	----
Ohio	6	4	----	2	14	14	----	----
Tennessee	6	3	2	1	9	2	7	
Middle States (I)	17	7	5	5	16	10	6	
Delaware	2	----	----	2	1	1	----	----
Maryland	9	2	5	2	9	3	6	----
New Jersey	6	5	----	1	6	6	----	----
Middle States (II)	50	37	5	8	60	50	9	1
New York	27	20	2	5	34	26	8	----
Pennsylvania	·23	17	3	3	26	24	1	1
Grand Total	182	88	54	40	213	107	102	4

NOTES

CHAPTER I

[1] Alexander S. Salley, Jr., *The Calhoun Family in America,* reprinted from *South Carolina Historical and Genealogical Magazine,* VII (1906), 81-98, 152-169; and "The Grandfather of John C. Calhoun," *ibid.,* XXXIX (1938), 50. Also photostats of Lancaster County records in Library of Congress. Although numerous other works have been consulted, Salley's account has been followed unless otherwise noted.

[2] Lyman Chalkley, comp., *Chronicles of the Scotch-Irish Settlement in Virginia,* I, 5 *et passim.*

[3] Calhoun to Charles H. Allen, Nov. 21, 1847, *Gulf States Historical Magazine,* I (1902), 439, is in error in stating that John Noble accompanied the Calhouns to South Carolina in 1756. He died in Virginia in 1752. Chalkley, III, 27.

[4] Calhoun to James Edward Calhoun, Sept. 15, 1846, *Correspondence of John C. Calhoun,* edited by J. Franklin Jameson, 707. (Cited hereafter as *Correspondence.*)

[5] Colonel W. Pinkney Starke, *Account of Calhoun's Early Life,* 66, is authority for Pat Calhoun's visit to Waxhaw. His account must be used with the greatest caution. For the early history of South Carolina the text follows David D. Wallace, *History of South Carolina;* and Robert L. Meriwether, *The Expansion of South Carolina, 1729-1765,* unless otherwise noted.

[6] The route is reconstructed from notes kept by William Calhoun on a business trip to the Reed Creek settlement six or seven years later. *Southern History Association Publications,* VIII, 180.

[7] John H. Logan, *History of the Upper Country of South Carolina,* I, 15-20.

[8] Salley, *Calhoun Family,* 4; Meriwether, 134-135. Where discrepancies exist, the latter work, being the most recent, has been followed.

[9] Calhoun to Allen, *loc. cit.,* 440. Accounts of the massacre with quotations from contemporary newspapers are in Salley, *Calhoun Family,* 5-6, and Wallace, II, 27.

[10] Salley, *Calhoun Family,* 9.

[11] George Howe, *History of the Presbyterian Church in South Carolina,* I, 331, 342.

[12] Janie Revill, comp., *Compilation of the Original Lists of Protestant Immigrants to South Carolina, 1763-1773,* 29-31, 34; Wallace, II, 44.

[13] *South Carolina Historical and Genealogical Magazine,* II (1901), 249. Also *ibid.,* XXXIV (1933), 55. (Cited hereafter as *SCHGM.*)

[14] John Drayton, *A View of South Carolina,* 196-197; Wallace, II, 57 ff.

[15] Starke, 66; William M. Clemens, ed., *North and South Carolina Marriage Records,* 53.

[16] William Moultrie, *Memoirs of the American Revolution,* I, 17, 44-45.

[17] *SCHGM,* II, 159-160; William A. Schaper, *Sectionalism and Represen-*

tation in South Carolina, 250. According to the census of 1790, Patrick Calhoun was the owner of thirty-one slaves, a number exceeded by only three others in all of Abbeville County, which then included most of the present counties of Greenwood and McCormick. *Heads of Families at the First Census of the United States: South Carolina,* 57.

[18] *Journal of the Convention of South Carolina Which Ratified the Constitution of the United States, May 23, 1788.*

[19] *Life of John C. Calhoun,* 4. (Cited hereafter as *Life.* For a discussion of its authorship, see Appendix A.)

[20] *Ibid.,* 5.

CHAPTER II

[1] *Life,* 6; Starke, 69.

[2] Howe, I, 654-655.

[3] The obituary in the Charleston City *Gazette* for March 7, 1796, gives the date of Patrick Calhoun's death as "the 15th ultimo," which would be February 15; but the date on his tombstone is that given in the text. "Inscriptions from a Calhoun Burying Ground," *SCHGM,* XXVII (1926), 185. Cf. *ibid.,* XXIII (1922), 155. The name "Carmel Academy" is given by George White, *Statistics of the State of Georgia,* 193 (Savannah, 1849).

[4] *Life,* 5.

[5] *Ibid.;* Starke, 74.

[6] *Life,* 6, is specific that the academy was reopened in Georgia in 1800, although the *Dictionary of American Biography,* "Moses Waddel," gives it as Vienna, S. C., in 1801.

[7] Augustus B. Longstreet, *Master William Mitten,* esp. chap. 8.

[8] Starke, 80, says that Martha Calhoun died shortly after John's matriculation at Yale. It seems evident, however, that it must have been before he left Carolina, since the date given on the tombstone is May 1802, and the term at Yale did not begin until October. See "Inscriptions from a Calhoun Burying Ground," *loc. cit.* Calhoun's statement in a letter to John Rodgers of March 28, 1825, that his mother died when he was sixteen years old is either a misreading or in error. *Virginia Magazine of History and Biography,* VIII (1901), 328.

[9] Franklin B. Dexter, "Student Life at Yale under the First President Dwight," *Proceedings of the American Antiquarian Society,* n. s., XXVII, 318-335. Also the same writer's *Sketch of the History of Yale University;* and *Biographical Sketches of the Graduates of Yale College with Annals of the College History,* V. Unless otherwise noted, the account of Yale during Calhoun's student days is based on these volumes.

[10] Anson Phelps Stokes, *Memorials of Eminent Yale Men,* II, 196-199.

[11] George P. Fisher, *Life of Benjamin Silliman,* I, 121. Cf. *Measures not Men,* 5; and Starke, 80.

[12] Albert J. Beveridge, *Life of John Marshall,* III, 235-236 n 2.

[13] Stokes, 199. The story is told in most of the early sketches of Calhoun's life and is vouched for by Silliman. Fisher, *Silliman,* II, 98.

[14] *Life,* 6.

[15] Calhoun to Alexander Noble, Oct. 15, 1804, *Correspondence*, 93-94. *Life*, 6.

[16] There is no foundation for the story that Colhoun was a compromise spelling adopted after correspondence with the head of the Highland Clan of Colquhoun, who urged the Senator to restore the name to its original form. The alleged correspondence took place toward the close of his life, but on the autograph roll of Drayton's militia company, dated 1775, the name appears in his hand as John Ewing Colhone. In the same year he witnessed a paper for his brother Patrick, spelling the name Colhoun. *SCHGM*, I (1900), 134-135; II (1901), 161. It was also spelled Colhoon, Cahoon and numerous similar ways, according to the fancy of the speller.

[17] Calhoun to Mrs. F. Calhoun, Aug. 29, 1804, *Correspondence*, 93.

[18] Starke, 83, has it that Calhoun read law that winter in the office of George Bowie in Abbeville, but an entry in the cash book of De Saussure and Ford seems conclusive:

"1804. Decr. 24th. Mr. John C. Calhoun Entered our office as a Student, fee 100 Guineas. . . ." *SCHGM*, XIII (1912), 177.

[19] Starke, 84. Jefferson was at Monticello from late March to the middle of April of the year in question, but not again until July, when Calhoun was already in Connecticut. The trip would hardly have been made as early as April, owing to the condition of the roads; but if it was, the party should have reached Newport long before July. The road, moreover, passed through Washington, where Calhoun might have called upon the President, had he wished to do so, without the fatigue and delay of a 200-mile detour.

[20] Calhoun to Mrs. F. Calhoun, Sept. 26, 1805, *Correspondence*, 98-99.

[21] Same to same, July 22, 1805, *ibid.*, 94-95.

[22] Samuel H. Fisher, *The Litchfield Law School*. Cf. Samuel H. Wandell and Meade Minnegerode, *Aaron Burr*, I, 34.

[23] John Cotton Smith to David Daggett, Jan. 1801, in *Proceedings of the American Antiquarian Society*, n. s., IV, 376; Reeve to Uriah Tracy, Feb. 1804, in Henry Adams, ed., *Documents Relating to New England Federalism*, 342-343. Also in Henry Cabot Lodge, *Life and Letters of George Cabot*, 442.

[24] New York *Patriot*, Nov. 1, 1823. Osborne was one of the editors of this paper, at that time a Calhoun organ.

[25] Calhoun to Andrew Pickens, Nov. 24, 1805, *Correspondence*, 99-100. Also to Mrs. F. Calhoun, Aug. 12, 1805, *ibid.*, 95-96.

[26] Calhoun to Mrs. F. Calhoun, Sept. 11, 1806, *ibid.*, 107. His diploma is dated July 29, 1806, Starke, 84.

[27] Calhoun to Mrs. F. Calhoun, Dec. 22, 1806, *Correspondence*, 107-108.

CHAPTER III

[1] *Charleston Year Book for 1880*, 258, 263.

[2] Wallace, II, 364.

[3] This is inference. James appears to have divided his time between Charleston and Abbeville until the middle of 1806, when he "thought it best to wind up his mercantile business in order to begin anew." Calhoun to Mrs. F. Calhoun, July 3, 1806, *Correspondence*, 106. We next hear of him as senior partner of Calhoun and Wilson in Augusta.

[4] Calhoun to Mrs. F. Calhoun, Oct. 1, 1807, *ibid.*, 109.

[5] *Life*, 7; Starke, 85-86.

[6] Starke, 85-86, and John Belton O'Neall, *Biographical Sketches of the Bench and Bar of South Carolina*, II, 284, both say that Calhoun was admitted to the bar in 1807. According to O'Neall, however, three years of legal study were required for admission, and Calhoun could not therefore have qualified before the end of December 1807. The authoritative *Life*, 7, says that the *Chesapeake* affair (June 22, 1807) occurred while he was a student at Abbeville; and he himself says that he was elected to the legislature the same year he was admitted to the bar; to Theodore Lyman, Sept. 8, 1828, *Correspondence*, 268. It was 1808 that he was elected to the legislature. The confusion of dates has probably arisen through careless reference to the winter of 1807-1808 by the first year only.

[7] Calhoun to Mrs. F. Calhoun, June 25, 1809, *Correspondence*, 111. See also Starke, 86.

[8] O'Neall, *Bench and Bar*, II, 284. Calhoun to Mrs. F. Calhoun, Apr. 6, 1809, *Correspondence*, 110.

[9] Benjamin F. Perry, "Judge Gantt," *Reminiscences of Public Men*.

[10] O'Neall, *Bench and Bar*, II, 390-392, 396-397.

[11] Edward Hooker, *Diary, 1805-1808*, 862-863.

[12] Louis M. Sears, *Jefferson and the Embargo*, 229-230; Charles Fraser, *Reminiscences of Charleston*, 14; John H. Wolfe, *Jeffersonian Democracy in South Carolina*, 222.

[13] *Life*, 7.

[14] Wolfe, 222.

[15] Sears, 237-238, 251-252; Victor S. Clark, *History of Manufactures in the United States*, I, 272.

[16] Wallace, II, 386. See also *Annals of Congress*, 10th Cong., 2d sess., 1483-1484.

[17] Wolfe, 230-231. De Saussure to Quincy, in Edmund Quincy, *Life of Josiah Quincy*, 189. (Cited hereafter as *Quincy*.)

[18] For political effect the measure was introduced by an upcountry member, Abram Blanding, and it was not generally known until after his death that Lowndes was its author. H. H. Ravenel, *Life and Times of William Lowndes*, 70-71.

[19] *Life*, 7. There is, of course, the usual amount of second guessing in this account, written long after the sequel had been revealed, but there is supporting evidence at least for the attitude of the caucus. See Wolfe, 231.

[20] *SCHGM*, II (1901), 163; O'Neall, *Bench and Bar*, II, 285.

[21] Calhoun to Mrs. F. Calhoun, June 25, 1809, *Correspondence*, 111. The material in the remainder of this section, unless otherwise noted, is drawn from Calhoun's letters to Mrs. F. Calhoun during 1809 and 1810, *ibid.*, 111-121.

[22] Longstreet, *Mitten*, chap. 15; Longstreet, "Review of Perry's Sketch of Calhoun," *XIX Century*, II (Jan. 1870), 625; John D. Wade, *Augustus Baldwin Longstreet*, 29, 33-34; Calhoun to Mrs. F. Calhoun, June 30 and July 27, 1810, *Correspondence*, 116, 118.

[23] Calhoun to Miss Floride Calhoun, Sept. 28, 1810, *Correspondence*, 121-122. This is the only letter from Calhoun to his fiancee known to exist, and but three of his letters to her after their marriage, all unimportant, are known.

These are among the Calhoun papers at Clemson College, hereafter cited as Calhoun Papers.

[24] Calhoun to Mrs. F. Calhoun, Sept. 7, 1810, *Correspondence*, 118-120.

[25] Based on casual references in letters, over a period of years. See especially Calhoun's letters to John Ewing Calhoun, 1818-1820, Calhoun Papers.

[26] See correspondence between Mrs. Calhoun and H. W. De Saussure in 1807, Calhoun Papers.

[27] *Life*, 8; Starke, 88. Also *Correspondence*, 117-122, *passim;* and E. S. Thomas, *Reminiscences*, II, 51.

[28] Starke, 89.

CHAPTER IV

[1] Calhoun to Mrs. F. B. Calhoun, Dec. 21, 1811, *Correspondence*, 124.

[2] Ravenel, *Lowndes*, 86.

[3] S. E. Morison, *Life and Letters of Harrison Gray Otis*, II, 32. Cf. Samuel Taggart, *Letters*, 1803-14, 361.

[4] Richard Crallé, editor of Calhoun's *Works*, believed the South Carolinian was the author of the report, and from both manner and matter he may well have been. Crallé includes it in the *Works*, V, 1-7, but his justification for so doing, as given in the introduction to the volume, rests largely on a confusion of events which took place in the second session of the Twefth Congress with those of the first session. Calhoun was by all odds the ablest phrasemaker among the concurring members of the committee, though the ideas were common to all the War Hawks.

[5] Lowndes to his wife, Dec. 7, 1811, Ravenel, *Lowndes*, 90.

[6] *Annals*, 12th, 1st, 422 ff.

[7] Richmond *Enquirer*, Dec. 24, 1811.

[8] Emory Upton, *Military Policy of the United States*, 92; *American State Papers, Naval Affairs*, I, 249-250. (Cited hereafter as *ASP*.)

[9] *Niles' Weekly Register*, II, 356 (cited hereafter as *Niles*); Henry Adams, *History of the United States*, VII, 14.

[10] Calhoun to Mrs. F. B. Calhoun, Dec. 21, 1811, *Correspondence*, 124; Ravenel, *Lowndes*, 100-101.

[11] Lowndes to his wife, Jan. 26, 1812, *ibid.*, 100.

[12] Calhoun to his wife, Mar. 1, 1812, *Correspondence*, 125.

[13] *Annals*, 12th, 1st, 803-824.

[14] H. Adams, *History*, VI, 205-207.

[15] Calhoun to Dr. James MacBride, Apr. 28, 1812, Ms. in Library of Congress. Also Macon to Nicholson, Apr. 30, 1812, *John P. Branch Historical Papers*, I, 139.

[16] *Annals*, 12th, 1st, 1399; *Works*, II, 20.

[17] Madison to Jefferson, May 25, 1812, Madison's *Writings*, Congressional Edition, II, 535. The often repeated story that Clay and other Congressional leaders called upon the President and forced from him the promise of a war message in return for the nomination has no basis in fact. Quincy seems to have given it currency, but long after the event. Federalists at the time merely thought that Madison was a compromise choice to insure party unity. See, for example, Taggart to Appleton, May 23 (misdated May 17), 1812, *op. cit.*,

401. If the President had traded a war message for the nomination on May 18, his hesitation on the twenty-fifth would have been an act of treachery. His determination was undoubtedly stiffened, however, by the assurances of Clay, Calhoun and others that a large majority in Congress favored war. The whole question is ably discussed by Theodore Clark Smith, "War Guilt in 1812," *Proceedings of the Massachusetts Historical Society*, LXIV (1932), 319-345, esp. 338 ff.

18 The actual authorship of the war report has generally been attributed to Monroe, following Gaillard Hunt, ed., "Joseph Gales on the War Manifesto of 1812," *American Historical Review*, XIII (Jan. 1908), 303-310; but there is a fair case for Calhoun. See C. M. Wiltse, "The Authorship of the War Report of 1812," *American Historical Review*, XLIX (Jan. 1944), 253-259.

19 The incident was described by Calhoun in the Senate in 1841. *Congressional Globe*, 27th Cong., 1st sess., 215. For the correspondence see *ASP, Foreign Relations*, III, 454-470.

20 Bernard Mayo, *Henry Clay*, I, 524.

21 Edward S. Delaplaine, *Francis Scott Key, His Life and Times*, 80; Susan Smythe Bennett, "The Cheves Family of South Carolina," *SCHGM*, XXXIV (1933), 132 ftn. 70. But cf. Perry, "Langdon Cheves," *Reminiscences*.

CHAPTER V

1 It has been estimated that from the close of the Revolution to the War of 1812 some 20,000 British seamen deserted to America, while 10,000 Americans or renegade British (they were often naturalized citizens of the United States) were impressed into the British service. Only ten percent of the impressed Americans were actually British deserters. See James F. Zimmerman, *Impressment of American Seamen*, Appendix.

2 William Sullivan, *Public Men of the Revolution*, 334-341. Cf. H. P. Prentiss, *Timothy Pickering as the Leader of New England Federalism, 1800-1815*, 80.

3 *Niles*, III, 22-23.

4 Charles Warren, *Jacobin and Junto*, 255; Story to Nathaniel Williams, Aug. 24, 1812, W. W. Story, *Life and Letters of Joseph Story*, I, 229; Morison, *Otis*, II, 61-62.

5 *Annals*, 12th, 1st, 1535-1542; *Works*, II, 20-31.

6 Charleston *Courier*, Sept. 8, 1812; Thomas P. Slider, *Memoirs of General William Butler*, 27; *Life*, 23.

7 *Life*, 12-13.

8 *Annals*, 12th, 2d, 315-321; *Works*, II, 31-42.

9 Ravenel, *Lowndes*, 116, 131.

10 Calhoun to Mrs. F. Calhoun, Nov. 23, 1812, *Correspondence*, 125.

11 Calhoun to Dr. James MacBride, Dec. 25, 1812, Ms. in Library of Congress.

12 *Annals*, 12th, 2d, 540-570; *Quincy*, 280-296.

13 Taggart, *Letters*, 418-419 (Jan. 17, 1813). Cf. *Quincy*, 296-300.

14 *Annals*, 12th, 2d, 813-821; *Works*, II, 43-56.

15 Ravenel, *Lowndes*, 142.

[16] Calhoun to Dr. James MacBride, Feb. 2, 1813, Ms. in Library of Congress.

[17] *Annals*, 12th, 2d, 1091-1099.

[18] Edward Channing, *History of the United States*, IV, 531-536; Morison, *Otis*, II, 52-53. Cf. *Niles*, II, 416.

CHAPTER VI

[1] Charles J. Ingersoll, *Historical Sketch of the Second War between the United States of America and Great Britain*, I, 123.

[2] *Ibid.*, II, 64.

[3] Monroe to Jefferson, June 28, 1813, S. M. Hamilton, ed., *Writings of James Monroe*, V, 271-273; Henry B. Learned, "Gerry and the Presidential Succession in 1813," *Am. Hist. Rev.*, XXII (Oct. 1916), 94-97.

[4] Ingersoll, I, 126; also 118 ff.

[5] *Life*, 13-14; Ingersoll, II, 50.

[6] New York *Evening Post*, Dec. 24, 1813.

[7] *National Intelligencer*, Dec. 28, 1813.

[8] *Charleston Courier*, Jan. 7, 1814.

[9] *Life*, 23.

[10] *ASP, For. Rel.*, III, 621-623; H. Adams, *History*, VII, 370-371; *Annals*, 13th, 2d, 855.

[11] *Annals*, 13th, 2d, 994-1002; *Works*, II, 56-69.

[12] Warren, *Jacobin and Junto*, 264.

[13] *Life*, 13.

[14] Calhoun to his wife, Feb. 7, 1814, *Correspondence*, 126.

[15] Taggart, *Letters*, 428 (Feb. 15, 1814).

[16] *Annals*, 13th, 2d, 1673-1694; *Works*, II, 69-103.

[17] *Niles*, IX, 35. The history of impressment is well summarized by Frank A. Updyke, *The Diplomacy of the War of 1812*, chap. 1.

[18] Morison, *Otis*, II, 66-67.

[19] H. Adams, *History*, VII, 389. Cf. Randolph to Quincy, Dec. 11, 1813: " 'Tis true we drive a little trade in tobacco, which pays for about the hundredth part of the dry goods which we import land-wise from the North. The balance is made up in specie. . . ." *Quincy*, 339-340.

[20] *Annals*, 13th, 2d, 1959.

[21] *Ibid.*, 1962-1965; *Works*, II, 103-110.

[22] *Annals*, 13th, 2d, 1966-1973.

[23] *Niles*, VI, 278.

CHAPTER VII

[1] *Niles*, VI, 313.

[2] Warren, *Jacobin and Junto*, 274-277.

[3] *Life*, 16; *Works*, III, 125.

[4] Wm. Wirt to his wife, Oct. 14, 1814, John P. Kennedy, *Memoirs of the Life of William Wirt*, I, 339.

[5] See *Works*, III, 125 ff, for his account of the affair. Also Ralph C. H. Catterall, *The Second Bank of the United States*, 10 ff.

[6] *Annals*, 13th, 3d, 622.

[7] *E. g.*, Taggart, *Letters*, 437-438 (Feb. 1, 1815).

[8] *Ibid.*, 434 (Nov. 22, 1814).

[9] This and other quotations from the New England press of the period not otherwise credited are from Frank M. Anderson, "A Forgotten Phase of the New England Opposition to the War of 1812," *Mississippi Valley Historical Association Proceedings*, VI, 176-188.

[10] J. S. Martell, ed., "A Side Light on Federalist Strategy during the War of 1812," *Am. Hist. Rev.*, XLIII (1938), 553-566.

[11] *Annals*, 13th, 3d, 482-491.

[12] *National Intelligencer*, Dec. 31; Ingersoll, II, 259.

[13] The incident has been overdramatized by Webster's biographers. George T. Curtis, *Life of Daniel Webster*, I, 143, says Calhoun burst into tears on receiving Webster's pledge of support; and Claude M. Fuess, *Daniel Webster*, I, 183, says Calhoun's action was taken because he "felt keenly the humiliation of the administration." The episode was not dramatic enough, however, to attract the notice of Ingersoll, although matters of lesser moment than the fiery and dominating Calhoun in tears did not escape the historically minded member from Philadelphia; and the South Carolinian could hardly have felt keenly a defeat he had helped bring about by voting against the bill.

[14] Warren, *Jacobin and Junto*, 280.

[15] Sullivan, *Public Men*, 363-364; Morison, *Otis*, II, 154-155.

[16] Calhoun, *Works*, III, 127-128; Taggart, *Letters*, 437-438 (Feb. 10, 1815).

[17] Calhoun to Mrs. F. Calhoun, Apr. 9, 1815, *ibid.*, 128-129.

CHAPTER VIII

[1] Calhoun to his wife, Nov. 29, 1815, *Correspondence*, 129.

[2] *Annals*, 14th, 1st, 430-431.

[3] *Ibid.*, 514-522.

[4] *Ibid.*, 829-840; *Works*, II, 135-153.

[5] *Annals*, 14th, 1st, 494-515; *ASP, Finance*, III, 57-61; Catterall, 17.

[6] *Annals*, 14th, 1st, 1060-1066; *Works*, II, 153-162.

[7] *Annals*, 14th, 1st, 1437, 1440-1451.

[8] Margaret Bayard Smith, *The First Forty Years of Washington Society*, 129. (Cited hereafter as Mrs. Smith.) It can never, of course, be positively proved that the chief killed by Johnson in a hand-to-hand encounter during the Battle of the Thames was indeed Tecumseh, but no contemporary doubted it. See, for example, the reference of Wright of Maryland in the House, March 8, 1816, *Annals*, 14th, 1st, 1181. Also *Niles*, XII, 80; and Leland W. Meyer, *The Life and Times of Colonel Richard M. Johnson of Kentucky*, 129-130, 132-133.

[9] *Annals*, 14th, 1st, 1127-1134.

[10] *Ibid.*, 1158.

[11] *Ibid.*, 1183-1184.

CHAPTER IX

[1] Jabez D. Hammond, who was one of the New York Representatives at the time, thinks Martin Van Buren, then a state senator, got the legislature to endorse Tompkins in the hope of taking enough New York votes away from Crawford to secure Monroe's nomination. *History of Political Parties in New York*, I, 409 ff. Henry Adams, *History*, IX, 123, attributes to Hammond a belief that the maneuver succeeded, and that "Martin Van Buren and Peter B. Porter, for reasons of their own, prevented New York from declaring for Crawford when such a declaration would have decided the result." There is little basis in Hammond for such a conclusion, and none at all for Stanwood's deduction from it that Van Buren and Porter "prevented the delegation from going to Crawford." Edward Stanwood, *History of the Presidency*, I, 109. In the actual voting, as Hammond is careful to make clear, the delegation did go for Crawford, with only three dissenting votes.

[2] J. E. D. Shipp, *Giant Days; or, the Life and Times of William H. Crawford*, 28-30; *Life*, 28.

[3] *National Intelligencer*, Mar. 14, 1816. The account of the proceedings is in the same paper for March 18 and 19.

[4] Crawford to Gallatin, May 10, 1816, Henry Adams, ed., *The Writings of Albert Gallatin*, I, 702.

[5] Cf. T. D. Jervey, *Robert Y. Hayne*, 66-67.

[6] Petitions and reports of Congressional committees are in *ASP, Finance*, vols. I-III.

[7] *ASP, Finance*, III, 85-99; *Annals*, 14th, 1st, 960-967.

[8] *Annals*, 14th, 1st, 1271-1272.

[9] *Ibid.*, 1328-1329.

[10] Edward Stanwood, *American Tariff Controversies of the Nineteenth Century*, I, 140-141.

[11] *Works*, II, 208-209. Crallé, in his preliminary note to the speech in *Works*, II, 163, seems hopelessly confused. He says the speech was made on April 6 instead of the fourth; that the preceding motion to strike out the minimum principle had been made by Tucker and not by Randolph; that Calhoun was at the time "busily engaged in framing his celebrated Report"; and that it was the chairman of the Committee on Manufactures who had called him to the floor. It is true that the *Annals of Congress* covering this session were not published until 1854, while volume II of Crallé's edition of Calhoun's *Works* appeared in 1853; but that can hardly excuse the error on the last point, which is contradicted by the evidence of one of the speeches in the very volume in question, even though it may excuse the first two. What "celebrated Report" may be referred to is not clear. Calhoun's only important report of the session was the bank report, presented three months before. He did introduce a bill on April 6 providing for the early resumption of specie payments, but it was not accompanied by a report. See also *Life*, 20.

[12] *Annals*, 14th, 1st, 1329-1336; *Works*, II, 163-173.

[13] *Niles*, XI, 284.

[14] See page 91 above.

[15] See Appendix B for tabular analysis of the voting in the House on the tariff of 1816.

[16] Gallatin to Madison, June 7, 1816, in Henry Adams, *Life of Albert Gallatin*, 561-562. Also *Niles*, XI, 31; and Ravenel, *Lowndes*, 157.

[17] Calhoun to Dallas, June 15, 1816, Ms. copy in Library of Congress; *Life*, 23; Charleston *Courier*, Sept. 16, 1816.

CHAPTER X

[1] H. Adams, *History*, IX, 144-145; *Annals*, 14th, 2d, 311-320.

[2] Lyon G. Tyler, *Letters and Times of the Tylers*, I, 290. John Tyler was the author of the simile.

[3] It will be recalled that Senators were at that time chosen by the state legislatures, and the President by electors, themselves usually at one remove from popular selection.

[4] *Annals*, 14th, 2d, 574-582; *Works*, II, 173-185.

[5] *Annals*, 14th, 2d, 621; *Life*, 23-24.

[6] Gallatin's report, dated April 12, 1818, outlined a ten-year program, to cost $2,000,000 a year and to be carried out by the Federal Government. Improvements were listed under four heads: (1) Canals paralleling the Atlantic coast to provide continuous inland navigation from Cape Cod to Cape Fear; and a great through turnpike from Maine to Georgia; (2) Improved navigation on four pairs of rivers, each pair consisting of one stream draining to the Atlantic and one flowing into the Mississippi River system. Each pair was to be joined by an east-west road. The pairs of streams selected were the Susquehanna and the Allegheny, the Potomac and the Monongahela, the James and the Kanawha, and the Santee and the Tennessee; (3) Canals to link the Hudson with Lake Champlain, and with Lake Ontario; and a canal around Niagara Falls; (4) Local improvements.

[7] Dec. 15, 1815, *Annals*, 14th, 1st, 16-17.

[8] *Annals*, 14th, 2d, 296-297, 361.

[9] *Ibid.*, 851-858; *Works*, II, 186-196.

[10] See, for example, James C. Jewett to H. A. S. Dearborn, Feb. 5, 1817, *William and Mary Quarterly*, XVII (1909), 143-144. Also Ingersoll, II, 258; and George Watterston, *Letters from Washington*, 50-56.

[11] See Appendix B for a tabulation of the voting.

[12] *Life*, 21. The date of the visit is fixed by the fact that it occurred while the internal improvement bill was still in Madison's possession. The President could not have received the bill before Saturday, March 1, when the Senate amendments were adopted by the House, and the bill and veto message came in on the third. The call could not have been made Saturday evening because the House remained in session and Calhoun was present. *Annals*, 14th, 2d, 1053-1055.

[13] H. Adams, *History*, IX, 131-132.

[14] Crawford to Gallatin, Mar. 12, 1817, Gallatin's *Writings*, II, 23-26.

[15] Jackson to Monroe, Oct. 23, Nov. 12, 1816, Jan. 6, 1817, J. S. Bassett, ed., *Correspondence of Andrew Jackson*, II, 261, 264, 272.

[16] Monroe to Jackson, Mar. 1, 1817, Monroe's *Writings*, VI, 4-5.

[17] Armistead Mason to John Thompson Mason, Jan. 14, 1817, and Feb. 18,

1817, *William and Mary Quarterly*, XXIII (1915), 234, 239. Also C. F. Adams, ed., *Memoirs of John Quincy Adams*, IV, 73. (Cited hereafter as Adams, *Diary*.)

[18] Calhoun to Monroe, Dec. 9, 1827, recalls the circumstances; *Correspondence*, 252. William M. Meigs, *Life of John Caldwell Calhoun*, I, 226 and ftn. 1, thinks the General Williams referred to is Colonel John Williams of Tennessee, but it is obvious from the context that the former South Carolina Representative and Governor is meant.

[19] Meigs, I, 226-227; Arthur Styron, *The Cast-iron Man; John C. Calhoun and American Democracy*, 97.

[20] Calhoun recalls the statement in a letter to Monroe, Dec. 9, 1827, *Correspondence*, 251-253.

[21] Rufus King to Jeremiah Mason, July 4, 1817, G. S. Hillard, *Memoir and Correspondence of Jeremiah Mason*, 162-163. (Cited hereafter as *Mason*.)

[22] J. Mason to C. Gore, Dec. 30, 1816, *Mason*, 148.

[23] Adams, *Diary*, IV, 15; Calhoun to Monroe, Nov. 1, 1817, *Correspondence*, 131.

[24] *Life*, 24-25.

CHAPTER XI

[1] Calhoun to Mrs. F. Calhoun, Nov. 15, 1817, *Correspondence*, 131; *Charleston Courier*, Dec. 13, 1817.

[2] Crawford to Gallatin, Apr. 23, 1817, Gallatin's *Writings*, II, 36.

[3] Adams, *Diary*, V, 497-498.

[4] Watterston, *Letters from Washington*, 50-56.

[5] Mills to his wife, Feb. 20, 1818, Elijah Mills, *Letters*, 24.

[6] Crawford to Gallatin, Mar. 12, 1817, Gallatin's *Writings*, II, 28; Monroe to Madison, Nov. 24, 1817, Monroe's *Writings*, VI, 33.

[7] *Annals*, 15th, 1st, 451-459; Glyndon G. Van Deusen, *Life of Henry Clay*, 119-121.

[8] Joseph Story to Ezekiel Bacon, Mar. 12, 1818, *Story*, I, 311; Christopher Gore to Jeremiah Mason, Mar. 20, 1818, *Mason*, 197; Rufus King to Mason, *ibid.*, 192-193.

[9] Monroe to Madison, Monroe's *Writings*, VI, 49.

[10] Mrs. Smith, 141-142; Daggett to Mason, Jan. 5 and Feb. 10, 1818, *Mason*, 181, 191; Rufus King to Mason, Mar. 1818, *ibid.*, 192; Elijah Mills to his wife, Jan. 6, 1821, Mills, *Letters*, 29.

[11] *ASP, Military Affairs*, II, 450. See also Edgar B. Wesley, *Guarding the Frontier*, 76-77.

[12] Jackson's *Correspondence*, II, 273-275, 277-282. Early in 1816 Jackson had himself similarly trespassed upon General Brown's authority by issuing orders to an officer attached to the Northern Division, but in his own case, of course, he was able to find ample justification for irregular procedure. See Wesley, 106-108.

[13] Jackson's *Correspondence*, II, 291-292.

[14] Monroe to Jackson, Aug. 4, 1817, *ibid.*, 319; also same to same, Oct. 5, 1817, *ibid.*, 329-332.

[15] *Ibid.*, 320-321.

16 *Ibid.*, 343; Upton, *Military Policy*, 145-147. *Niles*, XIII, 342, gives the order as follows:

Department of War, Dec. 29, 1817

ORDERS.—As a general rule, all orders will issue, in the first instance, to the commanders of division.

In cases where the nature of the duty to be performed, and the public interest may require it, orders will be issued directly to officers commanding department, post, or detachment, and to any officer attached to a division; but in such cases a copy of the orders shall be transmitted to the general of the division, for information.

17 *Life*, 30; Calhoun to Gen. Jacob Brown, Dec. 17, 1817, *Military Book No. 9*, 428-429, National Archives; *House Report* 79, 19th Cong., 2d sess.; *Reports to Congress, War Office*, I, 418-424, National Archives.

18 *Annals*, 15th, 1st, 210; *Life*, 25; *Cong. Globe*, 25th, 2d, app., 181; *ibid.*, 30th, 1st, app., 697. Also Calhoun to Williams, Feb. 5, 1818, *Correspondence*, 133-134; and Feb. 16, Mar. —, and Apr. 11, 1818, *Reports to Congress, War Office*, I, 439-440, 446-447, 448. For Van Deventer's share in it, see Virgil Maxcy to Calhoun, Mar. 2, 1827, *Correspondence*, 791-792.

19 *Annals*, 16th, 1st, 854. Cf. Calhoun to S. Smith, *Military Book No. 10*, 150; and Calhoun to John Fisher, May 26, 1818, *Confidential Letters, War Office*, I, 94, National Archives.

20 Wirt to Judge Carr, Jan. 21, 1818, John P. Kennedy, *Memoirs of the Life of William Wirt*, II, 68. Cf. Elijah Mills to his wife, winter, 1817-1818, *Mills, Letters*, 23.

21 Calhoun to John Ewing Calhoun, Dec. 26, 1817, *Correspondence*, 132.

22 *National Intelligencer*, May 29, 1818. The account of the inspection trip is based on reports in the Baltimore *American*, June 9; the Richmond *Enquirer*, June 9 and 12; and the Charleston *Courier*, June 22. Cf. Joseph G. Swift, *Memoirs*, 174-176.

23 *Southern Patriot*, June 29, July 3; Calhoun to Charles Tait, July 20, 1818, *Gulf States Hist. Mag.*, I (1902), 93. (Cited hereafter as *Tait Correspondence*.)

CHAPTER XII

1 *ASP, Mil. Aff.*, I, 689.

2 Adams, *Diary*, IV, 31; Calhoun to Jackson, Dec. 26, 1817, *ASP, Mil. Aff.*, I, 690; Monroe to Jackson, July 19, 1818, Monroe's *Writings*, VI, 55.

3 Jackson to Monroe, Jan. 6, 1818, Jackson's *Correspondence*, II, 345-346.

4 Jackson to Calhoun, Jan. 12, 1818, *ibid.*, 347.

5 For discussion from Jackson's side see J. S. Bassett, *Life of Andrew Jackson*, 245-249; and Marquis James, *Andrew Jackson, The Border Captain*, 408-411. The most recent and most detailed sifting of the evidence is by Richard R. Stenberg, "Jackson's Rhea Letter Hoax," *Journal of Southern History*, II, 480-496. Jackson's letter to Monroe was dated January 6 and Rhea's note was dated the twelfth, the interval being less than half of the customary mail time between Nashville and Washington.

6 *ASP, Mil. Aff.*, I, 745, 746.

7 Adams, *Diary*, IV, 36.

[8] *Ibid.*, 52-53.

[9] Jackson to Calhoun, Apr. 8 and 20, May 5, 1818, *ASP, Mil. Aff.*, I, 699-702 ff. Correspondence and papers dealing with the whole campaign are in *ibid.*, 689 ff. Also in *H. Doc.* 14, 15th Cong., 2d session.; and *Senate Document* 73, 16th Cong., 1st sess. Unless otherwise noted, the State Papers have been followed.

[10] Adams, *Diary*, IV, 87, 92; Calhoun to W. W. Bibb, May 13, 1818, *Niles*, XV, 304.

[11] Adams, *Diary*, IV, 101-102.

[12] Jackson to Monroe, Mar. 18, 1817, Jackson's *Correspondence*, II, 282-283. Major Lewis, Jackson's political mentor, expressed the opinion years afterward that knowledge of this letter had influenced Adams' opinion in the Seminole affair. It is not necessary to assume this, however, to understand his course. See William B. Lewis to Lewis Cass, 1844 or 1845, J. S. Bassett, ed., "Major Lewis on the Nomination of Andrew Jackson," *Proceedings of the American Antiquarian Society*, n. s., XXXIII, 27.

[13] Calhoun to Charles Tait, July 20 and Sept. 5, 1818, *Tait Correspondence*, 93-95. Cf. Calhoun to Jackson, Sept. 8, 1818, Jackson's *Correspondence*, II, 393.

[14] John Williams to Van Buren, Mar. 22, 1831, Van Buren Papers, Library of Congress. Jackson admits as much in his "Exposition against Calhoun" in 1831, Jackson's *Correspondence*, IV, 233, though he chose at the time to disregard it. See Jackson to Lewis, Jan. 30, 1819, *New York Public Library Bulletin*, IV, 160-161. Additional evidence is in Stenberg, *op. cit.*

[15] Calhoun to Jackson, Aug. 10, 1819. "I am persuaded . . . that it is only necessary to call your attention to the irregularities which I have stated to relieve me from the necessity of determining whether I shall permit the orders of the Government to be habitually neglected, or resort to the proper means of enforcing them. Should the alternative be presented I will not hesitate to do my duty." *Correspondence*, 160-162. See also Calhoun to Jackson, Dec. 22, 1818, *Confidential Letters, War Office*, I, 98-101.

[16] Adams, *Diary*, IV, 119.

CHAPTER XIII

[1] Calhoun to Swift, Apr. 7, 1818, *Military Book No. 10*, 51-53; *ASP, Mil. Aff.*, I, 810-813; II, 49-50; *House Report* 93, 16th Cong., 1st sess.

[2] *Works*, V, 40-54; *ASP, Miscellaneous*, II, 533-537.

[3] Calhoun to Hon. A. Smyth, Dec. 29, 1819, *Works*, V, 62-68, and *ASP, Mil. Aff.*, II, 33-34; *Correspondence*, 134-160, *passim*. Also Wesley, *Guarding the Frontier*, chapter 8.

[4] Calhoun to Gen. Thomas A. Smith, Mar. 16, 1818, *Correspondence*, 134-136; Smith to Calhoun, May 16, 1818, Secretary of War, Document File, National Archives.

[5] R. M. Johnson to Calhoun, Mar. 11, 1818; Smith to James Johnson, May 15; R. M. Johnson to Calhoun, May 29; James Johnson to Calhoun, May 29, 1818. Secretary of War, Document File.

[6] K. W. Porter, *John Jacob Astor*, II, 710 ff.; G. L. Nute, "Papers of the American Fur Company," *Am. Hist. Rev.*, XXXII (1927), 521.

[7] J. J. Astor to Calhoun, Mar. 14, 1818, Secretary of War, Document File.

[8] McKenney had been named Superintendent of Indian Trade early in 1816 by President Madison and was reappointed by Calhoun under the act of Apr. 16, 1818. See Calhoun to McKenney, Apr. 27, 1818, Indian Office, *Letter Book D*, 147, National Archives; also Aug. 17, *ibid.*, 201-202.

[9] *Works*, V, 8-24; *ASP, Indian Affairs*, II, 181-185.

[10] Swift, *Memoirs*, 178-181.

[11] Calhoun to Jackson, Dec. 22, 1818, *Confidential Letters, War Office*, I, 98-101; Calhoun to Macomb, Mar. 27, 1819, *Military Book No. 10*, 293; Calhoun to Jackson, Aug. 10, 1819, *Correspondence*, 160-162.

[12] Jackson's *Correspondence*, II, 325-345, *passim; Niles*, XVI, 121-127; Winfield Scott, *Memoirs*, 196-203.

[13] Calhoun to Winfield Scott, Mar. 5 and 11, 1819, *Correspondence*, 152, 154-155.

[14] *Niles*, XV, 91; *Works*, V, 25-40; *ASP, Mil. Aff.*, I, 779-782. Cf. Calhoun to Monroe, Aug. 22, 1818, *Correspondence*, 137. In 1826, when everything Calhoun had done in the War Department was subject to partisan criticism, this policy was bitterly assailed by Inspector General George Croghan, who charged that it was making soldiers into farmers to the destruction of all military spirit, and that it served no purpose save petty economy. Wesley, 115-116.

[15] *ASP, Mil. Aff.*, I, 834-837. The artillery school was suggested by Col. John R. Fenwick in a letter to Calhoun, Jan. 19, 1819, Secretary of War, Document File; but Calhoun's report on the subject preceded his receipt of Fenwick's letter.

[16] Meteorological observations had been kept for nearly twenty years by land office officials in the field, at the instigation of Commissioner Josiah Meigs, but the number of observation points was too limited to be of great value. See *Niles*, XV, Supplement, 16. The War Department records were compiled in 1839 by Dr. Samuel Forry of the Medical Corps, who also published two popular works based on the same data: *The Climate of the United States* in 1842, and *Meteorology* in 1843.

[17] Ravenel, *Lowndes*, 187.

[18] Calhoun to John E. Calhoun, Nov. 8, 1818, Calhoun Papers; Josephine Seaton, *William Winston Seaton*, 135; District of Columbia Land Records, Liber A. S. 43, 187-188. The deed was recorded Oct. 14, 1818.

CHAPTER XIV

[1] Samuel Rezneck, "The Depression of 1819-1822, A Social History," *Am. Hist. Rev.* XXXIX (1934), 30-33. Also Catterall, *The Second Bank of the United States*, 22-50.

[2] See, for example, the files of *Niles' Register* for 1819 and 1820.

[3] *Annals*, 15th, 2d, 583-597.

[4] Adams, *Diary*, IV, 221-222; Crawford to Gallatin, Apr. 26, 1819, Gallatin's *Writings*, II, 100.

[5] Mrs. Smith, 144-147.

[6] Adams, *Diary*, IV, 224.

[7] Nathan Sargent, *Public Men and Events*, I, 23; Lacock to Jackson, June 25, 1832, *Niles*, XLIII, 79-80.

8 Adams, *Diary*, IV, 239-240. Jackson argued that Crawford's hostility toward him stemmed from the caucus of 1816, in which the General's influence had been given for Monroe. The ill feeling was mutual, however, and on Jackson's side it grew out of Crawford's action when Secretary of War in allowing the claim of the Cherokees to certain lands which Jackson insisted belonged to the Creeks and had been ceded by them to the United States as a result of his conquest of the Creek Nation in 1814. See Jackson to Crawford, June 10, 1816, Jackson's *Correspondence*, II, 243; and Jackson to Monroe, Oct. 23, 1816, *ibid.*, 261. Also Jackson's correspondence with John Clark, Crawford's Georgia rival, in 1819, *ibid.*, 416-421; and Shipp, *Crawford*, 150.

9 Crawford to Gallatin, July 24, 1819, Gallatin's *Writings*, II, 116.

10 Adams, *Diary*, IV, 307. Cf. *ibid.*, 214-215.

11 *Ibid.*, 312.

12 Details of the trip are from the *National Intelligencer* and the *Southern Patriot*.

13 Secretary of War, Document File. The letters begin with one for Mar. 30, 1819, and run through the summer.

14 Calhoun to Gibson, June 9, 1819, *Military Book No. 10*, 309-311.

15 Monroe to Calhoun, and R. M. Johnson to Calhoun, July 5, 1819, Secretary of War, Document File; *H. Doc.* 65, 16th Cong., 1st sess., 11.

16 Calhoun to Jesup, July 19, 1819, *Military Book No. 10*, 315-316.

17 Calhoun to Johnson, July 20, 1819, *ibid.*, 317-318.

18 R. M. Johnson to Calhoun, July 19, 26, and Aug. 5, 1819, Secretary of War, Document File.

19 Wesley, 155; Sargent, *Public Men*, I, 24; Atkinson to Calhoun, Sept. 6 and Oct. 3, 1819, Secretary of War, Document File. See also *H. Doc.* 110, 16th Cong., 2d sess.

20 Adams, *Diary*, IV, 405, 406-407.

21 *ASP, Ind. Aff.*, II, 201; *Works*, V, 71. Also Thomas L. McKenney, *Memoirs, Official and Personal*, I, 34-35; Calhoun to Lewis Cass, Mar. 27, 1819, *Correspondence*, 157-158.

22 That the child was born at Pendleton is conjecture, based on a reference in a letter from Calhoun to John Ewing Calhoun, Sept. 5, 1819, in the Calhoun Papers. "I expect to be in Pendleton by the 4th of October." This is confirmed by another letter to the same brother-in-law, written November 1, shortly after his departure for Washington. The letter is dated from Pickensville, a town he would not have passed through had he been coming from anywhere other than Pendleton.

23 Ravenel, *Lowndes*, 198.

24 *National Intelligencer*, Nov. 23, 1819. It was another ten years before any distinction was recognized between typhus, typhoid and various similar diseases.

25 Calhoun to John Ewing Calhoun, Dec. 12, 1819, Calhoun Papers. Also to Col. Leavenworth, Dec. 29, 1819, *Correspondence*, 166; and to Charles Tait, Jan. 29, 1820, *Tait Correspondence*.

CHAPTER XV

1 See K. W. Rowe, *Mathew Carey*. By 1827 he was having to consider ques-

tions of pauperism, the sudden appearance of which disturbed him but did not shake his faith.

[2] The quotation is from Daniel Webster's speech before the Massachusetts constitutional convention of 1820. Fuess, *Webster*, I, 278.

[3] King to J. Mason, May 25, 1820, *Mason*, 243-244. Cf. Adams, *Diary*, IV, 506.

[4] Mrs. Smith, 148-149.

[5] Adams, *Diary*, IV, 509-511.

[6] Seaton, 145-146.

[7] Adams, *Diary*, IV, 524; V, 12. King's speech is not reported in the *Annals*, but a sketch of it appears in Charles King, *Life and Correspondence of Rufus King*, VI, 276-278. King, it should be noted, had not taken his seat until January 25 and so had not heard Pinkney's argument.

[8] See, *e. g.*, Judge Story's charge to a Boston Grand Jury, October term, 1819, *Story*, I, 335-348.

[9] One slaveholder estimated that capital invested in slaves did not pay as much as two percent. See Francis Corbin to Madison, Oct. 10, 1819, *Mass. Hist. Soc. Proc.*, XLIII, 261.

[10] Tyler, *Times of the Tylers*, I, 316. Also *Branch Papers*, II, 18, and Spencer Roane to Monroe, Feb. 16, 1820, *N. Y. Pub. Lib. Bull.*, X (1906), 174-175.

[11] *Annals*, 16th, 1st, 1588-1590; also William C. Bruce, *John Randolph of Roanoke*, I, 451-452.

[12] Adams, *Diary*, IV, 530-531.

[13] It was a change of front. In July 1819 Adams had written in his diary that he "did not approve of the attempted restriction upon the State of Missouri, because I believe it not compatible either with the Constitution of the United States or with the Louisiana Treaty." *Diary*, IV, 398.

[14] Adams, *Diary*, V, 3-6, 9. Adams is authority for the statement that Monroe requested written opinions from the members of his Cabinet, which were to be filed in the State Department. In 1848, when the slavery question occupied the center of the stage, the circumstances surrounding the original Missouri Compromise were recalled in a Senate debate; and the appropriate passage from Adams' diary, supplied by his son and editor, was read. Calhoun at that time could recall having given no written opinion, nor could any such opinions be found in the State Department. An envelope suitably labeled was found, but nothing was in it. *Cong. Globe*, 30th Cong., 1st sess., app., 1178-1180.

[15] Adams, *Diary*, V, 10.

CHAPTER XVI

[1] Calhoun to Jackson, Mar. 6, 1819, *Correspondence*, 152-154; to Atkinson, Feb. 7, 1820, *ibid.*, 168-171.

[2] *ASP, Mil. Aff.*, I, 810-813; II, 49-50. Also *H. Rept.* 93, 16th Cong., 1st sess.

[3] Adams, *Diary*, IV, 477.

[4] *Annals*, 16th, 1st, 727-732.

[5] *Ibid.*, 780.

[6] *Ibid.*, 82-84.

[7] *ASP, Mil. Aff.*, II, 32.

⁸ The account of the Mix contract is drawn from the testimony at a later investigation. See *H. Rept.* 79, 19th Cong., 2d sess., especially testimony of Capt. J. L. Smith, of Mix and of Van Deventer.

⁹ *National Intelligencer*, Feb. 4, 1820.

¹⁰ *Annals*, 16th, 1st, 1594.

¹¹ *New York American*, Mar. 11, 1820; Swift, *Memoirs*, 186.

¹² Calhoun to Samuel Smith, Mar. 1, 1820, *Reports to Congress, War Department*, II, 127.

¹³ *ASP, Mil. Aff.*, II, 70-71.

¹⁴ Calhoun to Senate Finance Committee, *Annals*, 16th, 1st, 548-551.

¹⁵ Mrs. Smith, 149-150; Calhoun to John Ewing Calhoun, Mar. 23, 1820, *Correspondence*, 172.

¹⁶ Adams, *Diary*, V, 34.

¹⁷ Col. Wm. A. Trimble to Calhoun, Mar. 2, 1818, and Oct. 20, 1818, Secretary of War, Document File. Calhoun to Trimble, Sept. 25 and Oct. 16, 1818, *Confidential Letters, War Office*, I, 95, 96. Also J. A. Trimble, "Memoirs of an Old Politician in the National Capital at Washington," *Journal of American History*, III, 617-618.

¹⁸ Calhoun to Tait, Jan. 29, 1820, *Tait Correspondence*, 95-96; Adams, *Diary*, V, 67-69; Monroe to Jackson, May 23, 1820, *Niles*, LXVII, 343. At a later date the South tended to blame Adams for his failure to get Texas as well as Florida in one treaty, but the failure was by no means his alone, nor could it have been avoided. Adams was not, however, as various historians have tried to make him appear, the innocent victim of Monroe's temerity, who yielded Texas only reluctantly after all the Cabinet had turned against him. (See, *e. g.*, Sargent, *Public Men*, I, 23-24; Carl Schurz, *Life of Henry Clay*, I, 164; Bennett C. Clark, *John Quincy Adams*, 149; Channing, *History of the United States*, V, 339.) He was as thoroughly convinced as were his colleagues that the claim to Texas could not safely be pressed. Jackson, too, was willing to let Texas go if Florida could be had. Jackson to Calhoun, Dec. 21, 1820, Secretary of War, Document File.

¹⁹ G. Van Deusen, *Clay*, 129; Thomas Hart Benton, *Thirty Years' View*, I, 15 ff.

²⁰ *Annals*, 16th, 1st, 1618-1620.

²¹ *Ibid.*, 2233.

CHAPTER XVII

¹ 3 *Statutes at Large* 582. I cannot agree with Carl Russell Fish, "The Crime of W. H. Crawford," *Am. Hist. Rev.*, XXI (1916), 545-546, that the act was a mere administrative measure. It afforded Crawford too ready a means of building a political machine for use in 1824; and it was too well timed to have been motivated by any other purpose than the creation of patronage. To me at least it follows logically the historic debates in the First Congress on the establishment of the Executive Departments, as a result of which the tenure of Cabinet officers was made dependent on the will of the President. (*Annals*, 1st, 1st, 372-616, *passim;* 1 *Stat.* 28, 65.) The act of 1820 extended the removal power to substantially all officers appointed by the President, at the same time relieving the Executive of the onus of exercising it by making it automatic. The

power to discharge is essential to good administration, but the power to reappoint after an automatic termination is the essence of the spoils system. Cf. also Fish, *The Civil Service and the Patronage*, 66 ff.; and Adams, *Diary*, VII, 424-425.

[2] Adams, *Diary*, V, 88-89.

[3] Calhoun to Tait, May 20, 1820, *Tait Correspondence*, 98. Cf. John A. Dix to Dr. G. C. Shattuck, Apr. 20, 1820, *Mass. Hist. Soc. Proc.*, L, 140.

[4] Calhoun to R. M. Johnson, May 14, 1820, *Military Book No. 11*, 38-40; R. M. Johnson to Calhoun, May 8, 1820, Secretary of War, Document File; Calhoun to Atkinson, May 13, 1820, *Military Book No. 11*, 38; same to same, May 20, *ibid.*, 45.

[5] R. M. Johnson to Monroe, May 25, 1820, Secretary of War, Document File; Calhoun to Johnson, June 24, *Military Book No. 11*, 61-62.

[6] *H. Doc.* 110, 16th Cong., 2d sess.

[7] R. M. Johnson to Calhoun, June 30, 1820, and July 13, 1820, Secretary of War, Document File; Calhoun to Johnson, July 22, 1820, *Military Book No. 11*, 79-80; same to same, Oct. 4, 1820, *Confidential Letters, War Office*, I, 125-128.

[8] A note in Adams' diary in the fall of 1822 indicates that Calhoun had seen Jefferson some time in 1820, and Calhoun's only absence from Washington not accounted for is one between June 1 and 9. Adams, *Diary*, VI, 70; Calhoun to R. M. Johnson, May 30, 1820, *Confidential Letters, War Office*, I, 117.

[9] Calhoun to Monroe, July 14, 1820, *Correspondence*, 174-176.

[10] *Albany Argus*, Aug. 22, 1820. Cf. Calhoun to Monroe, Aug. 11, 1820, *Letters to the President, War Office*, II, 13-14, National Archives.

[11] New York *American*, Sept. 13, 14, 1820.

[12] Calhoun to Tait, Oct. 26, 1820, *Tait Correspondence*, 98-99.

[13] Curtis, *Webster*, I, 176-177. Also New York *American*, Sept. 18; New York *Columbian*, Sept. 19; *National Intelligencer*, Sept. 27, 1820.

[14] William Wirt to his wife, Sept. 23, 24, 1820, Kennedy, *Wirt*, II, 102, 103.

[15] Calhoun to Tait, Oct. 26, 1820, *Tait Correspondence*, 98-100.

[16] Adams, *Diary*, V, 199.

[17] Ravenel, *Lowndes*, 208 ff. Recalling the circumstances of the compromise in a discussion in the Senate many years later, Calhoun said that "During the session of the compromise, Mr. Lowndes and myself resided together. . . . The subject was one of repeated conversation between Mr. Lowndes and myself. . . . After full reflection, we both agreed that Missouri was a State . . . and never could be remanded back to the territorial condition." It is thus clear that it is the second compromise to which he refers, placing the time as the second session of the Sixteenth Congress. *Cong. Globe*, 30th, 1st, app., 1179.

[18] Benton, *View*, I, 13.

[19] Porter, *Astor*, II, 710-714.

[20] Adams, *Diary*, V, 238.

[21] *Annals*, 16th, 2d, 607, 1715-1723; *ASP, Mil. Aff.*, II, 188-198; *Works*, V, 80-93.

[22] See pp. 105-106 above.

[23] *Annals*, 16th, 2d, 728.

[24] Upton, *Military Policy*, 150-153; Oliver L. Spaulding, *The United States Army in War and Peace*, 152-153.

CHAPTER XVIII

[1] Adams, *Diary*, V, 236; Calhoun to Jedidiah Morse, Apr. 2, 1821, *Correspondence*, 183-184; Calhoun to Timothy Pickering, Apr. 29, 1821, *ibid.*, 185-186.

[2] Adams, *Diary*, V, 314-316.

[3] Crawford to Tait, Sept. 4, 1821, Shipp, *Crawford*, 149.

[4] Adams, *Diary*, V, 291.

[5] *Ibid.*, 327.

[6] *Ibid.*, 333-334.

[7] Calhoun to Tait, Apr. 23, 1821, *Tait Correspondence*, 101-102; to Jackson, Apr. 8, 1821, Jackson's *Correspondence*, III, 46-47; to John Ewing Calhoun May 13, 1821, *Correspondence*, 188; to Ninian Edwards, July 3, 1821, N. W. Edwards, *History of Illinois*, 488-489; to Moses Waddel, Sept. 25, 1821. For a copy of the last mentioned letter I am indebted to Prof. A. G. Holmes of Clemson College.

[8] *Military Book No. 11*, 158 (Mar. 10, 1821).

[9] Calhoun to Monroe, June 18 and July 28, 1821, *Correspondence*, 189-190, 193. It is interesting to note, however, that when Waterhouse sought reinstatement during Adams' Presidency his plea was rejected, the President having "ascertained that his statement was essentially incorrect in point of fact, and, even if true, showed that he ought to have been dismissed." Adams, *Diary*, VII, 14-15.

[10] Calhoun to Monroe, Aug. 18, 1821, *Correspondence*, 193-195.

[11] *ASP, Mil. Aff.*, II, 411.

[12] Calhoun to John Ewing Calhoun, Nov. 26, 1820, *Correspondence*, 179-180. Cf. same to same, Oct. 23, 1820, and Jan. 8, 1821, *ibid.*, 178-179, 180-181.

[13] Calhoun to John Ewing Calhoun, July 23, 1821, Calhoun Papers. Also same to same, May 6, May 13, and Sept. 27, 1821, *Correspondence*, 187-188, 195-197; and to Monroe, Aug. 18, 1821, *ibid.*, 195.

[14] Crawford to Gallatin, May 13, 1822, Gallatin's *Writings*, II, 243; J. Q. Adams, *Parties in the United States*, 133.

[15] *Franklin Gazette*, Oct. 16, 1821; Calhoun to John Ewing Calhoun, Sept. 27, 1821, *Correspondence*, 195-197.

[16] Philip S. Klein, *Pennsylvania Politics, 1817-1832*, 125-130.

[17] Ingham to Calhoun, June 7, 1821, *H. Rept. 62*, 18th Cong., 2d sess., 112-113; Calhoun to Ingham, July 23 and Oct. 29, 1821, *Military Book No. 11*, 262, 310-311; to R. Tillotson and N. Gouverneur, Apr. 6, 1822, *ibid.*, 376.

[18] Calhoun to Tait, Oct. 1, 1821, *Tait Correspondence*, 103-104. Cf. Calhoun to Moses Waddel, Sept. 25, 1821, *loc. cit.*

[19] W. H. Sparks, *Memories of Fifty Years*, 219-221.

[20] Calhoun to Monroe, Oct. 14, 1821, *Correspondence*, 199-201.

[21] Adams, *Diary*, V, 361.

[22] *Ibid.*, 370-371.

[23] *Ibid.*, 434-435.

[24] *Ibid.*, 428-429, 436-438, 443, 474-475.

[25] Everett S. Brown, ed., *The Missouri Compromises and Presidential Politics, 1820-1825*, 74; also 66-67. While Taylor professed to be neither Clintonian

nor Bucktail, he had been elected on the Clinton ticket. His choice as Speaker was actively opposed by the Van Buren faction, and his defeat was necessarily their triumph. Cf. Adams, *Diary*, V, 438; and *King*, VI, 425-426.

26 Brown, *Missouri Compromises*, 67-68.

27 *Niles*, XXI, 204; Crawford to Gallatin, May 13, 1822, Gallatin's *Writings*, II, 243.

28 *National Intelligencer*, Jan. 10, 19, 21, 1822; Jervey, *Hayne*, 125-128; Ravenel, *Lowndes*, 223-229.

29 Lowndes to Hamilton, Dec. 29, 1821, Ravenel, *Lowndes*, 228.

30 Whether Calhoun's conference with Lowndes was before or on December 28 cannot be positively established. I have assumed it was before, because Lowndes' letter to James Hamilton, Jr., dated December 29, says it was "several days before I received your letter." Even had the letter referred to come on the very day Lowndes answered, that would still put the discussion with Calhoun well before the twenty-eighth. The impression given by Lowndes' letter is that Calhoun's decision was made before he spoke to Lowndes about it; but since it seems not to have been communicated to anyone else until he was "waited upon" by a "deputation from the Pennsylvania delegation" (or, as Adams put it two days later, a "deputation of members of Congress from the North and the South"), it may well be that he was asked by his partisans for a decision, appointed a time for them to come and hear it, and in the meantime consulted Lowndes. Cf. Adams, *Diary*, V, 466, 468; *Life*, 28; and Brown, *Missouri Compromises*, 70. The latter says the deputation that waited upon Calhoun was composed of "certain members of Congress from Pennsylvania and New York."

31 Ravenel, *Lowndes*, 126-128.

CHAPTER XIX

1 See, for example, Wm. Plumer, Jr., to Wm. Plumer, Dec. 30, 1821, Brown, *Missouri Compromises*, 69-70.

2 Hayne to Lowndes, Jan. 21, 1822, Jervey, *Hayne*, 126-127. Hayne disapproved the nomination and would have tried to prevent it, had he known in advance that it was contemplated. Once it had been accomplished, however, he accepted it as for the best.

3 Calhoun to Virgil Maxcy, Dec. 31, 1821, Galloway-Maxcy-Markoe Papers, Library of Congress.

4 Winfield Scott, *Memoirs*, 183 n.

5 Calhoun to Tait, Oct. 1, 1821, *Tait Correspondence*, 103.

6 Henry A. Wise, *Seven Decades of the Union*, 75.

7 Wm. Plumer, Jr., to Wm. Plumer, Jan. 3, 1822, Brown, *Missouri Compromises*, 70-75. Cf. Adams, *Diary*, V, 477-478.

8 H. Adams, *Gallatin*, 599. Cf. Crawford's letters to Gallatin in volume II of the latter's *Writings*.

9 James Brown to Henry Clay, Apr. 26, 1822, J. A. Padgett, ed., "Letters of James Brown to Henry Clay, 1804-1835," *Louisiana Historical Quarterly*, XXIV (Oct. 1941), 935.

10 Story to Mason, Feb. 21, 1822, *Mason*, 264-265.

[11] Webster to Mason, Mar. 23, 1822, *ibid.*, 265-266; *Writings and Speeches of Daniel Webster* (National Edition), XVI, 67-68.

[12] Martin Van Buren, *Autobiography*, 116.

[13] Ravenel, *Lowndes*, 230.

[14] See, for example, Elijah Mills to his wife, 1822, *Letters*, 37-38; and Hammond, *Political History of New York*, II, 126.

[15] Calhoun to Maxcy, Mar. 18, 1822, Galloway-Maxcy-Markoe Papers, Library of Congress.

[16] *Seaton*, 162.

CHAPTER XX

[1] *Annals*, 17th, 1st, 625 ff.; James Buchanan, "Autobiographical Sketch," J. B. Moore, ed., *Works of James Buchanan*, XII, 301.

[2] *Annals*, 17th, 1st, 724-728; *ASP, Ind. Aff.*, 260-264.

[3] Benton's speech in the Senate, Mar. 25, *Annals*, 17th, 1st, 318. The report is in *ASP, Ind. Aff.*, II, 326-364. Cf. Benton, *View*, I, 20-21.

[4] *Annals*, 17th, 1st, 317-331, 339; *National Intelligencer*, May 2, 1822; McKenney, *Memoirs*, I, 28-29.

[5] Porter, *Astor*, II, 714.

[6] The Indian Office files, now in the National Archives, are filled with complaints from agents and Indians. See, for example, Calhoun to Richard Graham, July 12, 1821, Indian Office, *Letter Book E*, 128; to Thomas Forsyth, Nov. 6, 1821, *ibid.*, 184-185; to Lawrence Taliaferro, Apr. 26, 1822, *ibid.*, 247. The last named implicates the American Fur Company.

[7] *Annals*, 17th, 1st, Executive Proceedings, 470-510; *ASP, Mil. Aff.*, II, 395-414; Adams, *Diary*, V, 517. *Reports to Congress, War Department*, II, 247-248.

[8] Sparks, *Memories of Fifty Years*, 89-90. The summary in *Annals*, 17th, 1st, 1143-1146, is thoroughly diluted.

[9] *H. Rept.* 109, 17th Cong., 1st sess. Cf. Swift, *Memoirs*, 189.

[10] *Annals*, 17th, 1st, 1198-1202.

[11] Calhoun to John Ewing Calhoun, Mar. 19, 1822, *Correspondence*, 202. If the numerous eulogies of Lowndes by contemporaries could be taken at face value, it would be all but impossible to doubt that only his untimely death kept him from the Presidency, so universally does he appear to have been beloved. It must be remembered, however, that in spite of all their good will, his colleagues had not elected him their Speaker, and he had refused to contest that post in 1821. He could not, or would not thrust himself forward; and the record will show that no man has ever been elected to the Presidency who did not actively seek that office.

[12] *Franklin Gazette*, Mar. 14, 28, Apr. 11, May 16, 22, 30, June 11, 27, July 11, 1822; Adams, *Diary*, VI, 42-43; Washington *Gazette* for May, June and July, 1822. Ingham, Dallas and Thomas Sergeant were all reputed to have a financial interest in the *Franklin Gazette*. See Adams, *Diary*, VII, 533, 537-538; and Francis P. Weisenburger, *Life of John McLean*, 58.

[13] Adams, *Diary*, VI, 17-18, 244.

[14] Calhoun to John Ewing Calhoun, May 14, 1822, *Correspondence*, 202.

[15] Calhoun to Major Milo Mason, Apr. 18, 1818, *Military Book No. 10*, 60; to Jackson, Apr. 22, 1818, *ibid.*, 62.

[16] Calhoun to Sterling, June 18, 1822, *Correspondence*, 203, facsimile in Meigs, I, 432 followed. Cf to Ninian Edwards, June 12, 1822, Edwards, *History of Illinois*, 490.

[17] Calhoun to John Ewing Calhoun, July 1, 1822, *Correspondence*, 204. Cf. same to same, May 14, 1822, *ibid.*, 202; and to Ninian Edwards, June 12, 1822, Edwards, *History of Illinois*, 490.

[18] Calhoun to Gov. Thomas Bennett of South Carolina, July 22, 1822, *Military Book No. 11*, 417-418; and orders to Col. Eustis and Major Bankhead, commanders at St. Augustine and Charleston, respectively, *ibid.*, 418.

[19] Jervey, *Hayne*, 130-136; "Denmark Vesey," *Dictionary of American Biography*.

[20] Calhoun to Ninian Edwards, Aug. 20, 1822, Edwards, *History of Illinois*, 492.

[21] Adams, *Diary*, VI, 46-48.

[22] *Ibid.*, 61.

[23] *Ibid.*, 66.

[24] McKenney, *Memoirs*, I, 26-27. Cf. Washington *Gazette*, Sept. 21, 24, 1822; and Washington *Republican*, Mar. 19, 1824.

[25] Adams, *Diary*, VI, 75, 76-77.

[26] *Ibid.*, 106-107.

[27] *H. Rept.* 81, 17th Cong., 1st sess., 10-11.

[28] Calhoun to W. P. Duval, Oct. 22, 1820, *Mass. Hist. Soc. Proc.*, LXIII, 16-17.

[29] Adams, in November 1822, referred tartly to "Calhoun, who has a candidate always ready for everything . . ." (*Diary*, VI, 112); and Crawford wrote in May of the same year that "every appointment in Florida was made without my knowledge, and even the appointments connected with my own department have been made without regard to my wishes, or rather without ascertaining what they were." Gallatin's *Writings*, II, 242. But Calhoun was writing in August to Ninian Edwards of his inability to convince the President of the necessity of distinguishing in his appointments between friends and foes. Edwards, *History of Illinois*, 491.

[30] Calhoun to John Ewing Calhoun, Oct. 8, 1822, Calhoun Papers.

[31] Plumer to Plumer, Dec. 27, 1822, Brown, *Missouri Compromises*, 82-83.

[32] Adams, *Diary*, VII, 205-206; and *Parties in the United States*, 130-132. For discussion of the latter volume, see C. M. Wiltse, "John Quincy Adams and the Party System," *Journal of Politics*, IV (Aug. 1942), 407-414. Cf. C. W. Elliott, *Winfield Scott*, 227-228.

[33] Adams, *Diary*, VI, 21-22.

[34] See especially Scott to Calhoun, Nov. 12, 1821; Dec. 14, 1821; and Sept. 12, 1822, Secretary of War, Document File; Calhoun to Scott, Apr. 4, 1822, *Military Book No. 11*, 374-375; and Memorandum by Van Deventer, August 1824, Secretary of War, Document File.

[35] The A. B. papers appeared at intervals in the daily edition of the Washington *Republican* (published in addition to the semiweekly edition during the session of Congress) from January 20 to March 3, and continued in four numbers of the semiweekly edition after Congress had adjourned. There were

altogether fifteen letters. The daily *Republican* published numbers on Jan. 20, 21, 23, 27, 29, Feb. 3, 6, 10, 17, 24, and March 3. The last is reprinted in the semiweekly issue of March 5, and further letters are printed in that edition for March 26 and 29 and April 2 and 9. The Library of Congress file is complete.

[36] Calhoun to John Ewing Calhoun, Apr. 14, 1823, *Correspondence*, 206.

[37] Ingham to Edwards, Aug. 20, 1823, Edwards, *History of Illinois*, 497.

CHAPTER XXI

[1] Calhoun to John Ewing Calhoun, Apr. 14, 1823, *Correspondence*, 205-206.

[2] Same to same, Jan. 16, 1823, *ibid.*, 205.

[3] Same to same, May 27, 1823, *ibid.*, 206-207; same to same, July 20, 1823, Calhoun Papers.

[4] These were among the periodicals taken by the War Department during Calhoun's incumbency. *H. Doc.* 68, 17th Cong., 2d sess.

[5] Fisher, *Litchfield Law School*, 16.

[6] Calhoun to Rev. Jeremiah Day, Dec. 2, 1822, Ms. in Yale University Library.

[7] Mrs. Smith, 147, 148, 152; George Ticknor to W. H. Prescott, Jan. 16, 1825, Anna Ticknor and G. S. Hillard, eds., *Life, Letters and Journals of George Ticknor*, I, 349-350; Rev. Charles Cotesworth Pinckney, "John C. Calhoun from a Southern Standpoint," *Lippincott's Monthly Magazine*, LXII (July 1898), 83.

[8] The identical phrase was used to characterize Calhoun by Wirt and by Clay at almost the same time. Wirt to Wm. Pope, Nov. 12, 1824, Kennedy, *Wirt*, II, 161; Clay to Francis Brooke, Dec. 5, 1824, Clay's *Works*, IV, 107.

[9] Mrs. Smith, 155-160.

[10] Calhoun to John Ewing Calhoun, Oct. 8, 1822, Calhoun Papers; District of Columbia Land Records, Liber W. B. No. 7, 286-289, and Liber W. B. No. 28, 68-69. Old Mrs. Calhoun borrowed heavily from the United States Bank to pay for the property. She still owed $4300 to the bank, and $1500 to a private individual in 1826, when both debts were assumed by Calhoun in return for which the rent of Bonneau's Ferry was transferred to him. A formal agreement to this effect, witnessed by her two sons, is among Mrs. Calhoun's papers.

[11] Bassett, *Jackson*, 748; Calhoun to Mrs. F. Calhoun, Nov. 12, 1824, *Correspondence*, 227.

[12] Seaton, 158; John Clagett Proctor, ed., *Washington Past and Present*, II, 826-827.

[13] Swift, *Memoirs*, 192; and see Calhoun's letters to Swift, T. R. Hay, ed., "John C. Calhoun and the Presidential Campaign of 1824; some unpublished Calhoun letters," *Am. Hist. Rev.*, XL (Oct. 1934, Jan. 1935), 82-96, 287-300, *passim.* (Cited hereafter as *Swift Correspondence.*)

[14] See Calhoun's letters to John Ewing Calhoun through the 1820's in the *Correspondence* and in the Calhoun Papers.

[15] Adams, *Diary*, VI, 301.

[16] McDuffie to ——, Jan. 13, 1823, A. R. Newsome, ed., "Correspondence of Calhoun, McDuffie and Charles Fisher, relative to the Presidential Campaign of 1824," *North Carolina Historical Review*, VII (Oct. 1930), 486. (Cited here-

after as *Fisher Correspondence*.) Cf. Elijah Mills to his wife, 1822, *Letters,*
37-38.

CHAPTER XXII

[1] The summary of Calhoun's activities and views during the 1824 campaign,
as given in this chapter, is drawn from so many sources that for the most part
no effort has been made to cite them individually. Most important of the
printed sources are the *Correspondence,* the "Calhoun-Gouverneur Correspondence," *N. Y. Pub. Lib. Bull.,* III, 324-333 (cited hereafter as *Gouverneur Correspondence*); the *Swift Correspondence;* and the *Fisher Correspondence.* Most important unpublished sources are the Calhoun Papers at
Clemson College, and letters of Calhoun and others in various manuscript collections in the Library of Congress. Newspapers used are mentioned in the
text, while monographs on particular phases of the campaign and biographies
of major and minor actors in it are listed in the bibliography.

[2] Story to Mason, Feb. 21, 1822, *Mason,* 264-265; John Taylor to Monroe,
Apr. 29, 1823, *Branch Papers,* II, 348-355. Also Virgil Maxcy to R. S. Garnett,
Nov. 16, 1823, *Am. Hist. Rev.,* XII (1907), 600-601.

[3] Calhoun to Maxcy, Mar. 12, 1823, Galloway-Maxcy-Markoe Papers,
Library of Congress.

[4] Morgan Dix, *Memoirs of John A. Dix,* I, 66-68; and letters of Dix to Dr.
G. C. Shattuck in 1822 and 1823, *Mass. Hist. Soc. Proc.,* L, 144-146.

[5] Wheaton to Webster, Nov. 30, 1823, E. F. Baker, *Henry Wheaton,* 48.

[6] Calhoun to Gouverneur, Apr. 28, 1823, *Gouverneur Correspondence,* 324-
325; to Swift, Aug. 24, 1823, *Swift Correspondence,* 89-90. A copy of the
prospectus of the *Virginia Times* was sent to Calhoun Jan. 30, 1823, by Charles
Yancey of Richmond, Secretary of War, Document File; and the first number
appeared Feb. 14.

[7] Signed "A Citizen of New York," *Measures, not Men* has generally been
attributed to General Joseph G. Swift, to whom the task of preparing it was
assigned, Swift, *Memoirs,* 192. It is in fact, however, little more than a reprint
of the sketches published in the *Franklin Gazette* during the spring and summer of 1822, believed by contemporaries to be the work of Dallas.

[8] McLean to Edward Everett, Aug. 8, 1828 (first draft, not sent), *Mass.
Hist. Soc. Proc.,* 3d series, I, 364 n.

[9] Calhoun to Ninian Edwards, July 20, 1823, Edwards, *History of Illinois,*
495. Cf. to Charles Fisher, Aug. 1, 1823, *Fisher Correspondence,* 482-483.

[10] Calhoun to Swift, Aug. 24, 1823, *Swift Correspondence,* 89-90.

[11] Calhoun to Swift, Nov. 9, 1823, *ibid.,* 96. Cf. New York *Patriot,* Nov. 21,
1823: "We can confidently defy . . . any . . . man, to show an instance in
which we have attacked any of the candidates except Crawford."

[12] See especially the letters of Calhoun and McDuffie to Charles Fisher during 1823, *Fisher Correspondence,* 477-504; and Virgil Maxcy to R. S. Garnett,
Nov. 16, 1823, *Am. Hist. Rev.,* XII (1907), 600-601. "Mr. C——n calculates
with great certainty upon Maine if Mr. Adams is withdrawn," wrote Crawford
to Van Buren, Aug. 1, 1823. "Indeed he calculates upon every bodies votes
when they are withdrawn." Van Buren Papers, Library of Congress.

[13] Richmond *Enquirer,* Oct. 24, 1823; *Seaton,* 159-160. Mrs. Smith, 162,

says Crawford was dosed with calomel; Shipp, 174 n, says lobelia. Cf. Sparks, *Memories of Fifty Years*, 60.

¹⁴ *New England Galaxy*, Sept. 5, 12, 19, 26, 1823.

¹⁵ Adams, *Diary*, VI, 177-222, *passim;* Plumer to Plumer, Dec. 3, 1823, Brown, *Missouri Compromises*, 83-88; Mrs. Smith, 163.

¹⁶ He was unseated in March, but was promptly re-elected and returned to the next session.

¹⁷ Sam Houston to Calhoun, June 4 and July 6, 1822, A. W. Williams and E. C. Barker, eds., *Writings of Sam Houston*, I, 10-11, 12-13.

¹⁸ Calhoun to Maxcy, Dec. 11, 1823, *Correspondence*, 216. Calhoun was told that only four or five votes had been against him, with 155 out of a total membership of 169 present. The Charleston City *Gazette* reported seven or eight opposed, but others said fifteen or twenty. Jervey, *Hayne*, 145.

¹⁹ McDuffie to ——, Dec. 26, 1823, *Fisher Correspondence*, 492-493.

²⁰ Duff Green to Ninian Edwards, Dec. 10, 1823, E. B. Washburne, ed., *Edwards Papers*, 212-215.

²¹ Adams, *Diary*, VI, 233-234. The emissary was Joseph Gales.

²² *Ibid.*, 241-242.

²³ Calhoun to John Ewing Calhoun, Jan. 30, 1824, *Correspondence*, 217.

²⁴ Adams, *Diary*, VI, 244-246.

²⁵ *Ibid.*, 235.

²⁶ Hammond, *Political History of New York*, II, 149; C. H. Ambler, *Thomas Ritchie*, 91-92.

²⁷ *National Intelligencer*, Feb. 17, 1824.

²⁸ Klein, *Pennsylvania Politics*, 153 ff.

²⁹ *Ibid.*, 132-150.

³⁰ *National Intelligencer*, Feb. 24, 1824; *Niles*, XXV, 407-408.

³¹ Calhoun to Maxcy, Feb. 27, 1824, Galloway-Maxcy-Markoe Papers, Library of Congress. Also in Meigs, I, 307-308; and in Bassett, *Jackson*, 334-335, with verbal differences. Cf. Calhoun to Jedidiah Morse, Apr. 15, 1824, Ms. copy in Library of Congress.

³² Cf. Jackson to Lewis, Mar. 31, 1824, *N. Y. Pub. Lib. Bull.*, IV (June 1900), 160-161.

³³ Webster, writing to J. Mason, Feb. 15, 1824, says that if Jackson should be nominated at Harrisburg, "Mr. Calhoun will be no longer a candidate." *Mason*, 281-282. Plumer thought him "virtually withdrawn from the course" in a letter written Feb. 29, Brown, *Missouri Compromises*, 102; and Clay asserted flatly, in a letter to Francis Brooke dated Feb. 23, that Calhoun had withdrawn, C. Colton, ed., *Works of Henry Clay*, IV, 87.

CHAPTER XXIII

¹ Adams, *Diary*, V, 309, 411; Maxcy to R. S. Garnett, Nov. 16, 1823, *Am. Hist. Rev.*, XII (1907), 600-601.

² "The Waltham company, and a manufacturing company at Hartford, Conn., have lately, respectively, divided at the rate of 25 and 17 per cent. per ann. on their capitals, leaving handsome surplusses." *Niles*, XXII, 225 (June 8, 1822). For the return from agriculture, see Taylor to Monroe, Apr. 29, 1823, *Branch*

Papers, II, 348-353; and Francis Corbin to Madison, Oct. 10, 1819, *Mass. Hist. Soc. Proc.,* XLIII, 261.

3 See Appendix C.

4 Calhoun to R. S. Garnett, July 3, 1824, *Correspondence,* 219-223.

5 *Annals,* 18th, 1st, 1308.

6 Fuess, *Webster,* I, 316 n.

7 Webster to J. Mason, Apr. 19, 1824, *Mason,* 288.

8 *Annals,* 18th, 1st, 3078.

9 *Ibid.,* 2207-2208.

10 *Ibid.,* 686-687.

11 *Ibid.,* 2361. See also the arguments of P. P. Barbour and R. S. Garnett of Virginia, 1918 ff., 2096-2097; and of John Carter of South Carolina, especially 2162-2163.

12 Adams, *Diary,* VI, 375-376. The documents published as the *Case of Ninian Edwards* have been relied upon unless other sources are cited. The identical material appears in three separate publications, namely: *H. Rept.* 133, 18th Cong., 1st sess.; *ASP, Finance,* V, 1-146; and *Annals,* 18th, 1st, app.

13 Adams, *Diary,* VI, 301-306, 389-395.

14 *Ibid.,* 397-398.

15 *ASP, Ind. Aff.,* II, 259-260.

16 *Ibid.,* 473.

17 Adams, *Diary,* VI, 255-256.

18 *ASP, Ind. Aff.,* II, 473; Adams, *Diary,* VI, 271-272; G. M. Troup to Calhoun, Apr. 24, 1824, E. J. Harden, *Life of George M. Troup,* 210-216.

19 *ASP, Ind. Aff.,* II, 502. The message and documents are in the same volume, 460-490.

20 *Annals,* 14th, 1st, 5-6; *H. Doc.* 146, 19th Cong., 1st sess.; *Works,* V, 112-114; Calhoun to McKenney, Mar. 11, 1824, *Military Book No. 12,* 33.

21 *ASP, Ind. Aff.,* II, 542-544.

22 Annie H. Abel, *History of Indian Consolidation West of the Mississippi,* 342-343.

23 Fisher, *Silliman,* I, 309; Sargent, *Public Men,* I, 26.

24 Calhoun to Monroe, Sept. 11, 1824, *Correspondence,* 225.

25 *Niles,* XXVI, 51 (Mar. 27, 1824).

26 "I have not the vanity to propose a plan to you—allow me tho to direct your attention to the plan upon which the War Dept. is organized—it was the work of Mr. Calhoun, & its *practical* operations are regarded as almost perfect. . . ." Commodore Kennon to Secretary of the Navy Thomas W. Gilmer, Feb. 22, 1844, *William and Mary Quarterly,* XX (1912), 120. The War Department was also the model followed by John McLean in reorganizing the Post Office.

CHAPTER XXIV

1 Dix, *Memoirs,* II, 309-314; Adams, *Diary,* VI, 252-417, *passim.* Adams' diary, unfortunately, has no entries between October 7 and November 10, during which interval the discussions reached their climactic stage, so that other accounts must be depended on.

2 Clay to Francis Brooke, May 28, 1824, Clay's *Works,* IV, 93; D. Webster

to E. Webster, June 5, 1824, Webster's *Writings*, XVI, 88; Adams, *Diary*, VI, 355.

[3] Adams, *Diary*, VI, 356-357.

[4] *Ibid.*, 417.

[5] *Niles*, XXVII, 148 (Nov. 6, 1824).

[6] Calhoun to Swift, Nov. 20, 1824, *Swift Correspondence*, 293-294; to Charles Fisher, Dec. 10, 1824, *Fisher Correspondence*, 484.

[7] Plumer to Plumer, Dec. 16, 1824: "It is in fact very much in Clay's power to make the President. . . ." Brown, *Missouri Compromises*, 123.

[8] When the Clay forces proposed a union with Adams in 1822, Clay to be Vice President and of course successor, Plumer wrote that "Clay, as Vice President, might be of great service to the administration, . . . or, what appears to me more probable, he might put himself at the head of the opposition. . . . Again, if Clay is Vice President, what shall be done with Calhoun? If made Secretary of State, he & Clay will, of course, be at the head of two parties, with one of whom the President must take part, & encounter the opposition of the other." Dec. 10, 1822, Brown, *Missouri Compromises*, 79. The situation was in no way altered by reversal of the offices. Adams took further note of the rivalry in his entry for Dec. 17, 1824: "Of the fourteen electors of Kentucky, seven voted for Calhoun as Vice-President; and this vote I thought . . . was more hostile to Clay than any vote for Jackson as President could be. It held up Calhoun as a future competitor against Clay. . . ." *Diary*, VI, 447.

[9] Adams, *Diary*, VI, 438-443, *passim;* Plumer to Plumer, Dec. 9, 1824, Brown, *Missouri Compromises*, 121

[10] Adams, *Diary*, VI, 444, 446-447.

[11] R. M. Saunders to Bartlett Yancey, Dec. 19, 1824: "Clay is either fixed against us or unites to force us into terms totally inadmissable—the declension of Crawford after four years in his favor. If he supports Jackson it will be under this understanding." A. R. Newsome, ed., "Letters of Romulus M. Saunders to Bartlett Yancey, 1821-28," *N. C. Hist. Rev.*, VIII (1931), 448. (Cited hereafter as *Saunders Letters*.)

[12] Adams, *Diary*, VI, 450-452.

[13] *Ibid.*, 442; Plumer to Plumer, Dec. 7, 1824, Brown, *Missouri Compromises*, 119.

[14] Adams, *Diary*, VI, 458, 462.

[15] *Ibid.*, 441, 443, 472. Calhoun knew nothing of this dickering. He had heard a rumor that Jackson meant to bring Clinton into the Cabinet, sought an explanation and received a denial. He had no notion that Adams was also flirting with the New Yorker. Calhoun to Smith Thompson, Nov. 10, 1824, *Swift Correspondence*, 293.

[16] Plumer to Plumer, Dec. 24, 1824, Brown, *Missouri Compromises*, 123-125; Adams, *Diary*, VI, 452-453.

[17] Clay to Blair, Jan. 8, 1824, Clay's *Works*, IV, 109-110; Adams, *Diary*, VI, 464-465; Brown, *Missouri Compromises*, 130-131.

[18] McLean to Edward Everett, Aug. 8, 1828 (first draft, not sent), *Mass. Hist. Soc. Proc.*, 3d series, I, 365 n.; Nathaniel Macon to Charles Tait, Jan. 7, 1824, Shipp, *Crawford*, 179; Mrs. Smith, 170-172.

[19] Adams, *Diary*, VI, 472-476.

[20] *Ibid.*, 495-496. Cf. 476.

[21] *Ibid.,* V, 466-467.

[22] *Ibid.,* VI, 480.

[23] G. Van Deusen, *Clay,* 188-190, gives the best account of the transaction.

[24] Van Buren, *Autobiography,* 150-152; Mrs. Smith, 184-186, 191-193; Hammond, *Political History of New York,* II, 190. Thurlow Weed, however, says Van Rensselaer had declared for Adams the day before the election. H. A. Weed, ed., *Life of Thurlow Weed including his Autobiography and a Memoir,* I, 172. Adams himself seems to have thought four or five days earlier that the patroon was inclining toward him, though wavering. *Diary,* VI, 493. Cf. also *King,* VI, 585-586.

[25] Edward L. Morse, ed., *Samuel F. B. Morse, His Letters and Journals,* 262-263.

[26] Edward Stanley, Earl of Derby, *Journal of a Tour in America, 1824-25,* 313.

[27] Monroe's memoranda are in the *Am. Hist. Rev.,* XLII (1937), 274-276. Cf. Adams, *Diary,* VI, 508-509. Denis T. Lynch, *An Epoch and A Man,* 282, says, but without citation, that the State Department was actually offered to Clinton, who declined it.

[28] Perry, "Poinsett," *Reminiscences of Public Men.* Adams, *Diary,* VI, 506-507, tells the story in negative rather than positive terms, recording a threat of systematic opposition if Clay should be appointed. According to his account, the informant was George Sullivan, a Massachusetts lobbyist, who quoted the South Carolinians as demanding a Cabinet of Poinsett, Cheves, McLean and Southard. Sullivan grew strangely hazy, however, when Adams said he would one day ask him to repeat the story in a court of law.

[29] "It is an essential part of this plan, as conceived by Clay, to throw Virginia & the South into the minority, & consequently into an opposition to the new administration. . . ." Plumer to Plumer, Dec. 24, 1824, Brown, *Missouri Compromises,* 124.

[30] He was not the oldest, as a matter of fact, but seems to have accepted the designation without argument.

[31] *Niles,* XXVIII, 30-31.

[32] *National Intelligencer,* March 5, 1825.

[33] "I really do believe that the common good is more concerned in Clay's being Secretary of State than in the question between Jackson and Adams." John J. Crittenden to David White, 1825, Ann Coleman, *Life of John J. Crittenden,* I, 70. Also Wise, *Seven Decades,* 77-79, 82-84. Clay's Address is in *Niles,* XXVIII, 71-79. Cf. Benton, *View,* I, 48.

[34] Adams, *Diary,* V, 325-326, *et passim;* VI, 116-118, 258.

[35] Clay resigned his connection with the bank to become Secretary of State, but Webster continued his affiliation as long as the institution lasted.

[36] Of the 107 Representatives who voted in favor of the tariff of 1824, 53 voted for Adams when the poll was taken in the House. Only 32 antitariff votes were cast in his favor, all but 10 of them from New England. Representatives from the critical states of Ohio, Kentucky and Missouri, "delivered" to Adams by Clay, were men who had stanchly supported the tariff. See *Niles,* XXVII, 387, for the Presidential vote.

[37] Calhoun to Swift, Mar. 10, 1825, *Swift Correspondence,* 294-295. Cf. to Gouverneur, Mar. 25, 1825, *Gouverneur Correspondence,* 328; and to Theodore

Lyman, Sept. 8, 1828, *Correspondence*, 267-269. Also *Life*, 30; and his speech on the Independent Treasury Bill, Mar. 22, 1838, *Works*, III, 293.

CHAPTER XXV

[1] Calhoun to Benjamin Silliman, Aug. 14, 1825, Fisher, *Silliman*, I, 325. A debt to Joel Poinsett appears to have been contracted about this time and was perhaps an outgrowth of the loss. The amount of the debt cannot be ascertained, but it was probably considerable since it was two years or more before Calhoun was able to repay it. Calhoun to Dr. Joseph Johnson, Dec. 11, 1825, and Feb. 25, 1827, copies in Library of Congress.

[2] District of Columbia Land Records, Liber W. B. No. 12, 277-278.

[3] *Niles*, XXVIII, 266-267.

[4] Calhoun to Gouverneur, June 10, 1825, *Correspondence*, 230; to Swift, June 27, 1825, *Swift Correspondence*, 296. Cf. to Van Deventer, June 10, 1825, *Correspondence*, 231.

[5] Calhoun to Van Deventer, June 24, 1825, *Correspondence*, 231-232. Cf. to Swift, Sept. 2, 1825, *Swift Correspondence*, 296-297.

[6] John McLean to Edward Everett, no date, *Mass. Hist. Soc. Proc.*, 3d series, I, 392; Saunders to Yancey, Feb. 12, 1827, *Saunders Letters*, 460.

[7] Weed, *Autobiography*, I, 177-181; *Niles*, XXIX, 16; Hammond, *Political History of New York*, II, 204-205.

[8] U. B. Phillips, *Georgia and State Rights*, 56-58; Harden, *Troup*, 254-424, *passim;* Benton, *View*, I, 58-59.

[9] Adams, *Diary*, VII, 56. Lee was a half brother of Robert E. Lee, then a cadet at West Point.

[10] Harvey T. Cook, *Life and Legacy of David Rogerson Williams*, 291. The date is conjectural.

[11] Adams, *Diary*, VII, 61, 67, 69.

[12] *Ibid.*, 72.

[13] *Ibid.*, 59, 61.

[14] Crawford to Clay, Feb. 4, 1828, Clay's *Works*, IV, 192; Jefferson to W. B. Giles, Dec. 26, 1825, *Niles*, XXXIII, 48; Richmond *Enquirer*, Dec. 8, 1825; William E. Smith, *The Francis Preston Blair Family in Politics*, I, 38.

[15] Calhoun to Swift, Dec. 11, 1825, *Swift Correspondence*, 298-299.

[16] *Register of Debates*, 19th Cong., 1st sess., 801-802.

[17] *Niles*, XXIX, 293; Jervey, *Hayne*, 188; Wallace, II, 425.

[18] *Senate Journal*, 18th Cong., 1st sess., 28.

[19] John Bailey to J. B. Davis, Dec. 16, 1825, *Mass. Hist. Soc. Proc.*, XLIX, 192; John McLean to Edward Everett, no date, *ibid.*, 3d series, I, 392; *National Intelligencer*, Dec. 29, 1825, and Jan. 2, 4, and 6, 1826. I am discounting the story that Calhoun influenced Senator McIlvaine to vote against Clay's confirmation, told at second-hand by Adams, *Diary*, VII, 69, and garbled by Sargent, *Public Men*, I, 107-108. It is at least balanced by the Vice President's stand in favor of confirming Rufus King. Adams, *Diary*, VII, 86.

[20] McLean to Everett, *loc. cit.;* Van Buren, *Autobiography*, 199-200.

[21] *Senate Journal*, 19th Cong., 1st sess., 415-439. The Richmond *Enquirer*, Mar. 28, 1826, is authority for Tazewell's authorship of the report.

²² Adams, *Diary*, VII, 111-112; Clay to Francis Brooke, Feb. 20, 1826, Clay's *Works*, IV, 137.

²³ Clay to Crittenden, Mar. 10, 1826, Coleman, *Crittenden*, I, 64; Webster to Mason, Mar 27, 1826, Webster's *Writings*, XVI, 125-127.

²⁴ Calhoun to Swift, Feb. 19, 1826, *Swift Correspondence*, 300. Cf. Saunders to Yancey, Jan. 10, 1826, *Saunders Letters*, 454.

²⁵ "Tazwell is at home—Gilliard is no more & the desertion of Homes of Maine & a few others leave our friends in the minority. . . ." Saunders to Yancey, Mar. 4, 1826, *Saunders Letters*, 455. And Judge Story, confidant of Webster, knew at this time that the mission would "ultimately be confirmed by a small majority." Story to P. P. Fay, Mar. 8, 1826, *Story*, I, 492-493.

²⁶ See, *e. g.*, Henry Adams, *The Degradation of the Democratic Dogma*, Introduction by Brooks Adams; Clark, *John Quincy Adams*, 241; and Charles T. Adams' preface to J. Q. Adams, *Parties in the United States*.

²⁷ Van Buren, *Autobiography*, 201; Benton, *View*, I, 66; Calhoun to Jackson, June 4, 1826, Jackson's *Correspondence*, III, 304. To this passage Bassett adds the following note: "It is one of the very unexpected things in our political history that John Quincy Adams, who consistently refused to make appointments that would serve to promote his re-election, should have been proclaimed as one who debauched the patronage. It is even more singular that the charge should be repeated by a man as intelligent as Calhoun." Most singular of all is the fact that so profound a student of the period as Professor Bassett should have been taken in by the Adams myth.

CHAPTER XXVI

¹ Adams, *Diary*, VII, 113.

² Memorandum dated May 20, 1826, in Jackson's *Correspondence*, III, 301-302.

³ Ben Perley Poore, *Perley's Reminiscences of Sixty Years in the National Metropolis*, I, 64. The story was denied by the stenographer and by the opposition press. Cf. Richmond *Enquirer*, Apr. 28, 1826.

⁴ *Register of Debates*, 19th, 1st, 400-401.

⁵ G. Van Deusen, *Clay*, 222-223.

⁶ Elijah Mills to his wife, April 8, 1826, Mills, *Letters*, 50.

⁷ Gore to King, Apr. 13, 1826, *King*, VI, 667; Webster to J. E. Denison, May 3, 1826, Webster's *Writings*, XVI, 129.

⁸ *Niles*, XXXII, 6-8; Sargent, *Public Men*, I, 119-120; *Register of Debates*, 19th, 1st, 1931-1959.

⁹ "It is already said, that if the Bill passes the Senate, the P. M. General is to be one of the Judges, & Mr. Speaker, P. M. General. The first arrangement I think likely—and that Webster is to be Speaker." Saunders to Yancey, Jan. 26, 1826, *Saunders Letters*, 454. Cf. Adams, *Diary*, VII, 84; Webster to Story, Dec. 31, 1825, Webster's *Writings*, XVII, 400-401; Webster to Mason, May 2, 1826, *ibid.*, XVI, 127-128; Weisenburger, *McLean*, 62-63.

¹⁰ *Register of Debates*, 19th, 1st, app., 133-138.

¹¹ The *National Journal* found it necessary to defend the action at some length, March 24, 25, 28, 1826. See also the *Telegraph* and the Richmond

Enquirer; and Culver H. Smith, "Propaganda Technique in the Jackson Campaign of 1828," *East Tennessee Historical Society Publications* no. 6, 44-66.

[12] Richmond *Enquirer,* Apr. 11, 21, May 30, 1826.

[13] *E. g.,* Saunders to Yancey, Apr. 17, 1826, *Saunders Letters,* 456.

[14] *Register of Debates,* 19th, 1st, 572-573. The rules referred to are:

When a member shall be called to order, he shall sit down, until the President shall have determined whether he is in order or not; and every question of order shall be decided by the President, without debate; but if there be a doubt in his mind, he may call for the sense of the Senate.

If the member be called to order, for words spoken, the exceptionable words shall immediately be taken down, in writing, that the President may be better enabled to judge of the matter.

[15] The Patrick Henry letters have generally been attributed to Philip R. Fendall, a clerk in the State Department, whose pen had often been used in Adams' service. They were universally believed by contemporaries, however, to be Adams' own, and Calhoun shared this view, continuing to hold it even after the *Intelligencer* of September 4, 1826 had published an "authorized" denial. See Onslow in the same paper, October 7. Adams' most recent biographer, Bennett C. Clark, *John Quincy Adams,* 243, also accepts his authorship of the letters.

Calhoun's second and third papers, those of June 27 and 29, were published as a pamphlet, probably immediately on their appearance. The lines are of the width of a newspaper column, as though the type had been left standing; and a note at the end informs the reader that he may find "Patrick Henry's" numbers in the *National Journal* for May 1 and June 7. After Adams had resumed the debate in August, Calhoun prepared his three final numbers, which seem to have been unknown to his editor, Richard Crallé, as well as to his various biographers. Crallé reproduces only the two from the pamphlet in *Works,* VI, 322-348; and William M. Meigs, *Life of Calhoun,* I, 315 n, says specifically that there were only three letters. Some time in 1827 the five Patrick Henry letters were brought out in pamphlet form as "An Argument on the Powers, Duties, and Conduct, of the Hon. John C. Calhoun, Vice President of the United States, and President of the Senate."

[16] See, *e. g.,* a letter signed "Observer" in the *Intelligencer* for Aug. 7, 1826, and the last of the Onslow letters in the same paper, Oct. 12. Also p. 75 above.

[17] Adams, *Diary,* IV, 532.

[18] *Register of Debates,* 20th, 1st, 278-341; Adams, *Diary,* VII, 433-434; *Life,* 32.

[19] Richmond *Enquirer,* June 9, 27, 1826; *Senate Journal,* 19th Cong., 1st sess., 785.

[20] Another choice bit, originating in the *Literary Cadet* of Providence, is the following: "Despised and condemned by the good, the virtuous and the just, he sits alone in the Senatorial chair, and listens without resentment to the reproaches of John Randolph, of Roanoke, and receives the merited execrations of an outraged people. Decency and morality shrink before the withering blasts of his malignity, and patriotism turns pale at the annunciation of his name." It is quoted here from the Richmond *Enquirer* of June 30, 1826.

[21] Calhoun to James Edward Calhoun, Jan. 23, 1828, *Correspondence,* 258-259.

22 Calhoun to Jackson, June 4, 1826, Jackson's *Correspondence*, III, 304-305.

23 Jackson to Calhoun, July 26, 1826, *ibid.*, 307-308.

24 Saunders to Yancey, Apr. 17, 1826, *Saunders Letters*, 457; Hammond, *Political History of New York*, II, 211-213; Ambler, *Ritchie*, 105-106.

CHAPTER XXVII

1 Calhoun to Mrs. F. Calhoun, Apr. 23, 1826, *Correspondence*, 233.

2 Same to same, May 28, 1826, *ibid.*, 235-255.

3 Calhoun to John Ewing Calhoun, June 14, 1826, *Correspondence*, 236-237; to Mrs. F. Calhoun, June 14, 1826, *ibid.*, 235-236.

4 Calhoun to James Edward Calhoun, Dec. 24, 1826, *Correspondence*, 238, says July 19, but this is undoubtedly a misreading of Calhoun's often difficult script. In a letter dated Georgetown, July 22, he says he expects to leave on Wednesday, which would be the twenty-sixth. The *National Journal* for Friday, July 28, says he did leave on Thursday morning. Cf. Calhoun to Van Buren, July 7, 1826, Van Buren, *Autobiography*, 514-515.

5 Calhoun to James Edward Calhoun, Dec. 24, 1826, *Correspondence*, 237-238.

6 A memorandum of account between Mrs. F. Calhoun and J. C. Calhoun for the year 1830, among the Calhoun Papers, gives the rental. For other details as to the Fort Hill estate I am indebted to Professor A. G. Holmes of Clemson College. The Lewis land was finally acquired by Calhoun in 1842. See also A. G. Holmes, "John C. Calhoun," *Southern Magazine*, II, #10 (1936).

7 Calhoun to James Edward Calhoun, Dec. 24, 1826, *loc. cit.*

8 *Niles*, XXXI, 94-95. The toast which precipitated his remarks was: "The vice president of the United States. The 12th congress witnessed his triumphant defence of American honor; the 19th his protection of liberty's citadel, the freedom of debate."

9 *National Journal*, Nov. 4, 1826.

10 Calhoun to John Ewing Calhoun, Jan. 15 and 31, 1827, *Correspondence*, 240, 241; to James Edward Calhoun, Jan. 23, 1828, *ibid.*, 257; District of Columbia Land Records, Liber W. B. No. 28, 68-69.

11 Perry, "William Smith," *Reminiscences of Public Men*, 80.

12 Richmond *Enquirer*, Dec. 21, 1826; *Senate Journal*, 19th Cong., 2d sess., 29-30. The *Enquirer's* story, while not otherwise verifiable, is in general upheld by a tabulation of the committee memberships. The conclusion that Ritchie's informant may have been Tazewell is based on the assumption that the information must have come from someone present at the balloting, presumably a member, and on the fact that Tazewell and Ritchie did correspond on political matters.

13 Calhoun to James Edward Calhoun, Dec. 24, 1826, *Correspondence*, 239-240. Van Buren, *Autobiography*, 514, is authority for the Virginia holiday. I have assumed that the "Ravenswood" referred to is "Ravensworth," the seat of the Fairfax County Fitzhughs.

14 *H. Rept.* 79, 19th Cong., 2d sess., 152.

15 Richmond *Enquirer*, Jan. 4, 1827.

16 *Register of Debates*, 19th, 2d, 575-576.

17 Calhoun to James Edward Calhoun, Feb. 14, 1827, *Correspondence*, 239.

The others on the committee were John C. Wright of Ohio, Lewis Williams of North Carolina, James Clarke of Kentucky, Ralph I. Ingersoll of Connecticut and Peleg Sprague of Maine.

[18] John Bailey to J. B. Davis, Jan. 3, 1827, *Mass. Hist. Soc. Proc.*, XLIX, 195; Calhoun to John Ewing Calhoun, Jan. 31, 1827, *Correspondence*, 241-242; to Jackson, Jan. 24, 1827, Jackson's *Correspondence*, III, 332.

[19] *H. Rept.* 79, 19th Cong., 2d sess.; *Register of Debates*, 19th, 2d, 1143.

[20] John Bailey to J. B. Davis, Feb. 17, 1827, *Mass. Hist. Soc. Proc.*, XLIX, 197; Virgil Maxcy to Calhoun, Mar. 2, 1827, *Correspondence*, 791.

[21] Saunders to Yancey, Jan. 20, 1827, *Sprunt Historical Publications*, X, No. 2, 61-62.

[22] Van Buren to B. F. Butler, Dec. 12, 1826, Van Buren Papers, Library of Congress.

[23] Van Buren to Ritchie, Jan. 13, 1827, Van Buren Papers, Library of Congress. Cf. Ambler, *Ritchie*, 107-108; and Van Buren, *Autobiography*, 514-515.

[24] Richmond *Enquirer*, Apr. 27, 1827.

[25] Ambler, *Ritchie*, 108-109.

[26] Calhoun to Van Buren, July 7, 1826, in Van Buren, *Autobiography*, 514-515. Van Buren confuses the two proposals.

[27] Hammond, *Political History of New York*, II, 241-247; Van Buren, *Autobiography*, 165.

[28] Saunders to Yancey, Feb. 12, 1827, *Saunders Letters*, 459-460.

[29] Webster to ——, Feb. 23, 1827, Webster's *Writings*, XVI, 145-148.

[30] *Life*, 34; *Register of Debates*, 19th, 2d, 496; *Senate Journal*, 245. Van Buren, in his *Autobiography*, says he missed his vote on the bill because he had "promised to accompany a friend on a visit to the Congressional Cemetery," 169. Stanwood, however, *American Tariff Controversies*, I, 258, says the New Yorker was in his seat but did not vote. As he had moved a vote on another measure a few minutes earlier, this seems likely.

[31] Cook, *Williams*, 242-243.

CHAPTER XXVIII

[1] Lewis C. Gray, *History of Agriculture in the Southern States to 1860*, I, 698-699; *Treasury Report*, 1854-5, 116; George R. Taylor, "Wholesale Commodity Prices at Charleston, South Carolina, 1796-1861," *Journal of Economic and Business History*, IV, part 2, 848-868; John G. Van Deusen, *Economic Bases of Disunion in South Carolina*, 331; Timothy Pitkin, *Statistical View of the Commerce of the United States* (1835), 58-82.

[2] *Niles*, XXXII, 237-238.

[3] Dumas Malone, *Public Life of Thomas Cooper*, 307-311; *Niles*, XXXIII, 28-32; Laura A. White, *Robert Barnwell Rhett*, 11-12.

[4] Malone, *Cooper*, 318-320.

[5] Calhoun to Van Deventer, July 23, 1827, *Correspondence*, 246.

[6] For the complete list and an account of the proceedings, see *Niles*, XXXII, 388-396.

[7] *Ibid*, XXXIII, 100-112, 123-128, 138-144, 149-160, 171-176, 188-192 and 203-208.

[8] Henry Orne, *Letters of Columbus*, 25; *Life*, 32; G. Van Deusen, *Clay*, 215.

[9] W. C. Rives to W. T. Gilmer, July 22, 1827, *Tyler's Quarterly Historical and Genealogical Magazine*, V (Apr. 1924), 231-237. The Coleman letter is in *Niles*, XXVI, 245, and Jackson's *Correspondence*, III, 249-251.

[10] Henry Lee, *Report of a Committee of the Citizens of Boston and Vicinity, Opposed to a Further Increase of Duties on Importations;* and Robert J. Turnbull, *The Crisis.* Cf. Thomas Cooper, *On the Constitution of the United States and the Questions that Have Arisen Under it* (1826).

[11] Calhoun to James Edward Calhoun, Aug. 26, 1827, *Correspondence*, 249-251.

[12] Calhoun to Van Deventer, July 23, 1827, *Correspondence*, 245-246; to same, Aug. 12, *ibid.*, 247.

[13] Calhoun to James Edward Calhoun, Jan. 23, 1828, *Correspondence*, 257.

[14] Calhoun to James Edward Calhoun, Aug. 26, 1827, *Correspondence*, 248-249.

[15] E. M. Carroll, "Politics during the Administration of J. Q. Adams," *South Atlantic Quarterly*, XXIII (Apr. 1924), 147-148.

[16] John McLean to Edward Everett, Aug. 8, 1828, *Mass. Hist. Soc. Proc.*, 3d series, I, 363-370. Everett admits frankly in his side of the correspondence that Hill had violated no statute or regulation but was to be removed on purely partisan grounds.

[17] Adams, *Diary*, VII, 349. The charges so often repeated that McLean abused the patronage of his department have been generally accepted, but there is an argument on the other side. Judge Hammond, who desired McLean's removal as ardently as Clay, states flatly that the Postmaster General was hampering the administration by his neutrality and impartiality. *Political History of New York*, II, 281-282. And the whole point of the controversy with Everett, cited above, is not that he appointed political opponents of Adams but that he would not remove such opponents without cause. To me, at least, the final proof of his innocence is that Jackson put him on the Supreme Bench for the very reason Adams longed to do so—he would not clean house in the department for political purposes. "John McLean," *Dictionary of American Biography.* See also *National Intelligencer*, Mar. 10, 1829: "We hope that the successor of Mr. McLean may . . . imitate . . . his resistance of proscription. . . ."

[18] Cf. Hammond, *Political History of New York*, II, 255. See above, p. 139.

[19] Smith, "Propaganda Technique," 50.

[20] Calhoun to Monroe, Dec. 9, 1827, *Correspondence*, 253; to James Edward Calhoun, Jan. 23, 1828, *ibid.*, 257.

[21] Adams, *Diary*, VII, 373-374, 378.

[22] "My system has been," he wrote on Dec. 28, 1827, "and continues to be, to nominate for re-appointment all officers for a term of years whose commissions expire, unless official or moral misconduct is charged and substantiated against them. This does not suit the Falstaff friends 'who follow for the reward,' and I am importuned to serve my friends and reproached for neglecting them, because I will not dismiss, or drop from Executive offices, able and faithful political opponents to provide for my own partisans." *Diary*, VII, 390. A few months later, after making certain appointments on frankly politi-

cal grounds, the President felt called upon to explain that though the men rewarded were not the best men, they could be counted on to "discharge the duties of their offices faithfully to the best of their ability. Nothing would induce me to compromise on that point; but in all short of that the right must in this, as in numberless other cases, yield to the expedient. . . ." *Ibid.*, VIII, 5. Naturally, he could always find partisans as able as his opponents.

²³ Adams, *Diary*, VII, 473-474; cf. *ibid.*, VI, 469, 511; also Webster to Mason, Mar. 1828, Webster's *Writings*, XVI, 175-176; and to E. Webster, *ibid.*, XVII, 453.

²⁴ Adams, *Diary*, VII, 404-405.

²⁵ See Madison to Monroe, Jan. 23, Feb. 26, 1828, Madison's *Works*, III, 612-613, 623; and to Brooke, Feb. 22, 1828, *ibid.*, 622. Cf. Brooke to Clay, Clay's *Works*, IV, 196; and Isaac Hill to Henry Lee, Sept. 16, 1828, *Mass. Hist. Soc. Proc.*, XLIII, 70.

²⁶ Calhoun to Monroe, Feb. 30 (sic!), 1827, *Correspondence*, 242-243.

²⁷ Calhoun to Monroe, Dec. 9, 22, 1827, and Jan. 3, 1828, *ibid.*, 253-256. The missing letter, italicized for the General's convenience, was forwarded to Jackson by Sam Houston, Jan. 13, 1827. See *Writings of Sam Houston*, I, 71-73.

²⁸ Calhoun to Jackson, July 10, 1828, Jackson's *Correspondence*, III, 413-415. Other letters will be found in this volume, in the Calhoun *Correspondence* and in Monroe's *Writings*.

²⁹ Crawford to Van Buren, Dec. 21, 1827, Van Buren Papers, Library of Congress. Also printed in Cook, *Williams*, 243-244. Cf. Crawford to Van Buren, Oct. 21, 1828, Jackson *Correspondence*, III, 446 n.

³⁰ Crawford to Alfred Balch, Dec. 14, 1827, Calhoun's *Works*, VI, 356-358.

³¹ Calhoun to James Edward Calhoun, Jan. 23, 1828, *Correspondence*, 259-260. Cf. Adams, *Diary*, VII, 427-428.

CHAPTER XXIX

¹ Channing, *History of the United States*, V, 13.

² Carl W. Mitman, "The Beginning of the Mechanical Transport Era in America," *Annual Report of the Smithsonian Institution, 1929*, 534; Lewis H. Haney, *A Congressional History of Railroads in the United States to 1850*, I, 26.

³ Edward Hungerford, *Story of the Baltimore and Ohio Railroad, 1827-1927*, I, 27-47.

⁴ *Niles*, XXXIII, 329-330, 353; Adams, *Diary*, VII, 412; Joseph T. Buckingham, *Personal Memoirs and Recollections of Editorial Life*, II, 17. Buckingham, who was editor of the Boston *Courier*, was "induced" by the "applicants for a protective tariff" to come to Washington for the 1827-1828 session of Congress "in order to keep our friends at home informed of whatever might be done or contemplated for the accomplishment of their purpose." He was one of many.

⁵ *ASP, Finance*, V, 778-845. The Treasury report, McDuffie's statement, and numerous memorials and petitions are in the same volume.

⁶ *Cong. Globe*, 28th, 1st, app., 747 (1843-1844). Calhoun's account is in *Works*, III, 47-51; *Cong. Globe*, 24th, 2d, 904-909; and *Life*, 33. Silas Wright

gives his version in the *Globe*, 24th, 2d, 921. See also Benton, *View*, I, 95-102; Stanwood, *Tariff Controversies*, I, 270 ff.; and F. W. Taussig, *Tariff History*, 88-108 (eighth edition).

[7] John Bailey to J. B. Davis, Mar. 8, May 10, 1828, *Mass. Hist. Soc. Proc.*, XLIX, 210, 212.

[8] Story to Ticknor, Feb. 2, 1828, *Story*, I, 534-535; Clay to Crittenden, Feb. 14, 1828, Coleman, *Crittenden*, I, 67.

[9] *Register of Debates*, 20th, 1st, 2471-2472. There is a tabulation of the voting in *Niles*, XXXV, 55-57.

[10] Malone, *Cooper*, 329.

[11] *Life*, 34.

[12] *Works*, III, 50-51; *Senate Journal*, 20th Cong., 1st sess., 355-363.

[13] Adams, *Diary*, VII, 531-536.

[14] Benton, *View*, I, 95; Stanwood, *Tariff Controversies*, I, 259.

[15] *Niles*, XXXV, 201. For various accounts of the proceedings, see *ibid.*, 183-185, 199-203.

[16] Upton, *Military Policy*, 148.

CHAPTER XXX

[1] Calhoun to James Edward Calhoun, May 4, 1828, *Correspondence*, 264-265. See J. Van Deusen, *Economic Bases of Disunion in South Carolina*, 30 ff. Niles, arguing the case for the tariff, cites various instances of lowered prices after the tariff (XXXV, 50, 116, 117, 136, 212), but they are trifling and local and mainly on hearsay. The bulk of the evidence is on the other side. For a review of the whole period, see Channing, *History of the United States*, V, 404 ff.

[2] Alfred H. Stone, "The Cotton Factorage System of the Southern States," *Am. Hist. Rev.*, XX (1915), 557-565.

[3] Ulrich B. Phillips, *History of Transportation in the Eastern Cotton Belt to 1860*, 77-80.

[4] Cf. Robert G. Albion, *Square Riggers on Schedule*, 49-76; and *The Rise of New York Port*, 95-121.

[5] Jervey, *Hayne*, 198.

[6] Calhoun to James Edward Calhoun, May 4, 1828, *Correspondence*, 265.

[7] *Niles*, XXXIV, 288-290; White, *Robert Barnwell Rhett*, 16-17. Born Robert Barnwell Smith, the name was not changed to Rhett until 1837. It is by that name, however, that he is known to history, and he will be so referred to in this work.

[8] Calhoun to Duff Green, July 1, 1828, *Niles*, XXXV, 61. As printed the letter is called an excerpt, and contains a final paragraph branding the tariff unconstitutional. This paragraph was later called an interpolation, *ibid.*, 113, 129, and XXXVI, 377; but there is no doubt that Calhoun did regard the tariff as unconstitutional at this time.

[9] Calhoun to Monroe, July 10, 1828, *Correspondence*, 266-267.

[10] Calhoun to Jackson, July 10, 1828, Jackson's *Correspondence*, III, 415. Cf. Calhoun's *Works*, III, 52-53; and *Life*, 34-35. Hayne wrote Jackson in similar vein two months later, specifically questioning the action of those

Jacksonians who had helped to make the tariff acceptable to New England. Jackson's *Correspondence*, III, 432-435, Sept. 3, 1828.

[11] Herman V. Ames, *State Documents on Federal Relations*, 144-145; Wallace, II, 427.

[12] Dice R. Anderson, *William Branch Giles*, 224-226; David F. Houston, *Critical Study of Nullification in South Carolina*, 70-71.

[13] *Niles*, XXXV, 60, 61-62, 141-142; Chauncey S. Boucher, *Nullification Controversy in South Carolina*, 23.

[14] Houston, *Nullification*, 69-70; Cook, *Williams*, 246-252; *Niles*, XXXV, 47-48; Wallace, II, 410.

[15] *Niles*, XXXVI, 319, XLI, 266.

[16] Library of Congress, Manuscript Register of Withdrawals. A fragment of the page containing the month is cut away, so the entry reads "—— 22, 1828." I have assumed this to be May 22, the day on which Congress adjourned. Before the passage of the tariff he would scarcely have drawn these particular volumes; and he did not return to the city until December 22, after the work in which he would have used them was completed.

[17] Linda Rhea, *Hugh Swinton Legaré*, 95-96. Articles were not signed, but a set of the *Review* with names attached was found among Elliott's papers. The list was published in the *Columbia State*, Nov. 30, 1924.

[18] Calhoun to Bartlett Yancey, July 16, 1828, *Sprunt Historical Publications*, X, #2, 75-76.

[19] *Niles*, XXXV, 203-208; Houston, *Nullification*, 77-79.

[20] The quotation is not correct, though it follows closely the sense of Jefferson's original draft. See Jefferson's *Writings*, Memorial Edition, XVII, 386-387. The word "nullification" does not appear in the Resolutions as adopted.

[21] *Niles*, XXXV, 315-321; also XXXII, 289. Cf. Adams, *Diary*, VIII, 56: "These blusterings of the South Carolina politicians about the dissolution of the Union are used for the purpose of carrying the election by intimidation, or, if they fail in that, of laying the foundation for forcible resistance to the laws to break down or overawe the Administration after the event. It is the counterpart of the New England dissolution project, which began with the purchase of Louisiana and ended by the Hartford Convention." Adams fails to grasp the economic basis of either movement.

[22] *National Journal*, July 25, 1828.

[23] Josiah H. Benton, Jr., *A Notable Libel Case;* Henry Adams, *Documents Relating to New England Federalism.*

CHAPTER XXXI

[1] Marshall to Clay, Nov. 28, 1828, Clay's *Works*, IV, 212.

[2] John E. Wool to Francis Baylies, Dec. 7, 1828, *Mass. Hist. Soc. Proc.*, XLV, 328; Crittenden to Clay, Dec. 3, 1828, Coleman, *Crittenden*, I, 71.

[3] Adams, *Diary*, VIII, 86, 89.

[4] Numerous verbal changes were made by the committee, mostly by way of making the document more concrete in expression; and there were one or two omissions of particularly abstract passages. It could hardly be called "greatly altered," however, as Rhett, who was a member of the committee, informed Crallé in 1854. It is not likely, either, that Calhoun disapproved of

the changes, despite Rhett's assertion that he did. The *Life*, 36, correctly calls them "not material." Compare "R. B. Rhett on the Biography of Calhoun," *Am. Hist. Rev.*, XIII (1908), 310-312. Calhoun's text is printed in *Works*, VI, 1-57.

[5] David R. Williams to Stephen D. Miller, Cook, *Williams*, 258-259.

[6] Thomas Cooper, *Statutes at Large of South Carolina*, I, 273.

[7] *E. g.*, Charleston *Courier*, May 7, 1829, and *Niles*, XXXVI, 324. Also *Life*, 36. In his speech on the Force Bill in 1833 he says Jackson knew his views before the election. "The doctrine which I now sustain, under the present difficulties, I openly avowed and maintained immediately after the act of 1828. . . ." *Works*, II, 217. And compare W. C. Rives to T. W. Gilmer, Dec. 5, 1828: "The last summer's proceedings in South Carolina have utterly annihilated Mr. Calhoun's prospects." *Tyler's Quarterly*, VI (July 1924), 100.

[8] A case was framed to test the constitutionality of the tariff of 1828 when Messrs. Holmes, Mazyck and Gadsden imported a bale of goods from Liverpool and refused to pay the duty. They were sued on their bonds, but the judge refused to admit evidence on any point save the validity of the bonds, thereby excluding the constitutional question. McDuffie defended the case against James L. Petigru. Edwin L. Green, *George McDuffie*, 97.

[9] See above, p. 133.

BIBLIOGRAPHY

ONLY the more important materials have been listed. The critical reader will note the omission of certain items which the circumstances of composition made it impossible to consult. Most important of these are the Lowndes and Clay Papers and the complete file of the *United States Telegraph*. Owing to the hazards of war, these items were withdrawn from the use of scholars before my work on them had been completed. It is believed, however, that the loss is not serious, since the Lowndes and Clay Papers have been fully explored by other writers, and the *Telegraph* is liberally quoted in contemporary papers.

MANUSCRIPTS

Calhoun letters in miscellaneous collections in the Library of Congress.
Calhoun Papers. Clemson College.
Calhoun Papers. Yale University Library.
Confidential Letters, War Office. National Archives.
Indian Office, Letter Books. National Archives.
Letters to the President, War Office. National Archives.
Military Books (War Department letter books). National Archives.
Reports to Congress, War Department. National Archives.
Secretary of War, Document File. National Archives.
Van Buren Papers. Library of Congress.

NEWSPAPERS

Albany (N. Y.) *Argus*.
Alexandria (Va.) *Gazette*.
Baltimore *American*.
Boston *Sentinel*.
Charleston City *Gazette*.
Charleston *Courier*.
Columbia (S. C.) *Telescope*.
Franklin Gazette (Philadelphia).
National Intelligencer (Washington).
National Journal (Washington).
New England Galaxy (Boston).
New York *American*.
New York *Columbian*.
New York *Evening Post*.
New York *Patriot*.
Niles' Weekly Register (Baltimore).
Richmond *Enquirer*.
Southern Patriot and Commercial Advertiser (Charleston).
Virginia Times (Richmond).
Washington *Gazette*.
Washington *Republican*.

443

BOOKS AND PERIODICALS

Abel, Annie H. *History of Indian Consolidation West of the Mississippi.* Annual Report of the American Historical Association, 1906. Vol. I, pp. 233-450. Washington, 1908.

Adams, Henry, ed. *Documents Relating to New England Federalism.* Boston, 1877.

——. *History of the United States of America during the Administrations of Thomas Jefferson and James Madison.* 9 vols. New York, 1889-1891.

——. *Life of Albert Gallatin.* Philadelphia, 1879.

Adams, John Quincy. *Memoirs of John Quincy Adams;* Charles Francis Adams, ed. 12 vols. Philadelphia, 1874-1877.

Adams, John Quincy. *Parties in the United States.* New York., 1941.

Alexander, D. S. "John W. Taylor," *Quarterly Journal of the New York State Historical Association,* Vol. I, No. 2 (January 1920), pp. 14-37.

Alexander, Holmes Moss. *The American Talleyrand; the Career and Contemporaries of Martin Van Buren, Eighth President.* New York, 1935.

Ambler, Charles H. *Thomas Ritchie, a Study in Virginia Politics.* Richmond, 1913.

American State Papers. Documents, Legislative and Executive, of the Congress of the United States. 38 vols. Washington, 1832-1861.

Ames, Herman V., ed. *State Documents on Federal Relations: The States and the United States.* Philadelphia, 1906.

Anderson, Dice R. *William Branch Giles: A Study in the Politics of Virginia and the Nation from 1790 to 1830.* Menasha, Wis., 1914.

Anderson, Frank Maloy. "A Forgotten Phase of the New England Opposition to the War of 1812," *Proceedings of the Mississippi Valley Historical Association,* Vol. VI (1913), pp. 176-188.

Annals of Congress. Debates and Proceedings, First Congress, First Session, March 3, 1789, to Eighteenth Congress, First Session, May 27, 1824. 42 vols. Washington, 1834-1856.

Bacot, D. Huger. "Constitutional Progress and the Struggle for Democracy in South Carolina following the Revolution," *South Atlantic Quarterly,* Vol. XXIV (January 1925), pp. 61-72.

Bacot, D. Huger. "The South Carolina Up Country at the End of the Eighteenth Century," *American Historical Review,* Vol. XXVIII (July 1923), pp. 682-698.

Baker, Elizabeth Feaster. *Henry Wheaton, 1785-1848.* Philadelphia, 1937.

Bancroft, Frederic. *Calhoun and the South Carolina Nullification Movement.* Baltimore, 1928.

Bassett, John Spencer. *The Life of Andrew Jackson.* 2 vols. in 1. New York, 1931.

——. "Major Lewis on the Nomination of Andrew Jackson," *Proceedings of the American Antiquarian Society,* n. s., Vol. XXXIII, part 1 (1923), pp. 12-33.

Bennett, Susan Smythe. "The Cheves Family of South Carolina," *South Carolina Historical and Genealogical Magazine,* Vol. XXXV (July and October 1934), pp. 79-95, 130-152.

Benton, Josiah H., Jr. *A Notable Libel Case.* Boston, 1904.

Benton, Thomas H. *Thirty Years' View.* New York, 1854-1856.

Beveridge, Albert J. *The Life of John Marshall.* 4 vols. Boston and New York, 1916-1919.

Bigelow, Abijah. "Letters of Abijah Bigelow, member of Congress, to his wife, 1810-1815," *Proceedings of the American Antiquarian Society,* n. s., Vol. XL (1931), pp. 305-406.

Boucher, Chauncey Samuel. *The Nullification Controversy in South Carolina.* Chicago, 1916.

Brown, Charles Raymond. *The Northern Confederacy according to the Plans of the "Essex Junto," 1796-1814.* Princeton, 1915.

Brown, Everett S., Ed., *The Missouri Compromises and Presidential Politics, 1820-1825.* St. Louis, 1926.

Bruce, William Cabell. *John Randolph of Roanoke.* 2 vols. New York and London, 1922.

Bryan, Wilhelmus B. *A History of the National Capital.* 2 vols. New York, 1914-1916.

Buckingham, Joseph T. *Personal Memoirs and Recollections of Editorial Life.* 2 vols. Boston, 1852.

Calhoun, John C. *Correspondence of John C. Calhoun;* J. Franklin Jameson, ed. Annual Report of the American Historical Association, 1899. Vol. II. Washington, 1900.

[———.] *Exposition and Protest, Reported by the Special Committee of the House of Representatives, on the Tariff; Read and Ordered to be Printed, Dec. 19th, 1828.* Columbia, S. C., 1829.

———. "John C. Calhoun and the Presidential Campaign of 1824; some unpublished Calhoun letters," Thomas R. Hay, ed., *American Historical Review,* Vol. XL (October 1934, January 1935), pp. 82-96, 287-300.

———. "Letters from John C. Calhoun to Charles Tait," *Gulf States Historical Magazine,* Vol. I (1902), pp. 92-104.

———. *Works of John C. Calhoun;* Richard K. Crallé, ed. 6 vols. N. Y., 1854-1857.

"Carolina." *An Address to the Citizens of North-Carolina, on the Subject of the Presidential Election.* Raleigh, 1823.

Carpenter, Jesse T. *The South as a Conscious Minority, 1789-1861; a Study in Political Thought.* New York, 1930.

Carroll, Eber M. "Politics during the Administration of John Quincy Adams," *South Atlantic Quarterly,* Vol. XXIII (April 1924), pp. 141-154.

"Cassius." *An Examination of Mr. Calhoun's Economy and an Apology for those Members of Congress who Have Been Denounced as Radicals.* 1823.

Catterall, Ralph C. H. *The Second Bank of the United States.* Chicago, 1903.

Chalkley, Lyman, comp. *Chronicles of the Scotch-Irish Settlement in Virginia; Extracted from the Original Court Records of Augusta County, 1745-1800.* 3 vols. Rosslyn, Va., 1912-1913.

Channing, Edward. *History of the United States.* Vols. 4-6. New York, 1937-1938.

Chitwood, Oliver P. *John Tyler, Champion of the Old South.* New York, 1939.

Clark, Bennett Champ. *John Quincy Adams, "Old Man Eloquent."* Boston, 1932.

Clark, Victor S. *History of Manufactures in the United States.* 3 vols. New York, 1929.

——. "The Influence of Manufactures upon Political Sentiment in the United States from 1820 to 1860," *American Historical Review,* Vol. XXII (October 1916), pp. 58-64.

Clay, Henry. *The Works of Henry Clay;* Calvin Colton, ed. 10 vols. New York, 1904.

Cleaves, Freeman. *Old Tippecanoe: William Henry Harrison and His Time.* New York, 1939.

Clemens, William M., ed. *North and South Carolina Marriage Records.* New York, 1927.

Coleman, Mrs. Chapman. *The Life of John J. Crittenden, with Selections from His Correspondence and Speeches.* 2 vols. Philadelphia, 1871.

Conger, John L. "South Carolina and the Early Tariffs," *Mississippi Valley Historical Review,* Vol. V (March 1919), pp. 415-433.

Cook, Harvey Toliver. *The Life and Legacy of David Rogerson Williams.* New York, 1916.

Cooper, Thomas. *Lectures on the Elements of Political Economy.* Columbia, S. C., 1826.

Curtis, George Ticknor. *Life of James Buchanan.* 2 vols. New York, 1883.

——. *Life of Daniel Webster.* 2 vols. New York, 1870.

Day, Clive. 'The Early Development of the American Cotton Manufacture," *Quarterly Journal of Economics,* Vol. XXXIX (May 1925), pp. 450-468.

Derby, Edward George Geoffrey Smith Stanley, 14th Earl of. *Journal of a Tour in America, 1824-1825.* London, 1930.

Dexter, Franklin B. *Biographical Sketches of the Graduates of Yale College with Annals of the College History.* Vol. V. New York, 1911.

——. *Sketch of the History of Yale University.* New York, 1887.

——. "Student Life at Yale College under the First President Dwight," *Proceedings of the American Antiquarian Society,* n. s., Vol. XXVII (1917), pp. 318-335.

Dix, Morgan, comp. *Memoirs of John Adams Dix.* 2 vols. New York, 1883.

Documents in Relation to the Claim of James Johnson for Transportation on the Missouri and Mississippi Rivers. 16th Cong., 2d sess., *House Document* 110. Washington, 1821.

Dodd, William E. "John C. Calhoun," *Statesmen of the Old South,* pp. 91-167. New York, 1911.

——. *The Life of Nathaniel Macon.* Raleigh, 1903.

Drayton, John. *View of South-Carolina, as Respects Her Natural and Civil Concerns.* Charleston, 1802.

Edwards, Ninian. *The Edwards Papers;* E. B. Washburne, ed. Chicago, 1884.

Edwards, Ninian Wirt. *History of Illinois from 1778-1833; and Life and Times of Ninian Edwards.* Springfield, 1870.

Elliott, Charles Winslow. *Winfield Scott: The Soldier and the Man.* New York, 1937.

Fish, Carl Russell. *The Civil Service and the Patronage.* New York, 1905.

Fisher, George Park. *Life of Benjamin Silliman.* 2 vols. New York, 1866.

Fisher, Samuel Herbert. *The Litchfield Law School, 1775-1833.* New Haven, 1933.

Ford, W. C., ed. "Letters to John Brazer Davis," *Proceedings of the Massachusetts Historical Society,* Vol. XLIX (1916), pp. 178-256.

Fraser, Charles. *Reminiscences of Charleston.* Charleston, 1854.

Fuess, Claude M. *Daniel Webster.* 2 vols. Boston, 1930.

[Gales, Joseph.] "Recollections of the Civil History of the War of 1812, by a Contemporary." *National Intelligencer,* June 9, 16, 25, July 14, 30, August 8, 15, 29, September 12, 1857.

Gallatin, Albert. *The Writings of Albert Gallatin;* Henry Adams, ed. 3 vols. Philadelphia, 1879.

Goodman, Warren H. "The Origins of the War of 1812: A Survey of Changing Interpretations," *Mississippi Valley Historical Review,* Vol. XXVIII (September 1941), pp. 171-186.

Goodrich, Samuel G. *Recollections of a Lifetime.* 2 vols. New York, 1856.

Gray, Lewis Cecil. *History of Agriculture in the Southern United States to 1860.* 2 vols. Washington, 1933.

Green, Duff. *Facts and Suggestions, Biographical, Historical, Financial and Political,* New York, 1866.

Green, Edwin L. *George McDuffie.* Columbia, S. C., 1936.

Green, Philip J. "William H. Crawford and the War of 1812," *Georgia Historical Quarterly,* Vol. XXVI (March 1942), pp. 16-39.

Hailperin, Herman. "Pro-Jackson Sentiment in Pennsylvania, 1820-1828," *Pennsylvania Magazine of History and Biography,* Vol. L (July 1926), pp. 193-240.

Hammond, Jabez D. *The History of Political Parties in the State of New-York.* 2 vols. Albany, 1842.

———. *Life and Times of Silas Wright.* Syracuse, 1848.

Harden, Edward J. *The Life of George M. Troup.* Savannah, 1859.

Hay, Thomas Robson. "John C. Calhoun and the Presidential Campaign of 1824," *North Carolina Historical Review,* Vol. XII (January 1935), pp. 20-44.

Holland, William. *The Life and Political Opinions of Martin Van Buren.* Hartford, 1835.

Holst, Hermann von. *John C. Calhoun.* Boston, 1882.

Hooker, Edward. *Diary, 1805-1808.* Annual Report of the American Historical Association, 1896. Vol. I, pp. 842-929. Washington, 1897.

Houston, David F. *A Critical Study of Nullification in South Carolina.* Cambridge, 1896.

Howe, George. *History of the Presbyterian Church in South Carolina.* 2 vols. Columbia, S. C., 1870.

Hungerford, Edward. *The Story of the Baltimore & Ohio Railroad, 1827-1927.* 2 vols. New York, 1928.

Hunt, Gaillard. *John C. Calhoun.* Philadelphia, 1908.

———. "Joseph Gales on the War Manifesto of 1812," *American Historical Review,* Vol. XIII (January 1908), pp. 303-310.

[Hunter, R. M. T.] *Life of John C. Calhoun.* New York, 1843.

Ingersoll, Charles Jared. *Historical Sketch of the Second War between the United States of America, and Great Britain.* 2 vols. Philadelphia, 1845-1849.

Ingham, William A. "Samuel D. Ingham, Secretary of the U. S. Treasury," *Bucks County Historical Society Papers,* Vol. IV (1917), pp. 19-30.

Jackson, Andrew. *Correspondence of Andrew Jackson;* John S. Bassett, ed. 7 vols. Washington, 1926-1935.

James, Marquis. *Andrew Jackson; the Border Captain.* Indianapolis, 1933.

——. *Andrew Jackson; Portrait of a President.* Indianapolis and N. Y., 1937.

Jenkins, John S. *Life of John Caldwell Calhoun.* Auburn and Buffalo, 1850.

Jervey, Theodore D. *Robert Y. Hayne and His Times.* N. Y., 1909.

Journal of the House of Representatives of the United States. 12th-20th Congresses. Washington, 1811-1828.

Journal of the Senate of the United States of America. 12th-20th Congresses. Washington, 1811-1828.

Kennedy, John P. *Memoirs of the Life of William Wirt.* 2 vols. Philadelphia, 1852.

King, Charles R., ed. *The Life and Correspondence of Rufus King.* 6 vols. New York, 1894-1900.

Klein, Philip S. *Pennsylvania Politics, 1817-1832: A Game without Rules.* Philadelphia, 1940.

Lee, Henry. *Report of a Committee of the Citizens of Boston and Vicinity, Opposed to a Further Increase of Duties on Importations.* Boston, 1827.

"Letters between Edward Everett and John McLean," *Proceedings of the Massachusetts Historical Society,* 3d series, Vol. I (1907-1908), pp. 359-393.

Lodge, Henry Cabot. *Life and Letters of George Cabot.* Boston, 1877.

Logan, John Henry. *History of the Upper Country of South Carolina.* Vol. I. Charleston and Columbia, 1859.

Longacre, James B., and Herring, James, eds. *The National Portrait Gallery of Distinguished Americans.* 4 vols. New York and Philadelphia, 1835.

Longstreet, Augustus B. *Master William Mitten.* Macon, Ga., 1889.

——. "Review of Ex-Gov. Perry's Sketch of J. C. Calhoun," *The XIX Century,* Vol. II (January 1870), pp. 618-630.

Lynch, Denis Tilden. *An Epoch and a Man; Martin Van Buren and His Times.* New York, 1929.

McCrady, Edward. *History of South Carolina in the Revolution, 1780-1783.* New York, 1902.

McKenney, Thomas L. *Memoirs, Official and Personal.* New York, 1846.

Madison, James. *Letters and Other Writings of James Madison;* Congressional Edition. 4 vols. Philadelphia, 1865.

Mahan, Captain A. T. *Sea Power in its Relations to the War of 1812.* 2 vols. Boston, 1919.

Malone, Dumas. *The Public Life of Thomas Cooper, 1783-1839.* New Haven, 1926.

Martell, J. S., ed. "A Side Light on Federalist Strategy during the War of 1812," *American Historical Review,* Vol. XLIII (April 1938), pp. 553-566.

Mason, Armistead Thomson. "Letters, 1813-1818," *William and Mary College Quarterly Historical Magazine,* Vol. XXIII (April 1915), pp. 228-239.

Mason, Jeremiah. *Memoir and Correspondonce of Jeremiah Mason;* G. S. Hillard, ed. Cambridge, 1873.

Mayo, Bernard. *Henry Clay; Spokesman of the New West.* Boston, 1937.

Meigs, William M. *The Life of Thomas Hart Benton.* Philadelphia, 1904.

———. *The Life of John Caldwell Calhoun.* 2 vols. New York, 1917.

Meriwether, Robert L. *The Expansion of South Carolina, 1729-1765.* Kingsport, Tenn., 1940.

Meyer, Leland Winfield. *The Life and Times of Colonel Richard M. Johnson of Kentucky.* New York, 1932.

Mills, Elijah H. "Letters," *Proceedings of the Massachusetts Historical Society,* Vol. XIX (1881-1882), pp. 12-53.

Mills, Robert. *Atlas of the State of South Carolina.* Baltimore, 1825.

———. *Statistics of South Carolina.* Charleston, 1826.

Mitman, Carl W. *The Beginning of the Mechanical Transport Era in America.* Annual Report of the Smithsonian Institution, 1929, pp. 507-558.

Monroe, James. *The Writings of James Monroe;* S. Hamilton, ed. 7 vols. New York, 1901.

———. "Monroe on the Adams-Clay 'Bargain,'" *American Historical Review,* Vol. XLII (January 1937), pp. 273-276.

Morgan, George. *The Life of James Monroe.* Boston, 1921.

Morison, Samuel Eliot. *The Life and Letters of Harrison Gray Otis, Federalist, 1765-1848.* 2 vols. Boston, 1913.

Morse, Edward L., ed. *Samuel F. B. Morse, His Letters and Journals.* 2 vols. Boston, 1914.

Moultrie, William. *Memoirs of the American Revolution, so far as it Related to the States of North and South Carolina, and Georgia.* New York, 1802.

Nettels, Curtis. "The National Cost of the Inland Frontier, 1820-1830," *Transactions of the Wisconsin Academy of Sciences, Arts and Letters,* Vol. XXV (1930), pp. 1-37.

Newsome, Albert R. *The Presidential Election of 1824 in North Carolina.* James Sprunt Historical Studies, Vol. XXIII, No. 1, Chapel Hill, 1939.

———, ed. "Correspondence of Calhoun, McDuffie and Charles Fisher, relative to the Presidential Campaign of 1824," *North Carolina Historical Review,* Vol. VII (October 1930), pp. 477-504.

O'Neall, John Belton. *Biographical Sketches of the Bench and Bar of South Carolina.* 2 vols. Charleston, 1859.

Orne, Henry. *The Letters of Columbus; originally Published in the Boston Bulletin.* Boston, 1829.

Parks, Joseph Howard. *Felix Grundy, Champion of Democracy.* University, La., 1940.

Perry, Benjamin F. *Reminiscences of Public Men.* Philadelphia, 1883.

———. *Reminiscences of Public Men.* 2d series. Greenville, S. C., 1889.

Phillips, Ulrich B. *Georgia and State Rights.* Annual Report of the American Historical Association, 1901. Vol. II. Washington, 1902.

———. "The Course of the South to Secession," *Georgia Historical Quarterly,* Vol. XX (December 1936), pp. 276-306; Vol. XXI (March, June, September, December, 1937), pp. 1-49, 113-141, 217-238, 309-344; Vol. XXII (March 1938), pp. 41-71.

Pinckney, Charles Cotesworth. "John C. Calhoun, From a Southern Standpoint," *Lippincott's Monthly Magazine,* Vol. LXII (July 1898), pp. 81-90.

Pinckney, Gustavus M. *Life of John C. Calhoun.* Charleston, 1903.

Pitkin, Timothy. *A Statistical View of the Commerce of the United States of America.* New Haven, 1835.

Plumer, William, Jr. "Extracts from the Journal of William Plumer, Jr.," *Pennsylvania Magazine of History and Biography,* Vol. VI (1882), pp. 357-359.

———. *Life of William Plumer.* Boston, 1857.

Poore, Ben Perley. *Perley's Reminiscences of Sixty Years in the National Metropolis.* 2 vols. Philadelphia, 1886.

Porter, Kenneth W. *John Jacob Astor, Business Man.* 2 vols. Harvard Studies in Business History, Vol. I. Cambridge, 1931.

Pratt, Julius W. *Expansionists of 1812.* New York, 1925.

Prentiss, Hervey P. *Timothy Pickering as the Leader of New England Federalism, 1800-1815.* Reprinted from the *Essex Institute Historical Collections* of January and April 1933 and April 1934.

Quincy, Edmund. *Life of Josiah Quincy.* Boston, 1867.

Quincy, Josiah [P.] *Figures of the Past; From the Leaves of Old Journals.* Boston, 1883.

Ramsay, David. *History of South-Carolina, from its First Settlement in 1670, to the Year 1808.* 2 vols. Charleston, 1809.

Ravenel, Harriott Horry. *Life and Times of William Lowndes of South Carolina, 1782-1822.* Boston and New York, 1901.

Register of Debates in Congress. 14 vols. in 29. Washington, 1825-1837.

Report of the Select Committee . . . to inquire into the Contract between the United States and Elijah Mix. 17th Cong., 1st sess., *House Report* 109. Washington, 1822.

Report . . . on a letter of John C. Calhoun . . . asking an investigation of his conduct while Secretary of War. 19th Cong., 2d sess., *House Report* 79. Washington, 1827.

Revill, Janie, comp. *Compilation of the Original Lists of Protestant Immigrants to South Carolina, 1763-1773.* Columbia, S. C., 1939.

Rezneck, Samuel. "The Depression of 1819-1822, A Social History," *American Historical Review,* Vol. XXXIX (October 1933), pp. 28-47.

Rhea, Linda. *Hugh Swinton Legaré, a Charleston Intellectual.* Chapel Hill, 1934.

Rippy, James F. *Joel R. Poinsett, Versatile American.* Durham, 1935.

Rives, William C. "Letters, 1823-29, to Thomas Gilmer," *Tyler's Quarterly Historical and Genealogical Magazine,* Vol. V (April 1924), pp. 223-237; Vol. VI (July and October 1924), pp. 6-15, 97-105.

Roane, Spencer. "Letters, 1788-1822." *New York Public Library Bulletin,* Vol. X (1906), pp. 167-180.

Rodenbough, Theophilus F., and Haskin, William L. *The Army of the United States.* New York, 1896.

Roseboom, Eugene H. "Ohio in the Presidential Election of 1824," *Ohio Archaeological & Historical Quarterly,* Vol. XXVI (April 1917), pp. 153-225.

Rowe, Kenneth W. *Mathew Carey: A Study in American Economic Development.* Johns Hopkins University Studies in Historical and Political Science, Vol. LI, no. 4. Baltimore, 1933.

Salley, Alexander Samuel, Jr. *The Calhoun Family of South Carolina.* Reprinted from *South Carolina Historical and Genealogical Magazine*, Vol. VII (April and July 1906).

————. "The Grandfather of John C. Calhoun," *South Carolina Historical and Genealogical Magazine*, Vol. XXXIX (January 1938), p. 50.

————., ed. *Journal of the General Assembly of South Carolina, 1776.* 2 vols. Columbia, 1906-1909.

Sargent, Nathan. *Public Men and Events from the Commencement of Mr. Monroe's Administration, in 1817, to the Close of Mr. Fillmore's Administration, in 1853.* 2 vols. Philadelphia, 1875.

Saunders, Romulus M. "Letters of Romulus M. Saunders to Bartlett Yancy, 1821-28," A. R. Newsome, ed., *North Carolina Historical Review*, Vol. VIII (October 1931), pp. 427-462.

Schaper, William A. *Sectionalism and Representation in South Carolina.* Annual Report of the American Historical Association, 1900. Vol. I, pp. 237-463. Washington, 1901.

Schauinger, Joseph Herman. "William Gaston: Southern Statesman," *North Carolina Historical Review*, Vol. XVIII (April 1941), pp. 99-132.

————. "Alexander Contee Hanson, Federalist Partisan," *Maryland Historical Magazine*, Vol. XXXV (December 1940), pp. 354-364.

Schurz, Carl. *Life of Henry Clay.* 2 vols. Boston, 1892.

Scott, Winfield. *Memoirs of Lieut.-General Scott, LL. D.* New York, 1864.

[————.] *Presidential Election.* Pieces copied from the Richmond Enquirer, having been published at different periods of the year 1823.

Sears, Louis M. *Jefferson and the Embargo.* Durham, 1927.

Seaton, Josephine. *William Winston Seaton of the "National Intelligencer."* Boston, 1871.

Shipp, John E. D. *Giant Days; or, The Life and Times of William H. Crawford.* Americus, Ga., 1909.

Simms, Henry H. *Life of John Taylor.* Richmond, 1932.

Slider, Thomas P. *Memoirs of General William Butler.* Atlanta, 1885.

Smith, Culver H. "Propaganda Technique in the Jackson Campaign of 1828," *East Tennessee Historical Society Publications*, No. VI (1934), pp. 44-66.

Smith, Margaret Bayard. *The First Forty Years of Washington Society;* Gaillard Hunt, ed. New York, 1906.

Smith, Theodore C. "War Guilt in 1812," *Proceedings of the Massachusetts Historical Society*, Vol. LXIV (1932), pp. 319-345.

Smith, William Ernest. *The Francis Preston Blair Family in Politics.* 2 vols. New York, 1933.

Sparks, William Henry. *The Memories of Fifty Years.* Philadelphia, 1870.

Spaulding, Oliver Lyman. *The United States Army in War and Peace.* New York, 1937.

Stanwood, Edward. *American Tariff Controversies in the Nineteenth Century.* 2 vols. Boston and New York, 1903.

————. *A History of the Presidency;* new edition, rev. by Charles Knowles Bolton. 2 vols. Boston and New York, 1928.

Starke, Colonel W. Pinkney. *Account of Calhoun's Early Life.* Annual Report of the American Historical Association, 1899. Vol. II, pp. 65-89. Washington, 1900.

Stenberg, Richard R. "Jackson, Buchanan, and the 'Corrupt Bargain'

Calumny," *Pennsylvania Magazine of History and Biography,* Vol. LVIII (January 1934), pp. 61-85.

———. "Jackson's 'Rhea letter' Hoax," *Journal of Southern History,* Vol. II (1936), pp. 480-496.

Stephenson, Nathaniel W. "Calhoun and the Divine Right of the Majority," *Lectures on Typical Americans and Their Problems.* Scripps College Papers, No. 3. Claremont, Calif., 1930.

———. "Calhoun, 1812, and After," *American Historical Review,* Vol. XXXI (July 1926), pp. 701-707.

Stokes, Anson Phelps. *Memorials of Eminent Yale Men.* Vol. II, "John Caldwell Calhoun," pp. 196-206. New Haven, 1914.

Stone, Alfred Holt. "Cotton Factorage System of the Southern States," *American Historical Review,* Vol. XX (April 1915), pp. 557-565.

Stone, Richard Gabriel. *Hezekiah Niles as an Economist.* Johns Hopkins University Studies in Historical and Political Science, Vol. LI. Baltimore, 1933.

Story, William W. *Life and Letters of Joseph Story.* 2 vols. Boston, 1851.

Styron, Arthur. *The Cast-iron Man; John C. Calhoun and American Democracy.* New York and Toronto, 1935.

Sullivan, William. *The Public Men of the Revolution.* Philadelphia, 1847.

[Swift, Joseph G.?] *Measures, not Men.* New York, 1823.

Swift, Joseph G. *The Memoirs of Gen. Joseph Gardner Swift.* Worcester, 1890.

Swisher, Carl Brent. *Roger B. Taney.* New York, 1935.

Taggart, Samuel. "Letters, 1803-1814," George H. Haynes, ed., *Proceedings of the American Antiquarian Society,* n. s., Vol. XXXIII (April and October 1923), pp. 113-226, 297-438.

Taylor, John. "Letters," *The John P. Branch Historical Papers of Randolph-Macon College,* Vol. II (June 1908), pp. 253-353.

Thomas, Ebenezer S. *Reminiscences of the Last Sixty-five Years.* 2 vols. Hartford, 1840.

Turnbull, Robert J. *The Crisis: or, Essays on the Usurpations of the Federal Government.* By "Brutus." Charleston, 1827.

Turner, Frederick J. *Rise of the New West.* The American Nation, Vol. XIV. New York, 1906.

Tyler, Lyon G. *The Letters and Times of the Tylers.* 3 vols. Richmond, 1884-1896.

Upton, Emory. *The Military Policy of the United States.* Washington, 1917.

Van Buren, Martin. *The Autobiography of Martin Van Buren;* John C. Fitzpatrick, ed. Annual Report of the American Historical Association, 1918. Vol. II. Washington, 1920.

———. *Inquiry into the Origin and Course of Political Parties in the United States; edited by his sons.* New York, 1867.

Van Deusen, Glyndon G. *The Life of Henry Clay.* Boston, 1937.

Van Deusen, John G. *Economic Bases of Disunion in South Carolina.* New York, 1928.

The Virginia Report of 1799-1800, touching the Alien and Sedition Laws; together with the Virginia Resolutions of December 21, 1798, the Debate and Proceedings thereon in the House of Delegates of Virginia, and Several Other Documents Illustrative of the Report and Resolutions. Richmond, 1850.

Waddell, Joseph Addison. *Annals of Augusta County, Virginia.* Richmond, 1886.

Wade, John D. *Augustus Baldwin Longstreet; a Study of the Development of Culture in the South.* New York, 1924.

Wallace, David Duncan. *History of South Carolina.* 4 vols. New York, 1934.

Wandell, Samuel H., and Minnegerode, Meade. *Aaron Burr.* 2 vols. New York and London, 1925.

Warren, Charles. *Jacobin and Junto, or Early American Politics as Viewed in the Diary of Dr. Nathaniel Ames, 1758-1822.* Cambridge, 1931.

Watkins, James L. *King Cotton.* New York, 1908.

[Watterston, George.] *Letters from Washington.* Washington, 1818.

Webster, Daniel. *The Writings and Speeches of Daniel Webster;* National Edition. Boston, 1903.

Weed, Thurlow. *Autobiography of Thurlow Weed;* Harriet A. Weed, ed. Boston, 1883.

Weisenburger, Francis P. *The Life of John McLean.* Columbus, 1937.

Wesley, Edgar B. *Guarding the Frontier; a Study of Frontier Defense from 1815 to 1825.* Minneapolis, 1935.

White, Laura A. *Robert Barnwell Rhett: Father of Secession.* New York, 1931.

Winthrop, Robert C. "Memoir of Hon. Nathan Appleton," *Proceedings of the Massachusetts Historical Society,* Vol. V (1861), pp. 249-307.

Wise, Henry A. *Seven Decades of the Union.* Philadelphia, 1872.

Wold, Ansel, comp. *Biographical Directory of the American Congress, 1774-1927.* Washington, 1928.

Wolfe, John H. *Jeffersonian Democracy in South Carolina.* Chapel Hill, 1940.

Zimmerman, James F. *Impressment of American Seamen.* New York, 1925.

PERSONAL ACKNOWLEDGMENTS

The bulk of the research and much of the writing of this volume was done at the Library of Congress, and my grateful thanks are hereby tendered to all those members of the library's staff—in the Reference Division, the Manuscript Division, the Periodical Division, the Rare Book Room, and the Reading Rooms—who helped to make my labors profitable and pleasant. My obligation to the National Archives and its competent staff is also great. To Yale University I am indebted for both manuscript material and illustrations; and to the authorities of Clemson College for permission to use the extensive Calhoun collection housed there.

Professor A. G. Holmes, of the Clemson faculty, and Mrs. Holmes have aided me almost from the beginning of my work, giving me generous assistance with the Calhoun papers, advice and counsel in matters of local history, and valuable criticism of my completed manuscript. The book was also reviewed in manuscript by Professor George E. Mowry of the University of North Carolina, and from the standpoint of the political scientist by Professor Ethan P. Allen of the State University of Iowa. To each of these, my thanks for encouragement and advice. Another who made my task easier was Miss Carolyn Feeley of Clemson, South Carolina, who copied many of the Calhoun letters for me.

Through all the years this book has been in process my wife has been a faithful and understanding collaborator, serving as need arose in the varying capacities of research assistant, typist, editor, proofreader and critic.

C. M. W.

INDEX

INDEX

A. B. plot, 262-263, 292-293.

Abbeville, 25, 39, 42, 54, 64, 72, 125, 182, 186, 316, 319.

Abolition, 176, 196. *See also* Slavery.

Adams, John, 27, 143; death of, 341.

Adams, John Quincy, 144, 146, 147, 148, 157, 178, 179, 180, 185, 189, 193, 231, 253, 257, 272, 276, 279-280, 282, 299, 330, 336-337, 343, 360, 361, 371; Minister to Russia, 78; Secretary of State, 138, 143; defends Jackson, 160-162; Calhoun trusts War Department affairs to, 180; on slavery, 196; offers Calhoun French mission, 200; campaigns for Presidency, 211-212; and patronage, 211-212, 327, 332, 361-362; on War Department attacks, 226-227; bids for Calhoun's support, 227-228; Report on Weights and Measures, 228; on Florida episode, 233-235; relations with J. W. Taylor, 236; relations with Calhoun, 238, 245-246, 261-262, 280-281; Calhoun's attitude toward, 240-242; attacks Calhoun, 277-278; and Calhoun's Vice Presidential aspirations, 299-301; political bargaining, 302-303; understanding with Clay, 302-306; charges against Calhoun, 304-306; and "corrupt bargain," 305 ff.; offers Clay State Department, 308; inauguration of, 309-310; inaugural address, 310-311; Cabinet appointments, 310-311; forms political party, 317-319; first annual message, 320-321; Onslow-Patrick Henry controversy, 333-336; and tariff agitation, 353; controversy with New England Federalists, 385-386; defeat of, 387-388.

Adams, Mrs. J. Q., 208.

Address to the People of North Carolina, 275.

Agriculture, 121, 122, 123, 191, 286; Calhoun's interest in, 231, 257.

Albany, 63, 165.

Alexander, Czar of Russia, 78.

Alexandria, D. C., 84.

Alexandria *Gazette*, 337, 344.

Alien and Sedition Acts, 97, 290, 381, 384, 395.

Alston, Joseph, 47, 181.

Ambrister, Robert, 158, 177.

Amelia Island, 157, 158.

American Fur Company, 150, 168, 221-222, 250, 251, 252.

"American System," 116, 131, 136; proclaimed by Clay, 288. *See also* Tariff, Internal improvements.

Annapolis, 85.

Arbuthnot, Alexander, 158, 177.

Archer, Major, 230.

Argus of Western America, 358.

Armstrong, John, Secretary of War, 75; resigns, 94.

Army, inadequacy of, 60; debates on increasing, 61; reduction of, 179, 206, 210; attacked in Congress, 203; Calhoun's plan for reduction of, 223-224; reorganization of, 230; reorganization attacked, 252. *See also* Military policy.

Artillery School, 172, 298.

Astor, John Jacob, 78, 150, 158, 222, 251; objects to Indian policy, 168.

Atkinson, Colonel Henry, 183-184, 215.

Augusta, Ga., 15, 182, 315.

Augusta County, Va., 12.

Bache, Richard, 232.

Bacon, Ezekiel, 55.

Bailey, John, 277, 278, 321, 369.

Baldwin, Henry, 189, 280.

Ballston Springs, N. Y., 217.

Baltimore, 68, 92.

457

Baltimore and Ohio Railroad, 366.

Bank, question debated as war measure, 94-96, 98-100; crisis, 175-176.

Bank of Missouri, 183, 185.

Bank of the United States, 138, 175, 176, 184, 190, 286; Calhoun sponsors incorporation of, 108-111.

Barbour, James, 192, 277, 308, 318; State Rights leader, 191; confers with Adams, 303; Secretary of War, 311, 317; and Mix contract, 345; Minister to England, 362.

Barbour, Philip, 191, 348; elected Speaker, 236.

Barlow, Joel, 79.

Barney, Commodore Joshua, 92.

Barron, John, 209.

Barry, William T., 184.

Barton, David, 221.

Bath, 142, 319. *See also* Willington, S. C.

Bayard, James A., 78.

Beaufort, S. C., 181.

Bedford Springs, Pa., Calhoun visits, 231-232.

Beecher, Lyman, 233.

Bell, Samuel, 354.

Belle Fontaine, Mo., 167, 168.

Benton, Thomas Hart, 273; attacks Missouri expedition, 185, 198; attacks Florida treaty, 210; and American Fur Company, 221-222; secures abolition of Indian trading houses, 250-251; critic of Adams, 327; and patronage, 331; tariff vote in 1828, 372.

Berlin and Milan Decrees, 56, 81.

Bernard, General Simon, 164, 171.

Berrien, John M., 344.

Bibb, Dr. William W., 50, 114, 159; member of War Mess, 54; Calhoun's second, 85.

Binns, John, 361.

Bladensburg, battle of, 92.

Blair, Francis P., 303, 321.

Blockade, 77, 87.

Bonaparte, Jerome, 60.

Bonaparte, Napoleon, 42, 58, 59, 86; Calhoun interested in career of, 38;

Bonaparte, Napoleon—*Cont.*
    Russian campaign, 78; abdication, 92.

Bonneau, J. E., 268.

Bonneau's Ferry, 34, 50, 51; Calhoun visits, 42.

Boston, 70; Calhoun visits, 217-218.

Boston Manufacturing Co., 120.

Bowie, George, 43; Calhoun studies law with, 41.

Braddock, General Edward, 13, 17.

Branch, John, 324, 328.

British, threaten Washington, 83-84; propose terms, 93-94. *See also* Great Britain.

Brooke, Francis, 362.

Brooklyn, 218.

Brown, General Jacob, 216, 233; commands Northern Division, 149; consulted on Army reorganization, 152; joins Calhoun on tour, 217; contributes to Army reorganization, 224, 229; ranking general, 229; illness of, 261-262; intermediary between Adams and Calhoun, 299; and election of 1824, 302, 303; wants Clinton in Adams' Cabinet, 308.

Brown, James, 247.

Bucktails, 237.

Buel, Jesse, 354.

Buffalo, N. Y., 217.

Bulfinch, Charles, 269.

Bull, Lieutenant Governor ——, 20.

Bureau organization, 152.

Burr, Aaron, 33, 37, 148.

Butler, General William, 72, 80.

Cabinet, Monroe's, 138-141, 142-146; Adams', appointments to, 310-311.

Caldwell, Major John, in Provincial Congress, 22.

Caldwell, Martha. *See* Calhoun, Martha Caldwell.

Calhoun, Andrew Pickens, son of John Caldwell Calhoun, 142, 265, 340, 342, 358; birth of, 53.

Calhoun, Anna Maria, daughter of

Calhoun, Anna Maria—*Cont.*
John Caldwell Calhoun, 142, 265,
340, 342.

Calhoun, Catherine, sister of John
Caldwell Calhoun, marries Moses
Waddel, 26-27.

Calhoun, Catherine Montgomery,
grandmother of John Caldwell Calhoun, 12, 14, 16.

Calhoun, Elizabeth, daughter of John
Caldwell Calhoun, birth of, 186;
death of, 208-209.

Calhoun, Ezekiel, uncle of John Caldwell Calhoun, 12, 13; land grants to,
15; moves to Waxhaw, 17.

Calhoun, Floride (Mrs. John Caldwell
Calhoun), 35, 48-49, 50, 101, 177,
186, 217; courtship of by Calhoun,
42-43, 48-49; marriage to Calhoun,
51-52; as hostess, 152, 173; accompanies Calhoun on southern trip,
180-182; popularity, 208-209; character of, 264 ff. *See also* Calhoun
and his family.

Calhoun, Floride, daughter of John
Caldwell Calhoun, birth of, 87-88;
death of, 101-102.

Calhoun, Floride Bonneau (Mrs. John
Ewing Colhoun), cousin and mother-in-law of John Caldwell Calhoun,
34, 48, 49, 186; at Newport, 34-35;
character of, 50-51, 267-269; pur-
chases Georgetown home, 268.

Calhoun, James, uncle of John Caldwell Calhoun, 12, 13; leads party of
refugees, 15; death of, 16.

Calhoun, James, brother of John
Caldwell Calhoun, 27, 44, 50, 213,
380.

Calhoun, James Edward, cousin and
brother-in-law of John Caldwell
Calhoun, 35, 231, 268, 356.

Calhoun, James Edward, son of John
Caldwell Calhoun, 358; birth of,
340.

Calhoun, John Caldwell, ancestry of,
12 ff.; birth of, 12, 22; learns politics from father, 24; early education, 25-26; studies with Moses

Calhoun, John Caldwell—*Cont.*
Waddel, 26; early interests in politics, 27; decides to study law, 27;
enters Waddel's academy, 27; studies at Yale, 29-36; undergraduate
interests, 31; elected to Phi Beta
Kappa, 31; adheres to Jeffersonians,
32-33, 37; illness prevents attendance at commencement, 33-34; visits Newport and Boston, 35; reads
law with H. W. De Saussure, 35;
enters Litchfield Law School, 35;
travels to New England with Mrs.
F. B. Calhoun, 35-36; arrives in
Litchfield, 36; studies at Litchfield
Law School, 36-39; resumes study
with De Saussure, 38; dislikes law,
38; visits Abbeville, 39; thinks
Charleston corrupt, 41; completes
legal training at Abbeville, 41; denounces Britain over *Chesapeake* attack, 42; admitted to bar, 42;
courtship, 42-43, 48-49; forms law
partnership with Patrick Noble, 43;
law practice of, 43-44; doubts value
of Jefferson's embargo, 44; elected
to state legislature, 46-47; attends
party caucus, 47; named aide to
governor, 47; elected trustee of
South Carolina College, 47; participates in constitutional compromise
in South Carolina, 48; visits Bonneau's Ferry, 48; attends commencement at Waddel's academy,
49-50; receives property settlement
from mother-in-law, 50-51; elected
to Twelfth Congress, 51; favors war
with England, 51; marriage to
Floride Calhoun, 51-52; buys plantation "Bath," 52; enters Congress,
53; intimacy with William Lowndes,
54; joins War Mess, 54; on Foreign
Relations Committee, 55, 72; drafts
Foreign Relations report, 55-56;
answers Randolph, 58-59; defends
embargo, 63; introduces war bill,
64; reads war report, 64; Chairman
of Foreign Relations Committee,
64, 81; and young Republicans, 69;

Calhoun, John Caldwell—*Cont.*

attempts to compromise quarrel with New England, June 1812, 70-71; achieves national prominence, 71; elected to Thirteenth Congress without opposition, 71-72; friendship with Cheves and Lowndes, 73; defends merchant class, 73; is homesick, 73-74; appeals to Federalists for unity, 75; opposes restrictive system, 76; becomes administration spokesman, 82; defends Madison, 83; opposes embargo but votes for it, 84; near duel with Grosvenor, 85; defends war, 86; declines to run for Speakership, 87; speaks on loan bill, 89; introduces bill to repeal restrictive system, 90; speaks against restrictive system, 91; illness, 94; refuses to sponsor administration bank bill, 94-95; proposes own bank bill, 95; bill defeated, 96; supports military draft bill, 97; seeks Webster's collaboration on bank bill, 99; influence in Fourteenth Congress, 103-104; heads Committee on National Currency, 104; proposes military program, 105-106; fears third war with England, 107; sponsors incorporation of Second Bank of the United States, 108-111; supports Compensation Act, 112-113; on the importance of Congress, 112-113, 129-130; supports Monroe for Presidency, 114-115; speaks in favor of protective tariff, 1816, 119-122; considered for Treasury, 124; attacked for support of Compensation Act, 124-125; re-elected to Fifteenth Congress, 125; opposes repeal of Compensation Act, 128-130; champions internal improvement bill, 132-136; antagonizes Lewis Williams, 136; attacks War Department administration, 136-137; Secretary of War, 139 ff.; and his family, 142, 180, 186, 208-209, 232, 264-271, 340-343, 357-358; in Mon-

Calhoun, John Caldwell—*Cont.*

roe's Cabinet, 144-145; reorganizes War Department, 151-152; makes southern trip, 1818, 153-154; and Seminole campaign, 155-163; approves occupation of Amelia Island, 157; disapproves Jackson's Florida conduct, 161-163; military policy, 164-174; outlines Indian policy, 168-170; opposed by fur-trading interests, 170; buys Washington home, 173; financial difficulties, 173, 230-231, 270; tries to save bank, 176; aids Jackson's defense, 178; breach with Crawford, 179; trusts War Department affairs to Adams, 180; accompanies Monroe on southern trip, 1819, 180-182; inspects fortification sites, 180-182; relations with Adams, 185, 238, 240-242, 245-246; serious illness of, 186-187; on Missouri Compromise, 195-196, 220; offered French mission by Adams, 200; and Mix contract, 203-205, 344-346; military policy debated, 206-208; figures in Adams' plans, 212; growing political strength, 213-214; political views, 1820, 214; and Johnson contracts, 214-216; visits Jefferson, 215; northern trip, 1820, 216-219; repudiates sectionalism, 219; plan for Army reduction, 223-224; military policy attacked, 225-227; blames Crawford for opposition to military program, 228; reduces Army, 229-230; interest in agriculture, 231; visits Bedford Springs, 231-232; on Jackson's conduct in Florida, 233-235; opposes J. W. Taylor for Speaker, 235-236; Presidential candidate, 238-239, 240 ff.; seeks defeat of Crawford, 241; nationalist attitude of, 243-244; qualifications for Presidency, 247-248; attacked in Congress, 249-250; interferes in state politics, 256-257; supported by Washington *Republican,* 257-259; attacked by Washing-

Calhoun, John Caldwell—*Cont.*
ton *Gazette,* 258; carries fight to
Crawford, 262-263; character of,
265-267; social life, 266-267; religious views, 268-269; unskilled as
politician, 270-271; campaign for
Presidency, 272-284; attacked by
Adams, 277-278; nominated by
South Carolina legislature, 279;
Adams' attitude toward, 280-281;
nominated for Vice Presidency
in Pennsylvania, 283; withdraws
candidacy, 283-284; on tariff of
1824, 285-286; connection with
A. B. plot, 292-293; and removal
of Cherokees, 293-296; and Indian migration, 296-297; achievements in War Department, 297-
298; negotiations with Adams on
Vice Presidency, 299-300; seeks
Vice Presidency, 299-301; elected
Vice President, 301; rivalry with
Clay, 302, 326; neutrality of, 304-
305; inaugurated as Vice President,
309; on functions of Senate, 309-
310; denounces Adams-Clay deal,
313-314; sells Washington home,
315; as Vice President, 315 ff.; political prospects, 315-317; com-
ments on Adams message, 321; attitude toward Vice Presidency, 322;
appoints committees, 322-323; attacked for committee appointments,
323-324; alliance with Van Buren,
324; opposes Panama mission, 326;
goes into opposition, 326-327; and
United States Telegraph, 328;
Onslow-Patrick Henry controversy,
333-336; makes common cause with
Jackson, 337-338; moves home to
Clergy Hall, 340-341; and North-
South alliance, 347-350; defeats
Woolens bill, 350-351; Radicals
seek elimination of, 351; on tariff
agitation, 356-357; position in
party, 362-364; correspondence
with Jackson on Seminole affair,
363-364; and tariff negotiations,
1828, 369; and South Carolina reac-

Calhoun, John Caldwell—*Cont.*
tion to tariff, 372-374; seeks constitutional solution for tariff question,
378-384; warns Jackson South
wants tariff reform, 379; accused of
disunion by National Republicans,
384-385; re-elected Vice President,
387; rivalry with Van Buren, 388;
becomes leader of State Rights
party, 390; writes *South Carolina
Exposition and Protest,* 390-397;
renounces economic nationalism,
397-398.

Calhoun, John Caldwell, son of John
Caldwell Calhoun, 342, 358; birth
of, 265; illness of, 340-341.

Calhoun, John Ewing, cousin and
brother-in-law of John Caldwell
Calhoun, 35, 142, 213, 231, 256,
260, 264, 268, 270, 340, 342-343.

Calhoun, Joseph, cousin of John Caldwell Calhoun, 23, 51, 124.

Calhoun, Lucretia, niece of John
Caldwell Calhoun, 358.

Calhoun, Martha Caldwell, mother of
John Caldwell Calhoun, marries
Patrick Calhoun, 22; death of, 29.

Calhoun, Martha Cornelia, daughter
of John Caldwell Calhoun, 342;
birth of, 270.

Calhoun, Patrick, grandfather of John
Caldwell Calhoun, 12.

Calhoun, Patrick, father of John Caldwell Calhoun, 12; visits Waxhaw,
14; land grants to, 15; returns after
Indian massacre, 16; Captain of
Rangers, 17; marries Jean Craighead, 17; surveyor, 18; takes part
in "Regulation," 21; sponsors protest, 21; elected to colonial assembly, 21-22; marries Martha Caldwell, 22; member of first Provincial
Congress, 22; elected to second Provincial Congress, 22; increases land
holdings, 23; acquires slaves, 23;
activities in Revolution, 23; objects
to Federal Constitution, 23-24;
death of, 26.

Calhoun, Patrick, brother of John Caldwell Calhoun, 27, 44, 49.

Calhoun, Patrick, son of John Caldwell Calhoun, 265, 340, 342; birth of, 231.

Calhoun, Rebecca, cousin of John Caldwell Calhoun, 17.

Calhoun, William, uncle of John Caldwell Calhoun, 12, 13; land grants to, 15; sponsors protest, 21; signs resolutions of Provincial Congress, 22.

Calhoun, William, brother of John Caldwell Calhoun, 44, 49, 50, 142, 213, 270, 358.

Calhoun family, 12; migrates to Virginia, 12; migrates to South Carolina, 14; land grants to, 15; backs John Caldwell Calhoun's education, 29.

Calhoun settlement, South Carolina, 15.

Calhoun's Creek, 15.

Callava, Colonel José, 233.

Cambreleng, Churchill C., 251, 351.

Campbell, George Washington, Secretary of Treasury, 88.

Campbell, James W., 345, 346.

Canada, 74.

Canals. *See* Internal improvements.

Cannon, Newton, 206, 207.

Cardozo, Jacob N., *Notes on Political Economy*, 382.

Carey, Mathew, 188, 352, 354.

Carmel Academy, Calhoun attends, 25-26.

Carroll, Charles, of Carrollton, 366.

Cass, Lewis, 169.

Castlereagh, Lord, 85-86.

Catawba Path, 14.

Catawba River, 14.

Caucus, 1812, 64; 1816, 114-115; 1820, 211; 1824, 281-282.

Cavaliers, 19.

Chambers, E. F., 327.

Chambers, Colonel Talbot, 168.

Charleston, 11, 15, 16, 54, 68, 181; dominates colony, 20; economic life of, 40-41.

Charleston and Hamburg Railway, 376.

Charleston *Mercury*, 353, 355.

Chef Menteur, 199.

Cheraw, 319.

Cherokees, treaty with South Carolina, 13-14; massacre by, 16; removal of, 293-296.

Chesapeake affair, 41-42, 56, 64.

Chesapeake and Delaware Canal, 132, 136.

Chesapeake and Ohio Canal, 365, 366.

Cheves, Langdon, 55, 62, 70, 72, 84, 104, 187, 190; in South Carolina legislature, 47; career of, 54; member of War Mess, 54; defends merchant class, 73; elected Speaker, 87; defeats bank bill, 98-99; becomes president of United States Bank, 176.

Cheves, Mrs. Langdon, 61.

Church of England, 19.

Circuit Court Act, in South Carolina, disallowed, 21.

Clark, John, 237.

Clark, Major Satterlee, 345, 346.

Clark, William, 169, 170.

Class legislation, 71. *See also* Restrictive system, Tariff, *South Carolina Exposition and Protest*.

Clay, Henry, 65, 71, 104, 115, 118, 125, 127-128, 135, 136, 137, 143, 148, 179, 192, 206, 207, 219, 227, 234, 253, 272, 330, 335, 336-337, 343, 345, 358, 362; elected Speaker, Twelfth Congress, 53-54; member of War Mess, 54; denounces Quincy, 75; elected Speaker, Thirteenth Congress, 81; Calhoun's second, 85; named peace commissioner 87; elected Speaker, Fourteenth Congress, 104; refuses Madison's offer of War Department, 124; refuses Monroe's offer of War Department, 138-139; elected Speaker, Fifteenth Congress, 146; attacks Monroe's administration, 147; speaks against Jackson, 177-178; attacks Florida treaty, 210; returned to Speaker-

Clay, Henry—*Cont.*
ship, Eighteenth Congress, 278;
proclaims American System, 288;
rivalry with Calhoun, 302, 326; understanding with Adams, 302-306;
and "corrupt bargain," 305 ff.; and
vote for Adams, 307; offered State
Department, 308; appointed Secretary of State, 311; and Panama
mission, 326; duel with Randolph,
329-330; and tariff agitation, 353;
and tariff of 1828, 370; seeks party
leadership, 387-388.

Clergy Hall, 186, 268, 315, 379, 383;
Calhoun moves home to, 340-341;
remodeling of, 340-341, 342.

Clinton, DeWitt, 227, 236, 237, 253,
276, 325; Calhoun fears ambition
of, 47; supported by Federalists,
72; and Erie Canal, 148; sectional
candidate, 272; and Calhoun's New
York campaign, 274; understanding
with, proposed to Adams, 303;
Brown seeks place for in Adams'
Cabinet, 308; offered British mission, 317-318; Van Buren makes
peace with, 319; death of, 361.

Clinton, George, 79; Calhoun opposes
for Vice Presidency, 47.

Cobb, Thomas W., 28, 177, 224.

Cocke, John, 202, 225, 345.

"Coffin handbill," 361.

Colhoun, John Ewing, cousin of John
Caldwell Calhoun, 34.

Colquhoun, Scottish clan, 12.

Columbia, S. C., capital moved to, 23.

Columbia, Tenn., 198.

Columbia River question, 222.

Columbia *Telescope,* 276, 382.

Columbian Observer, 305.

Commerce, 121, 122, 123, 285; in
New England, 67-68.

Commercial restrictions. *See* Embargo, Nonintercourse, Nonimportation.

Compensation Act, popular reaction
to, 124-126.

Condict, Lewis, 91.

Condict, Silas, 91.

Congress, importance of, 129-130.

Congresses, Twelfth, 53 ff.; Thirteenth, 80 ff.; Fourteenth, 104 ff.;
Fifteenth, 146 ff.; Sixteenth, 187 ff.;
Seventeenth, 235 ff.; Eighteenth,
278 ff.; Nineteenth, 319 ff.; Twentieth, 359 ff.

Congressional Committees, House of
Representatives, committee assignments, Twelfth Congress, 55; Fourteenth Congress, 104; Seventeenth
Congress, 236; Committee on Foreign Relations, 55, 56, 64, 72, 83,
84, 90, 114, 206, 210; Committee
on Indian Affairs, 250; Committee
on Manufactures, 189, 287, 367;
Committee on Military Affairs, 55,
72, 167, 177, 179, 236, 252; Committee on Naval Affairs, 55, 61, 360;
Committee on Ways and Means,
55, 71, 72, 96, 104, 118, 119, 206,
208, 360, 367.

Congressional Committees, Senate,
committees appointed by Calhoun,
322-323; election of committees,
344, 360; Committee on Agriculture, 323; Committee on Commerce, 322; Committee on Finance,
322; Committee on Foreign Relations, 322, 323, 325, 335, 360; Committee on Indian Affairs, 251, 323;
Committee on the Judiciary, 335;
Committee on Manufactures, 322,
371; Committee on Military Affairs, 152, 323; Committee on
Naval Affairs, 323, 335; Committee
on Public Lands, 322; Committee
on Roads and Canals, 323.

Conkling, Alfred, 318.

Connecticut, 32.

Constitution of the United States,
125, 129, 132, 191, 196, 220, 287,
320, 322, 330, 360, 373, 378, 382,
383, 395, 396; ratified by South
Carolina, 23; amendments proposed
by Hartford Convention, 99-100;
on currency, 109; Calhoun's view
of, in relation to internal improvements, 134-135; Madison's veto of

Constitution of the U. S.—*Cont.*
internal improvements based on, 137; intended to extinguish slavery, 191; liberal interpretation of, by Calhoun, 243; and tariff of 1824, 289-290. *See also* State Rights, Hartford Convention, *South Carolina Exposition.*

Constitutional compromise in South Carolina, 45-47; Calhoun participates in, 48.

Contract, inviolability of, 189 ff.

Cook, Daniel P., 211, 280, 292, 304, 305.

Cooper, Thomas, 355, 373, 390; attacks defense program, 275; "calculates the value" of the Union, 353; urges Van Buren to oppose tariff, 370; and Alien and Sedition Laws, 381; *Lectures on Political Economy*, 382.

Corporations, 191, 291.

"Corrupt bargain," 305-306, 311-313, 359, 362; denounced by Calhoun, 313-314; attacked by Randolph, 328-330; attacked by McDuffie, 330-331; charge renewed, 343.

Coryell, Lewis F., 232.

Cotton, 19, 44, 119, 248, 324, 352, 375-376; spread of in South, 45-46; manufacturing, 118; duties on, 124; factorage system, 375-376. *See also* Tariff.

Council Bluffs, 166, 168, 185, 198.

Cow Island, 168.

Craighead, Reverend Alexander, 17.

Craighead, Jean, marries Patrick Calhoun, 17; death of, 18.

Crawford, William H., 28, 50, 79, 143, 146, 147, 148, 157, 161, 178-179, 180, 227, 231, 237, 253, 272, 276, 299, 300, 308, 321, 325, 363, 364; Presidential candidate 1816, 114; becomes Secretary of Treasury, 124; remains in Treasury, 138; character of, 144; reveals Cabinet division on Seminole campaign, 162; breach with Calhoun, 179; attacks defense program, 200-208;

Crawford, William H.—*Cont.*
campaigns for Presidency, 211; thinks Calhoun supports Adams, 227-228; Calhoun seeks defeat of, 241; State Rights champion, 243-244; and A. B. plot, 262-263; illness of, 277-278; political maneuvers, 279; nominated by caucus in 1824, 281-282; wants Calhoun off Jackson ticket in 1828, 364.

Creek Nation, 318.

Crisis, The, 355-356, 377, 382.

Crittenden, John J., 370, 388.

Crooks, Ramsay, 168, 221-222, 251.

Crouch, Edward, 231.

Crowninshield, Benjamin, 139, 143, 145, 153, 159.

Cumberland Road, 132, 165, 175. *See also* National Road.

Cumming, Colonel William, 254.

Cunningham, Robert, 43.

Currency, Calhoun heads committee on, in Fourteenth Congress, 104.

Daggett, David, 190.

Dallas, Alexander J., 88, 96, 111, 117, 118, 124; becomes Secretary of Treasury, 94; induces President to veto bank bill, 100.

Dallas, George M., 242, 254, 274; supports Calhoun for Presidency, 232, 273; wants Mexican mission, 280; withdraws Calhoun's candidacy in Pennsylvania, 282-283.

Dartmouth College case, 190, 290.

Dauphin Island, 199, 206, 228, 253.

Davis, Warren R., 256, 343, 369.

Decatur, Stephen, 76, 209.

Democracy. *See* Democratic Party.

Democratic Party, 339, 350, 358-359, 370; divisions within, 346-347, 362-364.

Democratic Press, 254, 361.

De Onis, Luis, 157, 158.

Depression of 1818-1821, 175-177.

De Saussure, Henry W., Calhoun reads law with, 35; Calhoun resumes study with, 38; discusses

De Saussure, Henry W.—*Cont.*
property settlement with Calhoun,
50.

Detroit, 165.

Dickerson, Mahlon, 344.

Dismal Swamp Canal, 153.

Disquisition on Government, 393.

Dix, John A., writes newspaper articles in support of Calhoun, 274; and
Calhoun's Vice Presidential candidacy, 299, 300.

Draft bill, 97.

Drayton, William, urged for Secretary
of War by Jackson, 139; accompanies Van Buren to Charleston,
351; attends meeting of South
Carolina Congressmen in opposition
to tariff of 1828, 372-373; writes
on Georgia controvery, 382.

Dumbarton Oaks. *See* Oakly.

Dupont, E. I., 368.

Du Pont and Co., 207.

Duval, William P., 260.

Dwight, Timothy, 30; Federalist prejudice, 32; predicts Calhoun will be
President, 32-33.

Earle, Elias, 260.

Eaton, John H., and "corrupt bargain," 306; votes against confirmation of Clay, 311; financial backer
of *United States Telegraph,* 328;
carries Calhoun's message to Jackson, 337, 338; votes for tariff of
1828, 372.

Economic conditions, 1820's, 365-366.

Economic nationalism, 106, 285 ff. *See
also* American System.

Economic responsibilities of government, 131.

Edenton, N. C., 180.

Edinburgh *Review,* 265.

Edwards, Henry W., 32; supports Calhoun in House, 235; backs Calhoun's Presidential candidacy, 272;
in Senate, 279.

Edwards, Jonathan, 30.

Edwards, Ninian, 276; governor of

Edwards, Ninian—*Cont.*
Illinois Territory, 169; sounds out
Calhoun for Adams, 228; and A. B.
plot, 263, 292; supports Calhoun
for Presidency, 273; wants Mexican
mission, 280; supports Adams, 305.

Edwards, Pierpont, 31-32.

Election of 1824, 299-314.

Election of 1828, 387.

Elliot, Jonathan, 254, 361; *Debates,*
382.

Elliott, Stephen, 382.

Elmore, General John A., 51.

Emancipation. *See* Slavery.

Embargo, Jefferson's, 40, 46; Calhoun
doubts value of, 44; effects of, 44-
45.

Embargo, use of in War of 1812, 63,
70, 71. *See also* Nonimportation,
Nonintercourse, Restrictive system.

England. *See* Great Britain.

Eppes, John W., in Thirteenth Congress, 72; Chairman of Ways and
Means Committee, 81; revenue
measures, 88, 94.

Equality, irreconcilable with progress,
105.

Era of Good Feeling, 138, 209.

Erie Canal, 132, 136, 137, 148, 165,
365, 366.

Erwin, John P., 332.

"Essex Junto," 37.

Eustis, Colonel Abraham, 230.

Eustis, William, Secretary of War,
62-63; resigns, 74; in Sixteenth
Congress, 236; attacks Army appointments, 252; Governor of Massachusetts, 277.

Evans, Oliver, 69.

Everett, Edward, 319, 388.

Factions, rise of, 227.

"Family party," 232, 235.

Farnham, Russell, 222.

Federalist, The, 356, 382, 390, 395.

Federalists, 53; election gains, May
1812, 63; decline to debate war,
64; attitude toward War of 1812,

Federalists—*Cont.*
    68-70; increase strength, 80; hail
    British triumph, 92; join Jackson-
    ians, 359.
Fernandina, Fla., 157.
Findlay, William, 232, 323.
Fisk, Jonathan, 96.
Fitzhugh, William H., 344.
Fletcher vs. Peck, 189.
Florida, 154; treaty for, 206, 209-
    210; occupation of, 229; Jackson's
    activities in, 233-235. *See also* Sem-
    inole campaign.
Floyd, John, 225, 344, 348; and State
    Rights school, 191; and Indian pol-
    icy, 221-222; and A. B. plot, 292;
    defends Calhoun on Mix contract,
    345, 346.
Force, Peter, 277, 359.
Foreign Relations, Report on, 1811,
    55-57.
Foreign Relations, Committees on.
    See Congressional Committees.
Forsyth, John, 96, 104.
Fort Armstrong, 166.
Fort Barancas, 159, 160.
Fort Calhoun, 153, 180, 199, 226.
Fort Covington. *See* French Mills.
Fort Crawford, 166.
Fort Delaware, 226.
Fort Duquesne, 13; British victory at,
    15.
Fort Howard, 166.
Fort Independence, **217.**
Fort Loudoun, 16, 19.
Fort McHenry, 92.
Fort Meigs, 198.
Fort Niagara, 217.
Fort Prince George, **16.**
Fort Snelling, 198.
Fort Warren, 217.
Fort Washington, 226.
Fortifications, 164. *See also* Military
    policy.
Fortress Monroe, 153, 180, 199, 226.
Foster, Augustus, 60, 65.
France, 64, 69; relations with, 42, 56.
Franklin Gazette, 253-254, 273, 280,
    281.

Free trade, 285-286. *See also* Tariff.
French and Indian War, 13, 16.
French Mills, 199.
Fromentin, Eligius, 233-235.
Frontier. *See* Military frontier.
Fuller, Timothy, 212.
Fulton, Robert, 40.
Fur trade. *See* American Fur Com-
    pany, Indian trade.

Gaillard, John, 213, 306, 309, 323;
    death of, 327.
Gaines, General Edmund P., and Sem-
    inole campaign, 155; joins Monroe's
    party, 181, 182; advises Calhoun
    on Army reorganization, 230; dis-
    pute with General Scott, 261.
Gallatin, Albert, Secretary of Treas-
    ury, 62; nominated as peace com-
    missioner, 78-79; rejected by Sen-
    ate, 80; resigns Treasury, confirmed
    as peace commissioner, 88; plan for
    internal improvements, 132; Min-
    ister to France, 200; poor opinion
    of Calhoun, 247; nominated for
    Vice Presidency by caucus, 282;
    Minister to England, 332.
Gardener, Colonel Charles K., 274.
Gaston, William, 96, 273.
General Staff, 151.
Genesee Path, 175.
Georgetown, S. C., 181.
Georgia, 25, 293-296.
Georgia Advertiser, 254.
Gerry, Elbridge, 82.
Gibbons vs. Ogden, 291.
Gibson, Commissary General, 183.
Giles, William Branch, 318, 380.
Girard, Stephen, 78.
Goldsborough, Howes, 345.
Goodrich, Elizur, 31, 32.
Gore, Christopher, 330.
Gould, James, 37-38.
Gouverneur, Samuel L., Monroe's sec-
    retary, 181; supports Calhoun for
    Presidency, 247; financial contribu-
    tor to New York *Patriot,* 274; a
    Calhoun partisan, 316.
Graham, George, 124, 150.

Grant, Colonel, 16.

Great Britain, relations with, 41-42, 55-56, 86, 106-107, 179, 229.

Great Lakes, 165.

Green, Duff, 350, 359; supports Calhoun for Presidency, 273; favors Jackson if Calhoun withdraws, 279; editor of *United States Telegraph*, 328; renews "corrupt bargain" charge, 343; Senate printer, 360; launches weekly *Telegraph Extra*, 361.

Grosvenor, Thomas P., 96, 112, 132; Federalist leader in Thirteenth Congress, 80, 81; near duel with Calhoun, 85; in Fifteenth Congress, 104; praises Calhoun, 130.

Grundy, Felix, member of War Mess, 54; and war measures, 58; sponsors embargo bill, 84; fails to get Speakership, 87; out of Congress, 104.

Hagner, Peter, 217, 231.

Hamilton, Alexander, 173, 315; *Report on Manufactures*, 117.

Hamilton, James, Jr., notifies Lowndes of his nomination for Presidency by South Carolina Legislature, 239; in Eighteenth Congress, 278; opposes tariff of 1824, 289-290; among financial backers of *United States Telegraph*, 328; Randolph's second in duel with Clay, 330; McDuffie's second in near duel with Metcalfe, 331; accompanies Van Buren to Charleston, 351; on Democratic steering committee in House, 360; at meeting of South Carolina Congressmen to protest tariff of 1828, 372, 373; at Abbeville protest meeting, 380; proclaims nullification doctrine, 383-384; held back by Calhoun, 389.

Hamilton, Paul, 62-63.

"Hancock." *See* Clark, Major Satterlee.

Hanson, Alexander C., Federalist leader in Thirteenth Congress, 80, 81;

Hanson, Alexander C.—*Cont.* debate with Calhoun on bank bill, 96; in Fourteenth Congress, 104.

Harper, Robert Goodloe, 89.

Harper, Chancellor William, 382, 389.

Harrisburg caucus, 1824, 273-274.

Harrisburg Convention, for promotion of manufactures, 352-355, 367.

Harrison, William Henry, 57, 323, 327.

Hartford Convention, 96-97, 98, 100, 193, 385; adjourns, 99; results, 99-100.

Hartford *Times*, 354.

Hay, Mrs. George, 208.

Hayne, Robert Y., 242, 323, 344, 380; attorney general of South Carolina, 213; backed by Calhoun for Senate, 256, 260; electioneers for Calhoun, 273; in Eighteenth Congress, 279; leads fight against tariff of 1824 in Senate, 289; votes against confirmation of Clay, 311; and woolens bill, 351; holds meeting of South Carolina Congressmen to protest tariff of 1828, 372-373; among sponsors of *Southern Review*, 382.

Hendricks, William, 327.

Henry, John, 62.

Henry, Robert, 383.

Hill, Isaac, 358, 361.

Hobbes, Thomas, 382.

Holmes, John, 327.

Holy Alliance, 156, 229.

Hopkinson, Joseph, 118, 178, 190.

Houston, Sam, 279.

Hudson's Bay Company, 166, 168.

Huger, Benjamin, 181.

Huger, Daniel E., 343.

Huguenots, 18.

Hull, Isaac, 76.

Impressment, 42, 51, 56, 68.

India trade, in tariff debate, 1816, 119.

Indian affairs, 149-150, 249-252; education of tribes, 186; appropriation for, cut, 226; office of, created, 296; migration of tribes, 296-297.

Indian trade, 150, 221-222; Government trading houses abolished, 251.

Indigo, 19.

Industrial revolution, 103, 134.

Industry, 285. *See also* Manufactures, Tariff.

Ingersoll, Charles J., 354.

Ingham, Samuel D., 96, 132, 242, 360; moves tariff resolution, 90; in Fourteenth Congress, 104; and tariff of 1816, 118; in Fifteenth Congress, 146; supports Calhoun for Presidency, 232, 272; Calhoun's spokesman, 280; supports Jackson, 304, 305; among sponsors of *United States Telegraph*, 328.

Interests. *See* Sectionalism, State Rights.

Internal improvements, 131-136, 165, 176, 287, 297; Calhoun on, 132-135; and national defense, 133, 165; analysis of voting on, 1817, 403.

Irving, William, 118.

Isolationist doctrine, 91.

Jackson, Andrew, 139, 147, 148, 149, 154, 177, 184, 206, 221, 253, 272, 276, 299, 307, 308, 309, 310, 311, 325; defeats Creeks 93; victor at New Orleans, 100; dispute with War Department, 150-151; and Seminole campaign, 155-163; ignores orders, 171; quarrel with General Scott, 171-172; comes to Washington, 178; in Adams' plans, 214; made Governor of Florida, 229; activities in Florida, 233-235; nominated for Presidency by Tennessee Legislature, 256; in Senate, Eighteenth Congress, 279; nominated for Presidency in 1828, 319; coalition with Calhoun, 337-338; party for, organized, 347-350; and the tariff, 355; attacks on, 361; correspondence with Calhoun on Seminole affair, 363-364; election of in 1828, 387.

Jackson, Rachel (Mrs. Andrew Jackson), 361.

Jackson Day dinner, 346.

Jackson Republican, 385.

Jacksonborough, S. C., 12.

Jay's Treaty, 89.

Jefferson, Thomas, 27, 31, 32, 36, 37, 94, 97, 116, 132, 138, 145-146, 148, 195, 381; leads State Rights attack on Supreme Court, 189, 190-191; Calhoun visits, 215; death of, 341.

Jeffersonians, Calhoun adheres to, 32-33, 37.

Jefferson's Embargo. *See* Embargo.

Jesup, Quartermaster General ——, 182, 184, 202, 329.

Johnson, James, 182 ff.; gets supply contracts, 167.

Johnson, Richard M., 80-81, 96, 125, 139, 206, 327, 345; in Twelfth Congress, 58; in Fourteeenth Congress, 104; proposes annual salary for Congressmen, 112; seeks repeal of Compensation Act, 127; acts as his brother's attorney in getting War Department contracts, 167; defends Jackson's Seminole campaign, 177, 178; and Missouri expedition, 182 ff., 208; defends War Department, 202; attacks judicial review, 244; suggests political alliance with Jackson and Calhoun to Adams, 279; and election of 1824, 304.

Johnson contracts, 167-168, 182-185, 214-216, 225, 276.

Johnston, Josiah S., 329-330.

Jones, William, 79; becomes Secretary of Navy, 76; resigns presidency of United States Bank, 176.

Journal of Science, 173.

Journal of the Constitutional Convention, 382.

Judiciary bill, 331.

Julius Caesar, 181.

"Keowee," 343.

Key, Francis Scott, 85.

King, Charles, 359.

King, Rufus, 330, 332; Grosvenor's second in near duel with Calhoun, 85; Federalist candidate for Presi-

King, Rufus—*Cont.*
dent, 1816, 126; Northern leader in Senate, 192; speech on Missouri Compromise, 193; Minister to England, 318.
Kremer, George, and "corrupt bargain," 306.

Lacock, Abner, 178.
Lafayette, 301, 307.
Lake Champlain, 93.
Lake Pontchartrain, 198, 199.
Land warrant bureau, 152.
Latrobe, Benjamin, 138.
Lawrence, Abbott, 354.
Leavenworth, Colonel Henry, 186.
Lectures on Political Economy. See Cooper, Thomas.
Lee, Henry, Virginia journalist, 319.
Lee, Henry, of Boston, 355.
Legaré, Hugh Swinton, 28, 380, 382, 389.
Letcher, Robert P., 302, 303.
Levees, Presidential, 60, 65-66, 148, 179, 307-308.
Lewis, Meriwether, 169.
Lexington, Ky., 183.
Litchfield Law School, 383; Calhoun a student at, 35, 36-39.
Livingston, Edward, 279, 292.
Livingston, Chancellor Robert, 40.
Lloyd, James, 323.
Loan bill, 89.
Locke, John, and South Carolina constitution, 18-19.
Long, Major Stephen, 150, 185; heads scientific corps, 173.
Long Cane Creek, 14, 15.
Long Canes settlement, 14, 15, 17-18; Indian depredations at, 17.
Longstreet, A. B., 28, 50.
Lovell, Dr. Joseph, Surgeon General, 172.
Lowell, Francis Cabot, 120, 124.
Lowndes, Elizabeth (Mrs. William Lowndes), 73, 177.
Lowndes, William, 62, 84, 104, 146, 153, 187, 192, 201, 209, 225, 247; in state legislature, 47; description

Lowndes, William—*Cont.*
of, 54; member of War Mess, 54; defends merchant class, 73; friendship with Calhoun, 73; and bank question, 95, 96; revenue program, 106; objects to caucus, 1816, 115; defends tariff of 1816, 118; considered for Treasury, 124; refuses Madison's offer of War Department, 124; refuses Monroe's offer of War Department, 139; host to the Calhouns, 142; compares Palmerston unfavorably with Calhoun, 173; recommends occupation of Florida, 210; defeated for Speaker, 220; lives with Calhoun, 220; on Missouri Compromise, 220-221; nominated for Presidency by South Carolina Legislature, 237; and Calhoun's Presidential candidacy, 239; candidacy of, 242-243; death of, 253.
Lyman, Theodore, trial of, 385-386.

Machine politics, 244, 255, 271, 300.
Macomb, General Alexander, 171.
Macon, Nathaniel, 282, 323, 344, 360; chosen president pro tempore of Senate, 336-337.
Madison, Dolly (Mrs. James Madison), 60, 148.
Madison, James, 65, 70, 97, 138, 191, 195, 362; Calhoun endorses Presidential candidacy in 1808, 47; indecision of, 63; sends war message June 1, 1812, 64; signs war bill, 66; re-elected 1812, 72; names peace commissioners, 78; illness of, 82; favors internal improvements, 132; vetoes internal improvement bill as unconstitutional, 137.
Madisonville, La., 198.
Maine Argus, 358.
Mallary, R. C., 354, 367.
Mandan Village, 166, 167, 168, 198.
Manufacturers Journal, 188.
Manufactures, beginnings of in New England, 45; extent of, 116; effect of embargo on, 116-117; pressure

Manufactures—*Cont.*
for, 188-189; theory of government developed by advocates of, 396. *See also* Harrisburg Convention, Tariff.

Marbury vs. Madison, 189.

Marshall, John, 89, 310; and national supremacy, 189, 244, 381.

Marx, Karl, 393.

Mason, Jeremiah, 217.

Massachusetts militia, quarrel over, 93.

Maxcy, Virgil, supports Calhoun for Presidency, 273; seeks Maryland endorsement of Calhoun, 279; a Calhoun partisan, 316; withdraws congressional candidacy, 343.

McCord, D. J., 382.

M'Culloch vs. Maryland, 190, 191, 291.

McDuffie, George, 28, 29, 335, 344, 367; protégé of Calhoun brothers, 49-50, 213; in Seventeenth Congress, 235; defends War Department, 252-253; duel with Colonel Cumming, 254-255; supports Calhoun for Presidency, 272, 273, 279; and tariff of 1824, 288, 290; and election of 1824, 304, 305; attacks "corrupt bargain," 330-331; near duel with Metcalfe, 330-331; and Mix investigation, 346; on tariff policy, 353; on Democratic steering committee in House, 360; Chairman of Ways and Means, 360; and tariff of 1828, 369; at meeting of South Carolina Congressmen to protest tariff of 1828, 372, 373; speaks against tariff at Abbeville, 380.

McKean, Thomas, 143.

McKenney, Thomas L., 186; Superintendent of Indian Trade, 169; defends Indian policy, 250-251; editor of Washington *Republican,* 257; forced from editorship, 259; neighbor of Calhoun, 269; heads Office of Indian Affairs, 296.

McLane, Louis, 236, 307, 331, 335.

McLean, John, 318; Commissioner of Land Office, 260; Postmaster General, 269; supports Calhoun for Presidency, 272; urges Calhoun to withdraw, 276; believes Calhoun favors Jackson, 304; supports Adams, 305; retains Post Office, 311; and patronage, 331, 358.

Measures, not Men, 275.

Meehan, John S., 328.

Meigs, Return J., Postmaster General, 143.

"*Mercury* junto," 378.

Metcalfe, Thomas, challenges McDuffie, 330-331.

Middleton, Henry, succeeds Cheves in Fourteenth Congress, 104; confers with Adams on Calhoun's views, 180; visited by Monroe and party, 181; reports to Adams, 185.

Migration of Calhouns, 12.

Military academy, 105, 172, 201, 298.

Military appropriations, cuts in, 226.

Military frontier, 164, 166, 298.

Military policy, 164-174; attacks on, 206-208. *See also* Army, Fortifications, Indian affairs, Internal improvements, Missouri expedition.

Militia, 105.

Milledgeville *Gazette,* 254.

Miller, Stephen D., 389.

Mills, Elijah, 309, 323.

Minimum principle, in tariff of 1816, 119-120, 123, 124.

Missouri Compromise, 191-197, 219-221, 241, 242, 244, 296; Calhoun on, 220.

Missouri expedition, 166-168, 182-185, 200, 201-202; stopped, 208.

Mitchell, Thomas R., 373.

Mix, Elijah, 344 ff. *See also* Mix contract.

Mix contract, 203-205, 253, 276, 344-346.

Mobile Point, 199, 226, 232.

Monroe, Elizabeth (Mrs. James Monroe), 148.

Monroe, James, 65, 86, 89, 153, 168, 185, 195, 208, 215, 234, 236, 240, 247, 295, 308, 362, 363; dines with

Monroe, James—*Cont.*
War Mess, 57; becomes Secretary of War, 74; gives up War Department, 75; fails to defend Washington, 92; resumes War Department, 94; Presidential candidate 1816, 114; elected President 1816, 126; chooses Cabinet, 138-141; and his Cabinet, 142-146; first message to Congress, 147; and Seminole campaign, 155-163; inspects fortification sites, 180-182; makes southern trip, 180-182; orders advance on Johnson contracts, 184; re-elected 1820, 227.

Monroe Doctrine, 278.

Montgomerie, Colonel ——, 16.

Montreal, 217.

Morristown, N. Y., 199.

Morrow, Jeremiah, 115, 354.

Morse, Reverend Jedidiah, 186, 266.

Morse, Samuel F. B., 307.

National Bank. *See* Bank, Bank of the United States.

National defense, Calhoun's views on, 107-108, 120-121; internal improvements and, 133, 165.

National Intelligencer, 83, 115, 251, 305, 334, 385.

National Journal, 277, 278, 279, 281, 333, 337.

National Republicans, 343, 350; Adams' party called, 339; accuse Calhoun of disunion, 384-385.

National Road, 365.

Nationalism, growth of, 103 ff.; in Fourteenth Congress, 131. *See also* American System, Economic nationalism.

Naval victories, 75-76.

Navigation. *See* Commerce, Internal improvements.

Navy, inadequacy of, 60; debate on, 62.

New Bern, N. C., 181.

New England, attitude toward War of 1812, 67 ff.; carrying trade, 67-68;

New England—*Cont.*
begins shift from commerce to manufacturing, 77; refuses to take Government loan, 78; secretly negotiates with British, 97. *See also* Commerce, Hartford Convention, Sectionalism, State Rights, Tariff.

New England Galaxy, 277, 280.

New Hampshire Patriot, 358.

New Haven, 218. *See also* Yale.

New Orleans, 138.

New River, 12, 13.

New York *Advertiser,* 359.

New York *Advocate,* 218.

New York *American,* 218.

New York City, Calhoun visits, 218-219.

New York *Patriot,* 274.

Newport, 70.

Niebuhr, Barthold Georg, *History of Rome,* 383.

Niles, Hezekiah, 352, 353, 367; propagandist for tariff, 188; and Harrisburg Convention, 354-355.

Niles' Weekly Register, 143, 188, 384.

Ninety Six, 11, 12, 14.

Noble, John, 12, 13.

Noble, Mary, aunt of John Caldwell Calhoun, 12; land grants to, 15.

Noble, Patrick, cousin of John Caldwell Calhoun, 213, 380; Calhoun forms partnership with, 43.

Nominating convention, 282, 347-348; at Harrisburg, 282-283.

Nonimportation, 56, 70, 73. *See also* Embargo, Nonintercourse, Restrictive system.

Nonintercourse, 45, 87. *See also* Embargo, Nonimportation, Restrictive system.

Norfolk, Va., 180.

North. *See* Sectionalism, State Rights, Tariff.

North American Review, 265, 319, 382.

Notes on Political Economy. See Cardozo, Jacob N.

Nullification, 386. *See also* Sectionalism, State Rights.

Oakley, Thomas J., 96.

Oakly, Calhoun home in Georgetown, 269-270; sale of, 343.

Oliver Oldschool. *See* Sargent, Nathan.

O'Neall, John Belton, 380.

"Onslow," 333-334.

Orders in Council, 56, 63, 65, 73, 89.

Osborn vs. Bank of United States, 291.

Osborne, Selleck, 37.

Otis, Harrison Gray, 193.

Palatines, 18.

Palmerston, Lord, 173.

Panama Congress, 324-327, 328, 335.

Panama Mission. *See* Panama Congress.

Parish, David, 78.

"Patrick Henry," 333-334.

Patron of Industry, 188.

Patronage, Calhoun and, 260-262; Adams' use of, 317-319, 327, 331-332, 361-362; McLean and, 358.

Patterson, Betsy, 60.

Pawtucket, R. I., 76.

Peace treaty with Great Britain, signed, 100-101.

Pendleton, S. C., 34, 51, 186, 319.

Pendleton Farmers' Society, 342.

Pennsylvania, 12, 13, 18.

Pensacola, Fla., 159, 177.

Pension bureau, 152.

People's Party, 274-275.

Perceval, Spencer, 65.

Petigru, James L., 28, 380.

Phi Beta Kappa, Calhoun elected to, 31.

Pickens, General Andrew, 17.

Pickens, Andrew, son of General Andrew Pickens and cousin of John Caldwell Calhoun, 38, 213, 273.

Pickens, Francis, 358.

Pickering, Timothy, attacks War of 1812, 69; in Thirteenth Congress, 80; opposition leader, 81; offers Massachusetts "Remonstrance," 83; defends impressment, 89; approves British terms, 94; in Four-

Pickering, Timothy—*Cont.* teenth Congress, 104; defeated, 125; and internal improvements, 135; approves Calhoun's Army reduction plan, 224.

Pinckney, Charles, 24.

Pinckney, Charles Cotesworth, 181.

Pinckney, Henry L., 353.

Pinkney, William, 89; in Fourteenth Congress, 104; in Senate, 1820, 192; speech on Missouri Compromise, 193.

Pittsburgh, 165.

Plantation system, 192-193.

Plattsburg, 199, 217.

Pleasants, Governor James, 318.

Plumer, William, Jr., reports to Adams on Calhoun's Presidential candidacy, 245.

Poinsett, Joel R., 213; supports Calhoun in Congress, 235; on tariff of 1824, 290; and election of 1824, 308; ambassador to Mexico, 318.

Political machines. *See* Machine politics.

Pope, John, 211.

Pope, Nathaniel, 211.

Porter, Peter B., 58, 72, 80; in Twelfth Congress, 55; in Fourteenth Congress, 104; Calhoun visits, 217; becomes Secretary of War, 362.

Potomac River, 12, 83.

Potter, Elisha, 76.

Presidency, rivalry for in Monroe's Cabinet, 143-146, 148.

Presidential campaign, 1824, 249 ff.; 1828, 357-359, 361-362.

Presidential caucus. *See* Caucus.

Presidential politics, 1819, 179-180.

Presidential succession for 1824, 211 ff.

Preston, William C., 379.

Progress, irreconcilable with equality, 105.

Protection. *See* Tariff.

Providence, R. I., 76.

Quarterly Review, 265.

Quincy, Josiah, 55, 64, 80; attacks war measures, 74-75.

Radicals, name of Crawford's party, 211; attack military program, 224, 225; oppose Calhoun's candidacy, 249; Crawford's illness setback for, 277; wooed by Adams, 317-318, 332; join Jacksonians, 339; Calhoun defeated by in South Carolina, 343.
Railroads, 366.
Raleigh *Register*, 276.
Randolph, John, of Roanoke, 80, 112, 122, 335, 344, 362, 397; denounces War Hawks, 58; silenced by Clay, 64; defeated by Eppes, 72; in Fourteenth Congress, 104; warns against central power, 107, 108; and tariff of 1816, 120; defeated because of stand on Compensation Act, 125, 127-128; attacks constitutionality of internal improvements, 135; and State Rights school, 191; in Sixteenth Congress, 192; and Missouri Compromise, 194; and internal improvements, 287; and tariff of 1824, 290; elected to Senate, 321; attacks "corrupt bargain," 328-330; duel with Clay, 329-330; supports Jacksonians, 339; declines chairmanship of Ways and Means, 360; and tariff of 1828, 370.
Reapportionment, and the tariff of 1824, 286-287, 404.
Reed, John, 118.
Reed Creek, Va., 12, 13.
Reeve, Judge Tapping, 35, 36-38, 266, 383.
Regulators, 20 ff.
Relief, public, 175.
Restrictive system, 70, 76, 84; repealed, 90; Calhoun speaks against, 91. *See also* Embargo, Nonimportation, Nonintercourse.
Revolution, 12, 16.
Rhea, John, 156.
Rhett, Robert Barnwell, 381, 389;

Rhett, Robert Barnwell—*Cont.*
calls for forcible resistance to tariff, 377.
Rice, 19, 44.
Richardson, Reverend William, 17.
Richmond *Enquirer*, 191, 234, 275, 321, 344, 388.
Rigolets, 199, 226.
Rip Rap contract, *See* Mix contract.
Rip Rap Shoal. *See* Fort Calhoun.
Ritchie, Thomas, 275, 339, 359; praises Calhoun in Richmond *Enquirer*, 59; State Rights leader, 191; and caucus of 1824, 281; opposes Adams, 321; and North-South alliance, 347-350.
Ritner, Joseph, 354.
Roads and canals, 365-366. *See also* Internal improvements.
Roane, Spencer, 195, 244; leads in attack on Supreme Court, 191.
Roanoke River, 13.
Robbins, Ashur, 354.
Roberdeau, Major, 217.
Robertson, Thomas B., 118.
Rodney, Caesar A., 236.
Rogers, Thomas J., 242, 305.
Rowan, John, 372.
Ruggles, Benjamin, 327.
Rush, Richard, Madison's Attorney General, 139; Secretary of Treasury under Adams, 310, 317; report on tariff, 367.
Russia, offers to mediate War of 1812, 78; mediation refused, 84.

Sackett's Harbor, 199, 217.
St. Louis, 167, 183, 185.
St. Louis *Enquirer*, 185, 221, 273.
St. Marks, Fla., 158, 159, 177.
Salkehatchie River, 50.
Sanford, Nathan, 327.
Sargent, Nathan, 297.
Savannah, Ga., 181.
Scott, John, 220.
Scott, General Winfield, quarrel with Jackson, 171-172; prepares infantry tactics, 172; contributes to

Scott, General Winfield—*Cont.*
Army reorganization, 224, 229; seeks chief command, 261-262; supports Calhoun's candidacy, 272, 275; financial contributor to New York *Patriot*, 274.

Seaton, William Winston, 248.

Sectionalism, social and economic cleavage in South Carolina, 19; South Carolina compromise, 24; accentuated by Jefferson's embargo, 44-45; growth of in Monroe's administration, 148; Calhoun repudiates, 219; Calhoun warns against, 232-233; and Supreme Court decisions, 244; stimulated by Missouri Compromise, 256; in Presidential contest, 1824, 272; and tariffs, 286-287; and election of Adams, 308-309. *See also* Slavery, State Rights, Tariff.

Seminole campaign, 155-163; made a partisan issue, 177-179.

Senate, Calhoun and functions of, 309-310. *See also* Congresses, Congressional Committees.

Sergeant, John, 111, 232; in Fourteenth Congress, 104; candidate for Speaker, 220.

Shaftesbury, Earl of, 18.

Shawnees, 57.

Shelby, Isaac, 139, 184.

Silliman, Benjamin, 173, 266; Calhoun studies under, 31; calls on Calhoun, 297.

Simkins, Eldred, Calhoun's successor in House, 207; defends military policy, 207, 225; McDuffie law partner of, 213; in South Carolina Legislature, 322; Anna Maria Calhoun lives in family of, 342; marriage of daughter, 358.

Simkins, Eliza, marriage of, 358.

Slave revolt, 256.

Slave trade, 47, 51, 67; reopened, 40.

Slavery, origins in South Carolina, 19; and Missouri Compromise, 191-197; Calhoun on, 196, 219; Adams on, 196, 241; and Southern econ-

Slavery—*Cont.*
omy, 376-377. *See also* Sectionalism, State Rights.

Smilie, John, 72.

Smith, Margaret Bayard (Mrs. Samuel Harrison Smith), 177-178, 208-209.

Smith, Robert Barnwell. *See* Rhett, Robert Barnwell.

Smith, Samuel, in Fourteenth Congress, 104; and tariff of 1816, 118, 119; and internal improvements, 135; cuts War Department budget, 206; candidate for Speaker, 220; and tariff of 1824, 289; Adams' candidate for president pro tempore of Senate, 336-337.

Smith, General Thomas A., 167, 168.

Smith, William, 344, 380; Radical Senator from South Carolina, 213; Calhoun seeks defeat of, 256; defeats Calhoun faction in South Carolina, 322, 343; dislike for Calhoun, 343; votes for, for Vice President, 387.

Society, in Washington, 152-153, 173; the Calhouns in, 266-267. *See also* Levees, Presidential.

South. *See* Sectionalism, Slavery, Southern economy, State Rights.

South Carolina, 11, 71; Cherokee treaty, 13-14; origin of colony, 18-19; General Assembly of, 47-48.

South Carolina Exposition and Protest, origin of, 379-386; drafted by Calhoun, 389-390; analysis of, 390-398.

Southard, Samuel L., 318; on tariff of 1816, 118; supports Calhoun for Presidency, 272; becomes Secretary of Navy, 278; supports Adams, 305; in Adams' Cabinet, 311.

Southern economy, 352, 375-377.

Southern Review, 382, 383.

Sovereignty. *See* State Rights.

Spain, relations with, 147, 160-161, 162, 179, 207, 226, 229. *See also* Florida, Seminole campaign.

Speakership, importance of, 55.
Specie payments resumed, 138.
Speculation, 175, 366.
Spencer, Judge Ambrose, 273.
Springfield, Mass., 218.
Stamp Act, 22; tariff of 1828 compared with, 380.
Stanley, Edward, 307.
State Rights, 70, 108, 134-135, 148, 189-191, 243-244, 254, 287, 289-291, 321, 350-351. *See also* Hartford Convention, Sectionalism, Slavery, *South Carolina Exposition and Protest.*
State Rights party, Calhoun becomes leader of, 390.
State sovereignty. *See* State Rights.
Steamboats, on Missouri expedition, 168, 182-185.
Sterling, Ansel, 235.
Sterling, Micah, 235, 272.
Stevenson, Andrew, 368; elected Speaker, 360.
Story, Joseph, 247, 273, 369.
Strong, Governor ——, of Massachusetts, 70, 93.
Stuart, Colonel Philip, 83, 85.
Sturges vs. Crowninshield, 190.
Supreme Court, 190, 331, 362. *See also* Constitution; Marshall, John; State Rights.
Swift, General Joseph G., 270, 313; Chief of Army Engineers, 153; fortification surveys, 164; leaves Army, 171; and Mix contract, 204, 346; defends War Department, 205; supports Calhoun for Presidency, 272; financial contributor to New York *Patriot,* 274; Calhoun partisan, 316.

Taggart, Samuel, 75.
Tait, Charles, 144; Crawford's manager, 114; and Missouri Compromise, 192; influence in Alabama, 213; confidant of Calhoun, 219, 232.
Tallmadge, James, and Missouri Compromise, 191; Adams partisan, 275,

Tallmadge, James—*Cont.*
318; and Harrisburg Convention, 354.
Taney, Roger B., 273.
Tariff, lobby planned, 91; and the depression of 1818-1821, 176; pressure for, 189; and price of cotton, 248; and economic nationalism, 285-286; woolens bill defeated by Calhoun, 350-351; agitation to raise, 352-355; Southern reaction against agitation for, 353, 355-357; Calhoun on agitation for, 356-357. *See also* American System, Sectionalism, *South Carolina Exposition and Protest,* State Rights, Tariff of 1816, Tariff of 1824, Tariff of 1828.
Tariff of 1816, 106, 115-124; analysis of vote on, 123-124, 403.
Tariff of 1824, 285-291; and reapportionment, 286-287, 404.
Tariff of 1828, 365-374; lobby for, 366-368; reaction of South Carolina Congressmen to, 372-374; Calhoun seeks constitutional solution for, 378-384; reaction to in South Carolina, 377-384.
Tariff of Abominations. *See* Tariff of 1828.
Tattnall, Edward F., 330.
Taylor, John, of Caroline, 313, 390, 397; State Rights leader, 191, 194, 244; endorses Calhoun, 273; Calhoun visits, 275; and tariff of 1824, 289; thinks Adams' prospects good in Virginia, 300.
Taylor, John W., and Missouri Compromise, 192; chosen Speaker, Sixteenth Congress, 220; Calhoun prevents re-election as Speaker, 236; intermediary between Calhoun and Adams, 299, 300; elected Speaker, Nineteenth Congress, 319; loses Speakership, 360.
Tazewell, Littleton W., 323, 337, 344; Senator from Virginia, 311; reports on Panama Congress, 325; illness of, 327; joins Jacksonians, 339; and North-South alliance, 349-350.

Technology, 47.

Tecumseh, 57, 112.

Telegraph Extra, 361.

Telfair, Thomas, 119.

Texas, 209-210, 226.

Textile industry, 121. *See also* Cotton, Tariff, Woolens.

Thomas, Jesse B., 195, 332.

Thompson, Smith, 193; becomes Secretary of Navy, 143, 145; and Missouri Compromise, 196; opposes J. W. Taylor for Speaker, 236; appointed to Supreme Court, 278; candidate for Governor of New York, 362.

Thornton, William, 93.

Tibbits, George, 354.

Ticknor, George, 218.

Tippecanoe, battle of, 57.

Tod, John, 287.

Tompkins, Daniel D., 193; Presidential candidate, 1816, 114; Republican choice for Vice President, 1816, 115.

Tracy, Uriah, 37.

Transportation. *See* Internal improvements.

Trimble, William A., 184.

Truth's Advocate and Monthly Anti-Jackson Expositor, 361.

Tucker, Henry St. George, 104.

Turnbull, Robert J., 355.

Tyler, John, in Fourteenth Congress, 130; in State Rights party, 191; on Missouri Compromise, 195; friendly to Adams, 318; elected to Senate, 348.

Tyranny Unmasked, 291.

Unitarianism, Calhoun a believer in, 268-269.

United States, military unpreparedness of, 59-60.

United States Gazette, 297.

United States Telegraph, 328.

Utica, N. Y., 217.

Van Buren, Martin, 247, 251, 303, 344; political power of, 145; Sena-

Van Buren, Martin—*Cont.*
tor from New York, 236; skill as political manager, 237; secures political control of New York, 242; controls choice of New York electors for 1824, 274, 275; and caucus of 1824, 281; and election of 1824, 307; represents Radicals in New York, 318; makes peace with Clinton, 319; seeks alliance with Calhoun, 324; and Panama Congress, 325; on Adams' use of patronage, 327; and judiciary bill, 331; joins Jacksonians, 338-339; and North-South alliance, 347-350, 364; visits the South, 351; urged by Cooper to oppose tariff, 353; brings Federalists into Jackson party, 359; and tariff of 1828, 368, 370, 371, 372; elected Governor of New York 388.

Van Deventer, Christopher, 186, 357, Chief Clerk of War Department 152; and Mix contract, 203-205 253, 344 ff.; a Calhoun partisan, 273, 316, 317.

Van Rensselaer, Stephen, 344; and election of Adams, 307.

Virginia, 12, 13, 18.

Virginia Report on Alien and Sedition Laws, 383.

Virginia State Rights school, 189, 234, 273. *See also* State Rights.

Virginia Times, 275.

Waddel, Moses, 114, 144, 266; marries Catherine Calhoun, 25; as teacher, 27-29.

War bill, passed by House, 65; signed, 66.

War Department, chaotic state of, 149-150; reorganized, 151-152; attacks on, 225-227; Calhoun's achievements in, 297-298. *See also* Army, Indian affairs, Military policy.

War Hawks, 53 ff.; nostalgia of, 61.

War Mess, 54; entertains Monroe, 57.

War of 1812, 67-100, *passim*.

Ware, Nathaniel Alcock, 43.
Washington, D. C., taken by British, 92.
Washington, George, 116, 145, 227.
Washington, Ga., 182.
Washington *Gazette,* 254; attacks Calhoun, 258.
Washington *Republican and Congressional Examiner,* 262, 279; supports Calhoun, 257-259.
Waterhouse, Dr. Benjamin, 230.
Watertown Arsenal, 218.
Waxhaw, 14, 17.
We the People, 361.
Weather records, kept at military posts, 172-173.
Webster, Daniel, 104, 112, 190, 234, 292, 305, 313, 319, 330, 343, 358, 361, 385-386; enters House, 80; criticizes war, 81; leads opposition to War of 1812, 81-82; leader of Federalists, 86; proclaims isolationist doctrine, 91; opposes Calhoun's bank bill, 98; opposes bill to charter United States Bank, 111; supports duty on cotton, 1816, 119; entertains Calhoun in Boston, 217-218; supports Calhoun for Presidency, 273; returns to Congress, 278; opposes tariff of 1824, 288; and vote for Adams, 307; Adams' leader in House, 326; enters Senate, 360; and tariff of 1828, 371.
Webster, Ezekiel, 354.
Weed, Thurlow, and Adams' victory in New York, 317-318.
Weights and Measures, Report on, by Adams, 228.
Welles, Gideon, 354.
West. *See* Internal improvements, Sectionalism, State Rights.
Wheaton, Henry, 381; supports Calhoun for Presidency, 273; financial contributor to New York *Patriot,* 274; elected to New York Assembly, 275.
Whisky tax, 136.
White, Hugh Lawson, 323, 344.

Wilde, Richard H., 370.
Wilderness Trail, 175.
Wilkinson, David, 354.
Williams, David R., Chairman of House Committee on Military Affairs, Twelfth Congress, 55, 72; in Army, 80; considered for War Department, 139; urges acceptance of tariff, 380-381.
Williams, John, Calhoun discusses Army reorganization with, 152; Tennessee rival of Jackson, 179; given diplomatic post by Adams, 318.
Williams, Lewis, antagonized by Calhoun, 136; calls for Army reduction, 179; criticizes War Department, 200-201, 206, 207.
Willington, S. C., 29, 49, 52, 182, 319.
Wilmington, N. C., 181.
Winder, General, 92.
Wirt, William, 153; becomes Attorney General, 139; character of, 145; and Seminole affair, 157, 161; with Calhoun in New York, 218; in Adams' Cabinet, 311.
Woodbury, Levi, 344.
Wool, 353, 354, 368. *See also* Tariff, Woolens bill.
Woolens bill, 350-351, 356. *See also* Tariff.
Wright, Robert, 119.
Wright, Silas, 367.
Wythe, Chancellor ——, 53.
Wythe County, Va., 12.
Wytheville, Va., 12.

Yale College, Calhoun enters, 29; Calhoun studies at, 29-36; gives Calhoun honorary degree, 266.
Yancey, Bartlett, 332, 383.
Yancey, Benjamin, 43.
Yazoo land frauds, 144, 189.
Yellowstone, 198.
Yellowstone expedition. *See* Missouri expedition.
Yorktown, 301.

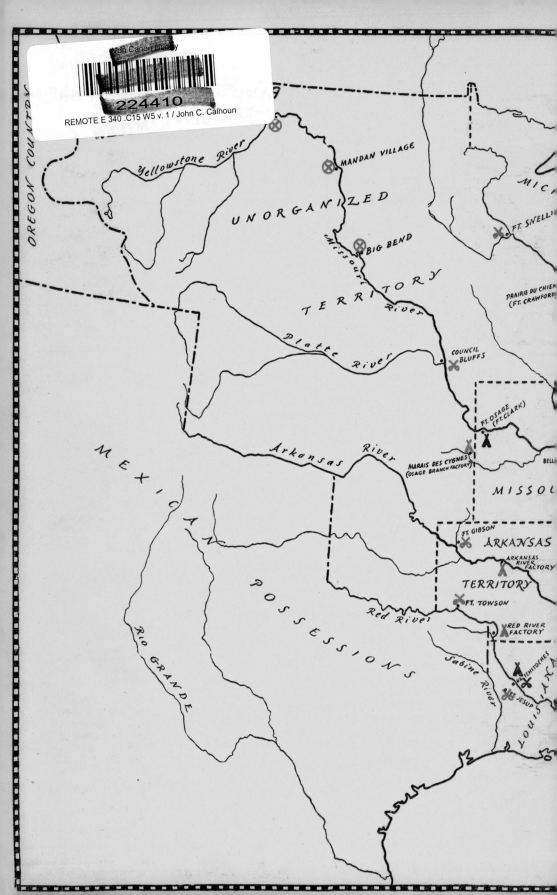

OREGON COUNTRY

Yellowstone River

⊗

⊗ MANDAN VILLAGE

UNORGANIZED

Missouri River

⊗ BIG BEND

TERRITORY

Platte River

● COUNCIL
✗ BLUFFS

MICH

✗ FT. SNELLI

PRAIRIE DU CHIEN
(FT. CRAWFORD)

M E X I C A N

Arkansas   River

FT. OSAGE
(FT. CLARK)
✗   ⚔

MARAIS DES CYGNES
(OSAGE BRANCH FACTORY)

BELLI

MISSOL

P O S S E S S I O N S

Red River

FT. GIBSON
✗

ARKANSAS

ARKANSAS
RIVER
FACTORY
⚔

TERRITORY

✗ FT. TOWSON

Rio Grande

Sabine River

✗ RED RIVER
FACTORY

⚔ CHITOCHES

✗ FT. JESUP

LOUISIANA